The Supreme Court in Crisis

The Supreme Court in Crisis

A History of Conflict

ROBERT J. STEAMER

THE UNIVERSITY OF MASSACHUSETTS PRESS 1971

Library of Congress Catalog Card Number 74-123544

Printed in the United States of America

Grateful acknowledgment is made for permission to reprint the following
material previously published by the author: "The Legal and Political
Genesis of the Supreme Court," reprinted with permission from the
Political Science Quarterly, 77 (December 1962), 546–569. "Congress and
the Supreme Court," from The Review of Politics, 27 (Jly 1965), 364–385.
"The Supreme Court and Constitutional Liberty at Mid-Century: The
1958–1959 Term as a Key," from Temple Law Quarterly, 34 (Winter
1961), 99–123. "Current Conflict Over the Supreme Court: Statesmanship
of Craftsmanship," from the Western Political Quarterly, 11 (June 1958),
265–277. "The Court and the Criminal," from the William & Mary Law
Review, 8 (Spring 1967), 319–342.

TO JEAN

Preface

THIS book had its origins in the late 1950s when the Supreme Court was under sustained attack from various influential quarters of the nation, not the least of which was a sizeable group of senators and representatives in the Congress. After writing an article for the *Western Political Quarterly* of June 1958 which dealt with some aspects of the judicial-legislative conflict of that day, I began to view the practice of judicial review in terms of the constitutional crises that it tended to produce. It seemed appropriate to write a history of the Supreme Court in which the emphasis would be on the recurring conflicts between the Court on the one hand, and one or both of the two great power centers of the American system, the Congress and the Presidency on the other. It is my contention that given the popular nature of the elective branches of government as opposed to the oligarchical character of the appointive branch, periodic constitutional crises are inevitable. Moreover, since the power of judicial review was not made explicit by the framers uncertainty surrounds its use, and the fact that the Supreme Court is exercising authority which the founding fathers may not have intended complicates the natural struggle among the forces responsible for fashioning public policy.

A study of the Supreme Court in the context of its conflicts with other political agencies in the American system suggests that uninhibited majority rule is sometimes unwise, unworkable, and even unwanted by very reasonable men who realize that willful desires of the moment need to be tempered by institutional arrangements which give consideration to the long view. The concept that all of the forces (individual and collective) that attempt to influence public decisions are compelled to operate within a set of rules subject to final interpretation by a small group of men—who make and defend their decisions within restricted judicial perimeters—has been accepted by most of the people most of the time. Even during those periods when the Court's theories of the Constitution were so at odds with popular thinking that Congress could have eliminated judicial review altogether, it was never able to muster the necessary votes. It might even be said that these recurring crises in American history have been not only inevitable but beneficial, for they have provided the people with extensive debates on the crucial issues of the day.

In writing a book of this kind one owes debts of considerable magnitude to many people—former teachers, colleagues and students (past and present) and to the scores of scholars whose work was read and digested prior to beginning the manuscript. For introducing me to the study of public law, I am grateful to two great teachers, George W. Spicer, recently retired from the University of Virginia and the late Robert E. Cushman, who led the Department of Government at Cornell for so many years. I wish to thank Professors David Fellman and Henry J. Abraham for their critical reading of the entire manuscript and for their valuable suggestions. I also appreciate the special encouragement and advice given by my former colleagues at Louisiana State University, Rene de Visme Williamson and William C. Havard. For making time available during the summer months I am indebted to the Research Council of Louisiana State University and to the Eli Lilly Foundation. I also wish to thank Mrs. Helen Hurd for converting difficult handwriting into a typescript and Mrs. Grace Lehnert and Mrs. Donna Coburn for their expert typing of the final manuscript. To my wife, Jean, I owe the greatest debt of all for her constant encouragement and intelligent assistance.

Contents

The Supreme Court in Crisis

1. The Legal & Political
Genesis of the Supreme Court

THE Supreme Court of the United States is unique among the world's judicial bodies because it is endowed not only with the ordinary legal authority that resides in other courts, but possesses, in addition, a vast reservoir of political power. This political power is exercised, however, within the limits of a carefully defined judicial procedure which is solidly rooted in centuries-old Anglo-American custom modified by statutory enactments in order to meet the changing needs of a dynamic society. The fact remains, nevertheless, that this admixture of law and politics has thrust upon the Court the unenviable constitutional duty of deciding cases between two litigants, the outcome of which not only determines the long-term constitutional direction of the nation, but also very often has a serious impact on contemporary public policies. This duality of functions, never perfectly differentiated, produces a fairly large penumbral area in which the Court's decisions become fair game for political attack by the uninformed, or misinformed, as well as by the well informed. Moreover, throughout the Court's history some of its critics have attempted periodically to destroy the institution itself by so stripping it of its powers as to leave a lifeless robot. In part, the extremely harsh criticism that has erupted from time to time has come from gored oxen, but to attribute all dissatisfaction with the Supreme Court to those who considered themselves injured by particular decisions is to oversimplify the matter. The problem is more basic and lies in the nature of the institution itself.

On the surface at least, the Court is a contradiction in American political theory. It is an oligarchy in a democratic polity, and although dissimilar to traditional oligarchies based on wealth and family with a strong element of preemptive privilege, it does in fact have an even less valid claim to political authority than wealth and family. A justice of the Supreme Court receives his appointment initially because he is a lawyer, or more probably a lawyer-politician, whom the president of the United States happens to like. The president may like a man's political views, his legal orientation, or it may be merely a matter of personal friendship. The president need not and does not say why a nomination to the nation's highest court is sent to the Senate. Furthermore, once the justice is on the bench, he is politically responsible to no one—certainly not to the president who appointed him, or to the Senate which confirmed him. As to that great mass called the people, a Supreme Court justice is so far removed from them that he need not respond to their current demands.

Careful students of American government are indeed aware that this surface picture is so highly superficial as to be downright inaccurate. But the masses are not profound students of American government, and very often they form their views from a veneer of knowledge. In addition, modern methods of communication furnish relatively easy means to those who would exploit mass emotions, whether out of sincere motives for the public good, or solely for individual gain. And the Supreme Court, because of its political role, is subject to fair or unfair comment by the mass communicators and by anyone at all who wishes to take pen in hand. Because of its legal role, however, which calls for a dignified, austere, and relatively disinterested judicial posture, the justices, unlike the president or individual congressmen, cannot answer back. It would be not only an impropriety but an absolute indignity for a justice of the Supreme Court to reply directly— even with a reasoned argument—to a critical journalist, and it is inconceivable that a justice moved to anger would toss off a profane epithet, no matter how well deserved, in the manner of one of America's twentieth-century presidents. By its very nature, then, the Court has produced in the American body politic an almost pathological ambivalence resulting in broad public attitudinal swings from reverence to condemnation and back to reverence again, often in one generation. Throughout American history, the

Court has always had able defenders to meet the periodic storms of protest, and it seems a safe prediction that this will be true in the future as it has been in the past.

Fundamentally, the Supreme Court has remained controversial because its role was imperfectly defined in the Constitution. This is partly because of the nature of constitutions and partly because of the nature of the judicial function. But the fact is that the power and authority of the Court are rooted as much in Anglo-American legal and political practice as in the phraseology of Article III. Consequently, an understanding of why the Court is what it is, and why it does what it does, is incomplete without a knowledge of its historical underpinning. This chapter will deal with the three main periods of the Supreme Court's prehistory. These are: (1) the American colonial period which may be dated from the beginning of the settlement of the colonies to 5 September 1774, when a congress first met to consider the grievances against the mother country and gradually prepared for the Revolution; (2) the period of government by a congress until 1 March 1781, when the Articles of Confederation were ratified; and (3) the period under the Articles of Confederation from 1 March 1781 to 4 March 1789 when the present Constitution of the United States became operative. In the period when creation of the judiciary began, three factors weighed heavily on later developments. These are: the general legal milieu of the colonial period; the influence of the vice-admiralty courts on judicial practice; and the general system of legal appeals.

Legal Milieu

Few, if any, observers of the American character question the proposition that Americans are a legally-minded people, perhaps the most law- and court-oriented of any people, past, or present. It is most interesting that this trait developed during the colonial period, reaching a plateau roughly at the time of the founding of the new nation. The tendency in America to litigate everything is spoken of by the Duc de la Rochefoucauld who traveled through the United States in the late 1790s. He pointed out that New Englanders were exceedingly litigious and that there were "few disputes even of the most trivial nature among them that can be terminated elsewhere than before a court of justice."[1] La Rochefoucauld wrote of Connecticut that "perhaps no equal number of people in the universe have such a multitude of lawsuits" and such a multitude of advocates. He observed, further, that these lawyers had a great political influence among the people.[2] Massachusetts, the more or less typical colony, shows us that the colonists had "a most disagreeable characteristic"—that of an unwillingness to end lawsuits. A study of court records in Suffolk County for the period 1671-80[3] indicates that a loser in the county court sought to appeal his cause as long as permissible, and that when the appeals failed, he began the litigation all over again from a different angle. The whole business, moreover, was encouraged by a consistent disregard of the principles of *res judicata* by juries and magistrates, and issues which early should have been settled forever took forever to settle.[4]

One factor contributing to the disregard of prior adjudications was the lack of availability of printed opinions, both English and colonial, to which the magistrate might refer.[5] The rapid development of the lawsuit *in extenso* seems particularly astonishing in view of the fact that the band of Pilgrims who landed at Plymouth in 1620 contained not one lawyer, and among the Puritans who founded Massachusetts Bay in 1628-40, only two had been admitted to the Inner Temple (comparable to admission to the American legal profession through successful passage of the state bar examination) and none had ever practiced law.[6] This phenomenon of litigation without lawyers is accounted for in part by the fact that, unlike today, educated men in England and America during the seventeenth and eighteenth centuries were generally familiar with the law and its administration.[7] Skill in the law had not yet been abandoned to the legal profession, and the colonists pursued a sort of rude natural justice popularly administered without the refinement of a later day.[8] The tradition of judicial action so deeply ingrained in the American character unquestionably had its roots in our early history.

What finally emerged in colonial America were thirteen variations of the same legal system, not thirteen different systems.[9] A not inconsiderable part of the English heritage was the confusion in the organization and procedure of the courts, and to a certain extent the American confusion resulted from adopting the English judicial organization when it was in its most chaotic form in the seventeenth and eighteenth centuries. The authoritative legal source for America during this period was Sir Edward Coke's *Fourth Institute*, and when Coke wrote, the English judiciary had not yet been set to any systematic or orderly pattern, and individual courts were often without clearly defined limits of jurisdiction.[10] For the rest, the colonial judicial systems developed *sui generis*. New courts and new procedures were added as needed, without any conscious attempt to copy the mother country.

Also contributing to the judicial disorder was the lack of any differentiation of governmental powers. The colonial legislatures, in addition to exercising administrative and lawmaking powers, acted as final courts of appeal.[11] Typically, in Massachusetts Bay Colony from 1629 until 1635 the governor and the assistants acted as legislators, magistrates, and judges, and until 1660 the General Court of Massachusetts acted as a legislature, a court of appeals, and even as a criminal court. As a matter of fact, it retained appellate jurisdiction in criminal causes and original equity jurisdiction until 1865.[12] In all of the colonies, New England, Middle and South, including New York with its Dutch beginnings, any meaningful separation of powers was virtually unknown until the late seventeenth century when the concept took rudimentary form.

Existing side by side with the colonial judicial systems after 1696 were the courts of vice-admiralty. These were established by the crown to try, in addition to the usual marine causes, other cases concerning commerce and revenue as provided by a parliamentary act of 1696.[13] Prior to this, lawsuits involving matters of a marine character were handled either by the existing common law courts, or by the governor and council, or other bodies sitting as admiralty courts with a jury. But the laws of England were not being enforced. In the common law courts both judge and jury were prone to acquit offenders, and in the makeshift admiralty tribunals jurisdiction was limited by the terms of the governors' commissions and in no wise extended to trials for breaches of the English navigation acts. British officialdom considered the situation critical since vessels and persons could carry on illicit trade with impunity, not to speak of the loss to the king's treasury.

So there came into being eleven vice-admiralty districts covering the American colonies. Judges, advocates, registers and marshals were appointed by the colonial governors with the approval of the High Court of Admiralty in England. Jurisdiction of the new courts fell roughly into three categories: the ordinary marine disputes, most of which involved suits for wages and salvage; those cases relating to breaches of acts of trade which were, of course, closely connected with England's colonial commercial policy; and, finally, prize cases. The system of crown-established courts operating alongside the colonial courts precipitated conflicts not unlike those of a later date so common under the American federal system. The major areas of jurisdictional dispute were those involving the proprietary governments and the courts of common law. The proprietary or corporate colonies operated under charters which contained undisputed grants of legal and judicial authority, generally conceded to be greater than the powers of the tenant-in-chief of the crown, and although it was not clear whether such charters conferred admiralty jurisdiction on the proprietors, the colonies of this class attempted to confine the jurisdiction of the vice-admiralty courts to narrow limits and to prevent encroachment on what they believed to be their charter prerogatives. Royal authority had its way, but the vice-admiralty courts contributed tensions which were to lead to the final break with England.

It was perfectly natural for the vice-admiralty tribunals to collide with the courts of common law since, in theory, the two systems were to exercise concurrent jurisdiction, although in fact, the jurisdiction of the king's courts was never succinctly and precisely defined. The situation was aggravated further because the vice-admiralty courts proceeded without juries. In some admiralty suits the defendant would raise the question of jurisdiction (normally overruled by the judge), but in others the judge would, of his own volition, turn a suit over to the common law courts. A vice-admiralty court might fine a seaman for assault, or order a vessel returned from master to owner, but the judge would then inform the injured party that he must sue at common law for damages. Occasionally, when a common law judge believed that an action lay outside the competence of a vice-admiralty court, he would issue a writ of prohibition. Sometimes the writ would be ignored, sometimes formally refused, depending upon which of the two courts was held in higher regard. More often than not writs of prohibition were obeyed since the common law courts were independent and were generally the more powerful.

An almost identical court struggle had gone on in England during the early part of the seventeenth century and there was no question that the common law courts in the mother country were first in power and prestige in the judicial structure. By statute, writs of prohibition could issue from a common law court to stay vice-admiralty proceedings, and a vice-admiralty judge who ignored the writ was subject to punishment for contempt. But the parliamentary statute did not extend to the colonies; the courts of common law in America merely *asserted* the authority to issue the writ. The judicial conflict in America deepened further as Parliament continued to increase the jurisdictional powers of the vice-admiralty courts. This was part of the well-known attempt on the part of Britain to tighten the loose bolts in the imperial structure, particularly after 1764 when the entire revenue system was revised with a view toward stricter enforcement of the trade laws.

Of all the grievances which the colonists held against the vice-admiralty courts, the deprivation of the right of trial by jury was the most persistent. In the official British view, the jury system had broken down since the colonials refused to bring in verdicts against violators of the trade and revenue laws. The colonists, on the other hand, in addition to their complaints against the revenue measures (taxation without representation), were able to argue that they were being denied an old and revered English constitutional right.[14] Later events were to prove that jury trials and admiralty law were not compatible. During the revolutionary period the states attempted to use jury trials in their admiralty proceedings but found them unworkable. The complexities involved in matters of the sea were just not within the competence of the average citizen, regardless of good intentions, and it was not long before the states returned to the old system of admiralty proceedings. Eventually admiralty jurisdiction passed to the appellate committee of the Continental Congress, from thence to an appellate court, and ultimately to the federal courts under the Constitution. It is noteworthy that the vice-admiralty courts were the forerunners of the federal courts, and that the establishment of the federal union created conflicts not very different from those of the colonial period. And it seems doubtful that any federated government containing a dual court system can ever be free of such jurisdictional disputes.

The third, and probably the most important, feature of the early period of judicial gestation is the system of appeals, primarily because it furnished the groundwork for the mature form of the doctrine of judicial review of legislative and executive acts. Common law methods of appellate procedure find their origins in three sources: the Roman law, the Canon law of the medieval church, and the Germanic law. Under the Roman republic and in the initial stages of the formation of the English common law, appeals from courts of original jurisdiction were unknown.[15] Appeals came into being in Rome during the period of the Empire when the Emperor became the supreme judicial magistrate, and Roman law eventually worked out four methods of insuring correct determination of facts, correct ascertainment of the law, and proper application of the law to the determined facts. These were: (1) inspection of the proceedings for legal error (*revocatio in duplum*); (2) rehearing the case in a higher court (*appellatio*); (3) referral of questions of law to the ultimate appellate tribunal for an authoritative answer; and (4) rehearing of the cause in the same court upon petition.

With many variations and refinements these became universal practice in legal systems.[16] The courts of the church in the Middle Ages took over the Roman appeals procedures and adapted them to ecclesiastical needs. Specifically borrowed from the Roman law were *supplicatio*, a petition to the ultimate legal authority for a rehearing, and *restitutio in integrum*, an extraordinary remedy in case of injury in the course of a judicial proceeding such as a judgment based on false testimony or forged documents.[17] Except in the Scandinavian countries, Germanic law contained no system of appeals. Its contribution to appellate procedure lay in what is called "impeaching a judgment," which was actually an attack on a proposed judgment, and not review after a decision had been rendered. When a judgment was proposed by the official court, any person attending the proceeding could impeach the judgment by proposing another, contending that his own proposal was the correct judgment. Ultimate settlement was made by a higher court.[18]

All of the above ingredients went into the formation of the English court system which took on a modern form after settling such crucial matters as keeping records, separating courts of record from the others, and clearly setting off finding of facts from questions of law, and applying law to the facts found.[19] During the American colonial period five types of review of judicial proceedings were in vogue in England and were available as models for American appellate procedure. They consisted of: (1) review of trials at circuit by the common law courts; (2) writs of error in Parliament (House of Lords) to review judgments of the King's Bench and Exchequer Chamber; (3) writs of certiorari to remove a case pending before an inferior court to a superior court of common law; (4) appeals from the ecclesiastical courts and admiralty; and (5) appeals in Parliament from chancery and to the Privy Council from courts of the colonies.[20] Prior to the advent of the eighteenth century, appellate procedures in the colonial courts followed the American judicial pattern generally and can be best characterized as informal and relatively crude. Throughout the eighteenth century, however, the colonies, using the King's Bench as a model, standardized somewhat their appellate courts and adopted common law practices.[21] By the time of the framing of the Constitution, modes of appellate jurisdiction and procedure were clearly imbedded in the judicial systems of colonial America, and it was consistent with the temper of nationalism which pervaded the constitutional convention that the framers create a final court of appeals to hear cases involving legal questions of national significance.

The precedents for judicial invalidation of legislative and executive acts are less compelling, but the constitutional relationships between colonies and crown, specifically the procedures governing judicial appeals from the member governments to the central authority of the British imperial edifice, furnish important antecedents for judicial review in its modern form.

Acts of the colonial legislatures were subject to several types of review in England.[22] First, the Board of Trade might, as a matter of administration, examine any colonial statute and recommend disallowance to the king in council. Acceptable statutes were confirmed by an order in council, based upon a report by the Board of Lords Committee, which in turn reported to the Privy Council. Objectionable statutes were rejected or "disallowed" by the same machinery, but until enacting colonies were notified, disallowed acts continued in force. In some instances acts were declared null and void *ab initio* in the routine legislative review process, and under these circumstances, all action taken under the provincial statute was without validity. The legal distinction between the two procedures is the difference between void and voidable. The legal effect of the former is non-existence of a law, past and present; the effect of the latter is identical with that of repeal which merely voids a law at a certain point in time. The Privy Council might disallow a law for any reason whatsoever, subject only to the limitation that the veto must apply to the whole of a statute and not to any item, clause, or part of it in itself.

Judicial annulment, on the other hand, was a different type of proceeding. This second generic type of review by the Privy Council occurred in the exercise of the appellate function under which an unfavorable determination was a declaration of nullity. Such a judicial power of voiding colonial enactments depended upon the charter or upon the terms of the governor's commission, whereas, in contrast, legislative review rested upon acts of Parliament. In short, the source of authority for the judicial voiding of a law is related to the prerogative, in contradistinction to legislative disallowance which is found in the supreme law-making power. Clauses were written into both the colonial charters and the commissions to royal governors declaring that laws should not be enacted contrary to or repugnant to the laws of England. This limitation was a basic rule of English law, fashioned by the courts and implemented by statute, with a history going back to the time of the Plantagenets.[23] In an effort to reduce the law of the realm to uniformity, the English courts developed the principle that local law, including customs and corporate bylaws, must conform to the common law. Since the early colonial settlements were legally corporations, and since the patents to the various proprietors were virtually identical, it was easy to apply the legal rules which obtained at home to the new plantations abroad.

Somewhat less clear were the effects of clauses in the commissions to the royal governors requiring laws to be agreeable to those of England, but English commissions generally from the early seventeenth century onward had to be exercised pursuant to English law.[24] In 1696 Parliament enacted a law providing that

all laws, by-laws, usages or customs, at this time, or which hereafter shall be in practice, or endeavoured or pretended to be in force or practice, in any of the said plantations, which are in any wise repugnant to the before mentioned laws, or any of them, or which are any ways repugnant to this present act or to any other law hereafter to be made in this Kingdom, so far as such law shall relate to and mention the said plantations, are illegal, null and void, to all intents and purposes whatsoever.[25]

Unfortunately, it is not possible to define precisely what was meant by "repugnancy" or "contrariety" to the laws of England. In some charters and commissions a different phraseology was used, namely: laws were to be "as near as may be agreeable" to the laws of England.[26] It is fairly clear that in order for a law to be repugnant or contrary to the laws of England, it had to be more than merely different from, or at variance with, English law. In all probability a prima facie presumption of repugnancy would exist if a colonial act ran counter to any viable common law or equity doctrine in England.[27] In some quarters in America the argument was propounded that repugnancy of colonial acts could not be tested by a vague standard of English law, but must be measured against acts of Parliament specifically intended to apply to and actually in force in the colonies.[28] But this argument seems far fetched. At the time of issuance of the colonial charters, hardly any acts of Parliament specifically applied to the crown's dominions,[29] and the clauses dealing with repugnancy in the charters were not limited to some laws of England while excluding others.[30]

What is important here is the existence of a dual legal jurisdiction over a single territory containing superior and inferior laws, plus the concept that repugnancy or contrariety of inferior to superior may be judicially determined, and the law of the inferior discarded. Of further significance to later American constitutional development is the fact that the power of judicial annulment was exercised solely in a lawsuit brought in a colonial court and carried on appeal to the Privy Council sitting as the highest court in the imperial system.[31]

In purely quantitative terms, precedents for executive disallowance clearly outweigh those for judicial annulment. Although we can only approximate, (precise data are nonexistent), better than 500 colonial statutes were disallowed by orders in council out of some 8,500 submitted.[32] On the other hand, the Privy Council assumed appellate jurisdiction in just four cases in which the issue was the validity of colonial statutes, [33] and in only one, *Winthrop v. Lechmere*, was the law judicially voided. In the latter case a Connecticut statute was set aside on the ground that the legislature had gone beyond its powers under the Connecticut charter, a document which was in actuality the constitution for the government of Connecticut.

In no sense can it be said that the Supreme Court of the United States exercises power identical with that of the Privy Council either in disallowance or annulment. At the same time, modern American judicial review is not an entirely different kind of power, but is, in fact, rooted in British imperial practice. Granted that the British colonial empire during the seventeenth and eighteenth centuries was not a federal system, and granted that twentieth century judicial supremacy in constitutional interpretation is unknown in England, nevertheless, the seed for American judicial review was sown in Britain. It could never germinate there for the simple reason that no formal limitations on the powers of Parliament existed. An American variety, however, was home grown for the simple opposite reason that limitations on the Congress, the president, and the states in the Union are unequivocally expressed in the American Constitution. The principle established, presumably first expressed by Sir Edward Coke in 1610, was that courts possessing proper jurisdiction might invalidate legislative acts when such acts ran contrary to some higher law. The American experiment with a superior written law set the stage perfectly for a refined application of that principle.

Admiralty Courts

The second period of judicial development can be best characterized as one of emergent national unity with a representative congress wielding all existing national authority on an *ad hoc* basis from 5 September 1774 until 1 March 1781. As a necessary consequence of the Revolution, the judicial power of the English crown ceased to exist in America, and, in general, each colony could boast a self-contained, independent judiciary, as no appeals lay beyond the highest court in each colonial judicial system. As is often the case, however, the solving of one problem creates others. With the surcease of British power came the end of the vice-admiralty courts and an ensuing vacancy which could not be left empty. By the fall of 1775 two classes of armed vessels were cruising in Massachusetts waters and capturing enemy ships as prizes. One group was authorized by the Continental Congress and the other by the Massachusetts Assembly.[34] Jurisdictional questions were unsettled, and General Washington, embarrassed and annoyed by requests concerning proper determination of these admiralty questions, wrote to the president of the Continental Congress on 11 November 1775. He asked that Congress set forth appropriate means of proceeding, including the establishment of a court "to take cognizance of prizes made by the Continental vessels."[35]

Reaction to Washington's letter was swift. Before the month was out, Congress had sanctioned the capture of English vessels of war, as well as service or supply ships, upon commission by Congress or with their authorization. In order to enforce these resolutions the Congress recommended that the colonial assemblies erect new courts, or give jurisdiction to those in being, to determine matters concerning captures. Various other provisions were made including the suggestion that jury trials be afforded the litigants, but most important, the Congress requested that in all cases an appeal should be allowed to Congress, or to such person or persons as they should appoint.[36]

There is no doubt that this action by a national authority to standardize admiralty procedure is a clear antecedent for a national judiciary. It also links together, for certain purposes at least, what were theoretically thirteen independent, sovereign states, and adds one factor to many others. When totaled up, these factors demonstrate that the states were always bound in some form of union and were never, in fact, independent or sovereign. But as one observer points out, this early resolve of Congress on matters of admiralty procedure created no tribunal, provided no method of procedure, and no means of enforcing decrees, was silent as to original jurisdiction, left the extent of appellate power in doubt, engrafted trial by jury upon admiralty proceedings (a novelty of uncertain value), and assumed an undefined authority. In short, it created "a crude and imperfect piece of legislation." [37] But the imperfections were dealt with in rapid succession, and there is a clear line of continuity from British judicial authority to congressional judicial authority to federal judicial authority under the Constitution of 1789.

Prompted by the resolution of the Congress, the colonies established courts of admiralty jurisdiction. Application to Congress on appeal was by petition, which at first was referred to an *ad hoc* committee of five members appointed for each case,[38] but on 30 January 1777, Congress resolved to appoint a standing committee of five members to hear and determine admiralty appeals. [39] This mode of operation came to an end in January, 1780, when Congress established a court for the trial of all appeals from the admiralty courts of the states in cases of capture. This court, appointed by Congress, consisted of three salaried judges, any two of whom constituted a quorum.[40] Trial procedure was to be according to the usages of nations, and juries were expressly forbidden.[41] The court continued to operate until 1786 when Congress resolved that "as the war was at an end, and the business of that court in a great measure done away, an attention to the interests of their constituents made it necessary that the salaries of the said judges should cease." [42] The last entry in the Journals of Congress relating to this court is on 24 July 1786, empowering it to hear an appeal against a decree in the Court of Admiralty of South Carolina, condemning the sloop *Chester*.[43] But this is moving us into the third period, that between 1781 and 1789 under the Articles of Confederation.

Legal Appeals

The Articles of Confederation were agreed to in Congress on 15 November 1777, but were not to be conclusive until approved by the legislatures of all the states.[44] All of the states but Delaware and Maryland ratified the articles by the end of 1778. Delaware consented to the new instrument of government in 1779, but Maryland, in an attempt to secure a provision for the holding of the unsettled public lands for the benefit of all of the states, held out until 1 March 1781. The new government began operations on 23 March. Although restricted to very narrow limits, the judicial power of the United States was defined and even extended in some particulars by Article IX. This article provided that Congress should have exclusive power: first, to appoint courts for the trial of piracies and felonies committed on the high seas; and second, to establish courts of appeals in cases of capture, provided that no member of Congress should be a judge of any of the said courts. Furthermore, the article declared that Congress was to be the last resort on appeal in all disputes then existing, or which might arise, between two or more states concerning boundaries or other causes, provided that no states should be deprived of territory for the benefit of the United States. Finally, it declared that all controversies concerning the private right of soil claimed under different grants of two or more states would be settled finally by Congress upon petition of either party.

Under the articles, Congress created no new court of appeals, but the old court, established in January, 1780, appears to have continued to hear prize cases until July, 1786. In the two remaining areas of national jurisdiction under Article IX, those of piracies and felonies committed on the high seas and those involving territorial disputes, the arrangements provided for were temporary and haphazard. This appears to be a natural consequence of the loose confederate form of government. Even the extent of the judicial powers of Congress under the Articles of Confederation in cases of capture was narrowed by the construction given the articles in state courts.[45] And in the matter of piracies and felonies committed on the high seas, litigation was actually handled by the states under authority of Congress. Courts for such cases were established by an ordinance of 1781, but the judges consisted of justices of the supreme or superior court of judicature and of the admiralty courts of the respective states. Trials were by jury under common law proceedings, and upon conviction, all forfeitures went to the state wherein the conviction was had. When holding such courts, the judges sat in the state court house, the prisoners were confined in the state jail under state officers, and upon conviction were executed by order of the sheriff.[46]

In the matter of boundary disputes, the record indicates that appeals were made to Congress in six instances,[47] and in only one did the controversy actually come to trial.[48] In the others, the differences were settled amicably. Even in those areas where Congress or its designate exercised an appellate judicial power, it possessed no power of enforcement, generally depending upon state enforcement machinery or, in boundary disputes, upon mere acquiescence. And in most matters of the national interest real judicial protection was unknown. At various times from 1776 until 1787, Congress recommended that the states lend a helping hand, but the national interest seemed less compelling than local autonomy. Among other things, Congress found it impossible to obtain action to punish infractions of the laws of nations in such matters as the violation of safe conducts or passports granted by Congress, acts of hostility against persons in amity with the United States, and infractions of treaties or of the immunities of ambassadors.[49] Nor would the states provide for damage suits for parties injured under the law of nations or for compensation to the United States for damages sustained from an injury done to a foreign power by a citizen.[50] In 1782, Congress enacted an ordinance to regulate the post offices of the United States, imposing penalties for misdemeanors, but of necessity made them recoverable by action of debt in the name of the postmaster general in the state where the offense was committed.[51] By resolutions, Congress called upon the states to empower congressionally appointed commissioners to settle the accounts of the military department, [52] and requested the states to enact laws to enable the United States to recover effects and individual debts due to the United States.[53] But the states refused to act. In July, 1784, the Committee of States, sitting during the recess of Congress in order to give national authority some continuity, met with a deaf ear when it declared that the states, by their inaction, had caused considerable damage to the national interest, and the Committee urged the adoption of measures which would enable the United States to sue for and recover their debts, effects, property and any damages which had been or might be sustained.[54]

From the foregoing analysis of judicial power during the period of the Articles of Confederation, the following observations seem appropriate. First, whatever central judicial power existed remained undifferentiated. Instead of establishing a clear-cut court or system of courts, Congress or its creatures looked after judicial matters. Second, even if there had been an independent judiciary under the Articles, it would have exercised only those powers which the member states would allow. Furthermore, there was no way in which such a court could have enforced its process, in any event, since there was no executive to bolster judicial authority. Judicial anemia was a natural consequence of a confederate form of government which really had no vital power of its own and generically, as an organizational form, could never be anything but weak and unstable.

However—and this brings us to the final generalization—the period 1781-87 did not break with past judicial history. Although no tribunal was vested with the appellate authority which before the Revolution was exercised by the king in council, continuity was preserved through the admiralty proceedings and interstate boundary disagreements. At least it can be said that a connecting link of *central* judicial authority was maintained in the sense that at no time did the state courts command the final word on *all* matters justiciable. Central authority was never totally absent. Most important in this regard was the Court of Appeals in cases of capture which had received 118 cases on appeal from the states.

The point was well made by constitutional historians over a half century ago that so large a number of appeals from state courts to a national tribunal would familiarize the public mind with the idea of a supreme national court to decide matters of national interest. This may have had an educative influence in bringing the people of the United States to accept such an institution under the new Constitution.[55]

Although it is clear that the American people were never without some form of central judicial authority, even during the period of confederation, it is certain that from the time of the break with Britain until several years after the Constitution had been in effect, a national judiciary did not exercise a prerogative of judicial annulment of legislative acts, state or federal. A few cases arose in the states which indicate that the *idea* of judicial annulment was still alive, although in no state was it a firmly established practice.[56] Constitutional historians differ over the exact number, or the precise importance, and even over the nature of the proceedings in the cases which are generally cited as precedents for judicial review in the state courts prior to 1789. I think it relatively unimportant whether these state cases are or are not clear-cut precedents since the Revolutionary-Confederation period was transitional and brief, a constitutional groping for ways of innovation without relinquishing ties with the past. The American Revolution was not a Jacobin or Leninist revolt, but was a conservative revolution, the intent of which was not to destroy authority, but to eliminate specific aggressions against the traditional rights of Englishmen. The movement toward a consolidated government which culminated in the Convention of 1787 had been underway for better than a quarter of a century, and among the constitutional ingredients available to the new government was a judicial check on legislative and executive authority.

Constitution and Court

Judicial power was by no means the central preoccupation of the framers of the Constitution. The great debates centered on the distribution of powers between the nation and the states, or federalism, and on the problems of executive and legislative authority, or the separation of powers. But it would be a mistake to conclude that the judiciary was of minor significance. In fact, the discussion of the nature, function and scope of central judicial authority cut across the broader issues of nationalism versus localism and checked and balanced government versus legislative supremacy. The matter of judicial review aside, the framers, when constructing the article on the judiciary, disagreed on four major questions, all of which, with the advantage of hindsight, appear to have been settled in the most appropriate manner. Judicial selection was a compromise between election by the legislature and appointment by the executive. Also a compromise was the decision to leave the creation of inferior federal tribunals to the legislative discretion. Invoking only token dissent were the decisions to establish the independence of the judiciary through life tenure and removal only by impeachment. Motivating the most prolonged debate was the proposal to create a Council of Revision wherein judges of the national tribunal would be associated with the executive in a revisionary power over legislative acts. In the final vote this provision was defeated by a narrow margin of four states to three, with two states dividing, and one state absent.

Judicial annulment, as it was used by the Privy Council and as it later developed in American constitutional practice, was never formally proposed at the Convention of 1787. It was, however, alluded to during the debates over the Council of Revision, and constitutional historians ever since have pointed to these debates and have arrived at directly opposing conclusions. One group closes the matter by contending that if the framers had intended that the judiciary have final authority on constitutional questions, they would have said so in unequivocal terms. The other side argues that the Constitution is, and ought to, be a broad outline of powers and limitations, and cannot detail everything without becoming a legal code. They contend that much of the authority of the judiciary arises by implication, and that, in any event, a majority of the framers either flatly asserted that they favored the court's assumption of this authority, or at the very least, were never on record as opposing it. [57] It is difficult to believe that the framers would not have prohibited the exercise of judicial annulment altogether had they held strong views against its exercise. There are, after all, clearly stated prohibitions on the

Congress in spite of the fact that the constitutional authority of Congress was to be contained by a specific enumeration of its powers.

Several historical facts, although not making American judicial review a foregone conclusion, weigh heavily in its favor. First and foremost, the system of disallowance of colonial laws in Privy Council had prevailed for several generations, and it was not likely that such a vital and mature doctrine would suddenly disappear because the American colonies had cut loose from Britain.[58] In the second place, the fact that governmental power had not, either in British or American practice, been carefully differentiated in the past made it unlikely that the newly created branches of government, although so meticulously separated in theory, would suddenly be thoroughly and completely separated in practice. The framers themselves, much concerned with checks and balances, specifically provided for some overlapping of power in the governmental structure and many of them assumed that the Supreme Court would check the legislative and executive branches on constitutional questions.

Third, as previously noted, a strong tradition of judicial action, of litigating matters public and private (the line between the two often being more apparent than real) developed early during the colonial period and became ingrained in the American character. This in itself did not necessitate judicial review, but it did serve to dramatize the importance of courts in the general scheme of government, and to produce a popular support for the judiciary. Combining these historical currents with the Federalist concept of a written constitution which is to be applied in the courts not only as law, but as supreme law, it is hardly surprising that the doctrine of judicial review was early enunciated by the Supreme Court. In an organic sense, the American constitutional system, by embracing a form of judicial annulment of statutes, "continued to breed true to its heredity."[59]

The Supreme Court, like the Congress and the Presidency, was not a brand new creation but the result of centuries of Anglo-American constitutional evolution. In the light of America's colonial and revolutionary history, and in view of the difficulties encountered under the loosely organized confederation, it would have been illogical for the framers of the Constitution to create a strong national government without providing for a national judiciary. But at the same time, any framework which specified judicial power too rigidly would have been something less than basic law. Constitution making is a high art, and the success and stability of a constitution hangs precariously on the subtle distinctions between what the organs of government *must* do and what they *may* do. That is, an enduring constitution must allow the men who are to operate the government just the right amount of leeway for creativity and imaginative statesmanship. It must allow those who govern to make choices from the heritage of a nation's past, innovating and discarding when and where prudence dictates. The article on the judiciary in the Constitution left open such great questions as appellate jurisdiction, judicial annulment, the number and qualifications of the justices, and the nature and extent of the lower federal courts. Other important matters such as judicial tenure and the Supreme Court's original jurisdiction were settled, that is, unless the Constitution were to be amended. It is natural and sensible that constitutions be indefinite and imprecise if they are to endure. Once the Supreme Court was established, its future place in the American system of government would depend, as would that of Congress and of the Presidency, as much upon the nature of the men who occupied its high offices as upon the document which gave it life. As it turned out, certain justices of strong will and firm political persuasion left a permanent mark upon the Court, plunging it periodically into vehement and mordant controversy. But in the final analysis, the Court remained both a captive and a maker of history.

2. Congress & the Supreme Court During the Marshall Era

ALTHOUGH the dynamics of American politics demand perpetual and creative alterations in the constitutional system, the building of the original complex of arrangements with the blueprint provided by the framers of the Constitution, was probably the most precarious undertaking in America's history. It was the task of Congress to turn the blueprint for a government into an operating reality, and all at one time. Any structural weakness might have brought down the entire edifice or, at least, would have forced some rebuilding at a later time under new stresses and strains. The establishment of the Supreme Court was peculiarly significant since, paradoxically, the Constitution deemed it a coordinate and coequal with the Presidency and the Congress, and yet the Court was a creature of Congress in the sense that its detailed form and substance depended upon a statutory enactment. Had the framers spelled out in Article III the precise structure of a federal judicial system, prescribed the detailed nature of the Supreme Court's appellate jurisdiction, and explicitly authorized judicial review, much of the conflict which continues to this day might have been avoided. Instead, while Article III of the Constitution provides for a Supreme Court, it leaves these important questions open to legislative discretion. The stage was set for frequent legislative-judicial altercations which at times have almost reached an irreparable constitutional crisis.

It would be an error, however, to lay the blame for all controversy on either the doctrine of the separation of powers or on the framers themselves. The power conflict growing out of the rise of political parties in America was equally responsible. The glorious system which the Federalists had envisioned—a system without widely organized political parties in which the wise and the well born would be chosen to occupy the executive and the judicial branches of the national government (and hopefully the legislature as well) was destined for oblivion from the beginning. It was unrealistic for the founding fathers to permit "popular government," along with guarantees of free expression and free association, and then to expect first, that the electorate would remain static, and second, that it would choose its representatives and leaders only from the aristocracy, an already loosely defined class in America.

Moreover, it was perfectly natural that the human predilection for power would have its effect upon constitutional practice, and as Congress became the arena for the interplay of partisan political forces and ideas, it drew the Supreme Court into the vortex of the struggle. As a result, ever since 1789 the Court's institutional security and its influence within the American system have waxed or waned in direct proportion to its involvement in partisan politics. How this apparent stepchild of the political system grew into a familial patriarch of great influence, the object of both love and hate, is a phenomenon which never ceases to excite the imagination of students of American government.

Federalists and Republicans

During the first twelve years of the Federalist domination of the national government, the Supreme Court heard only sixty cases, an average of five per year. One-third of the litigation involved matters of admiralty and maritime affairs, or questions growing out of war or foreign relations. With such a paucity of business the Court was required to meet for only a few weeks each year. In the one instance in which the Court had assumed a nationalist posture, it had been overruled by a constitutional amendment.[1] Such men of prominence as Edmund Pendleton of Virginia, Robert Hanson Harrison of Maryland, Charles Cotesworth Pinckney and Edward Rutledge of South Carolina had declined proffered appointments to the Court. Others, like Thomas Johnson of Maryland, John Blair of Virginia, and Alfred Moore of North Carolina served briefly and resigned. Even the chief justiceship offered little challenge to John Jay and Oliver Ellsworth who early abandoned it. Compared to the other branches of government the Court was insignificant, so much so that those who planned the capital had not included any structure to house it. On the day that President Adams nominated John Marshall for the chief justiceship, the District of Columbia commissioners wrote to Congress:

> As no house has been provided for the Judiciary of the United States, we hope the Supreme Court may be accommodated with a room in the Capitol to hold its sessions until further provisions shall be made.[2]

Just thirty years later Alexis de Tocqueville, in commenting favorably upon the power of judicial review, suggested that the Court had become a formidable power in its own right, observing:

> The peace, the prosperity, and the very existence of the Union are vested in the hands of the seven Federal judges. Without them, the Constitution would be a dead letter: the executive appeals to them for assistance against the encroachments of the legislative power; the legislative demands their protection against the assaults of the executive; they defend the Union from the disobedience of the states, the states from the exaggerated claims of the Union, the public interest against private interests, and the conservative spirit of stability against the fickleness of democracy.[3]

When de Tocqueville wrote, the Supreme Court had already survived the first great assault made upon it by the Congress, an assault which had been in the making since the election of 1800 when the "party battle" became a permanent fixture in the American system.

Although the first Congress contained an overwhelming majority of former members either of the Convention of 1787 or of the ratifying conventions in the states.[4] disagreement over the nature and the extent of judicial power was apparent from the beginning. While it is true that the Judiciary Act of 1789, drafted by a Senate committee of eight, five of whom had attended the Constitutional Convention,[5] passed with little opposition, it did not become law without *any* opposition. In the Senate six negative votes were cast[6] including that of Senator Samuel Maclay of

Pennsylvania who called the bill the "gunpowder plot of the Constitution" and a law system "calculated . . . to draw by degrees all law business into the Federal Courts."[7] If the Constitution permitted such legislation, it was indeed a dangerous document because it would eventually "swallow all the State Constitutions" and "all the State judiciaries."[8] In the debates in the House of Representatives there were similar forebodings. Samuel Livermore of New Hampshire contemplated "with horror the effects of the plan" and saw "a foundation laid for discord, civil wars, and all its concomitants."[9] A system of lower federal courts in the states would be "establishing a Government within a Government, and one must prevail upon the ruin of the other."[10]

Fundamentally, the opposition to the first Judiciary Bill concentrated on its concept of a dual court system in the states, and the two sections of the bill which were to arouse antagonism at a later date, the requirement of circuit riding by the Supreme Court justices, and the twenty-fifth section which explicitly permitted an appeal to the Supreme Court when a state court had denied a claim of federal right, were approved with little comment. Each of these sections favored expressly opposed groups, and taken together, they represented a compromise between those who distrusted a judiciary which sat at a distance from the environment in which the original conflict had occurred, and those who believed in a powerful judiciary which would provide uniformity of justice and generally aid in unifying the new nation. In brief, the Judiciary Act created a Supreme Court consisting of a chief justice and five associate justices, and a system of lower federal courts including thirteen district and three circuit courts. In the circuits a court, composed of two Supreme Court justices and one of the district judges of the circuit, was to sit twice a year in the districts comprising the circuit. In broadest terms the circuit courts were to handle diversity of citizenship cases, and the district courts became the nation's admiralty tribunals.[11] Not until 1869 was the irritating circuit riding abolished. But prior to that time three tiers of courts had been operated by two sets of judges, with the whole system pivoted on circuit riding by the Supreme Court justices. As Felix Frankfurter and James Landis point out, in their book on the Court, in addition to the problem of the justices effectively discharging their duties in both Washington and on circuit, the system's adaptability to the territorial expansion of the country was questionable. More territory implied more circuits, and additional circuits commanded either more circuit riding for the justices or more justices for circuit riding.[12] But if the nationalists had their twenty-fifth section which would force the states into line on matters of national law, the localists had their fourth section which ordered the justices into the hinterlands to hold court in the states. This compromise in the first judiciary act was a clear portent of things to come since it illuminated the power struggle which was to grow in intensity, a struggle epitomized by Hamilton and Jefferson, consisting roughly of nationalist aristocrats opposed by particularist democrats.

In the Sixth Congress political divisions over judicial organization with its concomitant overtone of ultimate control of public policy burst into prominence. To the first session which met in Philadelphia President Adams sent a message on 3 December 1799 requesting that Congress consider revision of the judicial system of the United States.[13] After some bickering the introduction of the bill was postponed until the second session, which met in Washington. The Federalists controlled both Houses of Congress, but they were painfully aware of the inroads of Republicanism, and they attempted to do, in the words of John Rutledge, "as much good as we can before the end of this session."[14] Just four days before the announcement that Thomas Jefferson was to be the next president of the United States, the Circuit Court Act of 13 February 1801 became law.[15] Realizing that Republicanism was on the ascendancy, the Federalists were undoubtedly motivated by the desire to retain principles of "sound government" in the judiciary, but there had been agitation for parts of the new law ever since the passage of the first judiciary act in 1789. Prior to 1801 there had been seventeen districts each of which contained a court presided over by a district judge. The act of 1801 added five new districts, four of which were created by dividing old districts in New York, Pennsylvania, Virginia, and Tennessee into two, and the fifth was made up of the territories of Ohio and Indiana. Of greater importance was the provision which relieved the Supreme Court judges of circuit riding, providing instead that the twenty-two districts be classed into six circuits and that incumbent district judges be appointed as circuit judges. Historian John Spencer Bassett suggests that "the Federalists committed one of the most damaging of their acts of foolish party manipulation,"[16] whereas Max Farrand, in his classic discussion of the act[17] concludes that it was not adopted solely out of political malice but was an administratively sound and convenient arrangement. Both are correct—Bassett on Federalist motives and Farrand on sound judicial practice. Ultimately, the principles of the act were to become a permanent feature of the federal judiciary,[18] but the bitterness of the party strife prevented so much as a trial period for the new law which "combined thoughtful concern for the federal judiciary with selfish concern for the Federalist party."[19]

In the Seventh Congress the Federalists were in a minority for the first time, and the Republicans pressed their political advantage. Although President Jefferson's message to Congress on 8 December 1801 had the surface appearance of a mild suggestion that Congress consider judicial reform, the Republican leadership turned the president's request into a mandate, which in all probability is what the politically artful Jefferson intended.[20] Ostensibly the Republicans proposed to repeal the Judiciary Act of 1801 which dealt with the federal judiciary as a whole and only peripherally with the Supreme Court. But the debates surrounding the question of repeal suggest the growing divisions in the country not only over the extent of judicial power, but over the broader questions of national power and judicial review. John Breckenridge of Kentucky, author of the Virginia and Kentucky Resolutions and able lieutenant of Jefferson, introduced the resolution for repeal in the Senate on 8 January 1802. He had sought the advice of John Taylor of Caroline County, Virginia whose long letter of reply became the basis for the repeal act of 1802.[21] In a full dress debate which continued for two months[22] the merits of the bill were argued mainly in terms of two themes: constitutionality and wisdom. The Federalists argued that the bill was invalid since the Congress would be removing judges from office by law rather than by impeachment, and furthermore that Congress would be abrogating a contract and enacting an *ex post facto* law.[23] The Republican answer was simply that the judge was not being removed but that the office was being abolished,[24] or as it was expressed in more general terms by Philip Thompson of Virginia, "It is an axiom in politics that an ordaining power always embraces a repealing power."[25] Another argument of the Jeffersonians was that the act being repealed was in itself unconstitutional since it had abolished the district courts in Kentucky and Tennessee by making them circuit courts, and the House of Representatives, by changing the titles of the judges, had exercised an appointing power which belonged only to the president and the Senate.[26]

Constitutionality aside, was it prudent to alter the judiciary in this fashion? The Jeffersonians contended that judicial business was decreasing and that additional courts were an unnecessary expense and burden to the people.[27] They also argued that law must be closely connected with the people, that the sources of law are properly environmental and popular. Federalist doctrine could not tolerate this rank heresy. In their view the proper source of law was knowledge—knowledge obtained from books, statutes, and prior decisions.[28] To popularize law was to vulgarize it. Circuit riding was bad on two counts. It necessitated the appointing of judges not for their wisdom but for their physical agility. Such a system, declared the Federalists, made it impossible for judges to discharge their duties. If it were to prevail, judges might as well be selected as one enlists soldiers.[29] The proposed system was also bad in that it blended inferior with superior responsibilities with the judges becoming as a "Proteus; constantly changing their character."[30]

If the Federalists, as Henry Adams said, "were altogether in the right" on the question of expediency and public convenience,[31] the Republicans were altogether in the right on the question of constitutionality. The repeal act of 1802 was imprudent from the standpoint of efficient judicial administration and the necessities of the day, but legislative abolition of an office of its own creation lay unequivocally within the purview of congressional authority under the new Constitution. As important as these questions were, they are, when placed in perspective, overshadowed by the Republican and Federalist views of organized government in general and of the American version in particular, and by the existence of a power conflict epitomized by the emergent political parties.

Gouverneur Morris urged the Federalist cause most eloquently. He predicted an end to all constitutions if public opinion "is to be our judge" and appealed to the "good sense," "patriotism," and "virtue" of the "host of assailants" against judicial power. Why are we here, asked Morris? We are "assembled here to save the people from their most *dangerous enemy*, to save them from themselves." [32] Morris pleaded with his colleagues:

> I stand in the presence of Almighty God, and of the world; and I declare to you, that if you lose this charter, never, no never will you get another! We are now, perhaps, arrived at the parting point. Here, even here, we stand on the brink of fate. Pause—Pause! For Heaven's sake, pause! [33]

In turning a deaf ear to Federalist importuning, the Republicans affirmed a belief in popular control of the government, including the judiciary, and ultimately they challenged the entire concept of judicial review. For, if this political power of the Supreme Court were admitted, the justices, all of a Federalist orientation, might well invalidate the repeal act.[34] Senator Breckenridge, in a reversal of the stand he had taken earlier as the author of the Kentucky Resolutions, now supported the doctrine of legislative supremacy. Contending that "this pretended power of the Courts to annul the laws of Congress cannot possibly exist," Breckenridge declared that " . . . the legislature have the exclusive right to interpret the Constitution, in what regards the lawmaking power, and the judges are bound to execute the laws they make." [35]

In all of the debates in Congress up to this time, the power of judicial review had been opposed only once. On 5 March 1800 Senator Charles Pinckney of South Carolina, arguing in behalf of a bill to prevent appointment of justices of the Supreme Court to any other official position while on the bench, said that "the dangerous right to question the constitutionality of the laws . . . is as unfounded and as dangerous as any that was ever attempted in a free government." [36] The fact that judicial review had not been more widely challenged militates strongly in favor of the conclusion that the disagreements over judicial annulment which became a matter of public record during the debates over the judiciary bill of 1802 were motivated by considerations of political power. Would the Republicans have supported judicial review if the membership of the Supreme Court had been of the proper political persuasion? Would the Federalists and the Republicans have reversed their fields if the Supreme Court had invalidated the Alien and Sedition Acts?

Although these questions are not susceptible of perfect answers, it is likely that with hindsight we can answer both questions in the affirmative without imputing lack of integrity to either group. Judicial review merely cut across the broader question of popular sovereignty as opposed to aristocratic rule. By 1800 the Federalist concept of a limited electorate had already passed from the American scene forever because Jeffersonian leadership had begun to understand and to apply the very modern political axiom of "getting out the vote." [37] Both groups lacked patience. The Federalists, failing to grasp the political realities of the day, seemed unable to perceive the necessities of fighting their opponents with their own weapons. On the other hand, the Jeffersonians, who controlled both houses of Congress after 1800, were unwilling to wait for the normal course of events— resignations and deaths—in order to control the judiciary as well. Finally, both groups were overly concerned with the theoretically possible misuse of judicial power. The Supreme Court might arrest public policy at a given moment in history, but to make its will prevail permanently over the combined wills of the president and Congress would have been, and historically has been, impossible.

If the disagreements in Congress from 1789 until 1802 were fundamentally over the nature of abstract judicial power, this was not the case during the period 1821-32. The first great judicial crisis occurred during this decade, when the Supreme Court became the object of a sustained congressional attack. This time, however, the court was reproached not for what it might do, but for what it had done. And the attack was not mounted because the Supreme Court was invalidating acts of Congress or asserting judicial supremacy, but because the Court was allowing too great an extension of federal power—national supremacy—over the states. In short, the Court was attacked for exercising judicial review of state legislation, a power strongly implied by Article III of the Constitution and expressly granted, under certain conditions, in the twenty-fifth section of the Judiciary Act of 1789. The controversy became highly personalized in terms of strong-willed Republicans in the Presidency and Congress who were in opposition to Chief Justice John Marshall, the hard-core Federalist with a dominating personality.

Judicial Review and the States

On 20 January 1801 President John Adams named John Marshall chief justice of the United States, the duties of which office he discharged with extraordinary vigor and distinction until he died on 6 July 1835. [38] John Marshall was born in a log cabin in the woods of Prince William County, Virginia, the first of fifteen children of Thomas and Mary Marshall. With scant formal education he joined the revolutionary forces in 1775 and served most of his four years with General Washington, including the trying winter at Valley Forge. After his discharge he entered William and Mary College and for a few weeks attended the lectures of the famous Virginia lawyer, George Wythe. After this brief academic experience he left for Richmond where he was admitted to the bar in 1780, the certificate having been signed by his cousin, Governor Thomas Jefferson. In 1783 Marshall married Mary Wills Ambler, the daughter of the treasurer of Virginia and a member of one of the wealthiest families of the state. Concurrently building a law practice and engaging in politics Marshall moved into a position of respect and authority in public life. He was elected to the Virginia House of Delegates in 1782 where he quickly espoused the nationalist cause. Later, as a delegate to the Virginia ratifying convention, he stood beside James Madison in opposition to such notables as Patrick Henry and George Mason. After the new national government had been formed, President Washington offered Marshall the post of United States attorney for Virginia, then the attorney generalship, and later the ministry to France. Marshall preferred to remain in the Virginia legislature where he had established a reputation as a leading spokesman for Federalist policies. Within a few years, however, President Adams persuaded him to act as one of three envoys to negotiate a *détente* with France, and he thereby became involved in the notorious X, Y, Z affair, so called because of President Adams' designation of the French representatives as Messrs. X, Y and Z. Because of his refusal to agree to what he considered outrageous terms to the United States including a bribe to the French Directory, Marshall returned home a hero in 1798. President Adams offered him an appointment to the Supreme Court, but he refused, choosing instead to run for Congress where he served for six months before accepting the presidential appointment as secretary of state in the late spring of 1800. Although Marshall received his official commission as chief justice on 31 January 1801, the president requested him to continue to discharge the duties of secretary of state "until ulterior arrangements can be made", which Marshall did until, as chief justice, he administered the presidential oath of office to Thomas Jefferson. Each of these great men disliked, distrusted and disdained the other, and each in his unique way gave the bulk of his life's energies to the new experiment in republican government.

To repeat the catalogue of descriptive flattery that historians have showered on John Marshall over the years would be an exercise in redundancy, but the fact is that his influence not only on the Supreme Court but on the future of American constitutional development cannot be overstated. He truly deserves being singled out as "the great Chief Justice." Perhaps, like Washington and Lincoln, he was the right man in the right place at the right time. As chief judge in a new nation, although able to draw upon English and American colonial constitutional practice, he had a unique opportunity for creativity, and he seized the chance to cover the Constitution with a permanent judicial gloss. Lesser men in the same environment might have failed miserably, or at the least, performed with only routine competence.

Marshall's unusual success can be attributed in part to his personal magnetism. He combined intelligence, charm, warmth, humor, an even temper, and that indefinable "common sense" with a penchant for hard work. He labored to move his colleagues toward unanimity on the tough issues of the times. The unusual social situation in which he and his associates lived, ate, worked and carried on their recreation in close personal proximity day after day, week after week, favored Marshall's special talents and enabled him to dominate the judicial scene. Professor John Roche suggests that important ingredients in his success were his exceptional ability as a manager of small groups combined with his

willingness to do most of the work.[39] Of a total of 1,215 cases
between 1801 and 1835, Marshall delivered the opinion in 519,
and of the sixty-two decisions involving constitutional questions,
he wrote thirty-six. And he spoke for the Court in eighty cases out
of 195 dealing with questions of international relations.[40] John
Marshall died at the age of eighty, having lived almost a decade
beyond Presidents Adams and Jefferson whose public careers had
been so interwoven with his own.

Any treatment of the Supreme Court under Marshall's leadership must begin with the case of *Marbury* v. *Madison*.[41] Growing
out of the factional struggles of the early nineteenth century the
lawsuit had its origins in an attempt by the Federalists to persuade
the Court to act against the Jefferson administration. After a
Federalist Congress had passed the Judiciary Act of 1801,
President Adams moved immediately to fill the new judicial posts
with Federalists. But, in the changeover of administrations, some
of the commissions were not delivered, including that of William
Marbury who had been named a justice of the peace for the
District of Columbia. President Adams' secretary of state, John
Marshall, should have completed the delivery, but failed to do so,
and President Jefferson's secretary of state, James Madison,
refused to carry out what the new administration considered to be
Federalist patronage. Marbury requested the Supreme Court to
issue a writ of mandamus compelling the secretary to transmit the
commission. In a paradoxical display of boldness and restraint
Marshall condemned the Jeffersonians for not doing their duty,
asserted the Supreme Court's authority to declare an act of
Congress unconstitutional, and at the same time berated Congress
for giving the Court more power than the Constitution permitted.

In his opinion Marshall asked three questions. Did Marbury have
a right to the commission? Was a mandamus the proper legal
remedy to obtain it? Could a mandamus issue from the Supreme
Court? After replying in the affirmative to the first two questions,
Marshall then ruled that unfortunately the Supreme Court could
not issue the writ. Why so? Because the Judiciary Act of 1789
which granted the Court the power to issue writs of mandamus in
an original proceeding was unconstitutional. Since the Constitution specifically outlines the original jurisdiction of the Supreme
Court and does not permit Congress to alter that jurisdiction,

Congress had gone beyond its powers by enlarging the Court's area of competence. (Actually the clause of issue in Section thirteen could be and logically should have been interpreted to mean that the Supreme Court might issue writs of mandamus when it had proper jurisdiction in a case. Under such an interpretation Marshall might have denied jurisdiction and sent Marbury to the district court. Section thirteen would then have remained intact and constitutional.) Even Jefferson whose concept of judicial review was a severely limited one, could not argue with the Court's assertion that it was protecting its own jurisdiction, protecting it, moreover, by telling the Congress that it was giving the Court *too much* power. At the same time Marshall's sweeping language justifying judicial review of acts of Congress was a strategic victory for judicial power and a pronouncement of enduring significance for the future of the Republic.

The argument in support of the Court's authority to declare acts of Congress unconstitutional closely followed Alexander Hamilton's logic in *The Federalist #78*. Essentially it encompassed the following points: (1) the Constitution not only grants powers but limits powers as well; (2) any legislative act that goes beyond the constitutional limits is void and not binding on the courts; (3) when hearing a case, if the courts are confronted with a law in opposition to the Constitution, they have no choice but to disregard the law in favor of the Constitution; and (4) this must be so because (a) the judges take an oath to support the Constitution, and (b) Article VI in declaring "what shall be the supreme law of the land, the Constitution itself is first mentioned; and not the laws of the United States, generally, but only those which shall be made in pursuance of the Constitution. . . ." Thus, by combining the judicial function with the phraseology of the Constitution that it must be applied not only as law but as supreme law, a logical case was made for judicial review.

Although *McCulloch* v. *Maryland* [42] and *Gibbons* v. *Ogden* [43] follow the general pattern of decisions rendered by the Court during the 1820s they deserve special attention both for their far-reaching implications and for the interesting rhetoric used by Marshall to support his constitutional position. In the *McCulloch* case, which involved the constitutionality of the Bank of the United States, the Chief Justice dealt with two questions. Had

Congress the power to incorporate a national banking institution? If so, was it within the powers of the states to lay taxes on its notes? Answering the first question in the affirmative Marshall announced the doctrine of implied powers. The ultimate affect of this was to give Congress the authority to meet national exigencies whether the Constitution enumerated the specific authorization or not. He did so by fashioning the "necessary and proper clause" into a grant of power endowed with infinite elasticity. As long as the end was "legitimate," "within the scope of the constitution," said Marshall, "all means which are appropriate, which are plainly adapted to that end, which are not prohibited, but consist with the letter and spirit of the constitution, are constitutional." Moreover, he continued, Congress might combine several powers to justify a legislative policy when no single power would suffice by itself. Clearly, if the justices of the future were to acquiesce in such an all-inclusive defense of legislative power, it would be a rare case indeed in which they might find legitimate grounds for invalidating an act of Congress. Was *Marbury* v. *Madison* that important after all?

In the second half of his opinion, however, Marshall had no compunctions about containing the powers of the states. Maryland's tax on a legitimate federal institution could not stand, for it was in conflict with federal law, and valid national laws "control the constitution and laws of the respective states, and cannot be controlled by them." Furthermore, "the power to tax involves the power to destroy," and the authority that legitimately creates something need not permit its destruction by a hostile hand. Many years later Justice Holmes was to quip that the power to tax was not the power to destroy "while this Court sits," but in 1819 there is little doubt that Maryland and other states as well were capable of taxing the national bank out of existence.

Gibbons v. *Ogden* is generally considered one of Marshall's greatest opinions, but its importance lies not in what it decided but in the Marshallian explication of that crisp phrase in Article I, Section Eight of the Constitution, "congress shall have power to regulate commerce . . . among the several states." The case had its origins in New York's grant of a monopoly to Robert Fulton and Robert Livingston to operate steam vessels on the state's rivers. They in turn granted exclusive rights to Aaron Ogden to run a commercial enterprise on the Hudson River, including stops at ports in New Jersey. Meanwhile New Jersey (and Connecticut) retaliated against the New York monopoly by forbidding boats licensed by Fulton and Livingston to enter the state's waterways, seemingly engaging in the very kind of commercial warfare that the commerce clause was designed to prevent. But the litigation actually entered the courts not over interstate rivalry but because of pocketbook competition that Ogden encountered when Thomas Gibbons began to cut into Ogden's profits by running boats along the same routes which he was licensed to do by the United States government under the Coasting Act of 1789.

Reversing New York's famed jurist Chancellor James Kent, Marshall declared that federal law superseded state law and that Gibbons could not be enjoined from plying his trade. For all practical purposes the New York monopoly was dissolved, and although national supremacy was again the basis for the ruling, the decision was one of the most popular ever rendered by "the great Chief Justice" since public support for the monopoly had always been minimal.

It was Marshall's elucidation of the constitutional phraseology—for the most part, obiter dicta—that is now revered by those who believe in comprehensive regulation of the economy. For, the general tenor of the opinion, although somewhat discursive, is the approval of congressional control over a broad range of activities. Commerce, said Marshall, is more than "traffic," it is "intercourse," and it encompasses navigation and commercial affairs generally. "Among the several states" means intermingled with, and commerce cannot stop at state lines, "but may be introduced into the interior" although the "completely internal commerce of a state . . . may be considered reserved for the state itself." "The power to regulate" is the power "to prescribe the rule by which commerce is governed," and it "is complete in itself, may be exercised to its utmost extent, and acknowledges no limitations, other than are prescribed in the Constitution."

To the supreme nationalist, then and now, the one great flaw in the opinion is its failure to state flatly that Congress has *exclusive* power to regulate interstate commerce, thereby removing the states from exercising any jurisdiction whatsoever over the subject matter. Such a pronouncement might have settled what soon became an interminable constitutional issue. At the same time the thrust of the opinion was on the side of national power, and in this and in his other major opinions, John Marshall continued to direct the American system on a course which the founding fathers intended but could not insure.

Both Presidents Washington and Adams had appointed Federalists to the Supreme Court, and Jefferson's hostility to the Court was as much personal as it was political. Had Republicans occupied the highest bench, Jefferson and his party might have viewed the judiciary and judicial authority in a somewhat altered light. It was not until March of 1804 that President Jefferson was able to present his first nomination to fill a vacancy on the Supreme Court. He chose William Johnson of South Carolina, characterized by the Federalist senator from New Hampshire, William Plumer, as a "zealous Democrat but . . . honest and capable." [44] Jefferson's second appointee was Henry Brockholst Livingston of New York, who filled the vacancy created by the death of Justice William Paterson in 1806. In the following year, in pursuance of an act of Congress creating a new associate justiceship to take care of the increasing business in the districts of Kentucky, Tennessee and Ohio, Jefferson appointed Thomas Todd of Kentucky, a lawyer from the new West who had been recommended by Republican members of Congress. But Jefferson had been unable to shake Federalist control of the Court, and upon his return to private life in 1809, the Court consisted of Federalist Justices William Cushing, Samuel Chase, Bushrod Washington, and of course, John Marshall and the three Republicans. When the Court met in 1812, however, it contained a Federalist minority for the first time. Justices Cushing and Chase had died, and Joseph Story and Gabriel Duval were their respective replacements. Although the Court was Republican in politics, John Marshall, as Charles Grove Haines points out, "continued to dominate the tribunal as fully as when the members were of his own political faith." [45] But the fact that former Republicans like Justices Johnson and Story came to espouse the cause of nationalism seems not too strange when one remembers that Jefferson in power, unlike Jefferson the critic, was instrumental in expanding federal authority, and that by the end of the War of 1812 John C. Calhoun fitted snugly into the Hamiltonian mold. Until the Jacksonian movement reached full flower America was in an era of virulent nationalism. The times, however, were not without dissent, and for a while the dissenters, the states'-righters, although unable to reverse the trend, were able to stay the movement for a few fleeting seconds of history.

The precipitating causes of the first concrete proposals in Congress to curb the power of the Court were the Court's decisions in the cases of *Cohens* v. *Virginia*[46] and *Green* v. *Biddle*[47] in the early twenties, but the crisis had been in the making for more than a decade. Sporadic proposals had been made beginning in 1806 which would have reduced judicial authority generally although the Supreme Court may have been the real target. Representative John Clopton of Virginia had proposed amendments to the Constitution which would have narrowed the meaning of the "necessary and proper" clause[48] and limited the jurisdiction of the federal judiciary.[49] A third constitutional amendment, introduced by Rep. David Williams of South Carolina would have given the states some control of the issuance of process in the federal district and circuit courts.[50]

The first hard assertion of federal judicial power over state authority came in 1809 in the decision in *United States* v. *Judge Peters*.[51] The legal issues had their origin in a dispute which had begun under the Articles of Confederation. The old Court of Appeals in Cases of Capture had awarded one Gideon Olmstead a prize claim which his home state of Pennsylvania refused to honor. Later, after the Supreme Court had authorized federal district courts to execute the decrees of the Confederation court,[52] District Judge Peters ordered that the prize money be paid to Olmstead. The Pennsylvania legislature reacted by directing the governor to protect the "just rights of the state" from any process issued by a federal court, but Olmstead applied to the Supreme Court for a mandamus compelling Judge Peters to enforce his earlier decision. In awarding the peremptory mandamus John Marshall declared for the Court that the ultimate right to determine the jurisdiction of the federal courts resided in the

Supreme Court and not in the state legislatures, and for good reason. Said Marshall:

> If the legislatures of the several states may, at will, annul the judgments of the courts of the United States, and destroy the rights acquired under those judgments, the constitution itself becomes a solemn mockery . . . the people of Pennsylvania, not less than the citizens of every other state, must feel a deep interest in resisting principles so destructive of the union and in averting consequences so fatal to themselves.[53]

When the United States marshal attempted to serve process against the holders of the prize money he was met by a body of the state militia which the governor had called into action. Ultimately, after the incident had come very close to causing bloodshed, Pennsylvania somewhat ungraciously acquiesced. The state legislature, in a resolution which recognized national supremacy, asserted nevertheless that the national government must operate within its constitutional limits and that the legislature could not permit an infringement of states' rights by an unconstitutional exercise of power in United States courts.[54] The doctrine of the Pennsylvania resolution was rejected by ten states, including the state of Virginia in which the legislature resolved that the Supreme Court of the United States was "more eminently qualified . . . than any other tribunal that could be erected" to decide such disputes.[55]

The Old Dominion, although refusing to support Pennsylvania, went through its own psychic shock just a few years later when, in *Martin v. Hunter's Lessee*[56] the Court ordered the Virginia Court of Appeals to reverse an original ruling. Georgia, too, had thought Pennsylvania in the wrong, but she bitterly fought the Marshall court after the ruling in *Fletcher v. Peck*[57] in 1810 in which Georgia had the dubious honor of being the first state to have one of its laws declared unconstitutional by the Supreme Court. The Supreme Court held that the state of Georgia might not sell state owned lands and then, at a later date, rescind the original sale, even though the original sale was tainted by fraud and bribery. Making three main points, the Court's opinion delivered by Marshall declared: (1) that the courts could not inquire into the motives of a legislature no matter how corrupt such motives might be; (2) that a legislative rescinding of a prior act of sale was a fundamental interference with private rights in violation of vested or natural rights in property; and (3) that the rescinding act impaired the obligation of contract and was thus forbidden by Article I, Section Ten of the Constitution. John Marshall gave the contract clause a far broader meaning than that intended by its framers since the overwhelming evidence indicates that the clause was intended to encompass private executory contracts and not executed contracts between a state and another party.

In *Martin* v. *Hunter's Lessee* the Court's argument with Virginia, as in the altercation with Pennsylvania, concerned the Supreme Court's appellate jurisdiction. Virginia had confiscated the vast land holdings of Lord Fairfax, a Virginia loyalist during the Revolution, and had made it illegal for an alien to inherit real property. Despite the right of Fairfax's English heir, Denny Martin, to inherit the estate under the treaty with Great Britain in 1894, the Virginia Court of Appeals upheld the laws of the state. On an appeal authorized by the twenty-fifth section of the Judiciary Act of 1789 the Supreme Court reversed the Virginia decision. Under the leadership of Spencer Roane, the Virginia court refused to abide by the Supreme Court's ruling, and declared the twenty-fifth section of the Judiciary Act unconstitutional. Once again the case went to the Supreme Court and Justice Story, for the Court, ordered Virginia to comply. He maintained that only if the Supreme Court might review the decisions of all inferior courts in the United States could the Constitution, treaties, and laws of the United States have uniform application as supreme law everywhere in the nation.

By 1820 the Court had invalidated laws in seven states, and by 1825 in ten. In addition to Pennsylvania, Georgia and Virginia, the Court had asserted national supremacy over New Hampshire (*Dartmouth College* v. *Woodward*),[58] New Jersey (*New Jersey* v. *Wilson*),[59] New York (*Sturgis* v. *Crowninshield*),[60] Maryland (*McCulloch* v. *Maryland*),[61] Vermont (*Society, etc.,* v. *New Haven*),[62] Kentucky (*Green* v. *Biddle*),[63] and Ohio (*Osborn* v. *Bank of the U.S.*).[64] It must be remembered that the Court could not deal with these questions on its own motion. Cases had to arise. And they arose out of the social, political and economic ferment of the times. The aftermath of the war of 1812 brought speculation, wildcat banking, and financial skulduggery which ultimately produced economic depression and hard times. Out of the financial chaos grew a natural conflict between debtors and creditors. The debtors appealed to the state legislatures for relief in the form of suspension of debts and contracts and for an increase of money in circulation. The creditors, unable to stem the affirmative legislative reaction to these appeals, turned to the courts for protection against what in their minds was imprudent and invalid legislation. As a result of these events, conservatism and nationalism were partners against radicalism and states' rights in a struggle which inevitably struck at the fundamental limits of both judicial and legislative power as well as the elemental nature of the union.

The decisions in *Cohens* v. *Virginia* and *Green* v. *Biddle*, which were handed down within a week of each other during the 1821 term of the Supreme Court, brought state-national antagonisms to a head. These cases ostensibly involved Virginia and Kentucky against the Supreme Court, but the issue was as much one of national supremacy as of judicial sovereignty.

In the Virginia case the Cohen brothers had been fined $100 by a local court for selling lottery tickets in violation of the state's laws. They carried on the enterprise under an act of Congress that had authorized a lottery in Washington, D. C., and after their conviction they maintained that the congressional statute protected their commercial activities in Virginia. On the merits of the case Marshall upheld the Cohens' conviction, observing that Congress had no intention of applying the ordinance beyond the boundaries of the District of Columbia and that Virginia had properly exercised jurisdiction in the matter. What propelled the case into a battle of crucial national significance, however, was Marshall's insistence—over Virginia's vehement protest—that the Supreme Court had jurisdiction in the case. In addition to reaffirming Justice Story's opinion in *Martin* v. *Hunter's Lessee*, the chief justice declared that the Eleventh Amendment to the Constitution does not preclude the appearance of a state as a defendant-in-error in the Supreme Court of the United States. It also furnished John Marshall a vehicle to answer the states' rights arguments of Spencer Roane, and he did so emphatically:

We think that in a government acknowledgedly supreme, with respect to objects of vital interest to the nation, there is nothing inconsistent with sound reason, nothing incompatible with the nature of government, in making all its departments supreme, so far as respects those objects, and so far as is necessary to their attainment. The exercise of the appellate power over those judgments of the state tribunals which may contravene the constitution or laws of the United States, is, we believe, essential to the attainment of those objects.

The case of *Green* v. *Biddle* arose out of the ordinance of separation between Virginia and Kentucky by which it was agreed that all private rights and interests in Kentucky lands derived from the laws of Virginia should be determined by the laws then in force in Virginia. Kentucky, however, in order to settle some of the many disputed land claims, enacted two statutes, one in 1797 and another in 1812. By their terms any person occupying lands who could show a clear title could not, without notice of adverse title, be held liable for rents and profits during his occupancy. Furthermore, a claimant who was subsequently awarded title to occupied land had to compensate the occupant for any improvements. If he did not the title would rest with the occupant who had originally paid for unimproved land. Justice Story invalidated the "occupant-claimant" laws in 1821. The case was reargued in 1822 and decided finally in 1823, affirming Story's original opinion. What the Supreme Court held was that the compact between Virginia and Kentucky was a contract, and as such, was entitled to protection under the Constitution.

Congress Acts

Although there had been occasional proposals offered in Congress to curtail federal judicial power from 1800 onward, when Richard M. Johnson of Kentucky arose in the Senate on 12 December 1821, he initiated a series of attacks on the Supreme Court that was not to cease until the last days of John Marshall. Despite the fact that the central issue was the nature and extent of state powers, the states were not able to act in concert[65] and any changes in the basic constitutional arrangements, either in the federal structure or in the power of the Supreme Court, would have to be made by Congress. Such changes might take the form of a statute or of a proposed constitutional amendment, depending upon the nature of the desired change. Senator Johnson urged the latter course of action when he introduced a resolution to amend the Constitution by giving the Senate appellate jurisdiction in all cases involving federal questions in which a state law is drawn in question.[66]

On 14 January 1822 in a long and tedious speech, Senator Johnson defended his proposal. He contended that the conflicts between the states and the federal judiciary had become "so frequent and alarming" that the public safety demanded an investigation to determine where the error lay. In addition to tracing and commenting on the cases in which the Supreme Court had invalidated state laws, Johnson made two major points. First, in his view, the union consisted of equal sovereigns within their spheres of power, and it was a "flagrant outrage to justice, a violation of every principle of equity" for one of the sovereigns to "arrogate to itself the exclusive power of judging in all cases of disagreement." Admitting the necessity of an umpire in cases of "serious collision," Johnson suggested that the Senate is the proper agency for this role. In theory, of course, such a proposal does not satisfy the requirement that the umpire of disputes be neutral, and in practice, the states would have had built-in protection.

Johnson's second point is an assault on the entire concept of judicial review. When courts declare laws unconstitutional, they are exercising political power. This is bad, said Johnson, not because judges are worse than other men but because they are not accountable to the people. Moreover, the Constitution nowhere grants the power to the judiciary to invalidate state laws, and "the States never designed so to impair their sovereignty as to delegate this power to the Federal judiciary." Furthermore, continued Johnson, the one time when the federal courts had the opportunity to safeguard our liberties, instead of striking down the statutes (Alien and Sedition Acts), the judiciary "was a willing instrument of Federal usurpation." The people found relief only in their own power, in the elective franchise which is "their only safe dependence." [67]

On 15 January, in a second speech devoted mostly to a refutation of the Court's decision in *Green v. Biddle*, Johnson suggested that the Senate might also consider: limiting the jurisdiction of the federal courts; subjecting federal judges to removal by address of both Houses of Congress; limiting judicial tenure; and vesting a controlling power in the Senate or some other elected body. At the conclusion of Senator Johnson's remarks Senator John Holmes of Maine suggested that the Johnson resolution be amended to eliminate the Senate as an appellate body and to empower the president to remove any federal judge, on the address of both Houses of Congress. [68] Debate on the proposals was postponed but they were returned to the calendar.

Andrew Stevenson of Virginia offered a resolution in the House on 26 April instructing the committee on the judiciary to prepare a bill repealing the twenty-fifth section of the Judiciary Act of 1789. His position was that the whole question of the Supreme Court's appellate jurisdiction ought to be debated, and that the resolution be ordered to lie on the table until the next session of Congress. [69] Actually, serious consideration of repealing the famed twenty-fifth section did not come until 1831. But the state of Kentucky and Senator Johnson were not silent. Kentucky had sent the Senate a remonstrance on 20 February 1823 against the decision in *Green v. Biddle* requesting Congress to enact a statute which would require a concurrence of two-thirds of the judges of the Supreme Court in all cases involving the validity of a law of any state. In the event that this failed of adoption, Kentucky urged that the size of the Court be increased. Senator Johnson proposed, on 10 December 1823, that the Court be increased from its membership of seven to ten, that three additional circuits be formed, and that at least seven judges must concur in any opinion involving the validity of laws of the United States or the laws of the states. [70] Ultimately two bills were reported by Senator Van Buren of New York from the committee on the judiciary, one of which would have required the concurrence of five of the seven justices in order to render a state law invalid; the other provided for the dividing of the United States into ten circuits in which the district judges would hold court and the Supreme Court justices would be relieved of circuit riding. [71] But Senator Johnson immediately proposed amending the bill to provide for ten Supreme Court justices, all of whom would continue circuit riding. Congress failed to act on any of these measures. Unfortunately the desires and needs of the new West to share in federal judicial administration equally with the rest of the country were intermingled with the desire to prevent the Supreme Court from declaring state laws unconstitutional. Many of the states were exercised over the Supreme Court's construction of the Constitution, particularly the doctrine of implied powers and the broad jurisdictional assumptions under the twenty-fifth section of the Judiciary Act of 1789, but there was little agreement on the method of curbing judicial power.

In 1825 Daniel Webster and Martin Van Buren introduced into the House and Senate, respectively, bills which would have increased the judicial circuits to ten and would have added three additional members to the Supreme Court. This touched off what constitutional historian, Charles Grove Haines, called "the second great debate on the judiciary system of the federal government." The debate was "great" in the sense that it was one of the most prolonged controversies over judicial organization in American history, lasting from 22 December 1825 until 18 May 1826 when the House, in a move that was equivalent to rejection, postponed the bill. [72] The basic disagreements in Congress, however, remained unchanged, and although the greater part of the debate was concerned with the demands of the West for a more equal share in judicial administration, the overriding issue of judicial authority and popular control of the courts and implicitly some state representation in the federal judiciary remained at the core of the discussion. There was no question that the federal court dockets were heavily congested. Representative Tristam Burges of Rhode Island pointed out that 180 cases lay over yearly on the docket of the Supreme Court, continuing to remain there from three to five years and that in the West some 1,700 to 2,000 cases lay over annually with the number actually increasing. [73] Although all parties recognized the need for judicial reform, the fear of judicial supremacy, with its concomitant lack of popular control over public policy produced deadlock and inaction. Strangely enough eleven years later, as though thousands of hours of debate had never occurred, Congress passed the act of 1837 with little discussion. The new law gave the West and Southwest two circuits by dividing the country into nine circuits, and it added two members to the Supreme Court. [74] Circuit riding, of course, remained,

The period 1826-36, the final decade of the Marshall judicial era, saw no change in the nationalist-particularist controversy which continued to focus on the Supreme Court as the ultimate in nationalist devilment, or salvation, depending upon one's viewpoint. Although the Court occasionally deferred to state authority, the general tenor of its decisions never ceased to be nationalistic during John Marshall's tenure. In the 1827 decision in *Brown* v. *Maryland* [75] the Court held that a Maryland statute imposing a license tax of fifty dollars on all importers and vendors of foreign commodities was an invalid interference with the power of Congress to regulate foreign commerce as well as a violation of the clause in Article I, Section Ten, prohibiting a state from taxing imports. In 1829 the Court held in *Weston* v. *City of Charleston* [76] that a city had no power to tax stocks and bonds of the United States since such a tax interfered with the government's borrowing power. In 1830 the Court decided the famous case of *Craig* v. *Missouri*, [77] holding unconstitutional a Missouri statute under the terms of which loan offices had been established with authority to issue promissory notes secured by personal or intangible property, which in turn could be used to purchase loan certificates by the state. The certificates were negotiable and served as a medium of exchange. In the opinion of John Marshall, speaking for the Court, the certificates were bills of credit and as such were forbidden by the Constitution. Marshall spoke only for a bare majority since he was unable to hold Justices Johnson, Thompson and McLean with him, and after reading their dissents, he wrote to Justice Story that it required "no prophet to predict that the twenty-fifth section is to be repealed." And while hoping that this could not occur in his time, he forecast nevertheless that "accomplished it will be at no very distant period." [78]

Marshall might better have predicted only the attempt, for in prophesying the success of repealing the twenty-fifth section he was indeed too gloomy. Possibly he was too close to the scene to perceive accurately, although his view is understandable in light of the incessant attempts to diminish the Court's authority. Even as he wrote the opinion in the *Craig* case the Congress was embroiled in a visceral debate over the nature of the union. The debate carried the names of Senators Daniel Webster and Robert Y. Hayne and had grown out of Senator Samuel Foote's resolution to inquire into the expediency of restricting the sale of public lands to those already in the market. The original question was virtually forgotten in the midst of the heated and mordant disagreements over the nature of the American Union. In the course of the debate the power of the Court to invalidate state laws was violently assailed and, of course, vehemently defended;[79] and shortly after the twenty-first Congress convened for its second session, Warren P. Davis of South Carolina submitted a report from the majority of the Judiciary Committee recommending repeal of the twenty-fifth section, accompanied by a bill to effectuate the change.[80] After relatively little discussion the bill was defeated by a vote of 138-51.[81] Another measure introduced by Representative Joseph Lecompte of Kentucky calling for a constitutional amendment which would limit the term of office of all federal judges was also defeated by a large majority.[82] The portent of the "irrepressible conflict" can be seen in the vote over repeal of the twenty-fifth section. All but five of the fifty-one votes cast for repeal came from Virginia, North Carolina, South Carolina, Georgia, Kentucky, Tennessee, Alabama, Louisiana and Missouri. Two votes from New York, two from New Hampshire and one from Maine were allied with the southern states. But even the South was by no means as solid as it later became. Two of the three members of the Louisiana delegation voted against repeal, as did some thirty other representatives from the southern contingent in the House.

Even as the Congress refused to curtail federal judicial power, the final and in some ways most serious challenge to the Supreme Court's authority during John Marshall's tenure was being made by the state of Georgia. The dispute grew out of a complex of arrangements under which the United States had, on the one hand, concluded a treaty with the Cherokee Indians which guaranteed them certain land titles, and on the other hand agreed to extinguish for the use of Georgia the remaining Cherokee land titles within the state's borders on peaceable and reasonable terms. On three different occasions the Supreme Court issued mandates to the state of Georgia only to be met with complete defiance. In two instances Georgia refused to honor writs of error in the Supreme Court,[83] and in a third, ignored the Court's decision which invalidated a Georgia law of 1830 requiring licenses and an oath of all whites in Cherokee territory.[84] It was in reaction to the latter case that President Jackson was alleged to have said that if the decision were to be enforced Marshall would have to do it.

Although it is true that Andrew Jackson never enforced the Court's decision, Charles Warren points out that the Supreme Court had not technically issued a mandate before it adjourned in March, 1832, and if a mandate had been issued in 1833 it would have been some time before the enforcement machinery, including the use of armed force, could have been set in motion.[85] Whether the president would have enforced the Supreme Court's decision is another question, but historical events of the day provided him with several sound reasons for not doing so. Most Americans, while not sympathetic with the methods, were in agreement with Georgia's and Jackson's policies of removing the Indians to lands west of the Mississippi. And apparently Jackson himself considered the Indian question temporary and hesitated to precipitate a national crisis over it.[86] Second, and more important, the Nullification controversy had reached the boiling point and the politically astute Jackson clearly understood a fundamental axiom in the use of power: it is most effective when it is concentrated. When the legislature of South Carolina enacted its Nullification ordinance, the president retaliated with a show of force which stunned the states' rights extremists. South Carolina received no official support from her sister states, and even Georgia, in a special state convention, condemned Nullification as unconstitutional.

At President Jackson's request, Congress enacted the Force Bill which included among its provisions an enlargement of the jurisdiction of the federal courts. The law provided for removal to the federal courts of any action commenced in the state courts against federal officers or against persons for acts committed under the federal revenue laws. The act also provided for habeas corpus in cases of prisoners in state jails held for acts done in pursuance of a federal law. Of greater significance to judicial power was Jackson's affirmation of judicial review during the Nullification controversy and his consistent refusal while president to recommend any measures which would have weakened the judiciary. On the crucial question of repeal of the twenty-fifth section of the Judiciary Act of 1789 he was persistently silent. [87] The vote on the Force Bill in Congress was, incidentally, not unlike the vote on repeal of the 25th section—almost unanimous in the northern delegations with about half the southern congressmen voting against it.[88].

The overwhelming defeat of the proposal to repeal the twenty-fifth section and the easy passage of the Force Bill brought to a close the first phase of a prolonged legislative-judicial controversy which, at bottom, was not an argument between Congress and the Supreme Court at all, but was, instead, a series of inevitable clashes among political, economic and social forces in a brand new experiment in man's evolution toward orderly but reasonably free government. In constitutional terms it was a fight for power between the states and the national government, an attempt by the United States to decide what kind of a governmental system to be. If the Supreme Court were to become truly the constitutional anchor of the system, it could do so only at the pleasure of the dominant pressures in the nation as expressed in Congress and in the Presidency. If the Court's pronouncements on matters of fundamental law were to be binding not only on the private parties to a lawsuit but on the states and on the other branches of government as well, a national consensus needed to be reached about the role of the Court in the American system. Such a consensus was visible by the 1830s. It was admittedly precarious—sometimes shifting in its elemental composition—but the basic agreement had been reached, and the consensus would not break down even when hanging on a hairspring balance in the 1850s or several generations later, in the 1930s and 1950s. The repeated assertions of nationalism in judicial decisions were a major factor making it impossible for Jackson to tolerate Nullification, and they further provided the constitutional theory which buttressed Lincoln's stand against secession.

The persistent argument that the Marshall court was anti-democratic and opposed to majority rule has little relevance to historical realities of that day. Such criticism presupposes that the United States was a democracy and that the Constitution was a democratic document. It also assumes that individual rights might be protected by the majority, and furthermore that the peoples' liberties would be safely kept by the states, but would be unsafe in the hands of the nation. This, in spite of the fact that the governmental powers of the states were considerably greater than those of the national government, and that a national government had appeared a necessity in part because of the irresponsible legislatures in the states. The extreme Anti-Federalists like Spencer Roane and John Taylor of Caroline, in opposing the developing nationalism, seemed to forget that the Constitution had been adopted, that it was intended to eliminate localist evils under the Articles of Confederation, and that to call the new system just another form of confederation was to belie the plain meaning of the framers. It might be wise to recall also that from 1789 into the late 1820s there was no such thing as the will of the electorate. The only popularly controlled agency of the nation was the House of Representatives, and even this, given the property qualifications for voting, was not *very* popular. In effect, there were in the first three decades under the Constitution three oligarchies—the Presidency, Congress and the Court—very often with differing intellectual viewpoints on the nature of the union and of the Constitution. More often than not all three branches were interested in partisan political goals, but the Supreme Court was able, given the nature of the judicial function, to identify itself with the fundamental law more closely than either of the other branches of the national government.

Moreover, the intellectual leadership of the nation had reached a decision in favor of nationalism. This is evinced by the inability of the localists to unite on any issue except slavery, which lay at the heart of an entire region's economic and social system. And by no means was there unanimity on the matter of secession among the people or their leaders in the seceding states. The movement toward nationalism might be slowed, cushioned perhaps, but to halt it, even temporarily, was difficult in the extreme, and to reverse the direction was impossible. The Jeffersonians could not do it when they controlled two branches of the national government—all three branches in fact in terms of numbers—for the simple reason that once in power the Jeffersonian radicals saw all too clearly that the destiny of the American people lay with a consolidated nation-state, and that the times had already passed over particularism and petty localism. Andrew Jackson, too, could not and would not alter the elemental trends of a dynamic people.

At any time Congress might have eliminated the Supreme Court as a political power in the basic governmental scheme, but at no time during the Marshall period could such a majority be mustered. Although the Court had its own constituency, "the inner republic of bench and bar"[89] who stood to profit from a stable, national government and who respected a judicially formulated rule of law, there must have been, among the nation's leadership generally and even among lesser political participants, the realization that elected officials more often than not act out of pure and simple expediency. But judges, as Americans well knew, are hemmed in by precedent, logic, and their perception of moral consequences, and in the final analysis, the judiciary must represent not the power of the state but its justice, wisdom, and mercy.

3. The Taney Court:
Consolidation of Power

ONLY during the period of John Marshall's tenure could the tone, the direction and the substance of the Supreme Court's work be attributed mainly to the chief justice. Over the years several of the chief justices have provided the Court with dedicated and effective leadership, and some have been great jurists, but it was only in John Marshall that the entire spirit of the Supreme Court was epitomized. Under Marshall's firm hand the Court had established itself as truly independent of legislative and executive control albeit remaining the focal point of controversy. Although not openly acknowledged at the time of Roger Brooke Taney's accession to the chief justiceship, it was clear to careful observers that the Supreme Court was as much a political institution as was Congress or the Presidency. The Court's method of operation, its constituency, and the means of selecting its personnel differed greatly from its sister branches, and while it did not initiate public policy, the Supreme Court put its stamp of approval or disapproval upon it, and in so doing enlisted friends and created enemies. It was clear also by 1835 that it was not the doctrine of *Marbury* v. *Madison* that had early set contentious forces in motion, but it was, instead, the successful marriage by the Court of property rights to national supremacy. The critics of the great Marshall decisions quarreled not, for the most part, with their assertions of federal power, but with their disallowance of attempts by the states to regulate the excesses of the new commercial class. What Marshall did was to make certain that the Supreme Court's interpretation of the Constitution reflected the ideas of Alexander Hamilton, John Adams, and Gouverneur Morris, reflected what in modern terminology would be called the right wing views of the old-line Federalists. These men were, after all, the Constitution-makers, and John Marshall, the oldest survivor in power who adhered to their views, was successful in translating and detailing the ideology into constitutional practice.

As the movement for popular sovereignty gained momentum, the Court's position became very difficult ideologically for two interrelated reasons. First, its check upon state power was in fact a veto on the popular will in the state legislatures, and although the more conservative elements in the original Federalist group had never intended an unchecked majoritarian system, they had, unfortunately for themselves and for the propertied class whose views and interests they represented, established a constitution which was flexible enough to permit an extension of the suffrage and the ultimate control of the Congress, the Presidency, and the state legislatures by the mass of voters. It was logical, therefore, that the new center of power, the numerical majority, would resent the institution whose views and practices conformed to a different era and supported the aspirations of a different class. Once the results of the Jacksonian revolution seemed to be permanently affixed to the American system, the Court was the one agency that remained out of step. But if the Court was putting its right foot forward when the nation generally was leading with its left, its role as a legal, political moderator was made doubly difficult because of the hardening sectionalism in the country. Any group of justices sitting on the nation's highest tribunal would have encountered opposition to some of their rulings whether or not they shared the old Federalist doctrines of John Marshall.

But by the mid 1830s, as the Court faced the formidable task of weaving the great public issues into the fabric of the Constitution, the enduring issues of propertied versus propertyless, minority versus majority, and nationalism versus localism were bound up in a perverse and delicate sectionalism which eventually became intractable. The Northeast, the leading center of power with its technological achievement coupled with corporate expansion, was ruled by a new aristocrat, the industrial capitalist. In many ways the kind of constitutional law desired by the eastern leadership was akin to that preferred by the land-holding aristocracy of the South. At least the ruling elite in both sections had a common bond, a vested interest in property, whether in land or in the new commercial ventures. In one sense the mutual interest even extended to slavery which, after all, involved property legally held and constitutionally protected. To some of the northern industrialists it was inconsistent to support a movement to abolish slavery while insisting on a virtually absolute right to ownership of property protected by law and enforced by the courts. Even the West, the third great section, was property conscious in the manner of a middle-class democracy, which it was. In spite of the property tie among the three sections, along with a certain amount of cultural cohesion, there were forces at work which constantly threatened the solidarity of the union. Cutting across all three sections was the social and political ferment resulting from the extension of the franchise to the masses, which, in essence, altered the face of the American system by diffusing political power. Naturally a voting, propertyless mass will exert pressures against existing privilege, and this is precisely what the common man in the East, South, and West began to do. Moreover, historical circumstances combined to create not only a democratic or egalitarian state of mind among the have-nots, but their numbers swelled abnormally fast. While the former was an effect of the westward movement with its strong democratic and almost anarchic tendencies, the latter resulted from the first wave of immigration into the Northeast, which amounted to a million and a half during the decade of the 1840s. In the South the slavery issue ultimately welded what would normally have been antagonistic whites, the propertied and the propertyless, into a monolithic mass in opposition to the other sections, particularly the Northeast, which at first hinted and then shouted that slavery must go.

When Roger Brooke Taney assumed the leadership of the Supreme Court in 1837, these great rivalries, or divisive forces, were at work in the nation: the rivalry between the rich and the poor, each possessing a rightful share of political power; the rivalry between the sections, potentially the most divisive; and the rivalry between the nation and the states. Added to these was a fourth rivalry—at the time by no means as serious as the other three but, as it turned out, equally significant for the future of the American system—the rivalry between the Supreme Court and the other branches of the national government. Taney's judicial leadership was just short of three decades, second in time and in importance only to that of John Marshall. Important despite the fact that not one of the rivalries, excepting slavery, was settled at the time of Taney's death, and the slavery question, though technically resolved, was merely replaced by a new racial rivalry which was in a hundred years to precipitate a crisis for the Supreme Court not dissimilar from that brought on by Taney himself.

What manner of man was Roger Brooke Taney? He was, like many of the practitioners of statecraft who contributed to the American political tradition, a curious mixture of conservative and liberal tendencies. He was a Jeffersonian, both in his agrarian bias and in his concern for the preservation of individual liberty. He was a Jacksonian in his opposition to special privilege, particularly in the sphere of corporate economic power. Yet, he was a Madisonian federalist in that he believed in a moderately strong national government—at least when acting in its defined sphere of competence—while at the same time he saw the states as preferable agents to the general government in regulating abuses, individual and corporate, for the public good. Daniel Webster, the prototype of the conservative mind in America, cried out that the Constitution was gone when Taney was appointed to the chief justiceship. What Webster meant was that John Marshall's Constitution was gone. But Webster's lament, even interpreted in that way, was too harsh a judgment. The great principles laid down by Marshall were, with slight modification, not only intact but even more deeply embedded in the system when Taney left the judicial scene than when he entered it. Taney brought to the Court a new emphasis, not a new philosophy. And at least the emphasis was more in tune with the times than had been the case during Marshall's twilight. Taney's concept of a proper mixture between public and private rights is best expressed in his first and one of his best constitutional opinions. He declared that:

> The object and end of all government is to promote the happiness and prosperity of the community by which it is established; and it can never be assumed, that the government intended to diminish its power of accomplishing the end for which it was created. The continued existence of government would be of no great value, if, by implications and presumptions, it was disarmed of the powers necessary to

accomplish the ends of its creation, and the functions it was designed to perform, transferred to the hands of privileged corporations, while the rights of private property are sacredly guarded, we must not forget that the community also have rights and that the happiness and well-being of every citizen depends on their faithful preservation.[1]

Perhaps the most important reason for the lack of extensive judicial innovation during Taney's leadership is to be found in the personal characteristics of the man. He simply could not and would not use power in the Marshall style, and in spite of the fact that every school boy thinks of the *Dred Scott* decision as an irresponsible and blatant misuse of authority, Roger Taney and his Court were essentially majoritarians. Ironically, Taney's chief legacy, as constitutional lawyer Wallace Mendelson points out, is the concept of judicial self-restraint.[2] Furthermore Taney's antilibertarian opinion in *Dred Scott* must be balanced against his ruling in the *Merryman Case*[3] which was the first significant defense of individual liberty in any federal court decision up to that time.[4]

When Taney took his place on the bench at the beginning of the 1837 term the Court should have been of a Jacksonian political persuasion, President Jackson having appointed five of the Court's members out of the full statutory complement of seven. But political viewpoint and judicial philosophy often become estranged when man the politician becomes man the judge. The longest tenured justice was Joseph Story, appointed to the Court at the age of thirty-two as President Madison's third choice for the vacancy. Story had been an avowed Republican in his youth but became virtually one with John Marshall in his views of the Constitution. He was, moreover, one of the finest legal scholars who ever graced the Court with his presence. He and Chancellor James Kent of New York founded the equity system in the United States, and Story's rules for equity pleading became the basis of equity proceedings in the federal courts. Andrew Jackson, nevertheless, is reputed to have called Story the most dangerous man in America.

Second in length of service was Smith Thompson of New York who had served President Monroe as secretary of the navy and who had been appointed to the Court by Monroe in 1823. Justice Thompson was among those who had disagreed with John Marshall toward the end of Marshall's tenure. He was in dissent in the famous, previously mentioned cases of *Brown* v. *Maryland*[5] and *Craig* v. *Missouri*,[6] and he helped to make up the majority which refused to follow the Marshall doctrine on contracts in *Ogden* v. *Saunders*.[7] Although personally opposed to slavery he voted to uphold the Fugitive Slave Act in *Prigg* v. *Pennsylvania*.[8]

The first of the Jackson appointees was John McLean of Ohio, former Postmaster General under John Quincy Adams and onetime judge of the Supreme Court of Ohio. The remaining Jackson appointees composing the Court at the time of Taney's accession were Henry Baldwin of Pennsylvania, a Yale graduate and former Congressman who acted so strangely in his later years as to be thought insane by some; James M. Wayne of Georgia who remained on the Union side and on the Court during the Civil War and became the last surviving colleague of John Marshall; and Philip P. Barbour of Virginia, a states' righter of the Spencer Roane school whom John Adams once described as a "shallow-pated wild-cat."

Eight more justices sat on the Court with Taney prior to the fateful *Dred Scott* decision in 1857. President Jackson's final appointee before leaving the Presidency was John Catron of Tennessee who was to concur in holding the Missouri Compromise unconstitutional. John McKinley of Alabama and Peter Daniel of Virginia were President Van Buren's contributions to the high bench. Presidents Tyler, Fillmore and Pierce named one judge each, and President Polk chose two. They were respectively: Samuel Nelson of New York, friend of James Fenimore Cooper and technician in admiralty, maritime and international law whose opinion in *Dred Scott* was the only one free of dicta; Benjamin R. Curtis of Massachusetts, who had characterized the Van Buren administration as "ambitious, selfish and ignorant men" and whose own conduct in the *Dred Scott* case led to his resignation from the Supreme Court; John A. Campbell of Alabama, Jeffersonian states' righter, who, although unsympathetic to secession, resigned from the Court and joined the Confederate cause at the outbreak of the war; Levi Woodbury of New Hampshire, a puritanical conservative who opposed slavery but believed that the statutes which supported it must be obeyed until national policy was altered; and Robert C. Grier who had been elevated to the Supreme Court after service as a Pennsylvania district judge. It was Grier who, on February 23, 1857, wrote a confidential letter to incoming President James Buchanan in which he detailed the attitudes of the justices on the *Dred Scott* decision and predicted the final outcome of the case. As a result of Grier's note Buchanan was prompted to declare in his inaugural address that he would "cheerfully submit" to the Supreme Court's decision "whatever this may be." President Buchanan was to place only one justice on the Court, Nathan Clifford of Maine, who was appointed upon the resignation of Justice Curtis immediately after the *Dred Scott* decision. Clifford had been associated with the pro-slavery wing of the Democratic party, and his nomination ran into bitter opposition. The Senate voted to confirm, however, and he served for twenty-three years, competently but without great distinction.

The Court which Taney led was hardly a monolith, and any broad generalizations concerning its doctrinal position would be foolhardy since they would collapse easily under rigorous analysis. What can be said with certainty is that the Taney court had by 1850 so ingratiated itself with the diverse elements in the nation that it was no longer a subject of attack and vilification in Congress. Serious attempts to destroy, or at least weaken, the Court's influence by cutting the heart out of its appellate jurisdiction—attempts which were prevalent during Marshall's day—had dwindled to insignificant proportions. The Court had not become all things to all men, but through Taney's shrewd political acumen it had been able to moderate the harsher conflicts without engendering excessive bitterness. If the decisions of the Taney Court moved in accord with the prevailing winds of public opinion, they did not, however, do so at the expense of institutional authority. As Supreme Court historian Louis Boudin observed many years ago, John Marshall was a mere pretender to the throne in comparison with Taney who "established a real kingdom." [9]

Economic Matters

The crucial areas of judicial construction were bound up in the three continuing and natural conflicts suggested above: between economic classes, between the nation and the states, and the sectional conflict over the slavery question. Not long after Taney's assumption of leadership, the Court decided the case of *Charles River Bridge* v. *Warren Bridge*,[10] a decision which suggested that the death of Marshall had marked the end of an era in judicial protection of vested rights. Those who concluded, however, that the contract clause had lost its strength as a barrier to state interference with corporate interests were premature in their judgments. The case originated in a conflict between public charters granted by the legislature of Massachusetts. Initially the legislature had granted the Charles River Bridge Company a charter under the terms of which the company was permitted to erect a toll bridge between Charlestown and Boston. Tolls were to be collected for a period of forty years. This was in 1785, and in 1792 the legislature granted a thirty-year extension to the bridge company authorizing at the same time the construction of a bridge across the river between Cambridge and Boston. Long after the company had recovered its original investment at a handsome interest, it continued to collect tolls. Public protest mounted. In 1818 the legislature was persuaded to charter the building of a new bridge, the Warren Bridge, which was to be erected sixteen rods from the old bridge on the Charlestown side and fifty rods away on the Boston side. It was to become a free bridge when sufficient tolls had been collected to pay for its construction or, in any event, to be a free bridge within six years. The prospect of the collapse of revenue prompted the Charles River Bridge Company to bring suit in which the company alleged that the chartering of a free bridge was an impairment of the obligation of contract, in contravention of the Constitution. The contract clause argument depended upon the proposition that the charter had made an exclusive grant to the original bridge company. No mention was made of exclusivity in the charter but, argued counsel, it was implied since all ambiguities in charters should be interpreted liberally in favor of corporate investors. For the Court to decide otherwise would be to undermine business confidence and create instability in economic affairs. The Court disagreed with the Charles River Bridge Company, Justice Taney holding that the charter did not confer the rights claimed by the company, and furthermore, that public contracts should be construed narrowly and any ambiguity in grants such as this must be decided in the interest of the public. "While the rights of private property are sacredly guarded," said Taney, "we must not forget that the community also have rights, and that the happiness and well-being of every citizen depends on their faithful preservation." Justice Story, in a long dissent, agreed with counsel for the Charles River Bridge, adamantly declaring that he stood "upon the old law."

But if Chief Justice Taney and a majority of his brethren held firmly to the Jacksonian rhetoric of special privileges for none, they by no means intended to weaken corporate privileges clearly held by statute. Writing for a majority of the Court in 1843, Taney handed down an opinion which would have brought him a letter of commendation from John Marshall, and indeed the opinion did bring such an approving letter from Justice Story who had not participated in the case. Illinois had enacted two distinct but related laws concerning the equity of a mortgagor. One provided that property could not be sold on foreclosure unless it brought a certain proportion of the appraised value. The other gave the debtor the right to repurchase foreclosed property within a certain time limit at a given rate. Similar laws for the relief of debtors had been enacted in eight states as a result of the economic collapse of 1837. Taney invalidated the laws on the ground that they interfered with the judicial enforcement of contracts, and while admitting that the rights of the creditors were not denied, he maintained that the interference with the legal remedy had the effect of impairing the contract itself. This was the first instance of the Court's invalidating a state law pertaining to a private rather than a public contract, and it is as clearly in line with Federalist concepts of natural and eternal rights in property as any opinion ever composed and delivered by John Marshall.[11] Yet the Supreme Court under Taney was not consistent on this question. It vacillated. It modified and altered its own doctrinal pronouncements. And most of all, it was divided, particularly from the late 1840s onward.

Indicative of the divisions on the Court over the question of protecting growing corporate power are the opinions in *Piqua Branch of the State Bank of Ohio* v. *Knoop*[12] and *Dodge* v. *Woolsey*.[13] Both cases deal squarely with the states' role in regulating the acquisition of wealth. Constitutionally they embrace rather narrow questions of state power and its limits; more broadly they concern majority have-nots against minority haves who wanted not only to protect but to increase their holdings. The *Knoop* case grew out of the Democratic party's attempts to curb privileges that had been granted to banks, railroads and corporations generally. Specifically, state legislatures had repealed exemptions from taxation which had been granted in earlier charters. In this case a bank had claimed that a tax imposed by the legislature was an impairment of the obligation of contract since its original charter had contained a tax exemption. A majority of the Court, speaking through Justice McLean agreed, and the Court voided the tax. In addition to the chief justice, Catron, Daniel and Campbell argued in dissent that no legislature has the authority to place a portion of the state's sovereign power beyond the reach of subsequent legislatures unless so authorized by the constitution of the state. But the class conflict is clearly recognized in Justice Campbell's words:

> The discussions before this Court . . . exposed us to the sly and stealthy arts to which state Legislatures are exposed, and the greedy appetites of adventurers for monopolies and immunities from the state right of Government. We cannot close our eyes to the insidious efforts to ignore the fundamental laws and institutions of the States, and to subject the highest popular interests to their central boards of control and directors' management.

After the decision in *Knoop*, Ohio assumed that if it repealed a tax exemption through amending its constitution, it would overcome the infirmities of an ordinary statute. But the Court held that the people of a state had no more authority to impair the obligation of contract by a constitutional amendment than they had by statute. Once again Justice Campbell cut through the constitutional issue to the question behind it. Arguing that in the end the doctrine of the case might overthrow the entire system of corporate combinations he bitterly condemned "these extraordinary pretensions of corporations [which] display a love of power, a preference for corporate interests to moral or political principles or public duties, and an antagonism to individual freedom, which have marked them as objects of jealousy in every epoch of their history." Continuing, he prophesied that "the establishment of this caste would be a new element of alienation and discord between the different classes of society."

The Court was not entirely consistent on the matter of tax exemptions. On two occasions it resolved ambiguities in legislative grants of tax exemptions in favor of the state,[14] but in at least one instance in which an exemption required clarification and might have been decided either way, the Court ruled against the public and in favor of the private right.[15] The old Marshall doctrines of vested rights in property, nurtured so well by the former chief justice in his contract clause decisions, remained intact throughout the Taney period. Still, the tone of some decisions, perhaps slightly off key, did open the door to later rulings (e.g. *Stone* v. *Mississippi*,[16] 1880) which put an end to corporate charter untouchability. To mention three there was the *Charles River Bridge Case*,[17] *West River Bridge* v. *Dix*[18] in which the Court held that a state could not bargain away its power of eminent domain, and dicta in *Phalen* v. *Virginia*[19] which suggested that a state might not bargain away its police power.

State v. Nation

In the area more narrowly construed as state versus national power, but often involving class conflicts, peripherally at least, the Court struck just enough of a balance between contradiction and consistency to ward off a concentrated attack on its work by those groups most able to curb its powers if they chose to do so. A fundamental issue which the Marshall Court had never clarified was the extent to which the states might regulate interstate commerce, if at all. Justice Story maintained to the end that the power to regulate commerce was exclusive with Congress and that John Marshall had said so. The Story position was inaccurate since Marshall had refused to make such a declaration when he was given a clear-cut opportunity to fashion that rule.[20] Sooner or later, the Taney Court had to face the question since various state regulatory measures were being attacked in the courts on the ground that they interfered with the commerce clause in what Marshall called its "dormant state." Although the Court upheld unanimously the laws of several states requiring a license for the privilege of selling intoxicating liquor, [21] it was divided between those justices who believed that the power of Congress over commerce was exclusive and those who thought it concurrent, but most of the justices could agree that in this instance the laws in question were not regulating interstate commerce anyway. They were either police regulations or controls over intrastate commerce, the effect of which on interstate commerce was either incidental or indirect. This, of course, begs the real question which is whether any regulatory state legislation, normally valid, ceases to be valid when it hits the subject matter of interstate commerce. Justice Woodbury urged his brethren to accept a compromise formula which would permit state regulations under certain conditions only. In 1851, the Court agreed with Woodbury when it announced the doctrine of selective exclusiveness in the now famous *Cooley* case.[22] The Court said in effect that when the subject matter of commerce required a uniform national rule, only Congress might regulate, but that the states might regulate local phases of commerce as long as such regulations did not burden traffic across state lines. The Court thus preserved state autonomy without limiting national power, and at the same time reserved for itself the right to determine qualitatively and independently when, and under what conditions, the states were in conflict with federal authority over interstate commerce. Everybody was happy.

In other cases in which the Court had to delineate powers between the national and state governments, it continued to perform the seemingly impossible task of pleasing everyone while strengthening its own position in the bargain. In *United States* v. *Gratiot* [23] the Court sustained a plenary national power over all public lands including those situated in states, but in *Holmes* v. *Jennison* [24] it dismissed a suit for want of jurisdiction. *Holmes* involved the right of a state to honor a request from a foreign nation, Canada in this instance, to return a fugitive from justice when no extradition treaty existed between the national government and the foreign nation involved. Three justices supported Taney in dissent. They would not have permitted the state action since the Constitution intended, in Taney's words, "to cut off all communications between foreign governments and the several state governments." Another case in which the states won a temporary victory was that of *Martin* v. *Waddell's Lessee* [25] which dealt with the authority of New Jersey to grant exclusive oyster bed rights in flats under its tidewaters. In an opinion by the chief justice, the Court upheld the state when it agreed with the New Jersey court's construction of the old royal charters and of the proprietors' deeds. However, Justice Taney took great care to point out that while the state court's rulings were entitled to great weight, they did not bind the federal courts.

Probably the decision which gave to federal judicial power its greatest expansive quality, and incidentally enhanced national power at the expense of the states, was *Swift* v. *Tyson*. [26] The immediate question was whether the Supreme Court was bound to follow the judicial interpretation by the courts of New York of the laws covering bills of exchange. The broader issue involved federal judicial independence in establishing the content of commercial jurisprudence. In interpreting the thirty-fourth section of the Judiciary Act of 1789 which provided that "the laws of the several states . . . shall be regarded as rules of decision in trials at common law" in the federal courts, the Court held that the section did not apply to decisions of courts on general questions not dependent upon local statutes or usages of a fixed and permanent nature. In this case, the Court refused to follow the law of negotiable instruments as laid down by the New York courts, but until 1938 when the case was overruled, its doctrine was extended to wills, torts, real estate, contracts and other such matters.

Another assertion of federal power through the enlargement of federal jurisdiction was brought about by Justice Taney's opinion in *The Genesee Chief* v. *Fitzhugh*. [27] The Court had ruled earlier that federal admiralty jurisdiction was limited to the ebb and flow of the tide [28] but the justices were now confronted with an act of Congress of 1845 which extended the federal court jurisdiction to certain cases arising on the Great Lakes. The chief justice painted with a broad brush in upholding the law by effectively extending admiralty jurisdiction to all public navigable waters. At the same time, however, the opinion had a soothing quality to it for the states since one of the bases for the holding was the necessity of state equality under the Constitution. As Taney so carefully observed, the "first principles on which the Union was formed" required that all citizens, including those living near internal waterways, have access to federal courts of admiralty jurisdiction, and not just those who live in states bordering on the Atlantic or on tidewater rivers connected to the ocean.

In spite of the clear assertions of national predominance in the federal system in the cases we have discussed and in others such as *Dobbins* v. *Commissioners of Erie County* [29] in which the courts extended, in fact distorted, the Marshall doctrine of intergovernmental tax immunity by holding that the salaries of federal officials were immune from a nondiscriminatory state income tax, the Taney Court was able to avoid areas where parochial emotions ran high. The one time when it might have become embroiled in a major political controversy, the Dorr rebellion in Rhode Island, it emerged from the fracas not only unscarred but with a renewed popular respect for its exercise of self-restraint. In 1841, Rhode Island's government was operating under its original charter from Charles II, a charter which had no provision in it for amendment. Protesting the restrictive suffrage in force at the time, a group of dissidents wrote a new constitution and held an election at which Thomas Dorr was chosen governor. The old government attempted to suppress what it regarded as a rebellion, and when one of its officers arrested an alleged revolutionary, he was sued for trespass. In order to give relief, the Court first had to decide which government was the legitimate authority in the state. Once again the chief justice performed the remarkable feat of pleasing both the state and national governments and preserving the integrity of the judicial process in the bargain. He pointed out that the political departments in Rhode Island had determined that the charter government was the legitimate one; that the state courts had acted in conformity with that determination; and that the Supreme Court would adhere to the decision of the courts of the state. Furthermore the clause in Article IV of the Constitution, under which the United States guarantees to every state a republican form of government, presupposed a political and not a judicial guarantor. Only Congress may decide which is the proper government of a state and whether it is republican in form. By admitting official senators and representatives from a state, Congress would be recognizing simultaneously the legality and the republican nature of the governing authority. Thus everyone but the Dorr supporters was happy with the outcome of the case. But even the Dorrites could not condemn the Court which had said, after all, that it was not competent to rule on the key issue.

Slavery

In view of the Taney Court's astounding success in accommodating the ofttimes bitter economic and political rivalries, it seemed inconceivable that at the height of its prestige it would stumble so badly when it attempted to adjust the great sectional dispute over slavery. Prior to its decision in the *Dred Scott* case the Court had handled the slavery issue with meticulous circumspection and it characteristically had been able, if not to please both sides, at least to refrain from espousing either the cause of slavery or abolition. It did so by deciding such cases on narrow legal and technical grounds. One of the earliest cases to come before the Taney Court was *Groves* v. *Slaughter* [30] which involved an interpretation of the constitution of Mississippi. The provision in question prohibited the introduction of slaves into the state as merchandise for sale after 1 May 1833, but it was not clear whether the language of the state constitution was self-enforcing. A majority of the Court held that the constitutional phrasing contemplated statutory implementation, and since the legislature of Mississippi had not acted in the matter, a purchase note for slaves given after 1 May 1833 was valid. Had the Court ruled that the Mississippi constitution was self-enforcing, it would then have had to face the possible conflict between state and national authority over interstate commerce. This, in turn, would have made it difficult for the Court to avoid some very controversial ancillary questions. Were Negro slaves commerce? If so, what were they precisely? Certainly not inanimate objects. Presumably, the Court would have had to designate them persons. Were they then citizens? In a strict legal sense the Court properly refused to face the constitutional issue in advance of the necessity of deciding it, and neither of the strong contending forces in America was helped or hindered.

The Court maintained a similar neutrality, at least on the surface, in the more celebrated case of *Prigg* v. *Pennsylvania* in

1842. [31] A slave owner in Maryland sent Prigg to Pennsylvania to capture a runaway slave. Such capture had been facilitated for many years under the National Fugitive Slave Law of 1793 which provided that an escaped slave might be seized by his master or a legal designee and, upon proof of ownership in a federal or state court, a magistrate might issue a certificate authorizing removal of the slave. Several states, North and South, had also enacted fugitive slave laws, thus establishing a cooperative arrangement that had worked reasonably well over the years. As the antislavery movement gathered momentum, however, some of the northern states, ostensibly to prevent kidnapping of free Negroes but actually to help runaway slaves into freedom, passed what were called "personal liberty laws." Pennsylvania had enacted such a law which prohibited the seizure of Negroes with intent to return them to slavery. Prigg, after being denied authorization to remove a captured slave from the state of Pennsylvania, forcibly carried the slave back to Maryland. Under amicable arrangements between Pennsylvania and Maryland, Prigg returned to Pennsylvania, was arrested and found guilty of kidnapping, thus furnishing the occasion for a test of a "personal liberty law." Speaking for the majority in a divided Court, Justice Story declared that the Pennsylvania law was in direct conflict with the federal fugitive slave law and was therefore unconstitutional. The federal law itself, said Story, was a valid exercise of congressional power under Article IV of the Constitution, the intent of which was to expedite the return of all runaway slaves. Had Story ended his opinion at this point he would have upheld national power while at the same time permitting the slaveholding states to buttress that power with their own fugitive slave laws. Instead he went on to say that the states had no authority over the subject at all since the power was exclusively national. As a result the free states could not hinder the capture of runaway slaves, nor could the slave states aid in their capture or return. Neither North nor South was particularly happy over the decision but in a sense both sides were appeased. The North, perhaps, benefited slightly from the decision in that state courts were no longer obligated to enforce federal law. In fact some states subsequently prohibited any official assistance in the return of fugitive slaves. But if no one was really happy with the doctrine of the *Prigg* case, all could live with it, and equally important, the Court could continue to live harmoniously in the American constitutional system.

In 1847 litigation reached the Court in two cases in which slavery was the underlying cause of action. In one [32] the Court had to deal with the effects of its decision in *Groves* v. *Slaughter* in which it had said that a provision in the Mississippi constitution was not self-enforcing. The Supreme Court of Mississippi disagreed and held that the state constitutional provision was effective without supporting legislation. The Supreme Court then had to decide whether it would accept the interpretation of the state judiciary on a matter of state constitutional law, the normal procedure, or adhere to its original position. Speaking through the chief justice, the Court followed its own ruling. Taney carefully pointed out that the Court was bound to respect the decisions of state courts but since in this instance the Supreme Court had ruled on the point prior to a decision in the state courts, it was not inconsistent for the Court to conform to its initial ruling. Although the usual outcries against national impairment of state sovereignty and dignity were raised in Mississippi, the decision had its popular aspects. As Taney's biographer, Carl Brent Swisher, points out, the opposite ruling would have added to the strife over slavery, and moreover, it would have permitted citizens of Mississippi to repudiate large financial debts owed to persons in other states from whom they had purchased slaves.[33] Perhaps this latter consideration influenced the Court as much as the slavery question in light of the prevailing judicial view of the sanctity of contracts.

The second case in 1847 involved another challenge to the fugitive slave law of 1793. Once again the Court upheld the power of the national government over the subject, but Justice Woodbury in writing the opinion, although personally a strong opponent of slavery, apparently deemed it necessary to distinguish for the abolitionists the difference between a man's opinion in the abstract and his constitutional duty as a judge. He said:

> Whatever may be the theoretical opinions of any as to the expediency of some of those compromises [in the Constitution], or of the right of property in persons which they recognize, this court has no alternative, while they exist, but to stand by the Constitution and laws with fidelity to their duties and their oaths.[34]

In the early 1850s the Court rendered opinions in two more cases in which slavery was at the base of the litigation. In the first the Court upheld an Illinois statute which provided criminal penalties for harboring and secreting a Negro slave.[35] Basing its opinion upon a strict interpretation of federalism, the Court saw no conflict with either the Constitution or with acts of Congress on the subject. At first glance this appears to be in conflict with Story's dicta in *Prigg* v. *Pennsylvania*, but actually the Illinois law, as the Court argued, did not affect any federal right or remedy of the slave or of the master, but merely prescribed a rule of conduct for the state's own citizens, and as such was a proper exercise of the state's police power. In *Strader* v. *Graham*[36] the Court confronted a set of facts similar to, but not identical with, those in the *Dred Scott* case. The question was whether slaves owned by a citizen of one state, Kentucky in this instance, who had been permitted to labor in a free state (Ohio), acquired their freedom either under the laws of Ohio or by virtue of the Northwest Ordinance of 1787 which had prohibited slavery in the Ohio territory prior to its acquiring statehood. In a unanimous opinion the Court dismissed the suit for want of a federal question. The status of a slave, said the Court, depended upon the laws of the state in which he was held in bondage, and Kentucky had the exclusive power to determine for itself whether employment in a free state should make a slave free upon his return.

Dred Scott's Case

Throughout the 1840s and into the 1850s the pattern of constitutional interpretation of the slavery question appeared to favor the slaveholding interests. What the Court had done in fact was to validate federal laws concerning fugitive slaves, laws which rested upon a secure foundation in Article IV of the Constitution. Even the strongly antislavery justices were not persuaded that the fugitive slave law, as pernicious as they may have thought it to be, was unconstitutional. And to a man, the Court studiously but with technical correctness, eschewed the question of a slave's changed status upon his moving from the legal system of one state to that of another. In short, the Court had sanctioned the status quo, and even if it had been able to stretch a clause in the Constitution to permit the rendering of an antislavery opinion, it is doubtful that such an opinion would have altered the seething forces of disunion in the slightest degree. It would instead have placed the Court in a politically partisan role and at cross purposes to Congress during the years when Congress was making the supreme effort to heal the sectional wounds in the nation. Evanescent though it was, the Compromise of 1850 closed the sectional breach. No sooner was it closed, however, than it began to reopen, and the Supreme Court, which had clearly established itself as a reasonably objective arbiter of all the great constitutional issues save one, hopefully took its turn at attempting to prevent America's most bitter division from escalating into a fatal disunion. The Court failed, as Congress had failed. The American people had failed.

Dred Scott belonged to those obscure millions of humanity whose individual existence is never a part of history's chronicle. For a fleeting moment the Negro slave born of slaves came into national prominence and his name shall be forever linked to a great but tragic episode in American judicial history. The case of *Dred Scott* v. *Sandford* [37] was argued in the Supreme Court on February 11-14, 1856, but the original litigation was begun in 1846. Peter Blow of Virginia had taken his Negro slave, Dred Scott, to Missouri where he later sold him to Dr. John Emerson, an Army surgeon. In his travels over a four-year period Emerson had taken Scott to a military post at Rock Island, Illinois, and to Fort Snelling in the Wisconsin territory before returning to Missouri with Scott and Scott's wife and daughter, whom he had acquired while at Fort Snelling. Both the Northwest Ordinance of 1787 and Illinois law forbade slavery in that state, and the Missouri Compromise of 1820 had outlawed it in the Wisconsin territory. Upon the death of Dr. Emerson, Mrs. Emerson moved to Massachusetts, literally abandoning Scott and his family, who then turned to his former master, Peter Blow. Blow consulted the law firm of Field and Hall, who saw an opportunity to earn a substantial fee and test the constitutionality of the Missouri Compromise at the same time. [38] If Scott's freedom could be established by reason of his residence in a free area, he could then claim back wages from the Emerson estate for the period in which he had been held in slavery. The litigation moved through the courts for a period of years, and in 1850 a jury in Missouri brought in a verdict in favor of Scott. On appeal by Mrs. Emerson, the Supreme Court of Missouri reversed the lower court, holding that whatever Scott's status may have been outside Missouri, upon his return he was once again a slave under Missouri law. In the meantime, Mrs. Emerson had married Dr. C.C. Chafee, a prominent abolitionist and Republican congressman from Massachusetts, who was interested in obtaining a ruling in the federal courts on the question of a slave's right to freedom upon being taken into free territory by his master. For reasons not precisely ascertainable, Chafee arranged for a dummy sale of the Scott family to his wife's brother, John F. A. Sanford of New York. A noted antislavery lawyer, Roswell M. Field (no relation to Scott's former counsel, Alexander P. Field) of St. Louis, was persuaded to institute new proceedings to secure the freedom of Dred Scott and his family, and more important really, to try and obtain a ruling in the Supreme Court of the United States that slaves became free when they moved into free territory. Since the federal courts had jurisdiction in a case of this kind only when the parties to the lawsuit were citizens of different states, Field's declaration to the Court averred that Dred Scott was a citizen of Missouri, and Sanford a citizen of New York. Sanford's attorneys argued in a "plea of abatement" that the Court had no jurisdiction of the case since Scott was a descendant of Negro slaves of pure African blood and was not a citizen of Missouri in the constitutional sense of the word. Field demurred to this plea but contended that Scott's racial origins neither prevented his being a citizen of a state nor his suing in the federal courts. The trial judge supported Field and overruled the "plea in abatement." The case went to trial and on 15 May 1854, the jury returned a verdict in favor of Sanford, holding Scott to be Sanford's slave. The case was taken to the Supreme Court on writ of error filed during the term beginning in December 1854.

The Court's docket had been overloaded, and Dred Scott's case was not reached until February, 1856, when it was argued at great length. Scott's appeal was based on the propositions that (1) he had become a free man under the provisions of the Missouri Compromise when his master had taken him into Illinois and into free territory, and (2) that as a free man he was a citizen within the meaning of the word as it was used in Article III of the

Constitution which extended jurisdiction of the federal courts to controversies between citizens of different states. It was theoretically possible for the Court to dispose of the case in summary fashion by affirming the holding of Missouri's highest court that Scott could not become a citizen.

There being no diversity of citizenship, the Supreme Court might then have dismissed the suit for want of jurisdiction. In so doing, the Court would have been following its own decision in *Strader* v. *Graham*, [39] in which the chief justice had said that each state has the right to determine the status of persons domiciled within its territory so long as such determination was not inconsistent with the Constitution of the United States. In general such a decision was the predilection of the Court when it first met in conference, but the pressures for a judicial pronouncement on the question of congressional powers over slavery were mounting, and in view of the great prestige enjoyed by the Court, it seemed to many that if it did choose to meet the substantive issues, its opinion would be accepted whether it condemned or upheld slavery. In terms of sectional representation on the Court, the South had a bare majority, the chief justice being from Maryland, Wayne from Georgia, Catron from Tennessee, Campbell from Alabama and Daniel from Virginia. Justices Grier, Nelson, Curtis, and McLean were respectively from Pennsylvania, New York, Massachusetts, and Ohio. In conference it became apparent that if the case were decided at that time, a cacophony of nine separate opinions would have been written. Although Justice Nelson was assigned the opinion, Taney readily accepted his request for a reargument of the case on the technical question of whether the Court could consider Scott's citizenship plea. At least the decision could then be postponed until after the 1856 election and the Court's opinions would not be involved in the partisanship of a presidential election. As matters turned out timing was probably not an important factor in the decision's impact upon the nation. After reargument a majority of the justices in conference were agreed that the precedent of the *Strader* case ought to be followed and Nelson again was appointed to write an opinion sustaining the lower court, and he did in fact write the opinion on this point.

It is difficult to ascertain precisely why Taney decided to write an opinion that dealt fully with every issue raised in the case rather than acquiesce in Nelson's judgment. Traditional reports of the Court's deliberations maintain that it was only after McLean and Curtis insisted on writing extended dissents that Wayne persuaded the chief justice to change his plans whereby he would deal fully with all the issues raised in the case. Nelson, who was absent at the final conference, later indicated that he would present the opinion that he had prepared as the opinion of the Court. Professor Allan Nevins argues persuasively that Wayne was the prime mover in convincing Taney to substitute a broad judgment for a narrow one, and that the southern contingent on the Court had sound reasons for coalescing at this time on the question of slavery in the territories. [40] The *Dred Scott* case was, after all, the first which had permitted a clear-cut decision on the Missouri Compromise, and with the respected Taney, now old and ailing, this was the "moment, if ever, to strike a blow for Southern rights in the Territories." [41] And the Democrats on the Court were being told from every quarter—press, politicians, and the president-elect—that a decision invalidating the Missouri Compromise would invigorate their party and give it renewed political life.

Nevins suggests further that McLean, for all his presidential ambition, could have had little motive for provoking his judicial antagonists to proclaim that Congress had no power over slavery in the territories since: (1) the Convention of 1856 had already nominated Buchanan; (2) he would be seventy-five years old by 1860 and out of the running; and (3) to take a step that would strengthen the new administration seemed downright perverse. As for Curtis, it made little sense for a conservative Whig of the Daniel Webster school, a man whom the abolitionists had called "a doughface," and an old representative of the business community, to become a sudden radical. In short, Nevins argues that it was Wayne and the southern justices who provoked McLean and Curtis to dissent in order that they might forge an answer in judicial terms.

Ultimately, Taney's long and complex opinion resulted in the dismissal of the case on jurisdictional grounds since Scott had no right to sue in the federal courts. In the course of his meandering he made three points. First, he observed that Negroes had been regarded as persons of an inferior order at the time the Constitution was adopted, that they were not citizens and were not intended to be included in the term "citizen" as used in the Constitution for the purpose of suing in the federal courts. Second, he said that Scott had not become free as a result of residence in territory covered by the Missouri Compromise because the Missouri Compromise was unconstitutional. It violated the Fifth Amendment in that it deprived slave owners of their property without due process of law. Third, whatever may have been the temporary effect of Scott's sojourn in Illinois, he had returned to Missouri where his status depended upon Missouri law. The courts of that state had held him to be a slave, and he was not, therefore, a citizen entitled to sue in the federal courts.

Each of the remaining eight justices wrote a separate opinion. Wayne filed a brief statement in support of Taney's position. Nelson filed the original opinion which he had prepared as the majority position. Grier concurred with Nelson and in general assented to Taney's opinion. Daniel wrote a long opinion in which he made virtually the same points as those made by Taney, and Campbell in another lengthy dissertation strongly denied that Congress had any power over slavery in the territories. McLean and Curtis wrote separate, long dissenting opinions. Technically, four of the eight associate justices (Wayne, Grier, Daniel and Campbell) concurred with Taney's reasoning on the Missouri Compromise. Catron argued that the Compromise was invalid rather than unconstitutional because of its incompatibility with the treaty under which Louisiana was ceded to the United States. Seven members of the Court (all but McLean and Curtis) agreed that it was up to the courts of Missouri to decide Dred Scott's status after his return to the state's jurisdiction, but only two of the justices (Wayne and Daniel) concurred in Taney's extravagant pronouncement that a Negro could not be a citizen of the United States under the Constitution.[42]

The *Dred Scott* case ended the term of the Court. It also ended one judicial era and opened another. Although Taney might have held firm to Nelson's position, denied the Court's jurisdiction and closed the ruling at that point, there are valid reasons for his not having done so. Motives aside, the fact that justices with strongly held and disparate views deemed it necessary to state them in a judicial decision was then and is now a normal aspect of the Supreme Court's role in providing the people with a full dress debate on constitutional issues. Furthermore, the charge by Abraham Lincoln and others that the latter part of the Taney opinion was pure dicta is not altogether true. Taney defended his position by asserting that it was common practice under a writ of error for the Court to consider all phases of a case even though a ruling on a single point might give relief to the litigants. While it might not actually have been common practice, it was not at all unusual to canvass several or all of the issues raised in a case. A leading example is Marshall's treatment of the issues in *Cohens* v. *Virginia* which was dismissed ultimately for want of jurisdiction although the opinion, as Professor Edward Corwin observed, "has always been regarded as good law in all its parts" and was enforced more than once in later cases.[43] To attack Taney as ideologically motivated and evil in his intent seems grossly unjust. He had opposed slavery for many years and had freed the slaves he had inherited except for two who could not support themselves and these he cared for until they died. Whether or not Taney's opinion was, in Professor Corwin's phrase, a "breach of trust" or an error in judgment is not easy to determine, but it was not a personal commitment to slavery. Some of the justices, including Taney himself, wrestled with the problems raised by the case in good conscience, and perhaps it was too much to expect that they would not accept the challenge to settle this terribly divisive issue. In a sense the Court may have been the victim of a decline in political leadership. Were there any truly imaginative presidents between Jackson and Lincoln? Congress had its giants, but they were dwindling in number and in stature. Given the fact that in the mid1850s the Supreme Court was held in the highest esteem in its entire existence by the bar and by the public generally, it seemed appropriate to many to make a plea for judicial intervention.

From the standpoint of judicial history, it is amusing and ironic that in this, the second time that the Court had declared an act of Congress unconstitutional, it had to go out of its way to do so. That is, in *Dred Scott* v. *Sandford* as in *Marbury* v. *Madison* the Court could have granted relief without exercising judicial review. But in *Dred Scott* judicial review received a needed impetus. It extended the frontier of the doctrine to something more than the preservation of judicial independence. The Court had now asserted that it was the final authority on the constitutionality of national policy. The case also laid the foundation for a judicial edifice of towering proportions, namely, the concept of substantive due process of law, which was destined to become a rigid bulwark for the protection of property rights and which now has become a strong device for the protection of individual liberty.

Congress Reacts

While I have emphasized the fact that the Supreme Court enjoyed unprecedented respect and prestige in the nation generally from the time of the death of Marshall to the day it rendered the *Dred Scott* decision, it was never altogether free from criticism by individual members of Congress. Attacks made on the Court during this period were not organized, and proposals for curbing the Court were introduced by senators or representatives from those states in which power had been limited in some way by judicial decisions. Senator Benjamin Tappan of Ohio, for example, at the request of the state legislature introduced several measures to alter the federal judiciary including a bill which would have limited a federal judge's term of office to seven years.[44] Indicative of some dissatisfaction with the Court was the brief exchange in the House of Representatives in 1850 over a resolution passed by the Senate authorizing the appointment of a special clerk by the Supreme Court. As a consequence of its growing business, the Court had requested the assistance of a clerk to transcribe opinions. Although the House passed the measure by a vote of 90-73, the large number of opponents indicates a latent hostility to the judiciary simply as an institution. Representative David K. Carter of Ohio delivered a derisive speech which suggests that a mood of irritation existed among some members of Congress. Carter declared that as he understood the bill it provided a clerk to aid the judges in their thinking and "when he became so old and inefficient that he could not do his own thinking without being supplied with a clerk for that purpose," he would be in favor of such a bill. The Supreme Court, he continued, wish to be "furnished with auxiliary brains to do their thinking which now, God knows, they [do] not do." But the way to correct such an evil was not through giving them a supplemental judge, but through reforming the Constitution, to "cut them off when old age, debility, or bad habits disabled them for investigating for themselves." [45]

An isolated speech here and there, a resolution introduced to limit tenure or jurisdiction on occasion—these were not serious enough to interfere with judicial independence. What they do tell us, however, is that in the very nature of the exercise of judicial review (and until the *Dred Scott* decision, it had been exercised exclusively over state legislatures under Taney's leadership and almost exclusively under Marshall's), some members of the national legislature will always disagree with the results. This very often produces a metamorphosis in which the distaste for an individual decision becomes a dislike of the doctrine, which becomes an attack on the institution that makes the doctrine a practical reality. In sum, whenever Congress has subjected the Court to a prolonged attack, the attack has had its origins in a disagreement with the outcome of a case or group of cases. But such disagreements reach serious constitutional proportions only when the issue is charged with deeply-held convictions and when the critics are numerous. One antagonistic senator does not provoke the Congress into a fight with the judiciary; nor does a large number of congressmen who are mildly disturbed over a decision of the Court. Numbers plus depth of feeling are the essential ingredients for a crisis, and the *Dred Scott* decision spawned both in a profusion never before witnessed.

The protracted debate in Congress extended through the thirty-fifth and thirty-sixth Congresses and was complex and discursive, wandering down every conceivable byway no matter how remotely connected to Dred Scott's case. At the heart of the verbal exchange were the great questions of slavery and the nature of the American union, but the proper role of the Supreme Court was, of course, a vital part of the discussion of the latter. Leading off for the anti-Court forces on 18 January 1858, was Senator John Parker Hale of New Hampshire. Hale, a product of Exeter and Bowdoin, began his political career as a Democrat, having been elected to the House under that party's label. When he denounced the annexation of Texas as promoting the interests of slavery, the Democratic party read him out of its ranks. The New Hampshire legislature elected him to the Senate in 1846 as the first dedicated antislavery senator. His strong antislavery position had secured him the nomination for president by the Liberty party in 1847, but he withdrew in favor of Van Buren when the party merged with the Free Soilers in 1848. In the election of 1852, Hale polled 150,000 votes as the standard bearer of the Free Soil Party. His eloquence, wit, and pleasant disposition combined to bring him a personal popularity in spite of his strong views on slavery.

Opening his remarks by pointing out that the Supreme Court had a rule that would not allow anyone arguing a case before them to speak disrespectfully of any other branch of the government, Senator Hale said that Congress had no such rule and that he intended to say of the Supreme Court that "which truth and justice" demanded him to say and that he would hold the Court "even as our fathers held the King of Great Britain—'enemies in war, and in peace friends.'" His hereditary respect for courts, he said, was gone. The Supreme Court had, in the *Dred Scott* decision, "come down from their place, and thrown themselves into the political arena, and have attempted to throw the sanction of their names in support of doctrines that can neither be sustained by authority nor by history," and he proposed to show it.[46]

For his support, Hale first drew upon the great apostle of democracy, Thomas Jefferson, quoting briefly from his letters to Spencer Roane, ("In denying the right they usurp of exclusively explaining the Constitution, I go further than you do, if I understand rightly your quotation from the Federalist, of an opinion that 'the judiciary is the last resort in relation *to the other departments* of the Government, but not in relation to the rights of the parties to the compact under which the judiciary is derived.' If this opinion be sound, then, indeed is our Constitution a complete *felo de se*."), to Dr. Jarvis ("you seem . . . to consider the judges as the ultimate arbiters of all constitutional questions—a very dangerous doctrine indeed, and one which would place us under the despotism of an oligarchy."), to Thomas Ritchie ("The judiciary of the United States is the subtle corps of sappers and miners constantly working underground to undermine the foundations of our confederate fabric."), to Archibald Thweat ("The legislative and executive branches may sometimes err, but elections and dependence will bring them to rights. The judiciary branch is the instrument which, working like gravity, without

intermission, is to press us at last into one consolidated mass."),
and to Dr. Hammond ("It has long, however, been my opinion
. . . that the germ of dissolution of our Federal Government is in
the constitution of the Federal judiciary—an irresponsible
body.").[47]

Implementing his case with an example from contemporary
history, Hale read an extract from a speech made just three years
previously by Senator Robert A. Toombs of Georgia in which
Toombs had said that he attached "little importance to the
political views" of the Supreme Court, since it had always found a
basis for the national government's assumption of power. In an
almost cynical reply to Hale, Toombs observed that what he had
said was correct when uttered but that the *Dred Scott* decision
had changed everything.[48] It was, of course, true that the Court
had invalidated for the first time an aspect of national policy, but
that decision had been in the interest of Toombs and the South
and slavery. Would Toombs and his southern brethren have
defended the Court had its decision, even though invalidating an
act of Congress, run counter to southern interests? It was obvious
that sectional interests took precedence over judicial doctrine, and
the men of the North were equally guilty of a lack of principle.

Continuing his remarks on 20 January Senator Hale refuted two
points of the Taney opinion. He disagreed with the Court's
affirmation that property in slaves is of the same right as all other
property and that the right to hold and to traffic in slavery was so
universally acknowledged in England and America at the time of
the American Revolution that no man thought of disputing it.
Hale argued that legally, as opposed to the moral question, there
was such a thing as property in slaves, but only within the
jurisdiction that imposed the servitude. In free states there was a
qualified property in human beings—criminals in the peni-
tentiary—who might be forced to labor within the state but not
outside it. Just as a confined criminal might not be forced to labor
outside the jurisdiction which held him, a slave was free when he
went beyond the boundaries of the state which legally bound him
to slavery.[49]

Furthermore, declared Hale, although man might hold inanimate things as property there was a universally accepted difference
between man and "the brute creature" which went back to the

beginning of recorded history. "When the Almighty created this broad earth and gave it to man for a home, He gave it to him to cultivate; He filled the land with cattle and the sea with fish and the air with fowls; then He made man and He gave him this commission: 'Have thou dominion over the fish of the sea, and the fowls of the air, and the cattle and over every creeping thing that creeps on the earth.' But man, sir, immortal man—made in the image of God—He never said, 'have thou dominion over him.' No; He reserved that last great work, man, for His own peculiar worship." [50] From universal morality as found in the revealed word of God, Hale moved to the courts and to the American founding fathers. He quoted from Lord [Sir John] Holt's opinion in a case in 1704 in which the English judge had said that "the common law takes no notice of Negroes being different from other men" and that men "may be the owners of property, and therefore, cannot themselves be the subject of property." Similar in tone were the documented words of American judges including those in the slaveholding states of Virginia, Maryland and Louisiana. Finally Hale repeated the criticism of slavery voiced by Washington, Mason, Madison, Jefferson, Henry, and Jay, concluding:

> If the opinions of the Supreme Court are true, they put these men in the worst position of any men who are to be found in the pages of our history. If the opinion of the Supreme Court be true, it makes the immortal authors of the Declaration of Independence liars before God and hypocrites before the world ... [I] f you believe the Supreme Court, they were merely quibbling on words. They went into the courts of the Most High, and pledged fidelity to their principles as the price they would pay for success; and now it is attempted to cheat them out of the poor boon of integrity; and it is said that they did not mean so, and that when they said all men they meant all white men and when they said that the contest they waged was for the right of mankind, the Supreme Court of the United States would have you believe that they meant it was to establish slavery. Against that I protest here, now, and everywhere, and I tell the Supreme Court that these things are so impregnably fixed in the hearts

of the people, on the page of history, in the recollections and traditions of men, that it will require mightier efforts than they have made or can make to overturn or to shake these settled convictions of the popular understanding and of the popular heart. [51]

William Pitt Fessenden, Senator from Maine, took care to distinguish between a *decision* of the Supreme Court and an *opinion* by judges on questions which were not properly before them. Fessenden, like Hale, was a graduate of Bowdoin, but his diploma had been withheld for a year on the ground that his general character, which included such bad habits as profane swearing and a disorganizing spirit, called for punishment. He was later to receive an honorary degree from his alma mater and to become a member of its Board of Governors. Fessenden, who began his political career as a Whig, assumed a conservative position on the slavery question, possibly in reaction to his abolitionist father, Samuel, who had sired him out of wedlock. Eventually his tolerance changed to hostility and an antislavery coalition elected him to the Senate in 1854. Abraham Lincoln called Fessenden "a radical without the petulant and vicious fretfulness of many radicals," and although Fessenden had little respect for President Andrew Johnson and disagreed with his policies after Lincoln's death, he voted for acquittal at Johnson's impeachment trial.

Fessenden admitted that he was bound to render obedience to the Supreme Court of the United States but he said, "When they undertake to settle matters not before them, I tell them those questions are for me as well as for them." [52] The question which was not before them was that of the power of Congress to exclude slavery from territory belonging to the United States. But the opinion on that point in any event, said Fessenden, rested on a fallacious assumption, namely that the Constitution recognizes slaves as property and protects slavery as such. Even if one were to admit that the Constitution so recognized slavery prior to 1808 by its protection of the slave trade, the fact that the Constitution did not protect it after 1808 denied that slaves were property after that date. However, the Constitution did not and does not recognize slaves as property; it merely recognizes slavery as an institution existing in certain states. And the institution does not extend to territories belonging to the United States since there is no such thing as a right of a state in a territory.[53] Fessenden seems to be saying that constitutionally slave owners may keep their slaves in those states where slavery is permitted, but they may not do so elsewhere in the United States including federal territory, where Congress may forbid slavery altogether.

On several occasions, Jacob Collamer, antislavery Whig Senator from Vermont, attacked the *Dred Scott* decision. Centering his criticism on the concept of a slave as property and offering essentially the same arguments used by Hale and Fessenden, he contributed little that was new to the debate. A strong speech which combined the decision and the Court as a single object of opprobrium was that delivered by New York's Senator William H. Seward, later to become Lincoln's controversial Secretary of State. Seward came from a political heritage of Jeffersonian democracy although he had cast his first presidential vote for John Quincy Adams in 1824. From this point he moved through anti-Masonism to Whigism and was at first conservative on the slavery issue. Gradually he began to espouse the antislavery cause and he was elected to the Senate in 1848 on the basis of his advanced views on the subject. Some historians suggest that his change in attitude toward slavery was the result of his marriage to Frances Miller, a liberal and humanitarian woman, but he might have arrived at his position independently since he was a man of considerable learning and of broad intellectual interests. In a long speech in which he traced the history of the slavery controversy, Seward said that the Supreme Court, in invalidating the Missouri Compromise, had committed an "ill-omened act" and had forgotten "its own dignity." The Court forgot also, continued Seward, that its province was simply *jus dicere* not *jus dare*. They forgot, moreover, that one "foul sentence does more harm than many foul examples; for the last do but corrupt the stream, while the former corrupteth the fountain." And they failed to remember that "judicial usurpation is more odious and intolerable than any other among the manifold practices of tyranny." Seward compared the justices of the Supreme Court to the English judges under Charles I who had subverted the statutes of English liberty, and he suggested that the entire affair was a conspiracy between the president and the Court against the forces of freedom. [54] It was just seven months later, on 25 October 1858 that Senator Seward delivered his prophetic speech in Rochester, New York, in which he declared that the slavery struggle was an "irrepressible conflict" between enduring and opposing forces.

In a characteristically narrow legalistic analysis, Senator Lyman Trumbull of Illinois attempted to separate what the Supreme Court legally could and did do from what it legally could not and did not do. Trumbull, who like Fessenden was to become one of the courageous seven who voted against President Johnson's conviction, argued this way. The *Dred Scott* case determined only that a person descended from Africans held as slaves had no authority to sue in the federal courts. The Supreme Court did not decide whether Scott was free or slave, and whether he was one or the other was immaterial to the decision. The Court decided that it had no jurisdiction to hear Scott's plea and then proceeded in "an extrajudicial manner" to pronounce on political questions not legitimately before it. The Court's opinion on congressional authority over slavery in the territories is pure dicta, and the fact that the judges did not say that it was not dicta does not make it law. No judge will ever declare in the course of an opinion that "what I am going to say is out of the case, and is of no authority whatever, but I will go on to say it." [55] Trumbull's position is interesting in that he does not say that the Court is a bad institution or even that the decision is an evil one; he contends only that the opinion is divided into two parts, a legal ruling and dicta, and that those who would construe the dicta as controlling law are giving the decision an erroneous interpretation. In short, Taney's essay on slavery and on the constitutional powers concerning its regulation is a private opinion and nothing more. Implicit, however, in Trumbull's analysis is the idea that the judiciary has a limited function, and that there is a definable distinction between law and politics, the latter being outside the domain of the Court.

More highly charged with emotion than most, and considerably more coarse and vituperative in tone, were the remarks of Senator Benjamin F. Wade of Ohio, an intense abolitionist who later became president pro tempore of the Senate and would have succeeded to the presidency upon Johnson's removal. So certain was he of the outcome of President Johnson's trial that he had begun to choose his cabinet prior to its conclusion. Wade contended that the Supreme Court in the *Dred Scott* case had done what no court had ever done before in the United States. This was no surprise to him, however, since he never had held the Court in reverence but thought it the "mere instrument of political power." It had always been so and *Dred Scott* had supplied further proof. But, intoned Wade, as evil as it is for the Court to tell us that "we have men among us so low that they can have no rights: that they are mere merchandise," there is yet another matter that must be dealt with. It is the pernicious doctrine, inadmissible in a free country, that judges appointed for life, vested with total immunity, have any right to decide the law of the land for other departments of the government. Such an interpretation of the Court's decisions, said Wade, would produce "the most concentrated irresponsible despotism on God's earth." Each department must act for itself; each senator is bound to follow his own interpretation of the Constitution. Dred Scott's rights have been determined forever, but no department of government and no other right was touched. "Talk about their deciding that slavery exists in Kansas as much as in South Carolina! Talk about the highest tribunal in the land deciding that slavery is in your territories! That every inch of ground outside of the free state is slave territory! I pity the weakness of the man who yields to any such idea as that. That court has no such transcendant power. It could bind nobody but the suitors in the court. It would be unfortunate if it could." [56] Thus spake Ben Wade. It was an old argument with a long line of respectable adherents including Thomas Jefferson and Andrew Jackson. It was not to be altogether without life one hundred years later.

In the House of Representatives, the criticism was no less bitter than it was in the Senate. Joshua Giddings of Ohio, an abolitionist of the Garrison-Sumner school submitted a resolution to the House on 18 January 1858 which began by declaring that the Supreme Court had purposefully denied the self-evident truth of the Declaration of Independence and ended with the phrase that "the court [has] brought discredit upon the judiciary of the United States." [57] Philemon Bliss, also of Ohio, took the opportunity to introduce a bill that would have repealed the twenty-fifth section of the Judiciary Act of 1789. [58] With feeling running high against the Court, this seemed a propitious time to reopen the old wounds shared by slave states and non-slave states alike. The movement came to nought, however.

One of the most thoroughgoing attacks on judicial review was made in a speech by Roscoe Conkling of New York on 17 April 1860. Conkling, who had been in the House for only two years, was later to be elected senator and to resign his seat in protest against President Garfield's policies. Two presidents, Grant and Arthur, proffered him appointments to the Supreme Court which he declined. Conkling was a noted physical culturist who, after the attack on Senator Sumner by his colleague, Preston S. Brooks, stood beside Thaddeus Stevens as a personal bodyguard. James K. Blaine once referred insultingly to Conkling's "grandiloquent swell, his majestic, supereminent, overpowering, turkey gobbler strut." [59] Conkling disavowed any intent to examine the arguments of the Supreme Court in the *Dred Scott* decision but declared that his concern was with the power of the Supreme Court, not its wisdom. [60] If the Supreme Court has the power ascribed to it by some, said Conkling, the Constitution and the institutions of the country are "nothing but wax in the hands of the judges: it amounts to a running power of amendment." Furthermore, if the Court may pronounce a final authority on the rights and powers of the legislative and executive branches of the government, it has an inflated supremacy which the framers of the Constitution in their fear of despotism would never have countenanced. Of the three branches, said Conkling, the Court "is the one removed furthest from the origin of all political power in the country; the one least in sympathy with the people; and restrained from trampling upon popular rights by nothing save that most unreliable of safeguards, the fidelity of unwatched human nature." [61] Such power, said Conkling, is irresponsible and is at best an oligarchy in the Republic. Relying primarily on the Convention's rejection of the Council of Revision, a judicial-executive composite which would have been able to veto acts of Congress, Conkling set out to prove that the framers never intended the Court to exercise judicial review. Secondly, he argued that if the only key to the Constitution were the document itself, nothing expressed therein or implied therefrom could grant such a power to the Supreme Court. If the right to interpret the Constitution is given to anybody, it is given to the inferior federal courts which were not even named in the Constitution. The purpose of the Supreme Court's appellate jurisdiction, according to Article III, is to review the action of inferior courts only to correct errors. This, however, would lead to the strange conclusion, continued Conkling, that "the district judges and juries of the land are our constitutional masters." Closing the argument, Conkling pointed to the fact that of the three branches of government, it is only the Supreme Court which the Constitution leaves undefined both in the number of its members and in their qualifications. Surely, he argued, the framers would not have created a "judicial regency," would not have conferred "political omnipotence" on the one department of government in which no qualifications of any kind are required. Conkling then concluded that the judgments of the Supreme Court are binding only upon inferior courts and on the parties litigant; and therefore the decisions of the Court are not in any sense binding on Congress but are merely addressed to its discretion. [62]

A speech which borders on the modern behavioral approach to the study of politics was delivered on 29 May 1860 by Representative James M. Ashley of Ohio. Ashley had acquired a deep-seated hatred of slavery, possibly through his experiences as a member of the crew on a river boat during his youth when he witnessed cruel treatment of slaves. Originally a Democrat, he went into the Free Soil Party in 1848, and then moved to the Republican organization in 1854. He entered the House in 1858. Ashley introduced the first resolution to abolish slavery through a constitutional amendment, and he initiated the impeachment trial of President Johnson. Both acts follow logically from the central theme of his speech in 1860 entitled: "Success of the Calhoun Revolution: the Constitution Changed and Slavery Nationalized by the Usurpations of the Supreme Court." Ashley argued that "the disunion school of Calhoun" had built a privileged class which had acquired and held virtual control of every department of the national government for the previous twenty years. It had done so, Ashley suggested, through a form of blackmail in which it threatened to dissolve the union if the people in the free states did not cooperate. While preaching compromise and concessions, this privileged class obtained complete control of the most dangerous department, the federal judiciary. The Calhoun group accomplished its task through its control of the Committee on the Judiciary, its strategy being the presentation of the appointment and confirmation of antislavery judges. This was done by the Committee's persuading the president to withdraw some nominations and persuading the Senate to reject others. The help of some northern senators was essential to the success of the scheme and many gave such help because of "carelessness, or incompetency, or criminal complicity," the latter being the case with those who owned southern plantations well stocked with slaves while claiming to represent a free people. A second element of control, Ashley contended, is demonstrated by the population and number of cases in the nine judicial circuits. The ninth circuit, composed of Arkansas and Mississippi, contained just over half a million white inhabitants whereas the seventh, consisting of Ohio, Indiana, Michigan and Illinois, contained over six million inhabitants. The second circuit (New York, Connecticut and Vermont) contained over five million freemen while the fifth (Louisiana and Alabama) had just over one million. In case load, the seventh circuit disposed of 1,782 cases in 1856 compared to 1,721 cases disposed of by the fourth, fifth, sixth, eighth, and ninth combined. The southern states comprised these five circuits. This state of affairs, said Ashley, was not the result of an accident, but the deliberate plan of the Calhoun faction which in effect had captured the Democratic party. Although Ashley contended, moreover, that Congress was not constitutionally bound by a decision of the Supreme Court, the central theme of his argument was that the entire federal judiciary had come under the control of a powerful minority, the slavocracy.

Speaking in behalf of the Court, or of the *Dred Scott* decision, or both, were Democrats, north and south, although those of the northern wing tended to defend the institution and judicial review as opposed to defending the particular ruling under attack. One of the South's most articulate spokesman was Judah P. Benjamin, United States senator from Louisiana. West Indian by birth, Benjamin had grown up in South Carolina, had attended Yale for a period, and had settled in New Orleans where he had secured a reputation as a leading member of the Louisiana bar. Elected to the Senate as a Whig in 1852, he moved into the Democratic party in 1856 where he became a leader of the secessionist wing. He later served the Confederacy as a member of the Jefferson Davis cabinet, and he fled to England at the war's end where he rose to great eminence in his second career as a legal practitioner.

In a long legalistic argument on 1 March 1858 Senator Benjamin attempted to refute the propositions that had been articulated by the northern contingent in the Senate, particularly those of Senators Fessenden and Collamer.[63] It was his duty, said Benjamin, to answer the charges brought against the highest judges of the land, charges made "with a violence, a recklessness, and . . . a disregard of the truth and decency," and he proposed to controvert the arguments that slavery was a creature of state statutes; that it had no existence outside the limits of those states where it was lawful; that slaves were not property outside slave states, and that slavery was not protected by the Constitution of the United States nor by international law. Through elaborate argument and detailed documentation, Benjamin demonstrated that slavery went far back into English history, and that at the time of the Declaration of Independence, it was protected by the Common Law of the Colonies and was supported by legislation and by judicial authority. Slavery was, in fact, "the common recognized institution of the New World."[64] Throughout his argument Benjamin emphasized the concept of slaves as property, thus appealing to the property instincts of his adversaries. He pointed out, for example, that slavery had been abolished in England by gradual emancipation and only by selling the slaves to themselves at a fair price. In the same view Benjamin suggested that the Constitution protected various kinds of property, including patent rights as well as slavery. He pointed to the millions of dollars in patent rights and asked what the condition of the northern inventor would be without this protection. Benjamin then turned to a discussion of the Supreme Court. He said that in *Prigg* v. *Pennsylvania* the Court had unanimously held that the Constitution protected property in slaves. Even Justice McLean, who had taken a different position in the *Dred Scott* case, joined the majority in *Prigg*. But more important, Benjamin argued in hairsplitting terms that every member of the Court had said that the Court had jurisdiction of the *merits* of the case, if not the parties. That is, Benjamin was saying, the Court had acted appropriately and normally in determining the broad issues of slavery even though Scott had no standing to sue. [65]

Neither Senator Benjamin nor his counterpart, Senator Fessenden, was wholly correct in his analysis. It was not true, as Benjamin had said, that the Court of necessity had to deal with both the jurisdictional question and the merits of the case. On the other hand, Fessenden was wrong in contending that once the Court had determined the jurisdictional point, it had no authority to look into the issues raised in the case. It was at bottom a matter of judicial discretion, and the pertinent question is whether the Court *should* have done what it did. This then is not a legal question at all but a matter of the judicial conduct of a judge or of the judges collectively.

Senator James A. Stewart of Maryland suggested that the Court had adjudged the slavery question "without regard to anything but the law and the Constitution applicable to its merits, with all becoming modesty and judicial propriety, and with distinguished learning and ability." [66] He reached this conclusion after presenting evidence that all of the states in the union had at one time excluded all nonwhites from the body politic. Negroes, along with Indians, had not been considered citizens. They could not vote, serve in the militia, or give evidence against a white person. If the Declaration of Independence included them, said Stewart, why did not our ancestors emancipate them? Had the Supreme Court ruled that Negroes were citizens, it would have done so only with "manifest disregard of all authority" and in the face of the "truth of history." [67]

One of the most objective defenses of the Supreme Court and of the exercise of judicial review was made by Senator William Bigler of Pennsylvania, a loyal Democrat who labored hard to prevent the breakup of the union. Bigler distinguished between a right and a power, maintaining that a people may have a power to do what is not their legal right. What is the right of a citizen in a territory worth, asked Bigler, if it cannot be enjoyed? What good is the right of a citizen to take his property into a territory if a majority can deprive him of the enjoyment and use of the property? "There is no constitutional right unless it can be enjoyed," and the right of a slave owner to reclaim his slave is almost destroyed by popular prejudice or public policy in certain states. It would appear that Bigler approved of slavery and all its trappings but such was not the case. He was arguing actually for adherence to established constitutional forms irrespective of one's personal view of particular decisions. As he phrased it, he had made it a rule in his political career "to maintain the Constitution of the United States as defined by the Supreme Court, and shall ever do so." While disagreeing with the *Dred Scott* decision, he said it was now his duty "to stand by that decision, regardless of any peculiar view I may have had on my own part, or of any prejudice I may thereby encounter." [68]

Another northern Democrat who hoped to compromise the slavery issue was Senator George E. Pugh of Ohio. He, like Bigler, spoke in terms of institutional loyalty and support. He reminded the Senate that they had defined the jurisdiction of the Supreme Court in such a way as to permit the owner of a slave to take his case to the tribunal for decision. Now that a decision had been made, many in the Senate refused to support it. Whatever an individual's opinion, said Pugh, the judgment of the Supreme Court must be carried into effect. Continuing, Pugh argued: "We cannot live for an hour under any other doctrine. It will not do to say that if the Supreme Court decided to please us, we execute that judgment; if it does not please us, we overturn it. No, sir; I say it is more important to the community, more important to the cause of good government, that a judgment once pronounced by the appropriate tribunal should go into effect, than that it should be decided rightly; far more." [69]

Essentially the same point was made by Senator Stephen A. Douglas of Illinois who said that he "would abide by the decision of the Supreme Court, not only as a matter of policy, but from considerations of duty." Douglas was first and foremost a constitutionalist who supported the properly constituted authority of government. His break with the secessionist wing of the Democratic party and his strong personal backing of President Lincoln after 1860 clearly demonstrates his consistency. Men like Douglas, Pugh and Bigler represented a middle ground, a position which very often seems to be devoid of any strong conviction and which is sometimes equated with lack of character. But in the final analysis it is a proper attitude for a constitutionalist to hold. It is a sound principle that organized government, if it is to be free must be orderly, and that even the harshest conflicts must be moderated within the existing rules. Constitutionalism in practice requires not only an agreement on what the rules are, but a consensus on great moral and ethical questions. Unfortunately, the rule concerning the Supreme Court's exercise of judicial review of acts of Congress was not written into the Constitution, and it had not yet been accepted as a customary practice. Furthermore, the slavery issue was the one major issue on which a consensus had not been reached. All of the compromises over slavery that had been made, including the symbolic approval of the institution when the Declaration of Independence was signed, had been in the name of expediency. The earlier the nation had faced the moral imperative of ending what never should have started, the easier would have been the transition. The abolitionist image of Roger Brooke Taney as a villain and the Supreme Court as a power-grabbing agent is a distortion of history, of logic and of fact, notwithstanding that what the Court said and did in *Dred Scott* was a great moral wrong. If Taney is guilty of a breach of ethics or of an inhumane attitude, so is George Washington, and James Madison, and every man who signed the Constitution and fought for its adoption since *that document* protected and nourished slavery. It is currently popular in some quarters to pronounce in reference to desegregation: "You can't legislate morality." This is a patent absurdity. If the whole Negro question teaches us anything it is that you (the government) cannot legislate immorality—at least not indefinitely. Ultimately the rules of constitutional government are with great moral questions, and statutes and judicial decisions are ways in which morals in the broadest sense are legislated. The Civil War was spawned as slavery was permitted to coexist with the professed American ideal of human equality. In short, the *Dred Scott* decision affected the coming of the Civil War only slightly, if at all. Had the case been decided differently, the war might have been delayed, but it is doubtful that armed conflict would have been avoided.

In the history of judicial review the *Dred Scott* case is more significant than *Marbury* v. *Madison*. In the latter case, the Court emphasized what had been generally recognized: that the judiciary was independent of the legislature and that the Supreme Court might protect its institutional integrity from legislative interference. And when the Court told Congress that the legislature was extending to the judiciary more power than the Constitution permitted, even the Jeffersonians could approve. For the Court to veto judicially a broad legislative policy of Congress was another matter. The difference in the two decisions was not merely one of degree but of kind, a difference between judicial independence and judicial sovereignty.[70] Judicial review of the congressional judgment became a vital principle of the American system after *Dred Scott* v. *Sandford* and not after *Marbury* v. *Madison*. Although Justice Oliver Wendell Holmes, many years later, in defending the Court's role as arbiter of the federal system, might suggest that the Court's power to invalidate acts of Congress was relatively unimportant, the doctrine can be defended in the abstract as well as in its historical context. In any event, it was not until the post Civil War period that it was used with some regularity. I would suggest, moreover, that the Taney Court may well have used the power at a propitious time and under circumstances favorable to its continuance. Had many more years passed without the Court's assertion of the power, it would have become a constitutional dead letter, and the fact that it was exercised on an issue over which the nation was divided so bitterly meant that Congress, in its disunited state, could not muster the kind of support needed to curtail the power of the Court. Moreover, since the law which the Court had held invalid had already been repealed, no actual policy conflict existed between Congress and the Court. The real controversy was over slavery, and it was already too late to settle it except by force.

Although the *Dred Scott* case closes a chapter in the history of judicial-legislative relationships, Justice Taney did not pass from the scene until October 1864, and in those final years he wrote two notable opinions. In *Ableman* v. *Booth*,[71] he asserted federal supremacy over the states and eloquently condemned defiance of federal judicial authority by the courts of Wisconsin. In *Ex parte Merryman*,[72] Taney, sitting in the United States Circuit Court, held that the president had no authority under the Constitution to suspend the writ of habeas corpus, thus rendering the very first American judicial decision condemning arbitrary military power and upholding individual liberty. Congressional critics, seemingly indifferent to the imperatives of constitutional government, again raised their voices in protest against "wrongly used" judicial power. Just prior to his death Taney wrote that he saw no hope that the Supreme Court would ever be "restored to the authority and rank which the Constitution intended to confer upon it." Like Marshall before him Taney was so intensely involved in his own times that he could not perceive the permanence of the structure to which he had contributed so much.

4. Chase & Waite:
The Period of Relative Calm

WHILE it is possible to divide the first seventy-five years of the Supreme Court's existence into two periods conforming to the service of Chief Justice Marshall and, to a lesser extent, to that of Chief Justice Taney, such is not the case for the fifty years following Taney's death. In part, the sheer length of service of thirty-four and twenty-eight years, respectively, for the two men is responsible for the special impact which each was able to make on the Court, on judicial history, and on the broadest phases of American constitutional law. No chief justice has even come close to the records of Marshall and Taney, and only Melville Fuller with his twenty-one years of service, can be placed in the category of long-tenured chiefs. But it is not simply length of service that compels historians to equate the Supreme Court's doctrines, its growth, and its contribution to American constitutionalism with its leadership. Time must be combined with those subtle and often indefinable personal traits which result in a man's name being linked to his era as opposed to his merely being identified with the institution in which he labored. Thus, we may talk of the Chase Court or the Waite Court, but these phrases connote little more than identification, and neither phrase suggests a particular doctrinal approach to the law, nor necessarily imputes a singular contribution to the Court's development. But if the Court's leadership was not of the highest quality during the half century following the Civil War, neither was the political leadership of the nation generally. The prime movers in the nation were concentrated in business, and for the most part, direction of the national government came from Congress.

There were no great presidents between Lincoln and Theodore Roosevelt, and there were no great chief justices between Taney and Charles Evans Hughes. Those justices to whom we must attribute intellectual dominance on the Court during the post Civil War era—Miller, Field, Harlan, and after 1901, Holmes—were associates. It is possible to break any study of the Court at the end of the nineteenth century and again at the end of Chief Justice White's tenure, for it is roughly at these points that minor squabbles with Congress appear, as preliminary bouts to the main event of 1936-37. There were, in fact, three serious judicial-legislative conflicts between 1865 and 1933. The first grew out of the aftermath of the Civil War and was primarily the result of the policies of a Congress determined to punish the former secessionists. The second and third, both more fundamental and enduring, were caused by the growing adherence of the nation to traditional democratic values, particularly to universal suffrage, and by the harsh results of a free-wheeling capitalism, especially the great inequities in the distribution of material wealth.

Post-Civil-War Crisis

Although Abraham Lincoln was committed to the reversal of the *Dred Scott* decision, he carefully distinguished between criticism of a specific ruling of the Supreme Court and criticism of the Court itself. His conception of judicial review was narrowly Jeffersonian. In his First Inaugural Address he argued that constitutional questions decided by the Court were binding upon the parties to a suit and "were entitled to a very high respect and consideration in all parallel cases by all other departments of government." [1] At the same time he warned that "the people will have ceased to be their own rulers" if the questions affecting the nation were to be irrevocably fixed by the Supreme Court the instant they were made. [2] He then suggested that he was not mounting an assault on either the Supreme Court or the individual judges since they were duty-bound to rule on cases properly before them. The real culprits were those who turned the decisions to a political advantage. Like Presidents Jefferson and Jackson before him, who had also assumed office in response to a political movement dedicated to alter the nation's direction, Lincoln had to contend with an authoritative branch of the government over which he had no coercive power. But in this one respect the fates were kinder to Lincoln than they had been to his predecessors. John Marshall remained on the bench to frustrate the will of both Jefferson and Jackson, but a majority of the judges, including the chief, were to pass from the scene during Lincoln's first term, leaving the President free to reconstitute the Court in his own image.

The first of the five southerners on the bench at the time of *Dred Scott*, Peter Daniel, had died early in 1860 prior to Lincoln's nomination and election. Justice Campbell had resigned to join the Confederate cause and McLean had died just one month after President Lincoln's inauguration. As a direct result of the president's deliberate slowness in making appointments, the Court operated at considerably less than full strength during the early years of the war. Those American presidents who have occupied the office during a time of great emergency have always viewed the Court, when staffed by men not of their choosing, as a hostile adjunct of the machinery of government. Lincoln was no exception. He desired a Court that would validate his policies. Congress might be led, legally and extralegally; but if the Supreme Court chose to disagree with the president, especially in regard to the constitutionally precarious use of emergency power, his leadership might be stalled, and even stilled. Therefore Lincoln moved cautiously, something he could afford to do under the circumstances, since out of the Court's membership of six, three looked favorably upon the president's ideas. Justices Catron of Tennessee and Wayne of Georgia were southern unionists who had remained loyal to the national cause, and Justice Grier of Pennsylvania believed wholeheartedly in the war. In opposition were the chief justice and Justices Nelson of Pennsylvania and Clifford of Maine.

President Lincoln's first nomination to the Court was Noah H. Swayne of Ohio. Virginia born, Swayne had attended a Quaker academy where he developed a violent hatred of slavery, so much so, in fact, that he left his native state and moved to Ohio where he acquired an outstanding reputation as a corporation counsel. Swayne's views on the war and on the slavery question made him acceptable to the president, but also influential in the selection was Lincoln's debt to the Republican organization in Ohio which had played a strategic role in his nomination at the convention. Swayne took his seat on 21 January 1862. Lincoln's second appointment, Samuel F. Miller of Iowa, had practiced medicine for more than a decade in Kentucky and, like Swayne, left the South because of his strong opposition to slavery. Miller studied law while administering to the sick, was admitted to the bar in 1847, and became a popular figure in Whig and Republican circles. He never had held a public office of any kind prior to his nomination to the Court in July 1862. Destined to become one of the Court's giants, he has been aptly described as "a big man—blunt as a hippopotamus and candid as sunlight"—to whom his rivals and friends alike accorded great respect. Lincoln's third appointment was his personal and political friend, David Davis of Illinois, who had done yeoman service for the president at the Republican convention of 1860. Davis took his seat on the bench on 1 December 1862, bringing the Court up to its statutory complement of nine. Congress and the president were soon to agree, however, that ten was a more "convenient" number than nine, and in the closing days of February 1863, the House and the Senate quickly enacted a law creating a tenth judicial circuit comprising California and Oregon, and providing for a Supreme Court consisting of a chief justice and nine associate justices.[3]

A sound case could be made for the additional circuit on the basis of the large number of cases arising out of the complexities of California land law, although it has been suggested that the real motive behind the move was the attainment of a Supreme Court that could be counted on to uphold those congressional and presidential actions which even those who believed wholeheartedly in the war might consider constitutionally marginal.[4] Congress had swung into action when the Prize Cases[5] were being considered, and the 5-4 division upholding presidential authority indicated how tenuous the Lincoln majority was, and the decision of the Court justified in the Republican mind the addition of an "insurance" justice. The president's choice was Stephen J. Field, a former Democrat who had joined the Union party in California out of distaste for the southern cause, and who had used his talents and energies successfully in the struggle to keep California loyal to the

Union. Connecticut born and a graduate of Williams College, Field practiced law in New York City for a time before moving to California in 1849 where he soon became one of the state's distinguished citizens. He was elected to the legislature in 1850 and to the Supreme Court of California in 1857 where he worked diligently to establish firm and lasting principles in California land law which had been in a chaotic state as a result of the conflicts between the common law and the Spanish code, a confusion which had been compounded by fraudulent and overlapping grants during the rough and tumble days of later California settlement. Justice Field was to give the Court able, strong-willed, but controversial intellectual leadership for thirty-four years.

On the morning of 13 October 1864 Secretary of the Treasury Salmon P. Chase received a telegram from his friend and cabinet colleague, Edwin M. Stanton, which read: "Chief Justice Taney died last night." [6] The way was now open for an additional Lincoln appointment to the Court, and a chief justice at that. Overtures were made to the president in behalf of many men, for the naming of the first Republican chief justice was an historic event, but none were so persistent as those in support of Lincoln's great political rival, Salmon P. Chase. Lincoln was reputed to have said that "he would rather have swallowed his buckhorn chair than to have nominated Chase," [7] but nominate him he did. Chase had sought the Republican nomination for president in 1856, 1860, and 1864, and he would have been delighted to run for and to serve in the nation's highest office at any time prior to his death in 1873. Even the chief justiceship could not quench his presidential thirst. Chase had been born in New Hampshire and reared in Ohio by an uncle. He returned to New Hampshire for his college education at Dartmouth, but began his legal career in Cincinnati where he soon became active in the antislavery movement. He served both as governor of Ohio and United States senator, and was named to Lincoln's cabinet largely as a reward for his record as an abolitionist, a record which had earned him the sobriquet "attorney general for fugitive slaves." Now the Republicans, like the Jacksonians before them and like the Jeffersonians of an earlier day, had finally gained control of the Supreme Court, the only branch of the government which could not be captured directly by winning an election. And like their political predecessors they could not be certain that the victory automatically carried judicial approval of Republican policies.

Many historians contend that the Supreme Court cowardly acquiesced in the unconstitutional picnic of an overbearing Congress in the immediate post Civil War years, and such an indictment contains an element of truth. The Court did retreat on occasion, but Chase's incumbency from 1864 to 1873 saw no less than ten acts of Congress declared unconstitutional, as compared with two during the entire history of the Court up to that time. The Court was equally active in its invalidation of state laws. Under Chase it annulled forty-six as compared with sixty between 1789 and 1863.[8] Not all invalidations were of equal significance, but some were controversial enough to irritate an already arrogant and self-righteous Congress. Both the quantity and quality of statutory invalidations during the years of Chief Justice Chase indicate that judicial review had really come into its own, although the Supreme Court is often remembered during this period for what it did *not* do. On the three occasions when it might have swept away the Reconstruction program,[9] it hesitated to act, and for this reason the Court is said to have "caved in, fallen through, failed."[10]

The bitterness engendered by the decisions in the *Dred Scott, Booth*, and *Merryman* cases had dissipated once the war was under way, but indicative of the intensity of feeling among the Republican radicals was the action of Senator Hale on 4 December 1861. On that day Hale, whose opposition to the judiciary went far beyond a disagreement with an individual decision, introduced a resolution requesting the Committee on the Judiciary to inquire into the expediency and propriety of abolishing the Supreme Court.[11] Hale's fellow radicals would not support him, for this was too much even for them. Lafayette Foster of Connecticut, a former editor of a Whig journal, the *Norwich Republican*, condemned Hale for undermining the confidence of the nation in the Court, and Senators Collamer and Orville Browning made the proper constitutional point that Congress had no power to abolish the Supreme Court even though a majority might desire it.[12] On 12 December Lyman Trumbull, chairman of the Judiciary Committee, asked the Senate to discharge the committee from further consideration of the Hale resolution, to which the Senate agreed.[13] It was not until after Lincoln's death, however, that the Court became subject to serious and successful legislative intrusions into its customary domain. For one thing the radicals did not take kindly to the justices' declination of circuit duty in those states which were under military domination. Chief Justice Chase's stubborn refusal to hold circuit court in Virginia, thereby preventing the trial of Jefferson Davis for treason, further inflamed the already offended radicals, and they retaliated by reducing the membership of the Court.[14] Representative James F. Wilson of Iowa introduced a bill to reduce the number of justices from ten to nine,[15] and Senator Trumbull, in a move to exert even greater control over the Court, offered an amendment which provided that no vacancy on the Supreme Court should be filled until the number of associate justices should be reduced to six, at which size it should remain.[16] The upshot was a bill which reduced the size of the Court from ten to eight, and the radicals had little difficulty in mustering the two-thirds majority to override President Johnson's veto. But for a time at least, the Court remained unintimidated. For it was in the midst of these proceedings that it rendered the decision in *Ex parte Milligan*.[17]

L.P. Milligan had been arrested in Indiana on 5 October 1864 by the military commander of the district, and he was subsequently convicted by a military tribunal of conspiracy to release and arm rebel prisoners for the purpose of aiding in an invasion of Indiana by rebel forces. He was sentenced to be hanged, but President Johnson commuted his sentence to life imprisonment. Milligan then petitioned the federal circuit court for a writ of habeas corpus, and the judges, unable to agree on the disposition of the case, certified the question of law to the Supreme Court. The Court ordered Milligan's release, holding that the military commission which had tried him was unlawful. While unanimous in its decision, the Court divided 5-4 over the reasons for its order. Speaking for the majority, Justice Davis declared that the Constitution did not permit either the president or Congress to institute a military commission to try civilians in areas outside the theater of military operations. Martial law, he said, "can never exist where the courts are open, and in the proper and unobstructed exercise of their jurisdiction" because such a proceeding is a violation of an individual's constitutional rights. "No doctrine," he argued, "involving more pernicious consequences, was ever intended by the wit of man than that any of its provisions can be suspended during any of the great exigencies of government. Such a doctrine leads directly to anarchy or despotism."

The chief justice, speaking for four dissenters, maintained that Congress possessed the power to establish the military commission, but had not exercised it in this instance. In answer to Davis and the majority, Chase observed that the civilian courts "might be open and undisturbed in the execution of their functions, and yet wholly incompetent to avert threatened danger, or to punish, with adequate promptitude and certainty, the guilty conspirators."

Firing a double-barreled volley; Thaddeus Stevens charged that the *Milligan* ruling was far more dangerous than the opinion of the *Dred Scott* case in its operation upon the "lives and liberties of the loyal men of this country" since it had "unsheathed the dagger of the assassin, and places the knife of the rebel at the throat of every man who dares proclaim himself to be now, or to have been heretofore, a loyal union man".[18] He urged, therefore, that Congress take immediate action on the question of the establishment of government in the rebel states. John A. Bingham of Ohio suggested that the Court's appellate jurisdiction be swept away and threatened the Court with "annihilation" through a constitutional amendment which would "abolish the tribunal itself."[19] Thomas Williams of Pennsylvania reiterated the suggestion that Congress ought to require that the Court be unanimous on all questions of constitutional interpretation. For the moment at least, the justices seemed impervious to the congressional shouting as they rendered decisions in *Cummings* v. *Missouri*[20] and *Ex parte Garland*,[21] both of which arose out of laws aimed at punishing former supporters of the Confederate cause. The *Cummings* case involved a clause in the Missouri constitution which required an oath of all voters, ministers, attorneys, and candidates for public office that they had not engaged in rebellion against the United States. Failure to take the oath resulted in disfranchisement or debarment from one's professional calling. In the *Garland* case the Court had before it the Federal Test Act of

1865 which imposed a similar loyalty oath on attorneys as a condition for admission to practice before the federal courts. In both cases the Supreme Court held that the oaths were bills of attainder and ex post facto and therefore expressly forbidden by the Constitution. Justice Field, the only Lincoln appointee in the majority, wrote the opinions and was joined by the Court's pre-Civil War members, Justices Wayne, Grier, Nelson, and Clifford. Chief Justice Chase and Justices Miller, Swayne, and Davis would have upheld both measures.

Once again the radicals in Congress reacted bitterly and moved to overrule the Court. Legislation was introduced in the House which provided that no person should be permitted to act as an attorney in any federal court if, among other things, he had engaged in rebellion against the government of the United States. According to the bill's author, Representative George S. Boutwell of Massachusetts, the purpose of the bill was "to declare by a rule, which I take it, under the Constitution and by decisions of the courts of the United States, it is entirely competent for the legislative department of the Government to declare, that certain persons shall not hold the office of attorney or counselor in any court of the United States." [22] Boutwell went on to suggest that the Supreme Court had failed in its duty, that its decisions in these cases were an offense to the "dignity and respectability" of the nation and that the Court had failed to protect itself from the "contamination of conspirators and traitors."

The Supreme Court was, as always, not without its eloquent defenders. Representative William E. Finck of Ohio said that the bill was intended to invade the "just jurisdiction" of the Court and to "subvert its just powers." The great danger, he argued, was what it had always been: that the more popular branch of the government will usurp the rights which belong to the other departments. The Court is attacked because "it has been faithful while others have been faithless; because it has had the . . . independence to rise above mere partisanship and to vindicate the great principles of the Constitution of our fathers." [23] Representative Andrew J. Rogers of New Jersey pointed out that the opinions in the cases under debate were written by an appointee of Lincoln, by a judge who had never resided in a rebel state, and he was moved to give warning against the irrational passions always present in popular government. We know, Rogers declared, that in times of excitement, reason and common sense give way to partisanship, usurpation and despotism. But in such times the only security which the citizens of the United States have is an appeal to the "august tribunal which is unfettered by partisan feelings in its decisions, given in a legitimate and constitutional manner to protect and defend them from impending ruin."[24] The arguments of Finck and Rogers are essentially those against unchecked majority rule; specifically they emphasize the necessity of standards to which even the majority must conform, an emphasis on adherence to established rules as opposed to the sheer force of numbers. Mr. Boutwell's bill failed of adoption, but the altercation which it provoked was merely a warm-up for the major event to come.

Another dispute had its origins in what should have been a routine action in the House when it was asked to fix a quorum of the Supreme Court at five, given a membership of eight. Congress had reduced the size of the Court from ten to eight immediately after President Johnson had nominated Henry Stanbery of Ohio in April 1866, for the vacancy created by Justice Catron's death. Since Catron was never replaced, the Court's membership fell to nine, and it was reduced to its statutory number of eight when Justice Wayne died on 5 July 1867. The bill fixing a quorum at five had been amended by the House Judiciary Committee to require a two-thirds vote of the Court to invalidate an act of Congress. On the floor of the House Representative Thomas Williams of Pennsylvania immediately offered a substitute amendment requiring unanimity of the Court to invalidate any law, state or federal. He contended that whatever arguments there were in favor of a quorum of two-thirds would apply with equal force to unanimity and that unanimity would give the country greater security.[25] Opposition to the Williams proposal was based on both policy considerations and constitutional grounds. Representative John Pruyn of New York said he thought himself to be in the "midst of a revolutionary tribunal" and urged a careful debate on the question.[26] Representative Samuel Marshall of Illinois went to the heart of the matter when he accused the bill's supporters of confessing their own guilt. It was evident, he argued, that they knew in their hearts that the legislation they had been enacting would not "bear investigation by a legal tribunal, made up now principally of members of their own party, placed there by their own favored President." [27] This bill, he declared, was crushing out of existence the Court's power to protect the constitutional rights of citizens. The argument against unconstitutionality was carefully composed by Representative George W. Woodward of Pennsylvania. While admitting the authority of Congress to make the Court any size, he observed that an attempt to tell the Court how many of its members must concur in a decision was an interference with the Court's power to decide, and "to decide" means "to decide every question that may come before them." This amounts to Congress prescribing a rule of decision for the Court, and this Congress may not do, for the Constitution vests such power in the Court itself. [28]

Representative Horace Maynard of Tennessee asked Woodward whence he derived the rule that a bare majority of the Court shall be sufficient to decide any question, [29] to which Woodward replied that it was derived from the nature of the body in which the Constitution vests power. All bodies composed of several members, he said, decide which part shall control the others. [30] Carrying the argument a step further Representative Richard Hubbard of Connecticut maintained that the Supreme Court is not a creature of Congress, but of the Constitution. Furthermore, he argued that when the Constitution created the Court, rules of common law were applicable, and the common law required majority voting. If Congress can alter the Court's internal procedures, it can change the implicit common law rules surrounding trial by jury. [31] Leading the debate on behalf of the bill Representative John Bingham of Ohio insisted that when the first Congress fixed a quorum in the Supreme Court for doing business it set ample precedent for the current bill. [32] Apparently he saw no difference between fixing a quorum and then determining a different number for deciding constitutionality. Representative James F. Wilson of Iowa went back to the simple argument of majority rule, observing that when the Court decides a case, it is making law from which there is no appeal except in an indirect way, and it is the duty of Congress to protect the people and the government from an accidental creation of organic law by the Supreme Court. [33] The strength of the radicals was such that the

Senate measure was approved with an amendment requiring a two-thirds vote on constitutional questions by a vote of 116-39, but the bill was shunted around in the Senate and never became law.

In February 1868 the Court agreed to take jurisdiction in the case of *Ex parte McCardle*. [34] William H. McCardle, a Mississippi newspaper editor, had been charged with seditious activity in 1867 for publishing libels about the military governors, inciting insurrection, and impeding Reconstruction in the South. After an unsuccessful petition for a writ of habeas corpus in the federal circuit court, McCardle's counsel appealed to the Supreme Court, a procedure permitted by the Habeas Corpus Act of 1867. This law was a Reconstruction measure which Congress had enacted to protect federal officials and other loyal unionists from adverse action by courts of the former Confederate states. Under the terms of this law, which McCardle was cleverly testing, federal courts might grant writs of habeas corpus in all cases in which a person was restrained of his liberty in violation of the Constitution, a treaty, or a law of the United States. It was originally designed to aid in the enforcement of Reconstruction legislation. When Congress became aware that the Supreme Court had docketed the case and might then rule on the validity of the Reconstruction program, it moved to forestall such a possibility.

On 12 March 1868 the House had before it a Senate bill which provided for the extension of the Supreme Court's appellate jurisdiction in cases involving customs and revenue officers. Representative Robert C. Schenck of Ohio obtained unanimous consent for its consideration, asserting that it was a routine matter. Representative James F. Wilson then rose and offered an amendment which repealed the Habeas Corpus Act under which McCardle's appeal had been taken. [35] The amendment also included an unprecedented provision prohibiting the Court from hearing cases of this nature which had already been docketed. Although the Democrats, asleep at the switch, made no objections to the bill at the time, it seems doubtful that they could have caused more than a temporary delay in its passage. Two days later they vented their anger on Schenck and his fellow radicals. Representative Benjamin M. Boyer of Pennsylvania charged that the bill had been shoved through without an adequate explanation of its meaning and that it was now plain that the object of the bill was to repeal the Court's jurisdiction in the *McCardle* case. [36] This, he suggested, indicated that the majority was so uncertain of the constitutionality of their handiwork that they would not permit it to undergo judicial scrutiny. Schenck replied that he had lost confidence in the majority of the Supreme Court since it was arrogating to itself the pretension of settling political questions, trampling upon the principle of decision in the case of the Dorr rebellion, and he held it to be not only his right but his duty as a representative of the people "to clip the wings of that court" whenever it attempted "to take such flights." [37]

After denying a request by Representative Charles R. Buckalew of Pennsylvania for postponement of action, the Senate passed the bill without debate by a vote of 32-6. On 25 March the Senate received President Johnson's veto message [38] in which he declared that he could not assent to a measure which proposed to deprive persons restrained of liberty in violation of the Constitution from the right of appeal to the highest judicial authority in the government. The message went on to say that the law, by its retroactive operation, would wrest from a citizen a remedy which he enjoyed at the time of his appeal, and would operate most harshly on those persons who believed they had been denied justice in the lower courts. President Johnson then observed that the Supreme Court had been viewed in the public mind as the true expounder of the Constitution, and rightly so, since it combined "judicial wisdom and impartiality in a greater degree than any other authority known to the Constitution." Thus, he concluded, any act which attempts to prevent a Supreme Court decision on a question of the liberty of a citizen may be justly held by many people as an admission of the act's unconstitutionality.

Senator Thomas A. Hendricks of Indiana, an ardent Douglas Democrat, a constant critic of Lincoln during the war and, later, vice president under Cleveland, opened the post-veto debate with an attack on the bill. It was wrong, he said, to prevent a man whose personal liberty is involved from taking an appeal to the Supreme Court, all particular circumstances aside, and equally pernicious was the principle of removing from the Supreme Court's jurisdiction a case which had already been docketed. Hendricks asked: "Do you, Senators, expect the people of this country to say that is right?" [39] He then pointed out that the very condition which the Constitution was supposed to prevent—the holding of all governmental power in the same hands—was now being effected. Why, he taunted, with five out of eight justices appointed by Lincoln and confirmed by the present senators, could they not risk the Court's ruling on Reconstruction legislation? [40]

Senator William H. Stewart of Nevada answered that the question was not how the Court might rule but whether the Court possessed the power to rule at all, and he contended that the Court had no power to determine the status of the southern states, which at bottom was what the *McCardle* case was all about. He then charged that the law was being used by the Democratic party to get their political questions before the Supreme Court, and that McCardle would not personally be affected substantially one way or the other. "The case is brought up here, not for the sake of liberty, but for the purpose of subserving political ends." [41] Stewart concluded his remarks with a mixture of high motives and conqueror's rights, declaring:

> I do not wish to see the judicial ermine dragged into political contests. If McCardle gets any relief in that court it will be because rebels have the right to dictate the terms of reconstruction and there is no power in this Government to secure the fruits of victory; it will be predicated upon the right of the conquered to dictate terms to the conqueror. [42]

Senator Reverdy Johnson of Maryland warned against dealing with the courts of justice in this suspicious spirit, holding that it was "dangerous to suppose that they can be governed by political and party motives." [43] Quoting de Tocqueville approvingly to the effect that judicial review was one of the most powerful barriers devised against the tyranny of political assemblies, Johnson maintained that without the Supreme Court's peculiar jurisdiction, the American system of government would have ended long ago.

Running throughout the criticism of the amendment repealing the habeas corpus act were the twin charges of political control of the judiciary and hypocrisy, both of which were combined in the sharply worded speech of Senator Willard Saulsbury of Delaware:

> Make no more Fourth of July harangues to your people. Tell them not what great blessings your fathers achieved for you

and for all their posterity by declaring their independence of the British Crown; but rather confess that you, the descendants of the fathers of the Revolution and the men who framed the Constitution, are denying to American citizens in time of peace that liberty which an English king could not deny to his subjects and retain his throne. [44]

Pass your bill, Saulsbury exhorted, and if the people have not lost their love for their cherished institutions by the time of the next election, "they will reverse your judgment." Senator Charles R. Buckalew cut through the partisan arguments to make the simple case that justice be done. He said that when Congress extended federal power over the South, it was essential that individuals be given protection through habeas corpus because the "protection of and advantages of our laws cannot be confined exclusively to our friends." It is "characteristic of justice herself" that general rules not discriminate but operate equally on friend and foe. [45] The Senate passed the bill over the president's veto by a vote of 33–9.

In the House the exchange over repeal of habeas corpus jurisdiction added little that was new to the debate, but some of the rhetoric is interesting. George W. Woodward said that McCardle had acquired a vested right which the act of 1867 "showed you were ready to respect when asserted by a Negro," and the right here involved concerned one of the highest interests of man—his liberty. If this legislation means anything, said Woodward, it means just this:

[T]he President shall not exercise the constitutional functions of his office, the judges shall not exercise the constitutional powers vested in them, but the legislative will shall be supreme; which I say is a repeal of the Constitution of the United States and a consolidation of all the political power of this Government into the hands of a legislative oligarchy to be wielded I know not by whom. [46]

A colorful and cogent analysis of the bill was made by Richard Hubbard who called the bill "a kind of centaur, or, to use a coarser metaphor, a Demerara team—a horse and a donkey yoked together." With one hand it opens the Court to any taxpayer whose property is subjected to taxation in violation of the Constitution or laws of the United States, and with the other it closes the door to anyone deprived of liberty. This means that "if a man's horse, his ox, or his ass is illegally distrained by the tax collector . . . he may travel clear to the Supreme Court . . . if, on the other hand, a man's wife or children are torn from him by violence . . . he cannot stir one step toward the Supreme Court." [47] James F. Wilson, however, contended that the bill involved nothing more than a matter of congressional judgment since constitutionally the power was clearly in Congress, and to document his case he went to the Supreme Court itself. He quoted from *Insurance Co.* v. *Ritchie* [48] in which the Court had held that when jurisdiction depended upon an act of Congress, jurisdiction granted may be taken away. [49] The House overrode the president's veto by a vote of 114-34 and the Supreme Court subsequently upheld the law and dismissed McCardle's case for want of jurisdiction. [50] Chief Justice Chase, speaking for a unanimous Court, declared that judicial duty "is not less fitly performed by declining ungranted jurisdiction than in exercising firmly that which the Constitution and laws confer." Maintaining that the Court's appellate jurisdiction is derived from the Constitution and not from acts of Congress, the chief justice observed, however, that the jurisdiction is conferred "with such exceptions and under such regulations as Congress shall make." Congress had chosen to make a specific exception and the Court is "not at liberty to inquire into the motives" behind the law. Without jurisdiction, said Chase, the Supreme Court's only function is to announce that fact and to dismiss the case.

In a broad sense the McCardle affair demonstrates the fundamental weakness of judicial power and its peculiar dependencies in the American system. Had the framers defined the Supreme Court's appellate jurisdiction in detail and then provided only for its expansion, and perhaps forbidden Congress to contract it, the McCardle dispute could not have arisen. But given the language of Article III, the radicals were on firm constitutional footing in denying appellate jurisdiction, or more specifically, in repealing jurisdiction once given. To snatch away a case already docketed is still another question. The spirit of the American constitutional heritage was certainly violated, and the Supreme Court might have said so. But American judicial power is partly political, and the

Court was forced to weigh political considerations in this instance. The question for the Court was that of deciding the circumstances under which it would apply the pressures of power and those under which it would acquiesce in the will of the legislature. It may be that the political judgment of the Court was unwise in the McCardle controversy, and if it had answered Congress with a firm no, it would have emerged a stronger institution with enhanced respect. It is possible, however, that it was wiser to "cave in" at this time in order to conserve its authority for use under more propitious circumstances. Given the strength and the mood of the radicals in Congress, it is likely that judicial review would have received a severe and perhaps final blow, if the Court, in its political discretion, had miscalculated a calculated risk.

As a matter of fact, the Court had no discretion when it docketed the case of *Ex parte Yerger* [51] in the fall of 1869. This suit, like the *McCardle* case, involved a petition for a writ of habeas corpus by another Mississippi editor, who had shrewdly taken his appeal under the original Judiciary Act of 1789. When the Court declared that it had jurisdiction of the case, the radicals again moved into action with extreme proposals. Senator Charles Drake of Missouri introduced a bill prohibiting the Court from exercising judicial review. [52] He asserted that from the day that the doctrine was announced in *Marbury* v. *Madison* it had become a professional dogma that such right exists, and "the dogma has been transmitted as an authoritative tradition and silently accepted, without investigation, without question, without even a superficial scrutiny." Drake raised the old, enduring argument that the Constitution nowhere provides the power of review, and that the legislature, in the nature of constitutional government, ought to be supreme. [53] The bill was referred to the Judiciary Committee where it died. Senator Sumner introduced a less drastic measure which forbade the Supreme Court from hearing political questions, the nature of such questions to be determined by the political branches. The Reconstruction acts were, of course, deemed political by legislative fiat. Senator Trumbull spoke on behalf of Sumner's bill, but like many legislative proposals, it never came to a vote. These proposals were not seriously considered, however, only because Yerger's attorney reached an agreement with the national government that Yerger would be protected from military harassment, thereby rendering the case moot, and a judicial decision unnecessary.

Prior to the death of Chief Justice Chase in 1873, the Court suffered a further loss in prestige as a result of its decisions in the *Legal Tender Cases.* [54] In 1870, with its membership standing at seven under the provisions of the Lyman Trumbull measure of 1866, the Court, speaking through the chief justice, declared the Legal Tender Act of 1862 unconstitutional. This measure had authorized paper money issues during the Civil War as legal tender in payment of debts, and Chief Justice Chase, over the protesting dissents of Justices Miller, Swayne, and Davis, declared that the law was invalid insofar as it applied to contracts made prior to its passage. At the very moment that the case was being decided, a confident Congress with Ulysses S. Grant in the White House, increased the size of the Supreme Court to nine. This move permitted the president to name two Republican justices who would, it was hoped, vote to uphold the constitutionality of Republican legislation. President Grant named William Strong and Joseph P. Bradley, both of whom joined with Miller, Davis and Swayne in 1871 to form a majority which directly overruled the original legal tender decisions.

Return to Power and Prestige

The appointment of Justices Strong and Bradley marked the beginning of a new era in judicial-legislative relationships, an era of good feeling which was to persist until the turn of the century. In addition to Strong and Bradley, President Grant appointed Ward Hunt in 1873, and Morrison R. Waite to the chief justiceship upon the death of Samuel Chase in 1874. The most distinguished of the four men at the time he joined the Court was Joseph Bradley whose intellect, knowledge of the law, and judicial acumen place him in the company of men like Story, Holmes, Cardozo, and Frankfurter. He was selected, however, on the assumption that he would vote to defend the conservative economic interests of the nation. His appointment satisfied the conservatives for whom he had labored as one of the most successful railroad lawyers in the country, but once on the bench Justice Bradley proved to be a man of thoroughgoing independence and unquestioned integrity, and often he voted to uphold economic controls over the very railroads whose interests he had earlier been paid to defend. William Strong, who was serving on the Supreme Court of Pennsylvania at the time of his appointment by Grant, had been urged upon President Lincoln as a candidate for the chief justiceship after Taney's death. He served as associate for ten years in contrast to Bradley's twenty-one, and wrote virtually no opinions of lasting importance, but his inherent conservatism pleased the business community for whose interests he usually voted. Ward Hunt of New York owed his appointment to Roscoe Conkling and must generally be classed as undistinguished—an "anonymous toiler"—but he alone dissented in one of the early cases involving the voting rights of Negroes at a time when the rest of the Court was unwilling to give the Civil War Amendments the broad scope that American democracy requires. [55]

In an unbelievable example of executive incompetence President Grant offered the chief justiceship to six men before Morrison R. Waite, Grant's seventh choice, accepted the appointment. Waite was called "His Accidency" and was described by Justice Field as a "man that would never have been thought of for the position by any person except President Grant . . . an experiment which no President has a right to make with our Court." [56] Grant had first offered the position to his personal friend, Roscoe Conkling, Senator from New York, who declined the post. Grant turned next to another close friend, Caleb Cushing, 84 years old at the time, but he was forced to withdraw Cushing's name after a great deal of publicity was given to a letter written by Cushing to Jefferson Davis on 21 May 1861 recommending to him a young man then returning to Texas. The president then nominated his attorney general, George H. Williams of Oregon, but withdrew his name after being subjected to a great deal of pressure from various quarters, including the influential New York Bar Association which had branded Williams unfit for the office. At some point during the course of events, Grant reportedly offered the position to Senators Oliver P. Morton of Indiana and Timothy O. Howe of Wisconsin, and to his Secretary of State, Hamilton Fish. Grant finally nominated Morrison R. Waite, a relatively obscure Ohio lawyer and unsuccessful politician, whose service to his country had consisted of an appointment as assistant counsel to

Caleb Cushing before the Geneva Tribunal which arbitrated the "Alabama claims" dispute, a controversy growing out of American charges that England had permitted the building and arming of Confederate cruisers, including the *Alabama*, in English shipyards to prey upon northern commerce. Making up the remainder of his public career were three unsuccessful runs for state office, one term in the state legislature, and a year as alderman in Toledo, a record which Waite's biographer calls "unimpressive."[57] Had he not been appointed chief justice of the United States, history would long ago have forgotten him. The appointment was confirmed quickly with an apparent sense of relief, but with little enthusiasm on the part of the Senate, the nation at large, or among the justices themselves. But history often turns accidents into assets and such was the case with Waite. Unquestionably not among the nation's great jurists, Waite nevertheless managed to perform creditably and competently, if not brilliantly. In a way he rivaled Taney in his ability to chart a course which, without sacrificing integrity and objectivity, remained in tune with the nation's mood. Consequently, although individual decisions of the Supreme Court under Waite were subjected to the normal criticism, the Court was free from the bitter congressional attacks of earlier years. Professor C. Peter Magrath, in his splendid biography, gives a succinct and fair estimate of Waite's judgeship:

> As an individual Morrison Waite was not spectacular. He wanted the intellectual brilliance of a Bradley, the boldness of a Field, the wit of a Harlan, and the aggressiveness of a Miller. And yet, perhaps more than any of his talented colleagues, he was the man ideally suited to lead the Court. For Waite had solid abilities as a lawyer and, most important, was a shrewd judge of people, a good amateur psychologist. He understood human nature and through a happy combination of hard work, tactful firmness, and an easy going kindness kept a strong-headed team of judges pulling together.[58]

During Waite's fourteen-year tenure, fourteen associate justices served under his leadership. The group included, in addition to those described above, John M. Harlan of Kentucky, William B. Woods of Georgia, Stanley Matthews of Ohio, Horace Gray of

Massachusetts, Samuel Blatchford of New York and Lucius Q.C. Lamar of Mississippi. All were able men; Harlan and Gray were outstanding judges; but only Harlan left an indelible impression on Supreme Court history.

John Marshall Harlan, appointed to the Court by President Hayes in 1877 at the age of forty-four, served thirty-four years on the bench, equaling the longest tenured justice, John Marshall, and his own colleague and intellectual adversary, Stephen Field. Like Marshall and Field his fame rests on considerably more than length of service. A man of great physical stature, aggressive personality and moral courage, Harlan was not lightly influenced by others. His great independence of mind resulted in strong dissents from the prevailing majority. Although a Whig in his early years, he did not support Abraham Lincoln for president. He did, however, support the Union cause, serving as a colonel in a Kentucky regiment. In 1863 he was elected attorney general of Kentucky, but was later defeated twice for the governorship. Harlan was not a legal craftsman, but in writing his opinions he relied on an intuitive common sense which simply dismissed the subtleties of legal reasoning. To the traditional, sharp legal analyst Harlan's mode of operation was unsettling, and Oliver Wendell Holmes, Jr., once described Harlan's mind as "a powerful vise the jaws of which couldn't be got nearer than two inches to each other" and he suggested that Harlan, although a man to be reckoned with, "did not shine either in analysis or generalization." [59] But Harlan was two generations ahead of his day and his dissents stamp him in the mold of a modern day liberal on the hard issues of racial equality and economic opportunity. Harlan was a likeable, friendly man with a ready wit and a delightful sense of humor who left his differences with his brethren in the conference room. All the justices, intellectual friend and foe, enjoyed Harlan's Kentucky bourbon at the whist parties which were a favored recreation for the Court during the 1880s and 1890s.

Horace Gray may be characterized as the Joseph Story of his day. Born of a distinguished Boston family (his half-brother was John Chipman Gray, the famous Harvard law professor and authority on real property), Gray graduated from Harvard at sixteen and spent his entire life in legal research. At twenty-six he was appointed reporter of the Supreme Court of Massachusetts, and ten years later became an associate justice, and eventually was named chief justice. In 1881, after seventeen years of service in the Massachusetts judiciary, Gray was appointed with virtually nationwide approval to the Supreme Court of the United States. Gray was a meticulous legal historian, and Justice Miller and later Chief Justice Fuller relied heavily on his painstaking research. Not of great originality, Gray had a capacity for synthesizing the work of others, and his unflagging devotion to the law was, in the words of Fuller biographer Willard L. King, like that of "a holy priest to his religion." At the age of sixty-one, Gray, until then a confirmed bachelor, married the daughter of his colleague, Stanley Matthews.

Stanley Matthews of Ohio had been a close friend of President Hayes since their student days at Kenyon College, and after Justice Swayne announced his retirement, the president sent Stanley Matthews' name to the Senate on 26 January 1881. Matthews and Hayes had fought together in the Union army and had been political associates for years. Matthews made a major contribution to Hayes' presidential campaign, and Hayes in turn supported Matthews against James A. Garfield for a Senate seat from Ohio. His brief stay in the Senate was at best undistinguished, but he had ingratiated himself with corporate wealth, particularly the railroads, by lobbying against the Thurman Act, a "sinking fund" law which required the Pacific Railroads to pay twenty-five per cent of their annual net earnings into the federal treasury. At the time of his nomination, Matthews was financier Jay Gould's chief counsel for the Midwest, and in the public mind was identified with corporate interests. The Judiciary Committee of the Senate refused to report out the nomination and it died with the Forty-sixth Congress. It hardly seemed possible that President Garfield, an old political enemy, would resubmit Matthews' name to the Senate, but less than two weeks after his inauguration Garfield did nominate Stanley Matthews, and after a struggle of two months, the Senate confirmed him by a vote of 24-23. Although not absolutely clear, it appears that Jay Gould was the political force behind the Garfield move,[60] but a Supreme Court justice cannot always be counted on to follow his known predilections, or more particularly, the predilections of the men who supported him for the job. Justice Matthews did not decide cases on the basis of an ideological commitment to big business;

often he sided with Chief Justice Waite and Justices Harlan, Gray and Blatchford to permit some government regulation of the economy. He served for seven years.

Samuel Blatchford of New York was one of the hardest working men ever to sit on the Court. He was appointed in 1882 by President Arthur after a career of public service which included fifteen years on the bench in New York. Specializing in admiralty and patent law, Blatchford often wrote more opinions in a given year than any of his colleagues, and can be fairly characterized as competent and colorless. Another man of modest talents but with a capacity for hard labor was William B. Woods of Georgia, an appointee of President Hayes in 1881. Woods, an Ohioan, had settled in Alabama after having fought on the Union side during the Civil War. He was one of those justices who came to the Court with many years of experience as a federal circuit judge but whose performance was not equal to that of many justices who were without prior judicial experience and who had been partisan politicians until the day they took office. Justice Woods died after six years on the Court. Lucius Quintus Cincinnatus Lamar, another short-term justice, was appointed a few months before Chief Justice Waite's death and served for only five years. Lamar was an exciting personality who was at home in many fields of learning. Before the Civil War he had been a professor of mathematics at the University of Mississippi and after the war rejoined the faculty, teaching at various times ethics, metaphysics and law. He wrote the Mississippi ordinance of secession and served in the Confederate Congress and as the Confederate envoy to Russia. He was elected to Congress in 1872 and to the Senate in 1876, and was Secretary of the Interior in President Cleveland's cabinet at the time of his appointment to the Court. He was the first Democrat to be appointed to the Court since Justice Field, and was the first appointee who had served in the Confederate army (he had surrendered at Appomattox as a Colonel). He would not be placed among the Court's "greats."

Throughout the period of Waite's chief justiceship the Court divided roughly between those justices, led by Waite and Miller, who would cautiously permit some government regulation of the mushrooming corporate enterprise, and those led by Field, who would not. It was not until the accession of Chief Justice Fuller that the Court became predominantly social Darwinist in its political persuasion and once again moved on to a collision course with Congress. The Civil War had eliminated slavery and had settled the fact of American nationhood, but the Fourteenth Amendment was the constitutional device through which the Supreme Court gave the nation a new direction. The American people had, in effect, created a different nation with a different constitution; they had made the transition from Madisonian federalism to Hamiltonian nationalism, but they had accomplished it with such subtlety and skill that the outward institutional framework appeared unaffected. Furthermore, the traditional assumption of constitutional historians that the Supreme Court from the 1870s onward undertook a new role and dealt with matters unlike those of the past, hardly fits the facts. In the main the Court continued to be the great defender and protector of private property that it had always been—although the protected property had taken a somewhat different form—and the Court remained the umpire-in-chief of the federal system through its interpretation of the key national powers of commerce and taxation. But most important of all, the justices erected a judicial edifice on due process of law which was to have repercussions far into the twentieth century.

The depressing aspect of judicial behavior during the period beginning in the latter 1870s and ending in the 1930s was the Court's indifference to the rights of Negroes. While Waite lived, the Taney tradition of judicial restraint prevailed over the activism of Field in the economic sphere, and in those cases involving the rights of Negroes, the chief justice and virtually the entire Court refused to give the Fourteenth Amendment anything but the narrowest possible scope. De-racializing the amendment's clauses, instead of giving them their intended meaning was our national catastrophe. With the exception of Justice Harlan, all of the justices seemed convinced that government in the United States, particularly the national government, had no power to act in behalf of liberty as it had acted against liberty since 1789 by protecting slavery.[61] If the Civil War amendments were supposed to eradicate the vestiges of slavery, and in a minimal sense this is what they intended, then why did the Supreme Court, for almost a century, ignore and distort their clear meaning and substitute a content which was, at most, a vague possibility in the minds of the men who framed the amendments? It seems reasonable to suggest that the Court reflected the national mood which, in the 1870s, was one of reconciliation of North and South, and reconciliation would not be affected so long as carpetbaggers and Negro majorities controlled the southern states. The old liberal idealism which had formed the intellectual base for the antislavery movement was spent, and some of the leading publicists as well as the politicians who spanned both eras, pre-and post-Civil War, had a change of heart and mind. In 1862 Horace Greeley had complained about Lincoln's moderation, but by 1868 he was suggesting an alliance between the commercial men of the North and South. And other journals of opinion, including *Harper's, Scribner's*, the *Atlantic*, and E.L. Godkin's *Nation* permitted the heroic image of the Negro to tarnish while at the same time they deloused the southern white.

At bottom the new attitude was based on economic and political motives of expediency, profits and power. A South beset by racial strife would not attract capital, and since the quest for Negro equality stood in the way of economic expansion and profit-making, stability soon took precedence over the Negro cause. [62] Furthermore, the party of Lincoln, originally an alliance of farmers and laborers, had been captured by the forces of big business during Grant's incumbency. [63] All matters of public policy were supported or condemned only as they served the cause of expansionist capitalism through the vehicle of the Republican party. When it became clear to the Republican leadership that power and profits could be maintained and extended through a nationally neutralized South which would return the whites to power locally by disenfranchising the Negro, the party dropped its original ideas, and the Supreme Court was unwilling to remind the nation's leaders that equality of condition in regard to fundamental political rights was as much a part of American democracy as the freedom to make money. Ironically enough, as constitutional historian Wallace Mendelson points out, the crucial economic issues that the Court faced during this period stemmed from the clashes of interest between the Eastern business establishment and the grain-growing West, the uneasy partners in the Republican hegemony. [64]

In looking at some of the major cases decided by the Court between 1874 and 1888, it is not difficult to see why Chief Justice Waite can be compared to Taney in terms of his ability to appease the warring political groups in the nation. The subject matter of litigation falls roughly into three broad categories: (1) questions of state power, perennial in a federal system, but now supposedly altered by the Fourteenth Amendment; (2) the effect of the Civil War amendments on the newly freed Negro; and (3) the extent to which national power might be used in an era of expansion in population, in economic productivity, and in territory, in an age of invention and novel scientific application.

It was in 1873, just prior to Waite's appointment, that the Supreme Court first dealt with the nature of the Fourteenth Amendment and the extent to which it altered the federal system. The Court's answer in the *Slaughterhouse Cases* [65] was that the American system had been changed little, if at all, by the amendment. It upheld the power of Louisiana's carpetbag legislature to grant a monopoly to a single firm of butchers in New Orleans. A majority of five, speaking through Justice Miller, rejected the argument of counsel for the ousted butchers (former Supreme Court Justice John A. Campbell) that the amendment had created a set of privileges and immunities which a state might not abridge, including the privilege of engaging in one's chosen occupation. Distinguishing between federal and state citizenship, Miller suggested that the states fundamentally might legislate in the police area as before unless they interfered with traditionally guaranteed federal rights. The monopoly was not a deprivation of property without due process of law within the traditional meaning of that clause, and, continued Miller, the Louisiana law did not run afoul of equal protection of the laws since that clause was intended to apply only to racial discrimination.

Justice Field, speaking for Chase, Bradley and Swayne, dissented with an opinion that portended the future. He declared that "the privileges and immunities designated are those which of right belong to the citizens of all free governments" and among them was the right to pursue a lawful calling, subject only to restrictions which apply with equal force to all similarly employed. Justice Field, who was to outlive Waite, eventually saw his ideas prevail, but until the death of the chief justice, Field often remained in opposition to the majority. The Court, under Waite, faced the privileges and immunities clause in 1875 and continued to construe it narrowly, holding unanimously that the privilege of voting was not a privilege of citizenship, and that this clause in the Fourteenth Amendment did not bar a state from granting the elective franchise exclusively to men. [66] In the same year the Court decided that the privileges and immunities clause did not guarantee a jury trial in common law cases. [67] Although the clause has been put forward many times over the years in oral and written briefs by lawyers who argued against the validity of various state laws, the Court has never amended the construction of the privileges and immunities clause made initially by Justice Miller.

While Waite led the Court, the due process clause seemed similarly destined for narrow construction, whether in the area of criminal procedure or in the novel substantive sense, with the result that the federal system seemed to be altered little, if at all, by the Civil War and the post-war constitutional amendments. In *Hurtado* v. *California*, [68] over the protest of Justice Harlan, the Court held that the Fourteenth Amendment did not prevent California from abolishing indictment by grand jury in felonies. After pointing out that in the Fifth Amendment due process of law and grand jury indictment were guaranteed separately, Justice Matthews argued that the former did not encompass the latter since the Court was "forbidden to assume, without clear reason to the contrary, that any part of this most important amendment is superfluous." It followed then, continued Matthews, that when the phrase "due process of law" was used in the Fourteenth Amendment, its meaning was identical to the same phrase in the Fifth Amendment, and that if it had been a part of the purpose of the Fourteenth Amendment to "perpetuate the institution of the grand jury in all the states, it would have embodied . . . express declarations to that effect." What, then, was the effect of the new due process clause? It was intended, said Matthews, only to secure "those fundamental principles of liberty and justice which lie at the base of all our civil and political institutions," but it was not to limit the states to those forms and procedures which had been sanctioned by usage. The implication of the opinion was that the Fourteenth Amendment had not overruled *Barron* v. *Baltimore* [69] and that the national Bill of Rights restricted only national power as in the past.

If the Supreme Court under Waite's direction was reluctant to admit that the Fourteenth Amendment had radically altered the federal system, the Court was consistently restrained in that it would not agree with the business community that due process of law added some new dimension to the protection of property, particularly corporate property. Between 1870 and 1890 the population of the United States doubled, and its character changed radically as the nation became more urban, more industrial, and more capitalistic. Quite naturally, the rapid economic and sociological alterations in America produced new tensions in the political system. In its early stages the conflict, which was to last well into the twentieth century, was primarily a struggle between the farmers and the railroads. But broadly speaking, it was a fight for political and economic supremacy between a new capitalistic class, on the one hand, and the worker, be he agrarian or urban, on the other. Social discontent was such that in the 1870s and 1880s state legislatures initiated regulatory policies over big business, including regulation of railroad and grain elevator rates and minimal labor laws. Unable to prevent the passage of such laws, large corporations mustered the greatest legal talent in the country to press the battle in the courts where they were certain they would win. The vehicle which would put an end to popular tampering with nature's economic laws, said the corporation lawyers, was the due process clause of the Fourteenth Amendment. They argued that the clause guaranteed certain private rights in property against legislative invasion, particularly in such matters as prices, rate schedules, and labor laws. But even assuming, although not admitting, that a legislature did possess such authority, corporation counsel maintained that it must exercise that authority "reasonably," and that the final judge of reasonableness is not the legislature but the courts. In essence, these were the arguments made in the landmark case of *Munn* v. *Illinois*, [70] but the Supreme Court refused to accept them.

In 1871 Illinois enacted a law, aimed at Chicago, which required a license for the operation of public warehouses in cities of not less than 100 thousand population, and provided maximum rates for the storage and handling of grain. For seven members of the

Court, Chief Justice Waite sustained the law as a proper exercise of the police power, a power which had been used in England "from time immemorial, and in this country from its first colonization" to regulate certain kinds of business enterprise. Furthermore, the common law recognized a category of businesses "affected with a public interest" which might be controlled for the public good, including the fixing of reasonable charges. Whether a business fell into the category, said Waite, was a matter for legislative, not judicial, determination and the reasonableness of rates was not subject to judicial review. "For protection against abuses by legislatures the people must resort to the polls, not to the courts." Supposedly, then, the whole question of business regulation was political and not legal. Justice Field, supported by Justice Strong, registered a characteristic dissent, calling the majority opinion subversive of the rights of both property and liberty.

A year after the *Munn* decision the American Bar Association was founded in Chicago and became, in Professor Edward Corwin's phrase, "a sort of juristic sewing circle for mutual education in the gospel of *laissez faire*." [71] To be sure, big business had suffered defeat in the first round with the Supreme Court, but the subtleties of the *Munn* opinion indicated that all was not lost. Had Chief Justice Waite simply held that the Fourteenth Amendment was in no way a bar to state policing regulations, business would have sustained total defeat. But in resurrecting the "business affected with a public interest" doctrine, Waite implied, or at least left open the inference that some businesses might not be so affected. In his dissent Field moved into the breach when he suggested that the door was open for judicial invalidation of state laws which purported to regulate businesses that were not affected with a public interest. Stephen Field, politically in the Federalist tradition, saw the unlettered masses as a constant threat to the stability of a free system and viewed the judiciary as a political safety valve which generally remained closed, but which might be opened occasionally to release a little Populist steam. Mixed with this Gouverneur Morris—attitude toward the mass of the people was a strong economic individualist strain that came with his successful rough-and-tumble career. It was not, however, until men like Melville Fuller, David Brewer and Rufus Peckham replaced Waite and Miller and Bradley that Field's construction of the

Fourteenth Amendment was to prevail. While Waite lived, the Court's decisions, with some exceptions, supported public regulation, both state and national. The Court upheld a Mississippi law under which the legislature had created a Railroad Commission to fix rates for railroads operating within its borders; but the chief justice in his opinion for the Court, wrote a qualification at the suggestion of Stanley Matthews, observing that the "power to regulate is not a power to destroy; and limitation is not the equivalent of confiscation." [72] Furthermore, said Waite, the state cannot require a railroad to operate without reward, nor can it take private property without due process of law. While thought by some to be a modification of the *Munn* case and a concession to the principle that the due process clause substantively limits state regulatory powers, [73] the fact remains that Waite and a majority of his brethren upheld state authority over business enterprise. Not only did the Court in the 1870s and 1880s uphold a variety of state and local regulatory laws against the claim that due process of law was violated, [74] but it also deferred to state power in *Stone* v. *Mississippi* [75] when Chief Justice Waite sharply modified an old Marshall doctrine on contracts in holding that a legislature may not bargain away its police power, and that a charter that permits acts against the public welfare which a legislature deems harmful may be rescinded.

Perhaps the greatest failure of the Waite Court, one that was to set off social as well as constitutional reverberations some seventy-five years later, was the handling, or more accurately, mishandling, of the Negro question. For all its self-restraint in general in the area of Negro rights, the Court chose to assume an activist posture by restraining the national government's attempt to enforce the Fourteenth Amendment. In a series of cases between 1876 and 1884, the Court first devitalized the Enforcement Act of 1870, [76] later invalidated a major provision of the Enforcement Act of 1871, [77] and finally nullified the Civil Rights Act of 1875, [78] the total effect of which was to prohibit meaningful national protection of Negro rights, and to permit brutal aggressions against Negroes in the South. Only in the area of voting did the Court sustain federal protective authority for the Negro. It upheld a conviction of state election officials accused of stuffing a ballot box in violation of the Enforcement Acts [79] and affirmed a lower court's conviction of nine men who had beaten a Negro because he had voted in a federal election. [80] Doctrinally the Court had declared that the right to vote in a national election was a constitutionally guaranteed right and that Congress might protect it from interference, either private or public. Although fundamentally the Court's holdings said that the Fourteenth Amendment was intended to restrict the states and not to enlarge the sphere of congressional authority, in only a few instances did the Court clamp down on discriminatory practices by the states. [81]

During these years the Supreme Court displayed a strong nationalist orientation, and when state laws were in conflict with national authority, the justices deemed the national interest paramount. Very often the cases did not involve a conflict between federal and state statutes, but between a state law and the constitution in its dormant state. The commerce clause, for example, was held to prohibit various local schemes of taxation [82] as well as to bar certain police measures. [83] In the matter of the power of the states over commerce itself, the Court severely restricted the area of state competence when it held in the famous *Wabash Rate Case* [84] that a state may not regulate intrastate railroad rates when the transportation involved is a part of an interstate system. Chief Justice Waite dissented from this holding, emphasizing the local character of the regulation and adhering to his opinion in the *Granger* cases (*Munn* v. *Illinois*) that, unless Congress had acted, the states had plenary control over rate-fixing and that an indirect effect on interstate commerce did not invalidate a state regulation of a railroad operating within its borders.

However, the chief justice joined the majority of his Court to pronounce judicial blessings on legislative incursions into new fields, a policy that caused violent reactions in the business community whose activities were allegedly affected adversely. The Court, for example, upheld the power of Congress to levy an income tax, [85] to make treasury notes legal tender, [86] and in the famous *Sinking Fund Cases* [87] it approved the Thurman Act which required that the Pacific Railroads pay twenty-five percent of their annual net earnings into the federal treasury. The American business oligarchy, particularly the railroad leadership, had attained considerable power, often through buccaneering methods.

In order to maintain and to extend its favorable position, it had to find ways to prevent public regulation, and if it could not dominate state legislatures or Congress, its only hope was to throw up a legal barrier around its activities through the device of judicial intervention. Until 1888 the Court—at least a majority of its members—would not buy the businessman's *laissez faire* product, but in the normal course of affairs, one's wares are most easily peddled to those who evince the desire to buy them in the first place. Accordingly business received a warmer reception in the judicial house when some of the old occupants moved out and some new faces moved in.

5. Fuller & White:
Conservatism & the Revival of
Judicial Activism

CHIEF Justice Fuller came to the Supreme Court at a time when the American nation was undergoing unprecedented alteration in its social and economic character. Stimulated by the Civil War, industrial activity had surged forward in one continuous boom, and by 1900 the United States had forged the greatest industrial complex in the world, surpassing the combined efforts of Great Britain and Germany in iron and steel production. At the time of Abraham Lincoln's election capital invested in manufacturing was about one billion dollars; by 1900 it had increased to ten billion while the number of workers engaged in manufacturing quadrupled, the latter phenomenon heralding the end of Jeffersonian agrarianism. Over half the population lived in cities by 1900 contrasted with sixteen percent in 1860, and the total population of the nation had increased from 31 million to over 70 million. The little agrarian republic of less than 4 million people was rapidly becoming a world power as it exploited its natural resources and created a new kind of material wealth. Men who dealt in steel, coal, meat packing, milling, lumber, textiles and the railroads were creating a technological machine with infinite capacities for good and evil in the lives of mankind, and the extent to which one might surpass the other depended in large measure on the way in which politics and law, always so intermingled in the American system, would handle the problems that accompanied such rapid and revolutionary change.

The chaos that resulted from such swift-moving events was reflected in the condition of the Supreme Court's docket when Fuller took his seat on the bench in 1888. The Court had more than a three-year backlog of cases, and by 1890 the arrears were actually increasing. In 1888 the docket contained 1,571 cases; in 1889, 1,648; and by 1890 the Court was facing no less than 1,816 cases. Contributing to the increased number of appeals was a large assortment of patent, copyright, and trademark cases, although the greatest increase in appeals resulted from the diversity of citizenship jurisdiction. For better than a decade various proposals had been offered in Congress to relieve the Supreme Court's congested docket,[1] including bills to create a special court of patent appeals, to insert an intermediate court of appeals between the trial courts and the Supreme Court, and to divide the Supreme Court into three panels of three judges each. In January of 1890 Chief Justice Fuller gave a dinner in honor of David J. Brewer to celebrate his appointment to the Court, and along with his colleagues on the bench the Chief invited Senators George F. Edmunds, William M. Evarts, James Z. George, John J. Ingalls, George F. Hoar, George G. Vest, and James L. Pugh. Within a few weeks the Judiciary Committee of the Senate, of which Fuller's senatorial guests were members, sent the chief justice a compendium of all the proposed measures dealing with the Supreme Court and suggested that the committee would be willing to entertain the views of the justices. At the request of Fuller, Justice Gray prepared a report embodying nine proposals in which the entire bench had concurred. Three dealt with the establishment of a court of patent appeals and urged that pending patent appeals be transferred to the new court; the remaining six contained detailed recommendations for creating intermediate courts of appeals. As a result of Fuller's careful planning Congress enacted the Circuit Court of Appeals Act of 1891 embodying most of the proposals of the justices. Although it did not establish a court to hear patent appeals, the act of 1891 was comprehensive enough to be ranked with the Judiciary Act of 1789 as a major piece of organic legislation dealing with the federal judiciary. Just prior to the act's passage in 1890 the Court received 623 new cases. By 1892 the number of new appeals had diminished to 290.

Melville Weston Fuller, Jacksonian Democrat, Episcopalian, lawyer, and local Illinois politician, was elated when Grover Cleveland carried his party's standard to victory in 1884, although little did he dream that the president would offer him the prestigious office of chief justice. President Cleveland had been attracted to this amiable and charming attorney from Chicago and had selected him for the sensitive position as chairman of the Civil Service Commission. This was an unusually critical spot in the administration since Cleveland, who had advocated civil service reform, now had to face an army of office seekers as the first Democrat to occupy the Presidency since Buchanan. Fuller declined on the ground that with a family of nine children he could not afford a $20 thousand a year drop in income. He also refused a second appointment, that of solicitor general, but like most men, he was unable to say no to the highest judicial office in the land, even though it too would entail a considerable financial loss.

Born in Augusta, Maine, in 1833 Fuller graduated from Bowdoin College in 1853. He then attended the Harvard Law School for one year, during which time he sat in lectures with fellow students Joseph H. Choate and James Bradley Thayer. He was admitted to the bar in 1855. Deciding to cast his future with the developing West he moved to Chicago in 1856, a year that also saw the arrival of a Yankee store-keeper named Marshall Field. George M. Pullman, the inventor who introduced the railroad sleeping car, had come to the bustling city just a year earlier. Although not a man of brilliance or of great learning in the law, Fuller possessed a singular talent—the ability to persuade men with antagonistic views to accept compromise.[2] He was a supreme diplomat with a passion for conciliation, partly because of a personal dislike of disputation and rancor. His biographer suggests that an essay written by Fuller in his junior year in college furnished the key to his career. He addressed the subject: Are great intellectual powers preferable to energy and decision of character? Espousing the negative, Melville Fuller concluded that it was far better to have a firm and indomitable will than to be endowed with high intelligence. His life gave proof to the thesis. It was his character and not his intellect that brought him to a position of national leadership, and there is little question that he managed the Court's business with great skill. Theodore Roosevelt called him the "most popular" though not the strongest or the most famous chief justice. Justice Holmes, who sat under Fuller, White, Taft, and Hughes, said that Fuller was the best presiding officer; Justice Miller who sat under Taney, Chase, Waite, and

Fuller, agreed with Holmes. With all due respect to Fuller's courage, dignity, independence, and administrative skill, the fact remains that as a judge Fuller was competent but unexciting. His judicial opinions have been characterized accurately as "labored," containing no "lofty phrases," no "grandiloquent passages," [3] and his political ideas were unimaginatively conservative, consisting of a belief in "sound money, free trade, states' rights, no paternalism, governmental economy, and the preservation of the civil rights of the individual." [4] They were well suited to an age of enterprise.

The first Court over which Chief Justice Fuller presided consisted of the titans, Miller, Field, and Harlan, and the lesser lights, Gray, Bradley, Blatchford, and L.Q.C. Lamar. Stanley Matthews, while technically on the Court, was gravely ill when Fuller took his seat and he never returned to duty. Of the eight only Harlan was to outlast the chief, and ten additional men were to serve during his tenure. Appointed in 1890 and serving almost as long as Fuller was David J. Brewer. An honors graduate from Yale in 1856, Brewer had studied law for two years in New York in the office of his uncle, David Dudley Field. A second and more famous uncle was Justice Stephen Field of the Supreme Court. At the age of thirty-three Brewer, who had settled in Leavenworth, was appointed to the Supreme Court of Kansas where he served for fourteen years until he accepted a post on the federal circuit court of appeals. In 1890, after five years on the federal bench, he was elevated to the Supreme Court of the United States. Tall, powerful, jovial, witty, and self-disciplined, Brewer rose at five o'clock every morning and began to work in his library. Both on and off the bench he eagerly and ably discussed the public issues of his day, always from an ultraconservative viewpoint, and his intense desire to preserve freedom of economic enterprise pervaded his life including his judicial opinions. In a commencement address at Yale delivered to the June graduating class of 1891 Brewer articulated his beliefs. [5] He declared that from the time when "Eve took loving possession of even the forbidden apple, the idea of property and the sacredness of the right of its possession has never departed from the race. . . . [H]uman experience . . . declares that the love of acquirement, mingled with the joy of possession, is the real stimulus to human activity." It was therefore, said Brewer, the special obligation of popular governments to preserve the rights of property. In fact, he argued, "the demands of absolute and eternal justice forbid that any private property, legally acquired and legally held, should be spoliated or destroyed in the interests of public health, morals or welfare without compensation." But a concern for the preservation of private property was not Brewer's sole preoccupation. He had a strong interest in international law as a means for securing international peace, and with logical consistency opposed imperialism, American as well as European. Occasionally he could take an advanced position, as he did in publicly supporting woman suffrage. During his tenure he wrote the opinion of the Court in 526 cases and authored fifty-three dissents.

Henry Billings Brown was a classmate of David Brewer at Yale. Born in Massachusetts of well-to-do parents, educated at Yale and the Harvard Law School, Brown built a successful law practice in Detroit prior to accepting an appointment by President Grant to the United States District Court in Michigan. When he was appointed to the Supreme Court by President Harrison in 1890, it was believed by close observers of the federal scene that Brown would be utilized primarily in admiralty cases since, at the time of his nomination, he was considered the nation's foremost expert in admiralty law. But being a man of industry and independent mind, he participated actively in the important public law cases of his time. Over the protesting dissents of Brewer and Peckham he wrote the carefully reasoned opinion in *Holden* v. *Hardy*[6] upholding a law providing for a maximum eight-hour work day for miners; but he joined the majority in *Lochner* v. *New York*[7] to strike down the New York maximum hour law for bakers. In an official memoir Charles A. Kent wrote that Brown's life demonstrated how a man without "extraordinary abilities ... might attain and honor the highest judicial position by industry, by good character, pleasant manners, and some aid from fortune."[8]

Another Yale honors graduate was George Shiras Jr., successful Pittsburgh lawyer, whom Harrison appointed to the vacancy created by Justice Bradley's death in 1892. Amiable, sprightly, but generally not regarded as a distinguished judge, Shiras served for ten years. Both he and Fuller were devotees of Charles Dickens, and they would occasionally exchange notes on the bench designating the lawyer arguing a case as Micawber, Uriah Heep or some other Dickens character.[9] President Harrison's choice to succeed Justice Lamar in 1893 was Howell E. Jackson, a Tennessee Democrat who, although he had opposed secession, later held office under the Confederacy. After the war he served in the Tennessee legislature, and then in the United States Senate, until President Cleveland made him a federal circuit judge. Justice Brown once said that it was Howell Jackson who persuaded Harrison to appoint him (Brown) to the Supreme Court, and thus, when Lamar died, Brown returned the favor by prevailing upon Harrison to appoint Jackson. Although a man of sound judgment, careful learning and unquestioned integrity, his brief service of two years does not give us enough time to measure his judicial ability. His small stature and white goatee led some journalists to suggest that he looked like a miniature Uncle Sam.

When Justice Blatchford died in the summer of 1893 President Cleveland nominated William B. Hornblower, a New York lawyer and nephew of former Justice Bradley. Because of a disagreement between the president and Senator David Hill of New York, Hornblower's nomination was rejected by the Senate. Cleveland's next choice, Wheeler H. Peckham of New York, was also turned down as Senator Hill once again invoked senatorial courtesy. Flipping the senatorial courtesy coin, the president nominated a senator, Edward Douglass White of Louisiana, whom the Senate confirmed the very day his name was submitted. White, a forty-six year-old bachelor, former Confederate soldier, devout Irish Catholic, son of a former governor of Louisiana, and a wealthy sugar planter, took his seat in March 1894. He was to serve for twenty-seven years. In 1910 President Taft broke with tradition and promoted White to chief justice. He was an energetic, able presiding officer who speeded up the work of the Court. Although White had a keen intellect, a prodigious memory, and monumental energy, his opinions—all 700 of them—leave something to be desired. They have been characterized as "models of what judicial opinions ought not to be."[10] To his colleagues White was always humble, genial, and likable. To students of constitutional law his judicial writing, although obviously learned, is difficult and dreary.

Of the remaining five justices who served under Fuller, Oliver Wendell Holmes, Jr., surrounded himself with followers to the point where he had a cult of worshippers rivalling that of John

Marshall himself. Justice Joseph McKenna, if not downright incompetent—and he may have been that—was barely able to do the work, although with the aid of White and Fuller he survived on the Court for twenty-six years. The other three, Peckham, Day and Moody, were thoroughly competent but not outstanding. Had Moody not been forced to retire due to ill health after only three years' service, he might well have established a brilliant and enviable record.

William Henry Moody was often mistaken for Theodore Roosevelt. He looked like him and he acted like him. Within one five-year period of his life he had served in all three branches of the national government: in Congress, in the executive as secretary of the navy and attorney general, and in the judiciary as associate justice of the Supreme Court. He was one of those individuals whose favorable personal endowments won him success in everything he did. Massachusetts born, educated at Andover and Harvard, he read for a time with Richard Henry Dana before entering the practice of law. Holmes and Gray were impressed with him when he argued cases before the Supreme Court of Massachusetts, as was President Roosevelt, who rewarded him with a justly deserved appointment to the Supreme Court. Moody had, incidentally, acquired a good deal of public notoriety as the prosecutor in the Lizzie Borden murder case.

William Rufus Day, it would seem, was destined to be a judge—he was the son of the chief justice of Ohio, and the great grandson of the chief justice of Connecticut. He built a solid reputation as a trial lawyer in Ohio, and became a good friend of another Ohio attorney, William McKinley. President McKinley later appointed him respectively, secretary of state and justice of a federal circuit court of appeals. It was Theodore Roosevelt who elevated him to the Supreme Court. A man of slight stature and plagued by ill health, he was an ardent baseball fan who never missed a game in Washington and who was often seen scurrying from bench to ball park. Modest, courteous, well-liked, he preferred the quiet of home, family, and a good book to all social diversion other than baseball. He resigned from the Supreme Court in 1922, having served almost twenty years.

Less moderate than his brethren in the tone of his opinions and in his attitude toward national or state regulation of business was Rufus W. Peckham of New York. Peckham had not attended college but had been admitted to the New York bar in 1859 after having "read" (apprenticed) law for a period. He remained a practicing lawyer for twenty-four years until he was elected first to the New York Supreme Court and then to the New York Court of Appeals. He served ten years on the New York bench before being appointed to the Supreme Court in 1896 where he remained for slightly more than thirteen years. A conservative Democrat of the Cleveland school, he repeatedly held to a social Darwinist bias, typically expressed in his opinion in the *Lochner* case. [11] He was an able judge who wrote with clarity and in a straightforward, outspoken manner.

Interested in the Catholic priesthood in his early years, Joseph McKenna changed his mind in favor of law and politics. As a practicing attorney, he worked his way through the political ranks to become a congressman from California. His future seemed to be the work of fate or chance. While he was on the Ways and Means Committee it was chaired by William McKinley. Later, as president, McKinley appointed McKenna attorney general of the United States. Rumor had it that the president sought an Irish Catholic for a top cabinet post in order to allay fears that he was friendly toward the American Protective Association, an anti-Catholic society of that time. Prior to his selection as a member of the president's cabinet, McKenna had spent five years on the federal circuit court in California, and the lawyers as well as his fellow judges thought him unfit for the Supreme Court. Once on the Court he managed to survive, according to one observer, because he had the good sense to attach himself to a stronger judicial mind, usually Justice White, and because the chief justice was considerate enough to assign him the less difficult cases. [12]

Oliver Wendell Holmes, Jr., was a man of great learning, wit, and mental energy. His physical constitution was equally superior, permitting him to fight in the Civil War, to recover from three serious wounds, and to live long enough to be acquainted with both presidents named Roosevelt. By any standard, he is one of the towering figures ever to sit on the Court. After graduating from Harvard Holmes went off to war, but he returned to complete his law degree in 1866. He practiced law in Boston for fifteen years and found time to edit the *American Law Review* and to prepare the twelfth edition of Kent's *Commentaries on American Law*. His classic work on the common law was published in 1881. He served briefly on the faculty of the Harvard Law School in 1882, resigning to accept an appointment to the Supreme Court of Massachusetts. He served in that post for twenty years (three as chief justice) until President Theodore Roosevelt named him to the Supreme Court in 1902. Had he died at that point in his career, at the age of sixty-one, he would have been relatively unknown outside academic legal circles.

In one sense Holmes exemplified the democratic ideal. He cared too little for public office to seek it, but performed his duties in such a way that the office sought him. When Senator Henry Cabot Lodge suggested that he run for governor of Massachusetts from which office he might go directly to the United States Senate, Holmes retorted that he didn't "give a damn to be a senator." This was not from any sense of modesty; in fact, it is more likely that his attitude was a result of arrogance. To Holmes politics was transient and trivial. Ideas were paramount, and if posterity were to remember him, it must be for his ideas, not for his political performance. As he phrased it in a speech at Harvard in 1886, it was the thinker who possessed a "secret isolated joy" in knowing that "a hundred years after he is dead and forgotten, men who never heard of him will be moving to the measure of his thought." What Holmes brought to the Court, in the words of Wallace Mendelson, was "skepticism and intellectual humility—perfect solvents for the economic dogmatism which had permeated both bench and bar." [13] Holmes was intellectually humble, however, in the sense that he was a philosophical relativist and paid due respect to the ideas of others. At the same time his violent rejection of any moving force in nature ("a brooding omni-presence in the sky") and of the humanness of man (he saw "no reason for attributing to man a significance different in kind from that which belongs to a baboon or to a grain of sand") indicate an intellectual thrust which can hardly be called humble. He was a social Darwinist who respected the Spencerian doctrine of the mechanistic evolution of the cosmos from the relatively simple to the relatively complex. He nevertheless refused to read his own views into the Constitution. As Mendelson suggests, he did not "confuse his personal tastes and distastes with constitutional necessity." [14] Admirable as that may be under some circum-stances, it may be a dereliction of duty under others, and Holmes' relativism and restraint in refusing to interfere with majorities who would curb the excesses of capitalism might be thought less admirable if used to justify majorities who wished to curb the legitimate aspirations of a minority group. Holmes was, however, an exciting and an unusually competent judge. His greatness, as one of his many biographers suggests, "lay most of all in his manner of meeting life. He had a genius for living, a genius for finding himself, using himself wholly." [15] Holmes was a man of quality to whom the act of learning was a supreme joy. In his own words, "To know is not less than to feel. . . . A valid idea is worth a regiment any day." [16] Holmes retired from the Court at the age of ninety-one and died in 1935, two days before his ninety-fourth birthday.

Due Process and State Power

Such were the men who served with Melville Weston Fuller. Although they held disparate views toward law and public policy, a majority of them could generally combine to overturn legislation, state and national, which was designed to regulate a sector of the economy. The significant litigation before the Court between 1888 and 1896 falls roughly into two categories: that dealing with the due process clause and the extent to which it limited state power; and that concerning the use of national power, a part of which involved fiscal and regulatory measures. With the exception of its attitude in the latter category, the Court's views were attuned to the expanding nationalism of the times, and the justices carefully built a structure on the Marshall bedrock of national supremacy and implied powers. Indicative of this position are such cases as: *In re Neagle* [17] in which Justice Miller interpreted presidential power so broadly as to go beyond the concept of enumerated powers and imply an inherent power in the executive; *Fong Yue Ting* v. *United States* [18] which held (over the protests of Fuller, Brewer and Field) that the deportation of aliens in peacetime was as much an attribute of sovereignty as the exclusion of such aliens upon their arrival, and that constitutional guarantees such as due process were not applicable in deportation proceedings; *Chinese Exclusion Case* [19] which upheld the power of Congress to exclude aliens even if, as in these instances, Congress had abrogated agreements permitting them to enter, or reenter, the United States, and had contravened a treaty with China. There was also *Leisy* v. *Hardin* [20] in which Chief Justice Fuller apparently persuaded the Court to overrule *Peirce* v. *New Hampshire* [21] and to apply the original package doctrine to interstate commerce, thus preventing the states from excluding commodities of commerce from their borders; *In re Rapier* [22] which upheld the right of Congress to exclude lotteries from the mails; *Public Clearing House* v. *Coyne* [23] which approved the extension of congressional power over the mails in upholding a fraud-order law; *Swift* v. *Tyson*, [24] a landmark case later to be overruled, which insisted that on questions of general law the Supreme Court might ascertain for itself what the law is and would not be bound by the state courts; and *United States* v.*Texas*, [25] upholding the power of the United States to sue a state in order to fix boundaries, a power which, incidentally, had been denied by many members of Congress. These cases, while confirming the nationalist sentiment of the day, were not among those which led to a clash with Congress.

If one may name a single case that marks the turning point in the rise of a new constitutionalism or new judicialism, by which is meant the conservative alignment that resulted after the replacement of Waite and Matthews by Fuller and Brewer, it would be the *Minnesota Rate Case* [26] decided on 24 March 1890. A Minnesota statute of 1887 had established a Railroad and Warehouse Commission empowered to fix rates finally without any appeal to the courts. Declaring the law invalid Justice Blatchford for the majority argued that it deprived the railroad of the "right to a judicial investigation, by due process of law, under the forms and with the machinery provided by the wisdom of successive ages for the investigation judicially of the truth of a matter in controversy, and substitutes, therefore, as an absolute finality, the action of a railroad commission." [27] The question of reasonableness of rate charges for transportation, said Blatchford, is a question for judicial investigation, requiring due process of law for its determination. In short, the Court held that due process must be judicially, not legislatively or administratively determined. Justice Bradley wrote a dissent for himself, Gray, and Lamar in which he bemoaned the fact that the majority had practically overruled *Munn* v. *Illinois*. [28] As he saw it, the *Granger Cases* had held that the "settlement of the fares of railroads, and other public accommodations is a legislative prerogative and not a judicial one." [29] In answer to the argument that the law was bad since it provided for no appeal from decisions of the commission, Bradley replied that there must be a final tribunal somewhere for deciding all questions, that all human institutions are imperfect and that injustice may occur at whatever level is the final one. [30] It was theoretically possible, now that the Court had assumed the final determination of the reasonableness of rates, that it was simply attempting to insure fair regulation and would not set aside regulation itself. For cases involving such enterprises as railroads, grain elevators, and the like this was true since they were "affected with a public interest," but eventually some businesses were held to be outside government control altogether. This was a logical position for the Court once it had been established by implication in *Munn* v. *Illinois*—that some business might be regulated under certain conditions. If the conditions and the enterprise were not properly "public," then the judiciary might stay the hand of government control.

Although the business community in concert with the legal fraternity would have moved the Supreme Court to that end, they were not quite able to succeed, in part because of counter pressures in the system. The *Minnesota Rate Case* had been decided in 1890, and in 1892 two significant events took place which, although hardening conservative attitudes (and arteries), portended an intensification of the American version of the class struggle that was to be an integral part of American law and politics for many years. On 4 July a vehicle of agrarian discontent, the newly formed Populist party, celebrated Independence Day by setting forth its demands: free coinage of silver; credit inflation; government ownership of railroads, telegraph, and telephone; and a graduated income tax. On 6 July striking unionists of the Amalgamated Association of Iron and Steel Workers in Homestead, Pennsylvania, rioted at the Carnegie Steel plant and battled with 300 Pinkerton guards, shocking most Americans in the same way that they were to be shocked by the Negro rioters of the 1960s. The following year saw the beginning of an industrial depression and a financial panic that further exacerbated the widening rift between the haves and the have-nots.

Just prior to these events the Supreme Court handed down the opinion in *Budd* v. *New York*. [31] In a 6-3 decision the Court returned to the principles of *Munn* v. *Illinois* by upholding a New

York law that regulated rates and charges in warehouses, elevators, and shipping facilities generally on the state's waterways. Justices Brewer, Field and Brown, however, dissented. Said Brewer:

> The paternal theory of government is to me odious. The utmost liberty to the individual, and the fullest possible protection to him and his property, is both the limitation and duty of government. If it may regulate the price of one service, which is not a public service, or the compensation for the use of one kind of property which is not devoted to a public use, why may it not with equal reason regulate the price of all service, and the compensation be paid for the use of all property? And if so, 'Looking Backward' is nearer than a dream. [32]

Two years later in *Brass* v. *North Dakota* [33] the majority that favored some regulatory measures was reduced from six to five. A North Dakota statute, while similar to the Illinois and New York laws that had been upheld in *Munn* and *Budd*, differed somewhat in that it was statewide in application whereas the latter applied to geographic centers like Chicago and Buffalo. Counsel for the grain elevators in North Dakota claimed that the dissimilar circumstances negated the principle of "virtual monopoly" which was the basis for invalidating the laws of Illinois and New York. Without the presence of monopoly, it was argued, the law was an invasion of private property rights. But Justice Shiras, for the majority, discarded the monopoly idea, holding that once it had been established that legislatures might regulate grain elevators, it was not up to the courts to challenge the legislative judgment of the circumstances that warranted legislation. Now it appeared that the Court was permitting broad regulatory powers by the states, but it will be recalled that the majority on the Court was the slimmest possible and was less than that in *Budd* and *Munn*. Two new appointees, Jackson and White, joined Brewer and Field in dissent, and Brown, who had been with Brewer and Field in *Budd*, moved to the majority side. Justice Brewer stoutly maintained his position. The country, he said, was "rapidly travelling the road which leads to that point where all freedom of contract and conduct will be lost."

In another case decided in 1894, *Reagan* v. *Farmers Loan and Trust Co.*, [34] the Court approved the principle of regulation while condemning a specific regulatory order. Aware of the doctrine of the *Minnesota Rate Case* that the state law had been invalidated because it did not permit judicial review of a railroad commission's conclusions, the Texas legislature established a regulatory commission in 1891 but provided carefully for notice, hearing and an appeal to the courts. Unless found otherwise the commission's schedules were to be conclusive. The railroads took the position that the latter section of the law deprived them of due process and therefore rendered the entire law invalid. This was so, it was argued, because the railroads were forced to carry on business until the courts made a final determination, and even then the commission might set new rates only slightly different from the old, thereby putting the railroad to further expense and financial loss. Speaking for a unanimous court Justice Brewer upheld the law but at the same time ordered the commission's rates set aside. Clarifying the Court's position in the *Minnesota Rate Case*, Brewer pointed out that the fixing of charges for a common carrier was an administrative or legislative function, but that there was no doubt of the power of the courts "to inquire whether a body of rates prescribed by a legislature or commission is unjust and unreasonable . . . and if found so to be, to restrain its operation." While it appeared that the Court would not interfere with the concept of rate fixing, it would be the final authority on the question of the reasonableness of rates, and having taken that position, it effectively repudiated Chief Justice Waite's earlier assertion that "the people must resort to the polls, not to the courts" to remedy legislative abuses.

Although the pronouncements of the Supreme Court on the questions of state regulation of business set the tone of judicial review during the 1890s, and may have contributed to the eventual quarrel with Congress, the decisions that precipitated the discordant notes were three in number, all handed down during the winter and spring of 1895. The first of these was *United States v. E.C. Knight Co.*,[35] decided on 1 January. On the ground that the company had acquired a monopoly of over ninety percent of the sugar refining facilities in the United States, the government brought suit under the Sherman Act requesting dissolution of the American Sugar Refining Co. Originally the suit had been instituted by William H.H. Miller, attorney general under President Harrison, but it was actually prosecuted by Richard Olney. Olney had opposed the passage of the Sherman Act and had later worked for its repeal. In fact, it was suggested in some quarters that Justices Gray and Brown may have joined the majority in denying the request for dissolution because of Olney's weak presentation of the case—he offered no direct proof of interstate control of sales and prices, but merely submitted evidence concerning the purchase of stock.

Speaking for the Court, Chief Justice Fuller agreed that the American Sugar Refining Company might well be a monopoly, but if so, it was not a monopoly of commerce but of manufacturing, and while control of an object involves, in a sense, control of its disposition, it is a secondary not a primary consideration. In Fuller's view, although the power over manufacturing might bring the "operation of commerce into play, it does not control it, and affects it only incidentally and indirectly. Commerce succeeds to manufacture, and is not a part of it." If the people desire protection from manufacturing monopolies, it is to the states that they must take their grievances, said Fuller, for Congress can act only against a monopoly of commerce. To permit congressional regulation of manufacturing is to weaken the federal system through interference with the reserved powers of the states. Whatever restraint combinations in manufacturing may have upon commerce is simply an "indirect result, however inevitable and whatever its extent."

Alone in dissent was Justice Harlan who argued that the majority opinion was destructive of the Marshall doctrine in *Gibbons* v. *Ogden* [36] which held that the national power was intended to be sufficient for national objectives. In Harlan's judgment an unlawful restraint on the free course of trade which affected the people of all the states was properly a matter for national regulation. In Harlan's words:

> [T]he general government is not placed by the Constitution in such a condition of helplessness that it must fold its arms and remain inactive while capital combines . . . to destroy competition, not in one state only, but throughout the entire country, in the buying and selling of articles—especially the necessaries of life—that go into commerce among the states. [37]

Over Harlan's objection the economic conservatives and social Darwinists won a major victory which, translated into constitutional terms, was a victory for states' rights. Justices Fuller, Brewer and Field who unswervingly believed in *laissez faire* could join with staunch states' righters Shiras and White to create the essential majority.

The Tax Question

Attracting considerably more attention, as much attention in fact as any case in the history of the Court, was *Pollock* v. *Farmers' Loan and Trust Co.*,[38] involving the validity of a federal income tax. On 7 March argument in the case began with several days of old-time oratory on behalf of the business community which had enlisted some of the best legal talent in the nation. Opening the hearing was William D. Guthrie who declared that the constitutional requirement of uniformity for indirect taxes was violated by the various exemptions in the law. The exemption of the first $4 thousand of personal income discriminated against corporations, which naturally did not come under the exemption, and against individuals with income over $4 thousand per year, who bore the entire tax burden while constituting only two percent of the population. Uniformity, said Guthrie, meant equality of burden and not simply geographic sameness, but most important, "the requirement of approximate equality inheres in the very nature of the power to tax, and it exists whether declared or not in the written Constitution."

Guthrie was followed by Clarence A. Seward who asked the Court to examine a question which supposedly had been settled, namely, the nature of a direct tax. Dismissing precedent with a wave of his hand, Seward said that the *Hylton* case[39] had been predicated on Alexander Hamilton's ideas, and that the *Springer* case[40] dealt with a wartime tax and was not binding during peacetime. Furthermore, he maintained that the framers' objective in requiring apportionment of direct taxes was to make their use by the national government unlikely, and to reserve to the states this mode of taxation. Completing the logic of the argument, Seward said that to exempt income taxes from the direct tax rule would weaken the position of the states in the system and defeat the purpose of the framers. Seward's argument was imaginative but historically inaccurate—it is impossible to show that the framers ever contemplated an income tax.

For the government, Assistant Attorney General Edward B. Whitney argued that previous decisions of the Court defining direct taxes should stand, and that uniformity was geographical and nothing more. But, he observed, if a broader interpretation were given to constitutional language, the $4 thousand exemption, although admittedly discriminating against the rich, was defensible as a balance to the consumption taxes which hit the poor most heavily. On 11 March argument became highly emotional when Senator George F. Edmunds maintained that the income tax was "intentionally and tyrannically and monstrously unequal," that it not only violated the direct tax and uniformity clauses, but the Fourteenth Amendment as well since that amendment applied to the national government by inference. Unless the Supreme Court invalidated the tax, said Edmunds, "one evil step will lead to another . . . until by and by we will have revolution, then anarchy and then a tyrant to rule us."

Although Attorney General Olney may have been lax in the *Knight* case, he performed with exceptional competence in *Pollock*. As "an impeccable conservative who had relentlessly harassed the Coxey marchers and the Debs railway strikers . . . [he] now turned out a smoothly reasoned, even brilliant defense of the income tax." [41] He asserted that the direct tax question was settled, and that to reject the precedent after a century's duration "would go far to prove that government by constitution is not a thing of stable principles, but of the fluctuating views and wishes of the particular period." In answer to the inequality argument, he maintained that perfect equality of taxation was impossible. He wound up his argument with an appeal for judicial self-restraint, pointing out that the Court was being asked to "supplant the political [departments] in the exercise of the taxing power; to substitute its discretion for that of Congress."

Another spokesman for the government was James C. Carter, a distinguished advocate of the day, who argued that equality of taxation meant apportionment of the burden where it could most easily be borne. If the appellants complained that two percent of the population would pay the entire income tax, said Carter, they might reflect that this same two percent had been receiving over fifty percent of the national income and paying only slightly more than two percent of the tax bill.

Last to speak against the tax was the most skillful orator of them all, Joseph Hodges Choate, who called the law "communistic in its purposes and tendencies . . . defended here upon principles as communistic, socialistic . . . populistic as ever have been addressed to any political assembly in the world." He said much more in this vein before addressing himself to the constitutional argument, which was essentially that since a tax on real property is admittedly a direct tax, then a tax on income from real property is a direct tax, and a tax on personal property differs in no important way from a tax on real property, therefore a tax on income derived from all personal property is a direct tax.

In a 6-2 opinion (Jackson was ill) the Court, speaking through Chief Justice Fuller, declared unconstitutional that part of the income tax imposing a tax on income or rents from real estate on the ground that it was a direct tax and needed to be apportioned. Fuller also declared the tax on income from state and municipal bonds invalid as a burden on the borrowing power of the states. On the three remaining issues—whether invalidating tax on rents or real estate invalidated the entire tax; whether a tax on income from personal property was a direct tax; or whether any part of the tax was invalid for want of uniformity—the Court divided 4-4.

Chief Justice Fuller's opinion attempted to answer three questions. The first question: were the direct-tax clauses put into the Constitution to prevent a majority of the states from voting a tax on a minority? Answering yes, Fuller argued that on the basis of the debates in the ratifying conventions, and in the "Grand Convention" itself, representation and taxation went hand in hand as a general constitutional principle, and the direct tax provision was simply a compromise over slavery. Fuller also marshaled evidence to prove that the framers contemplated raising revenue normally by duties, excises, and imports, and that only in extreme emergency should the government resort to direct taxes. Since the requirement of apportionment would necessitate inequality of burden in certain instances, the framers must have contemplated such inequality, and therefore intended the direct tax requirement to operate only in emergencies, and designed it "to prevent an attack upon accumulated property by mere force of numbers." [42]

In answer to the second question, what is a direct tax?, Fuller began by quoting Madison's notes: "Mr. King asked what was the precise meaning of direct taxation. No one answered." He then went on to suggest that the distinction between direct and indirect taxes was well understood by the framers and needed no prolonged discussion in the convention. Fuller's critics say that he began by noting that the phrase "direct taxes" had no "precise meaning" and ended by saying that the words were "well understood." Fuller's biographer, Willard King, however, defends the language with the observation that "[w]ords with well understood meanings are many; words with precise meanings are rare. The failure of any person in a group to volunteer an answer to a request for a precise definition of a word does not give rise to any inference that the word has no well understood meaning." [43]

Fuller now had to deal with the third question: Did not precedent dictate that an income tax was not a direct tax? Fuller reasoned that in none of the previous cases dealing with the subject [44] had income from real property been involved, and that whatever was said concerning the meaning of direct taxes as they affected rents was purely dicta. Thus, none of the previous cases was overruled, but simply distinguished from the case at hand.

There is, of course, no support in history for Fuller's assertion that the framers intended the direct tax clause to be a barrier against an attack on property by force of numbers, but as Professor Arnold Paul suggests, there may have been an inner core of truth to Fuller's contention, since the framers might well have placed such a prohibition in the Constitution had they foreseen popular majorities, operating through universal suffrage, levying a tax that would bear heaviest on the wealthy states.

Since the inconclusiveness of this decision satisfied no one, the Court granted a petition for rehearing with the date set for 6 May. Although ailing, Howell Jackson assured the chief justice that he would be present. On 20 May Fuller, now speaking for a bare majority of five, delivered a second opinion declaring the entire tax unconstitutional. After repeating his original arguments the chief justice extending his ruling to include income from personal property. While admitting that a tax on business, the professions, or employment was not a direct but an excise tax, Fuller argued that with so much of it invalidated, the entire taxing scheme must fall. As he observed, "what was intended as a tax on capital would remain in substance a tax on occupations and labor." Justices Field, Brewer, Shiras and Gray joined the chief. Separate dissents were written by Harlan, Brown, Jackson and White. All condemned the majority for reversing judicial precedents, and all were critical of the social and political aspects of the opinion. Harlan called the decision a "judicial revolution that may sow the seeds of hate and distrust among the people of different sections of our common country," and he deplored the fact that the national government was now denied "a power which is, or may become, vital to the very existence and preservation of the Union in a national emergency."[45] Justice Brown characterized the decision as "a surrender of the taxing power to the moneyed class. . . ." and he condemned the emotionalism of the propertied classes. "Even the spectre of socialism is conjured up to frighten Congress from laying taxes upon the people in proportion to their ability to pay them. . . . I hope it may not prove the first step toward the submergence of the liberties of the people in a sordid despotism of wealth."[46] Justices White and Jackson dissented primarily on the ground of breaking with precedent. Their arguments were constitutional and legal and dwelled little on the public policy question.

Fuller's biographer adds an interesting footnote to this case in pointing out that the line of cleavage on the Court was in strict accord with the per capita wealth of the states in which the individual justices resided. In view of the $4 thousand exemption virtually none of the income tax would have been collected in the home states of Harlan, Brown, Jackson or White.[47] In general members of Congress divided similarly along economic lines with the representatives from the poorer states voting for the income tax in opposition to the representatives from the wealthier states.

The final of the trilogy which furnished Congress with ammunition for sniping at the Court was the *Debs* case.[48] During the Pullman strike of 1890, labor organizer Eugene Debs had disobeyed an injunction issued by a district court, commanding him and others to stop obstructing trains engaged in interstate commerce, and stop interfering with the mails. He had been imprisoned for contempt, and his case went to the Supreme Court on a petition for habeas corpus. Arguing for Debs and other officials of the American Railway Union were attorneys Lyman Trumbull, Clarence Darrow and S.S. Gregory. The brief for the defense made the following points: first, if an indictment in a federal court declares no offense against federal statutes, a judgment pronounced upon such an indictment could not justify imprisonment; second, since the government carries the mail in its sovereign function, equity may not apply since it may not be invoked in political matters; third, the jurisdiction of the federal courts depends exclusively upon the laws of the United States and has no common law basis; and finally the federal law relied upon in Debs' case confers no right upon the government to abate a public nuisance on an interstate highway, it only allows restraint by injunction of the violation of a penal statute. For the government Richard Olney, Edward B. Whitney and Edwin Walker argued that only one question was present in the case: whether or not the lower court had jurisdiction to issue the injunction. It did, they argued, on two grounds: the attorney general of the United States may sue in chancery to protect the interests of the public, and the Sherman Act authorizes the injunction.

For the majority Justice Brewer wrote the opinion upholding the injunction, and he suggested that the answers to two questions would dispose of the case. First: Are the relations of the federal government to interstate commerce, and to the mails, such as to authorize a direct interference to prevent forcible obstruction thereof? Second: if such authority exists, has the court of equity jurisdiction to issue an injunction in aid of its authority? On the first point Brewer argued that the entire strength of the nation may be used to enforce "the full and free exercise of all national powers and the security of all rights entrusted by the Constitution to its care."[49] But, he asked, in answering the second question, is there not an alternative to armed force? Of course! It is the right of appeal to the courts for a judicial determination and for the exercise of all their powers of prevention. Even if it were true that the equity jurisdiction may be used only to protect property, as the defense contended, the United States has property in the mails, the protection of which was one purpose of the injunction. Furthermore, the injunction was not simply a matter of enjoining mob violence but of restraining "forcible obstructions of the highways along which interstate commerce travels and the mails are carried." [50]

Thus, at every turn, the Supreme Court frustrated the popular forces that had gained access to the legislative halls and had written regulatory legislation aimed at big business. And at the same time the Court thwarted labor's attempts to pressure industry into recognition of unions and to bargain collectively with them. No doubt the Court's decisions of this period gave the forces of capitalism in America a "vital period of incubation." And it came at a time when corporate development was most vulnerable, during the years of expansion and consolidation. [51] It should be noted that the *Debs* case involved the first successful criminal prosecution based on the Sherman Act, and that the act was used not against business but against labor. It was an unfriendly judiciary that had given the Sherman Act a perverse twist. As Eugene Debs saw it, it "was not the soldiers that ended the strike. . . . It was simply the United States courts." [52]

The Court and Darwin

But the social Darwinism that permeated the Fuller court had repercussions far beyond the advantages it afforded business to the disadvantage of labor. It infected the Fourteenth Amendment as it applied to the race question, and it was no more clearly apparent than in the opinion in *Plessy* v. *Ferguson* [53] which the Court wrote in 1896 following closely on the heels of *Knight, Pollock* and *Debs*. Writing for the majority of seven (Justice Brewer did not participate), Justice Henry Billings Brown upheld a Louisiana statute requiring railroads to provide "equal but separate" accommodations for Negro and white passengers. He suggested that a statute which implies merely a legal distinction between two races, a distinction based on color which is ineradicable, does not destroy the legal equality of the two races, and does not necessarily imply the inferiority of either race. But his social Darwinist assumptions can be seen in this passage: "Legislation is powerless to eradicate racial instincts or to abolish distinctions based upon physical differences, and the attempt to do so can only result in accentuating the difficulties of the present situation." [54] Law apparently can have no effect upon social control, in this instance, race relations. The tragic paradox in this case is that law, bad law, did have an effect upon race relations—an adverse effect. Justice Harlan, the only dissenter, movingly and eloquently protested, predicting accurately that the decision would "stimulate aggressions more or less brutal and irritating" against the rights of Negroes and would vitiate the Civil War amendments. [55]

It was not the Supreme Court's attitude toward the Negro, however, that sparked the clashes with Congress. It was the Court's continuing attitude toward property rights, and a new movement, the Progressive protest, was to become not only the opponent of certain of Supreme Court decisions, but of judicial power itself. The Progressive movement, while it gathered into its fold the ideas and followers of the old Populist party, had a grass roots origin of its own in the cities. Wealthy manufacturers, like Samuel M. Jones and Thomas L. Johnson, who had turned to urban reform, were in the forefront of the movement which eventually included such influential United States Senators as Robert M. LaFollette of Wisconsin, Hiram Johnson of California, Albert J. Beveridge of Indiana, Jonathan Dolliver and Albert B. Cummins of Iowa, Moses D. Clapp of Minnesota and William E. Borah of Idaho. Progressive leaders in the House included Charles S. Lindbergh of Minnesota, Victor Murdock of Kansas, and George W. Norris of Nebraska who was elected to the House in 1908 and quickly assumed the leadership of Republican insurgents. From the turn of the century onward the Progressives had forged a program that aimed at national regulation of the economy through democratic liberalism, and eventually the liberals in both parties could unite to enact into law the desired reforms. At first the programs encountered the intransigence of the Fuller Court, but ultimately even the Court was to give way to the claims of majoritarian rule, in part because of changes in personnel after 1900. Still present during the period 1896-1910 were Fuller, Brewer and White who had voted to strike down the income tax law, but Shiras and Brown were replaced by Day and Moody in 1903 and 1906, both of whom were moderate in their views of government regulation. Holmes replaced Gray in 1902, and although different in temperament, both tended toward judicial restraint. With these changes in personnel, a majority could be mustered to uphold, on occasion, national regulatory measures.

The first indication that such a majority could be obtained came in 1903 with the case of *Champion* v. *Ames* [56] in which the Court upheld an act of Congress of 1895 which forbade the shipment of lottery tickets in interstate commerce. Although the real intent of the law was to control gambling, the Court, through Harlan, ruled that regulation of commerce includes prohibition, and that Congress might reasonably prohibit articles from inter-state commerce that might have a harmful effect, not on the commerce, but on society at large. Chief Justice Fuller spoke in dissent for himself, Brewer, Shiras, and Peckham, arguing that the law was not a regulation of commerce but a suppression of lotteries, and that it clearly intruded upon the reserved powers of the states. The following year in *McCray* v. *United States* [57] the Court upheld a tax on artificially colored oleomargarine, the intent of which was to suppress the sale of oleo colored to look like butter. Justice White, for the Court, upheld the tax as a revenue raising measure on its face, reiterating the old doctrine that the Court would not inquire into the motives of the legislature. In the application of the Sherman Act in the first decade of the century, the Roosevelt administration met with some success when litigation reached the Supreme Court. In *Northern Securities Co.* v. *United States*, [58] decided in 1904, a majority of five upheld the government in ordering the dissolution of the Northern Securities Company, a creation of E.A. Harriman and James J. Hill, owners of competing railroads who had organized the company in order to secure a terminal line into Chicago. Attorneys for the company relied on the doctrine of the *E.C. Knight* case that the Sherman Act did not cover activities that were not strictly in interstate commerce, but Justice Harlan for the majority declared that the law covered any combination which operated to restrain commerce. It was in this case that the recently appointed Holmes dissented, thereby enraging President Roosevelt who had appointed him. Holmes joined Peckham and White to support Chief Justice Fuller's opinion adhering to the *Knight* doctrine. Just a year later, however, Holmes wrote the opinion in *Swift & Co.* v. *U.S.* [59] in which the Court first arrived at the "current" or "stream" of commerce doctrine, a judicial formula that was to lead eventually to the end of the distinction between manufacturing and literal commerce across state lines. The government had sought an injunction against a group of meat packing houses that had allegedly combined to control prices in the stockyards. Although the combinations in question had occurred locally, and all sales were local, Holmes, for the majority, held them to be a restraint on commerce. In doing so, he emphasized the nature of the industry, namely, that the live animals moved into the area and the finished product moved out, and that the local combination actually was an interference with interstate commerce. As he phrased it, this was a "typical, constantly recurring course," a "current of commerce among the states."

Even at the time that some of the justices were moving toward some liberality in construing the Sherman Act as a true check on the emerging monopolists, the Court was destroying the act's effectiveness. It did so by applying the "rule of reason," an English common-law concept of monopoly, which held that not all business combinations were illegal, but only those that unreasonably restrained trade or worked against the public interest. Corporation counsel had suggested the idea in 1897[60] and again in 1904 in the *Northern Securities* case, but the Court did not formerly recognize the concept until it decided the *Standard Oil*[61] and *American Tobacco Company*[62] monopoly cases in 1911. Applying the rule of reason to those two cases which involved alleged monopolies in restraint of commerce, the Court was actually extending the "reasonableness" doctrine that it had been applying to due process cases for some time. It was a useful device that might be employed to check government regulation at both the state and national levels. Although we shall turn shortly to the congressional reaction to the decisions of the Fuller Court, most of which came as a result of the *Pollock, Knight* and *Debs* cases, a portrait of the Court under Fuller would be incomplete without mention of a few key decisions rendered between 1905 and 1911, the latter date being the time when Edward Douglass White was elevated to chief justice.[63]

One such case was *Lochner* v. *New York*[64] in which Justice Peckham, speaking for a majority of five, invalidated a New York law that limited working hours in bakeries to sixty hours per week or ten hours per day. The constitutional basis for the ruling was the due process clause which was held to include "freedom of contract," that is, the liberty of employer and employee to enter into a contract of labor without interference by the government. Bakers are not "wards of the state," said Peckham, and there is no "reasonable ground for interfering with the liberty of person or the right of free contract, by determining the hours of labor, in the occupation of a baker." [65] This was a novel idea, and four of the justices said so, including Holmes who wrote that the "Fourteenth Amendment does not enact Mr. Herbert Spencer's Social Statics." Both the majority opinion and Holmes' dissent have been overemphasized in the past by constitutional historians. Although the majority extended the concept of "reasonableness" to its outermost limits in interfering with the legislative will, the principle of the *Lochner* case was modified in practice [66] and was applied in only three major cases. [67] Furthermore, Holmes' dissent, while rhetorically sweet sounding to the Progressives, is a negation of judicial review in that it gave carte blanche to majority rule. If the majority can embody whatever opinions they please into the law, which is what Holmes said, then the Fourteenth Amendment is a meaningless limitation on the states, and the Bill of Rights a similar meaningless limitation on Congress. What is really at issue is whether constitutionalism limits legislatures, supposedly the embodiment of the popular will, as well as the tyrannical executive; and secondarily, whether due process has a substantive as well as a procedural meaning. By 1905 it was clear to all students of government that implicit in the concept of constitutional government is a limitation on *all* institutions of government, including those that abide by majority rule. Whether due process was to have a substantive meaning was a point of disagreement among the justices.

In 1908 the Court continued to interpret the commerce clause narrowly when it held the Employers' Liability Act unconstitutional. [68] This act of Congress of 11 June 1906 had made every common carrier engaged in interstate commerce liable for on-the-job injury or death of any employee. The statute had superseded the old common law "fellow-servant rule" which held an employer not liable for injuries to an employee suffered through negligence of a fellow workman. The law also modified the "contributory negligence" rule under which an employer was not liable for injury to an employee suffered through the carelessness of another injured person. This was a public policy that recognized that the old rules no longer were in accord with necessities of modern industrial society. But, a majority of the Court did not see it that way. They held that while Congress might regulate carrier liability, the statute was so broad in its language that it covered employees whether or not they were directly engaged in commerce. Justices Moody, Harlan and McKenna believed that all employees of carriers were rightly covered by the act, and Holmes argued that the statute itself could have been construed narrowly enough to be held valid. As a result of the decision Congress was impelled to enact another law, this time with language carefully applying only to employees specifically engaged in interstate commerce. It was upheld in 1912 [69] when the make-up of the Court was slightly different. In the same year that the Court decided the *First Employers' Liability Cases* it also decided *Adair* v. *U.S.* in which it invalidated an act of Congress that prohibited railroads from discriminating against union labor. Specifically, the Erdman Act of 1 June 1898 had prohibited contracts by which any employee promised not to join a union as a condition of employment (yellow-dog contracts), and a majority believed this an interference with "liberty of contract." A final case of importance decided prior to Fuller's death was *Ex parte Young* [70] in which the Court held that a state official may be enjoined from enforcing a state law that is allegedly unconstitutional. In this instance the injunction had been used to prevent enforcement of a railroad rate law against the Northern Pacific Railroad. Later Congress modified the ruling by forbidding the enjoining of a state officer from enforcing a state law unless it was heard by a court composed of three federal judges.

When Fuller died in 1910, President Taft elevated Edward Douglass White to the chief justiceship and in doing so, broke several long-standing precedents. White, at sixty-five, was six years older than any other chief justice had been at the time of his appointment, and he was not of the president's political party. But more important from the standpoint of custom, White was the first chief justice to be promoted successfully from the bench. [71]

Speculation was that Hughes would be the new chief, and Taft at one time had written Hughes that if the office of chief justice were to become vacant, he would promote Hughes to it. Why did President Taft change his mind? No one knows precisely, but what we do know is that Taft coveted the office of chief justice more than any other worldly honor, including the presidency; that Hughes was forty-eight and in perfect health, and in the normal course of events would have held the post for many years beyond Taft's lifetime. On the other hand, White, at an advanced age, might occupy the office for only a short period. If a Republican president were to be in office at the time of White's retirement or death, he would almost certainly appoint Taft, and if a Democrat were president he, too, might appoint Republican, Protestant, northern Taft since Taft magnanimously had chosen Democrat, Catholic, southern White. In any event, hindsight tells us that Taft executed a perfect political maneuver that returned to him what he had yearned for his entire adult life.

President Taft was not only able to appoint a chief justice who would in effect hold the post for him, but also had the opportunity to reshape the Court by naming in addition to White, five associate justices. The least distinguished of the group were Horace Lurton, Joseph Lamar and Mahlon Pitney. Willis Van Devanter, while not among the unusual, possessed a certain style and ability which was to endear him to other members of the Court if not to the Court's observers. Taft's finest appointment was without question Charles Evans Hughes whose public service had been exemplary and who probably would have been treated well by history had he never served on the Court at all.

Horace Harmon Lurton was a professor in the Vanderbilt University Law School at the time President Taft selected him. Born in Kentucky, educated privately in his early years and later at the University of Chicago and Cumberland University, veteran of the Confederate army, Lurton had served on the Supreme Court of Tennessee for some years before President Cleveland made him a federal judge in the sixth circuit. During his federal service he apparently impressed the presiding judge of the circuit, William Howard Taft, who subsequently was in a position to reward him. Taft said that Lurton possessed the faculty in judicial conference of first analyzing his own judicial processes and then

patiently helping his colleagues to analyze theirs, and he characterized Lurton as "high-minded, earnest, self-sacrificing, and able."
Had Lurton been on the Court for a long period, he might have
made a greater contribution to judicial history, but as the record
stands, his slightly less than five years service was competent but
unimpressive. He was devoted to precedent and established rules
of law and he believed in judicial self-restraint and a strict
construction of the Constitution.

When President Taft chose Charles Evans Hughes for associate
justice of the Supreme Court on 25 April 1910 the nomination
was approved in general by both the public and Congress, in
contrast to the dispute in Congress and in the press in 1930 when
he was reappointed to the Court as chief justice. Whatever else
may be said of Hughes, there can be no disagreement that he set
the highest standards for himself in all that he did, and he did a
great deal. [72] Alpheus Mason suggests that his life represents at
least eight careers: law teacher and eminent lawyer, investigator,
governor, associate justice of the Supreme Court, presidential
candidate, secretary of state, World Court judge, and chief justice
of the United States. In this day of permissive child rearing
Hughes' early life is a testament to the Spartan-like, tough,
ordered existence. He was an only child and he received
considerable attention, all of it designed to produce a virtuous
man with a disciplined mind and a high sense of morality. At the
age of five his mother gave him a copy of the New Testament and
Psalms in order that he could take his turn reading verses at family
prayer, and when he reached the advanced age of eight his father
presented him with a Greek New Testament with lexicon. Always
his educational slogan was: BE THOROUGH! At an early age he
evolved what he called "The Charles Evans Hughes Plan of Study"
to guide his reading and research, and at thirteen he wrote essays
with such titles as "The Limitations of the Human Mind" and
"The Evils of Light Literature." When he was fourteen he entered
Colgate University (then Madison College) intending to follow the
occupation of his father, the ministry. Two years later, however,
he transferred to Brown University, having decided to prepare for
law. He graduated fourth in his class of forty-three, a standing that
earned him a Phi Beta Kappa key. Moving on to Columbia Law
School he graduated with highest honors and took a position with

Chamberlin, Carter and Hornblower, a firm in which he soon became a partner. With the exception of a two-year period (1891-93) in which he taught at the Cornell Law School, he remained in the private practice of law until 1905. In that year Hughes began his public career as counsel to the Stevens Committee set up by the New York legislature to investigate gas rates. Thereafter he remained a public figure until his death.

Hughes' philosophy of government was a mixture of conservative and liberal elements. He supported government regulation of utility rates, the merit system in public employment, the direct primary, and progressive social legislation such as workmen's compensation and child-labor laws. At the same time he opposed the ratification of the income tax amendment. He was economically conservative but a thoroughgoing civil libertarian both on and off the Court. In the twentieth century, he remained a consistent nineteenth century liberal. Judicially he would be classified as a moderate activist. He believed the Supreme Court to be the final arbiter of constitutional questions and he considered courts the "expert agents of democracy." The task of the Supreme Court, in Hughes' view, was "to preserve and enforce the primary and fundamental conceptions of justice." It may be a tribute to his objectivity that the Progressives were not in agreement at the time of his appointment. Senator Borah strongly approved of his selection as did the *Nation*, but William Jennings Bryan charged that Hughes was "a shining illustration of that peculiar type of citizen developed in this country during the present generation— the citizen who personally opposes vice and is a punisher of small crimes, but shows no indignation at the larger forms of legalized robbery." Until he resigned on 10 June 1916 Hughes wrote 151 opinions for the Court and dissented thirty-two times. In only three cases in which Hughes wrote for the majority was there more than one dissenter, and in only nine instances was there any dissent at all, a situation that suggests that Hughes either reflected the sentiment of the Court or was able to persuade his brethren that his was the only tenable position.

President Taft named Willis Van Devanter to the Court in 1910. A native of Indiana, graduate of DePauw University and of the Cincinnati Law School, Van Devanter went to the territory of Wyoming at the age of twenty-four where he became a close friend of Territorial Governor Francis E. Warren. He became successively commissioner in charge of revising the territorial statutes, city attorney of Cheyenne, member of the territorial legislature, and at age thirty, the chief justice of the Wyoming Supreme Court. He resigned the latter position to form a law firm with his brother-in-law, a firm which was to have as its clients some of the wealthiest corporations in the West including the Union Pacific Railroad. His federal public service began with his appointment as assistant attorney general in charge of cases for the Public Lands Division of the Interior Department from which President Roosevelt appointed him a judge on the Eighth Circuit Court of Appeals. He served for seven years before President Taft elevated him to the Supreme Court. When Taft later served as chief justice, he called Van Devanter his "mainstay" and "the most valuable man" in conference. [73] All of his colleagues defended him and paid tribute to his usefulness, even when the number of his written contributions to the Court's work was considerably below the average. For example, he wrote only five opinions in 1930, one each in 1931 and 1932, nine in 1933, three in 1934, none in 1935 and three in 1936.[74] During these years the other members of the Court were writing, on the average, twenty opinions each year. Van Devanter was apparently one of those persons who is fluent and precise in any oral exchange but for whom writing is a formidable enterprise.

President Taft's remaining two appointees, Joseph Rucker Lamar and Mahlon Pitney must be classified as undistinguished and are virtually unknown outside the circle of judicial historians. Lamar, plantation-born Georgian, schoolmate of Woodrow Wilson in Augusta in his early years, graduate of Bethany College, and law student at Washington and Lee, except for two terms in the Georgia legislature and two years on the Georgia Supreme Court, practiced law in Augusta until he joined the Supreme Court of the United States. He served for five years. Mahlon Pitney was chosen by Taft to replace John Marshall Harlan in 1912. Extremely conservative, he served for eleven years. A graduate of Princeton and a practicing lawyer, Pitney saw service in both the New Jersey legislature and on the Supreme Court of the state. Just prior to his appointment to the United States Supreme Court he had served for four years as chancellor of the state. Among his more notable opinions, all conservative, were the limiting of the common right of workmen to combine, [75] invoking the Clayton Act to restrain a labor union from boycott, [76] and denying to Congress the right to tax stock dividends on the ground that they constituted a capital increase and not income. [77]

The three remaining justices to serve under Chief Justice White were James Clark McReynolds, Louis Brandeis and John H. Clarke, all of whom were appointed by Woodrow Wilson. All were Democrats but of widely divergent views, and Brandeis and McReynolds were to become adversaries, both personally as well as in terms of judicial and constitutional orientation. McReynolds has been called "the Supreme Court's greatest human tragedy" [78] since he had become a rather tragic, lonely figure during his years on the Court, but all of it appeared to be of his own making for he was compulsively rude and unpleasant to many people with whom he came in contact. Moreover, he appeared to be an open, anti-Semite, seemingly hating Brandeis and Cardozo for no other reason than their being Jewish. His and Brandeis' careers had crossed in an interesting way prior to their becoming colleagues on the Court. President Wilson had appointed Brandeis attorney general but withdrew the appointment after the furor raised, for the most part, by the Boston Bar Association. Turning to Secretary of the Treasury William Gibbs McAdoo for advice, Wilson thereupon appointed McReynolds, an old friend of McAdoo and a fellow Tennesseean. He was, at the time, practicing law in Tennessee, although he had served without distinction as assistant attorney general under Theodore Roosevelt. He had been, in addition, a real estate operator, a teacher at Vanderbilt University and secretary to Howell E. Jackson when the latter was on the Supreme Court. When Justice Lurton died in 1914, President Wilson appointed McReynolds to the Court where he was to remain for twenty-six years, an unswerving conservative at a time when Progressivism, and later New Dealism, were capturing the loyalties of the American people.

Entirely different in temperament, personality and political persuasion was Louis Brandeis, [79] McReynolds' contemporary and judicial opponent. Born in Louisville, Kentucky, of a Bohemian-Jewish immigrant family, Brandeis entered the Harvard Law School without any college training at the age of nineteen. Physically frail and possessed of bad eyesight, he was advised by a physician to abandon the study of law, but he graduated at the top of his Harvard class at the age of twenty, among the first Harvard students to be taught law by the case method. He built up a highly successful law practice in Boston, and twenty years after his entry at Harvard he was almost a millionaire. Brandeis, however, was always a reformer at heart, albeit a conservative one. He did not believe in tearing down but rather in making institutional adjustments to fit new social and economic conditions. By the early 1900s he had all but abandoned his lucrative corporate law practice to devote himself to community service. Unlike many reformers of his time Brandeis was less interested in bringing about material comforts for all and more concerned with a fuller realization of a democratic way of life. In his view the new economic conditions—excessive hours of labor, irregular employment, low wages, employers' use of oppressive power, absentee ownership, and bigness manifested by monopolistic practices—led to a demoralized and irresponsible citizenry, making derelicts out of the very people who are presumed to be the rulers in a democracy. Business, he declared, had become too large, and as a consequence, socially irresponsible. His remedies seemed simple enough to achieve—restore sound competition, make administration responsible and efficient, and check the exercise of power. He was never an enemy of capitalism or private property or profit -making. He simply wished to redress the economic and political imbalance of power, and he worked hard to bring about social justice. He did so primarily by arguing cases in the courts, and his name will be forever attached to the new type of lawyer's brief which minimizes legal precedent and relies primarily on sociological, psychological and economic facts in support of an argument.

The Brandeis brief was first used in the case of *Muller* v. *Oregon* [80] in which he marshaled evidence drawn from hundreds of reports of legislative committees, bureaus of statistics, commissioners of hygiene and factory inspectors to prove that long hours were *in fact* dangerous to women's health, safety, and morals. He was of the new school of sociological jurisprudence, but we might point out that such methodology works only in a society that is reasonable, civilized, and genuinely concerned with social justice. President Wilson nominated him to the Supreme Court on 28

January 1916, but he was confirmed on June 1 only after a long, bitter fight in the Senate during which time the privileged classes in America, and more particularly those in Boston, raised false issues about a dedicated American whose ability and integrity were really unimpeachable. He served until 1937 and died in 1941. He must be placed among the Court's great and influential judges.

When Charles Evans Hughes resigned from the Court to accept the Republican nomination for the Presidency, Wilson appointed John H. Clarke of Ohio to the vacancy. Clarke was a bachelor, corporation lawyer and a political associate of Newton D. Baker who had originally recommended him to Wilson for appointment as a federal district judge in 1914 and as a Supreme Court judge two years later. Clarke had made only one major incursion into politics, and that was in 1903 when he opposed Mark Hanna for the Senate and lost. He was, incidentally, among the first to advocate direct election of senators. From a reading of the newspapers of the day one receives the impression that Clarke was a very able man and would have made a fine judge, but he resigned after only two years on the bench to devote full time to persuading America to enter the League of Nations, although one source reports that Clarke told his friends that a reason for his early resignation was the presence of McReynolds whom he could not stand.[81] While on the Court he generally voted to dissolve monopoly and he dissented in both of the child labor cases in which a majority struck down federal regulatory laws. Under Chief Justice White the Court was one of considerably broader vision than it had been under Fuller. Although usually divided, it was occasionally unanimous, and much of the time a majority could agree to uphold federal regulatory measures. It was during this period moreover, that the Court first began to deal with significant civil liberties questions in increasing numbers.

In 1907 Congress enacted the Hours of Service Act which provided that railway employees could not work more than sixteen consecutive hours. The law was challenged on the ground that it went beyond the scope of the power of Congress to regulate commerce as well as depriving both employers and employees of due process of law.[82] For a unanimous Court Hughes wrote the opinion sustaining the law as a proper regulation of commerce in the interest of safety. It was competent, he argued, for Congress to consider and to seek to reduce the dangers to the employees incident to the strain of excessive hours of duty. To the contention that the law interfered with state authority over intrastate commerce, Hughes replied that because those employees who worked intrastate could not be singled out was not a bar to the law. The power of Congress may not be defeated "by the comingling of duties relating to interstate and intrastate operations."

Some of the justices, however, saw the need to distinguish an obvious safety measure from one involving an economic advantage for labor. After an attempt to arbitrate a dispute between the railroads and their employees who had demanded a reduction from a ten- to an eight-hour day, President Wilson, in order to avert a general strike, sponsored the Adamson Act which established the maximum eight-hour law for railroad workers. Shortly after its passage a United States district court held it unconstitutional, but the Supreme Court speaking through the chief justice reversed the lower court and upheld the law. [83] White emphasized the public character of rail transportation and the concomitant right of public regulation. Since the railroads were forbidden to reduce wages below those in effect for the previously longer day until a special commission should observe the eight-hour day and report to the president, the act had the effect of fixing wages. But White argued that given the temporary nature of the wage-fixing, the law did not violate due process. Justice Day dissented, saying he believed that it achieved "the taking of the property of A and giving it to B by legislative fiat." Pitney, Van Devanter and McReynolds held that the law was not a proper regulation of commerce. The following year Chief Justice White joined the dissenters to make up the majority of five that struck down the congressional attempt to regulate child labor. [84] Justice Day for the majority distinguished the line of cases upholding prohibition from commerce of lotteries, impure foods and the white slave traffic on the ground that those transactions had contaminated commerce in some way, but that such could not be said of child labor. The purpose of the law, Day argued, was not to regulate commerce but to prohibit child labor. It was a subterfuge, and furthermore, the statute invaded the reserved powers of the states. If Congress can "regulate matters intrusted to local authority by prohibition of the movement of commodities in interstate commerce, all freedom of commerce will be at an end, and the power of the states over local matters may be eliminated, and thus our system of government be practically destroyed." Justice Holmes wrote a dissent, concurred in by Justices Brandeis, McKenna and Clarke. While it is perfectly true that, constitutionally speaking, precedent held that regulation of commerce included prohibition of articles, Day's point was essentially correct. The evil aimed at had nothing to do with interstate commerce, and the eventual constitutional tying of the most tenuous transactions to interstate commerce did destroy the old style federalism. And it needed to be destroyed. But logic and the past were with the majority whereas the political necessities of the future were plainly seen by the dissenters.

If a majority doggedly stuck to an outdated notion of federalism, they were not completely rigid. After the Fuller Court had invalidated the first Employers Liability Act [85] because it allegedly invaded the sphere of intrastate commerce, a new law was drafted which applied specifically to employees engaged in interstate commerce, and the Court unanimously upheld it. Van Devanter, for the Court, declared that commerce is performed by men and with the help of things, and these men and things are the instruments and agents of commerce. [86]

Another example of judicial permissiveness of congressional power under the commerce clause was the Court's upholding of the Webb-Kenyon Act of 1913. [87] As a result of the prohibition movement Congress, in an attempt to make state prohibition laws effective, forbade the shipment of liquor in interstate commerce into those states that prohibited its manufacture, sale, or even possession. Whether or not the federal law took effect depended upon the laws of the states, a situation that raised the question of invalid delegation of legislative power to the individual states. The Court ruled that the statute did not actually delegate power to the states since Congress had fixed the conditions under which the law took effect, and in this sense, it applied equally to all parts of the United States. Practically speaking this ruling allowed Congress to divest any commodities moving in interstate commerce of their interstate character, thus permitting those states whose laws forbade the sale or use of such commodities to confiscate them at the state line. Permitting the states to regulate was in itself federal regulation.

It was during this period that the Court approved broad powers for the Interstate Commerce Commission, including the power to fix intrastate railroad rates. The commission had found that interstate rates out of Shreveport, Louisiana, to points in Texas were higher than intrastate rates within Texas. The commission ordered the carriers to cease charging higher rates for interstate transportation from Shreveport to points in Texas than it charged for equal distances wholly within the state. The effect of the order was to force carriers to ignore the rates fixed by state law and to adjust to the federal order. In a suit brought by the carriers it was alleged that Congress lacked the power to control intrastate charges, even if to prevent discrimination against interstate traffic. For a majority of seven, Justice Hughes declared that the purpose of the commerce power was to make impossible the evils which had overwhelmed the Confederation, and the fact that carriers are both intra- and interstate does not derogate from the complete and paramount authority of Congress over the latter or preclude national power from being exerted over the former. In Hughes' words, "wherever the interstate and intrastate transactions of carriers are so related that the government of one involves the control of the other, it is Congress and not the state, that is entitled to prescribe the final and dominant rule." [88]

With the significant exception of the child labor case [89] the Court during the period of White's chief justiceship approved national regulatory measures while invalidating state regulations of interstate commerce at the same time, [90] thus affording the vast majority of Congress only meager grounds for complaint. Even the substantive due process bugaboo was minimized as a basis for voiding state police regulations. In three instances Justice Hughes spoke for a unanimous Court upholding state regulatory measures dealing with labor relations. In one, the Court upheld an Iowa law that barred a railroad from setting up as a defense to an action in negligence brought by an employee, any contract of insurance entered into by the employee prior to the injury or an acceptance of a benefit after the injury. [91] In another the Court sustained a state child labor law, [92] and in the third, upheld a California law that forbade the employment of women in selected establishments for more than eight hours per day or forty-eight hours per week.[93] All were attacked by employers on the ground that they denied liberty (of contract) without due process of law. Only in *Coppage* v. *Kansas*[94] did a divided court use the due process clause to invalidate a labor statute. In this instance the law made it a criminal offense for an employer, as a condition of employment, to require an employee to enter into an agreement not to become a member of a labor union while employed. In addition to the standard argument in defense of liberty of contract, Justice Pitney observed that it was not a legitimate exercise of the police power to seek to strengthen labor organizations which "are not public institutions."

Although the bulk of the cases arising under the Civil War amendments up to 1930 involved economic regulation and an allegation of denial of substantive due process, the White Court decided three significant cases involving racial discrimination. In *Bailey* v. *Alabama*[95] the Court invalidated an Alabama statute, the purpose of which was to force Negroes to work out contracts of labor. The law provided that any person, who with intent to injure or defraud, entered into a written contract for the performance of service, and thereby obtained money from his employer, and with like intent failed to perform such service, was guilty of a crime and punishable as in the case of theft. Furthermore, the refusal or failure to perform the service without just cause and without refunding the money was prima facie evidence of the intent to injure or defraud. While the presumption of fraud might be negated by evidence, the law did not permit the employee-defendant to testify that he did not intend fraud. Bailey, a Negro, had agreed to work at twelve dollars per month for a year and received an advance of fifteen dollars. After working shortly over a month, he quit and was then sentenced to a fine of thirty dollars and costs, and in default of payment, to serve in prison at hard labor for 136 days. For the majority, Justice Hughes stated that the law was a violation of the Thirteenth Amendment's prohibition of involuntary servitude. Although the statute had as its purpose the punishment of fraud, Hughes observed, its "natural and inevitable effect is to expose for conviction for crime those who simply fail or refuse to perform contracts for personal service in liquidation of a debt." Not only was the Alabama statute at odds with the Thirteenth Amendment, said Hughes, it was also in direct conflict with an act of Congress of 2 March 1867 forbidding peonage or involuntary servitude.

In *McCabe* v. *Atchison, Topeka & Santa Fe R.R.* [96] the Court, again speaking through Hughes, began to look at segregation with a more critical eye than ever before. Invalidating a state law that authorized intrastate carriers to provide sleeping cars, chair cars and diners for white persons only, Hughes dismissed the argument that lack of demand by Negroes for such accommodations justified the law. While adhering to the doctrine of "separate but equal," the Court stated emphatically that it did not follow that accommodations for the Negro could be dispensed with altogether. In the following year, again in an opinion by Hughes, the Court struck down an Arizona law that had been enacted to protect the white labor market from being undercut by aliens who would work for lower wages. [97] The law required employers of more than five workers within the state to employ not less than eighty percent qualified electors or natural born citizens. In extending the equal protection clause of the Fourteenth Amendment to aliens Hughes reasoned that a state may not deny to lawful inhabitants, because of their race or nationality, the ordinary means of earning a livelihood.

Although the Court began to display a tinge of modern liberalism in its attitude toward equal protection of the laws, such was not the case in its early interpretations of freedom of speech. In a series of three important cases, *Schenck* v. *United States*, [98] *Abrams* v. *United States*, [99] and *Pierce* v. *United States* [100] the Court refused to interpret the First Amendment literally or liberally. In *Schenck* the Court unanimously upheld the Espionage Act of 1917 and the conviction of Charles T. Schenck who had circulated anti-draft leaflets for men eligible for conscription. Schenck had declared that the draft was unconstitutional and urged men to assert their rights and to refuse to comply with conscription orders. In the Court's opinion Justice Holmes declared that the right of free speech was not absolute and that during a war the utterance of things normally acceptable will not be endured. Holmes went on, however, to enunciate the clear and present danger rule as an administrative and judicial test which might determine whether speech or writing was constitutionally permissible. In Holmes' words: "The question in every case is whether the words used are used in such circumstances and are of such a nature as to create a clear and present danger that they will bring about the substantive evils that Congress has a right to prevent. It is a question of proximity and degree."

Involved in the *Abrams* case was the act of Congress of 1918 which made it a felony to "incite mutiny or insubordination in the ranks of the armed forces" or to "utter, print, or publish disloyal . . . or abusive language about the form of government, the Constitution, soldiers and sailors, flag, or uniform of the armed forces, or by word or act support or favor the cause of the German Empire or its allies in the present war, or by word or act oppose the cause of the United States." Jacob Abrams and others had been convicted for publishing pamphlets in which they condemned the government for sending troops to Russia in 1918 and called for a general strike of munitions workers. Again the Court found no violation of First Amendment rights when it upheld both the statute and the conviction of Abrams, but Justice Holmes, joined by Brandeis, dissented in a notable display of rhetoric. He believed that the government had failed to show that the pamphlet had any immediate effect upon the war effort or that it had been Abrams' purpose to have any. In an attempt to establish the clear and present danger rule as a protective device, Holmes declared:

[W]e should be eternally vigilant against attempts to check the expression of opinions that we loathe and believe to be fraught with death, unless they so imminently threaten immediate interference with the lawful and pressing purposes of the law that an immediate check is required to save the country . . . Only the emergency that makes it immediately dangerous to leave the correction of evil counsels to time warrants making any exception to the sweeping command, 'Congress shall make no law abridging the freedom of speech.'

In the *Pierce* case the Court once again voted to uphold the conviction of the author of a socialist pamphlet attacking conscription and the war even though there was no showing of intent to interfere with the draft or any evidence that the pamphlet had any effect on the war. Justice Pitney, speaking for seven members of the Court, observed that the pamphlet might "have a tendency to cause insubordination, disloyalty, and refusal of duty in the military and naval forces of the United States." This time it was Justice Brandeis who spoke for himself and Holmes, urging that clear and present danger ought to be proved, and that mere bad tendency was not enough. In other cases growing out of the war the Court consistently upheld the government when personal or property rights were at stake. [101]

Two remaining decisions of more than passing interest were handed down prior to the death of Chief Justice White. In one the Court for the first time faced an attack on the constitutionality of a constitutional amendment. [102] The Eighteenth Amendment which prohibited the manufacture, transportation and sale of alcoholic beverages in the United States was proclaimed a part of the Constitution on 29 January 1919 and became the subject of litigation soon afterward. There were two points at issue. First, it was alleged that the amendment had been improperly ratified since the vote for proposal in Congress had been two-thirds of those present and voting and not two-thirds of the entire membership. Second, it was contended that the control of intoxicating beverages was a state matter and that the invasion of the state's powers destroyed the Tenth Amendment, and thereby fundamentally altered the federal union. Van Devanter, for the Court, made no attempt to analyze the substantive points but simply stated that proposal of an amendment by two-thirds of a quorum satisfied Article V of the Constitution, and that the amendment was binding on the courts.

The second case also involved a fundamental question with far-reaching implications: the nature of the treaty-making power. [103] At issue in the case was the validity of the Migratory Bird Act of 1918 and a treaty with Great Britain of 1916. By the terms of the treaty the two countries had agreed to protect certain species of migratory birds that moved back and forth between the United States and Canada. The state of Missouri argued that the subject matter of the treaty and the statute was not within the enumerated powers of Congress, and therefore invaded the reserved powers of the states. Missouri seemed to have a tenable argument since the earlier Migratory Bird Act of 1913, which had attempted to accomplish the same result in the absence of a treaty, had been invalidated by a lower court. Justice Holmes pointed out that while acts of Congress must be made in pursuance of the Constitution, treaties are made under authority of the United States, and that the limits to the treaty-making power were somewhat broader than those restricting the ordinary law-making power. Treaty-making, he declared, must be construed in the light of America's national development.

The period from 1882-1921 is not one in which the Court can be said to have maintained a consistent posture on constitutional questions, although prior to Fuller's death the tendency of the justices was to find reasons for striking down economic regulatory measures, state or national. But it is interesting that even at the height of the Court's "carnival of unconstitutionality," even after *Pollock, Debs* and *Knight*, there was no sustained attack on the Court in Congress, but merely a feeble thrust here and there. Senator Wilkinson Call of Florida introduced a resolution to create a committee of seven senators to inquire into the imprisonment of Debs for an "alleged contempt of court" and to recommend such legislation as shall be necessary for the just enforcement of law and the "protection of citizens from arbitrary and offensive exercise of judicial power." [104] Senator Marion Butler of North Carolina, on at least three different occasions, introduced a resolution to amend the Constitution relating to direct taxes, [105] suggesting that the Court had perverted the Constitution [106] and that the income tax decision was "most monstrous." [107] Butler also proposed a constitutional amendment that would have altered Article III so as to require that Supreme Court justices, and those of the other federal courts, be elected by popular vote, the chief to be chosen by the entire country, and the others to be elected from the circuits. [108] There was no visible support for a popularly elected judiciary.

A strong component of the political theory of the Progressive movement held that judicial review was not only unsound—an oligarchic and undemocratic element in an otherwise democratic system—but also that it was never intended to be a part of American constitutional arrangements anyway. All the old arguments against the Supreme Court's exercise of the power were raised again and all were answered again. The debate took place, however, outside the legislative halls, and it was carried on by lawyers like Louis B. Boudin and Louis Brandeis, constitutional historians and scholars like Charles Warren, Andrew C. McLaughlin, Edward S. Corwin and Charles A. Beard, and by Progressive politicians like Theodore Roosevelt and Senators Albert Beveridge, Norris, La Follette and Borah. As in the past those who attacked the system were, at bottom, unhappy over the outcome of particular cases, and this is manifestly clear in the speeches and writings of the time. Senator Borah wrote an article in the *New York Times* in which he suggested the Court would be more likely to have popular approval if at least seven judges concurred that an act of Congress was unconstitutional. [109] The intrinsic merits of the proposal aside, it became obvious when Borah listed some 5-4 decisions of the past such as the *Pollock* and *Lochner* cases, that the requirements of an extraordinary majority on questions of unconstitutionality would have produced the result that Borah desired.

Similar in tone to the Borah article was a speech given by Senator Robert M. La Follette to a political rally of 14 thousand people in Madison Square Garden in 1924. [110] Amidst the political oratory and invective La Follette enunciated the Progressive proposals including "restriction of the veto power of federal judges over Congressional action" and "election of federal judges for fixed terms." He also suggested that the Constitution should be amended to provide that Congress, by reenacting a statute, would make such a measure effective over a judicial veto. Like Borah, he argued that the 5-4 decision was a menace to democracy, and that such 5-4 decisions as in the *Income Tax* case, the *Standard Oil* and *American Tobacco Trust* cases, *Hammer* v. *Dagenhart*, *Bailey* v. *Drexel Furniture Co..*, and *Adkins* v. *Children's Hospital* are always "on the side of the wealthy and powerful and against the poor and weak."

But even as the debate raged, the Congress moved to broaden the basis of appeals to the federal courts and, in a sense, increased the power of the Supreme Court. Under the Judiciary Act of 1789 appeals could be taken to the Supreme Court from a state court only when a claim of federal right had been denied, but there was no appeal beyond the highest court of a state when a claim of federal right was sustained. After the due process clause of the

Fourteenth Amendment became a barrier to some forms of state regulation, an interesting problem arose. If a state legislature attempted to protect labor in some way and an employer raised due process as a bar to the state legislation, the state courts might strike down the legislation as a denial of due process of law, thus sustaining the employer's claim of a denial of a federal right. But for the state and the employee, whom public policy was attempting to protect, the state court was the end of the line. The situation became critical in 1911 when the New York Court of Appeals held the New York state employer's liability act unconstitutional [111] and the state courts of Washington [112] upheld similar legislation. In practice, then, the federal guarantee of due process meant one thing in one state and the opposite in another. Congress remedied the situation by an act of 1914 that permitted the Supreme Court to accept cases on writs of certiorari from state courts in which the highest court of the state had sustained a federal right as well as in those in which a federal right had been denied. The Supreme Court ultimately upheld the concept of employers' liability, but more important, the Congress had actually expanded the jurisdiction of the Court even as it criticized much of the Court's work.

6. Taft & Hughes:
The Road to a Major Crisis

IN relative terms the Supreme Court seemed insignificant during the 1920s. In part this was because national attention was focused elsewhere, and in part, it was because the Court under Taft was in the mainstream of a conservative trend. After a slight downturn in the economy in 1921 the nation embarked upon a period of unprecedented economic expansion, and the national government under the prevailing *laissez faire* philosophy generally remained passive while corporate enterprise had its way. And all three departments cooperated to validate Calvin Coolidge's declaration that the United States "is a business country and it wants a business government."[1] In Congress there was a general decline after two decades of progressive and regulatory legislation. While progressivism was not dead and in fact would have a vengeful resurgence in the 1930s, it was impotent for the moment. Presidents Harding, Coolidge and Hoover were deliberate stand-patters, believing in unhampered corporate enterprise, and the Supreme Court's composition was such that a probusiness majority could be predicted on any major test of government versus business.

President Harding appointed four conservative, property-oriented lawyers to the Court: William Howard Taft and George Sutherland in 1922, and Pierce Butler and Edward T. Sanford in 1923. In most of the litigation pitting government against business these men joined Justices McReynolds, Van Devanter and McKenna to form a majority in favor of business. Holmes and Brandeis were often in dissent and, after McKenna's death in 1925, were joined by Harlan F. Stone.

It will be recalled that President Taft had appointed Edward Douglass White Chief Justice at the advanced age of sixty-five when Charles Evans Hughes, then forty-eight, seemed the logical choice. We have speculated that since Taft coveted the office of chief justice, he hoped that he might have a chance at it after his retirement from the Presidency, and as it turned out, the scheme, if it were that, worked perfectly. Chief Justice White died on 19 May 1921 and to no one's surprise President Harding offered Taft the job immediately. In fact Taft in a postelection talk with Harding reportedly told the president that White had said that he was holding the office for him and would give it back to a Republican administration. [2] No one could argue that Taft was not qualified for the office, for he came to it after forty years experience in public life, including having been president of the United States. In 1887, at the age of twenty-nine, he had been appointed to the Superior Court of Ohio to fill a vacancy and was subsequently elected to a full term. In 1889 President Harrison chose him for the post of solicitor general and three years later elevated him to a federal circuit court. Taft left the bench in 1900 to accept President McKinley's offer to become chief commissioner to the Philippine Islands, a post which he enjoyed, for during his tenure he twice refused what he wanted most, an appointment to the Supreme Court. Reluctantly he agreed to serve as President Roosevelt's secretary of war from which he went on to the presidency in 1908. Taft was a supreme conservative in his view of the American system, which included a strong belief in private enterprise but also a belief in using judicial review to shape the law to meet new situations. In his day, as in John Marshall's, judicial activism went hand in hand with conservatism. In the words of T.S. Pringle's biography, "To Taft, clearly, the difference between conservatism and radicalism was the difference between right and wrong, between the known and the unknown, between the sound and the unsound." [3] In Taft's view personal liberty and private property were all of a piece, were "indispensable to any possible useful progress of society," and like all respectable conservatives he believed strongly in stability—stability in society and stability in judicial decisions. [4] He strove for unanimity—"massing the Court" as he called it—during his leadership, although he occasionally wrote a dissent himself (twenty in all).

When Taft took over the Court it was badly divided and was far behind in its calendar, and the chief justice met both problems with success, moderate in the former, fairly complete in the latter. By the end of 1922 the Court had broken all records in disposing of cases and had reduced the time period between the filing and the hearing of a case by three months. In spite of Taft's constant pressure on the justices to work harder they could not decongest the docket. Litigation had increased rapidly because of prohibition and the income tax laws, but more important, there were more lawsuits as a result of regulatory legislation enacted under Progressive leadership, including, among others, those laws dealing with safety appliances, food and drugs, meat inspection, narcotics, white slavery, packers and stockyards, automobile theft, kidnapping, and grain futures. On 18 February 1922 the chief justice delivered a speech in which he analysed the problem. When the Court adjourned in June 1921, Taft said, there were 343 undisposed cases and now, seven months later, the number of cases had increased to 516. When the Court opened the October term in 1925 the number had again increased to 533. As a direct result of Taft's efforts Congress enacted two major pieces of legislation dealing with the judiciary, one in 1922 and the other in 1925. The first act created more judges for the lower courts than the original Judiciary Act of 1789. In addition it gave the federal judicial system a sense of direction and a much needed administrative unity by creating the Conference of Senior Circuit Judges to advise Congress on legislation governing the judiciary and to promote effective standards of judicial administration in the lower federal courts. The Judiciary Act of 1925 was called the Judges' Bill since its basic ideas were those of Taft and his brethren on the Supreme Court. Justice Van Devanter wrote the final draft, but the entire Court had been consulted and concurred in the proposal. By acquiring broader discretionary powers of review the Court would now be permitted to conserve its time for handling cases of national significance. Much of what the Court had been doing was to be left to the state courts and the circuit courts of appeal. Specifically, most decisions of the federal courts of appeals were made reviewable in the Supreme Court only by writ of certiorari and most direct appeals from the district courts to the Supreme Court were abolished. Only two classes of cases could be taken from the state courts to the Supreme Court as a matter of right: (1) when the validity of a state statute was challenged on federal constitutional grounds and its validity was sustained; and (2) when a federal statute or treaty was invoked and its validity was denied by a state court.

Thus Taft not only led the Court in the sense that he motivated the individual justices to become more productive, but also he was able to convince Congress to enact legislation that would permit a more efficient use of the Court's time. In terms of sheer hard work, Taft set the pace for his colleagues. He rose daily at 5:15 and began work at six o'clock. At eight o'clock he had breakfast and then worked for an hour and three quarters before walking to the Capitol. After the Court closed at four-thirty he worked until ten with an hour out for dinner at seven. His biographer suggests that he worked far too zealously and paid the penalty of impaired health, but for the chief justice there was no easy way. As he put it, "I am never free from the burden of feeling that whenever I attempt to do anything else I am taking time from my judicial work. The exhausting character of it everyone testifies to. I was talking with my brother Brandeis yesterday, and he spoke of the comment that Judge Hughes made on the matter. He had been through a presidential campaign, and he has had as active a practice at the bar as anybody possible since he left the bench. He had been governor, but he said that he never found anything that took the 'gimp' out of him as service on the Supreme bench." [5] Despite Taft's somewhat dogmatic conservatism, and it grew more so as he became older, his innate ability combined with a love of judicial power and a real learning in the law surely place him close to Marshall and Taney, where no other chief could be ranked prior to Taft's tenure. And he was flexible enough to affirm much legislation that expanded the powers of the national government.

During July, 1921, William Howard Taft wrote to George Sutherland, "I look forward to having you on the bench with me. I know, as you do, that the President intends to put you there." [6] When John H. Clarke resigned on 5 September 1922 President Harding appointed Sutherland to the Court, and he was confirmed the same day. George Sutherland was born at Stoney Stratford in

Buckinghamshire, England, in 1862. He was the first justice in over 100 years to be of foreign birth.[7] His father joined the Church of Jesus Christ of Latter Day Saints and emigrated in 1863 to Springville in what is now the state of Utah. Since his father was never more than a moderate economic success, George worked hard as a youth on the family farm while receiving a rudimentary public education from McGuffey's readers and Webster's spelling books. He left school at the age of twelve in order to earn a living, first taking a job in a clothing store in Salt Lake City, later becoming an agent for the Wells-Fargo Company. In 1879 he entered Brigham Young Academy in Provo and came under the influence of its president, Karl G. Maeser, a powerful Mormon leader who indoctrinated Sutherland with two ideas that he never forgot—that the United States Constitution was a divinely inspired instrument, and that Herbert Spencer ranked with Plato, Aristotle, Bacon, Newton, Leibnitz and Kant as one of the great philosophers of all time.

Spencer's social Darwinism, the concept of the survival of the fittest in a *laissez faire* economic system, became the anchor for virtually all of Sutherland's social, political and economic ideas. Sutherland went on to study law with the greatest constitutional lawyer (Spencerian also) of the day, Thomas M. Cooley, and to practice law first with his father and later with Samuel R. Thurman who was to become chief justice of the Utah Supreme Court. He also began to take an interest in politics in the 1880s and 1890s as he helped to organize the Republican Club of Central Utah and attended the Republican National Convention of 1892. In 1896 he was elected to Utah's first state legislature, four years later was chosen Utah's lone representative to the national House, and in 1905 was elected to the United States Senate. Although he defended the Supreme Court's position in the income tax case, he supported the eight-hour day for federal government workers, the Children's Bureau, Postal Saving Banks and Workmen's Compensation for interstate employees. Essentially, Sutherland's Spencerian orientation, however, kept him in a conservative mold, and he became a national figure as he opposed Woodrow Wilson's domestic reforms and accepted frequent invitations to address powerful conservative groups, including bar associations, chambers of commerce and trade associations.

Although he was held to be one of the ablest men in the Senate by friend and foe alike, he was defeated for reelection in 1916 after having served two terms. He practiced law in Washington, D.C. until Harding nominated him to the Supreme Court in 1922 where he remained until his retirement in 1938. He died in 1942.

George Sutherland was, like Taft, a *laissez faire* conservative who saw great evils in the control of the individual by government since in his scheme of values the ultimate good was human freedom and any diminution of it was bad. Therefore, government restraint must be kept to a minimum, and the most effective way of doing so in the American system was through judicial power. He was, perhaps, too rigid, too "intellectually parochial" and so immersed in the Spencerian philosophy that he could not transcend his own experience.[8] In spite of his bias he was a judge of great power and learning, and in the thirties was the intellectual leader of the conservative wing of the Court. Moreover, some of his opinions, particularly those in foreign affairs, continued to have a vital influence on the American system. He will be remembered also for his enlightened views on the administration of justice, for it was his opinion in *Powell* v. *Alabama*[9] that laid the foundation for the contemporary revolution in the law of criminal justice.

President Harding's third appointee to the Court was Pierce Butler of Minnesota, a Roman Catholic, self-taught lawyer, member of a politically inactive family and citizen of a state that never before had produced a Supreme Court justice. Pierce Butler was born in a log cabin near Northfield, Minnesota, on St. Patrick's Day, 1866, the sixth of nine children. Butler's parents, Patrick and Mary Ann, had left Ireland after the potato famine of 1848 and were married in 1855 in Galena, Illinois. Later they acquired a homestead in Dakota County, Minnesota Territory. Pierce went to a one-room schoolhouse and attended Carleton College, just five miles from his home, prior to studying law with the firm of Pinch and Twohy in St. Paul where he was eventually admitted to the bar. Throughout his life Butler was intensely devoted to the United States, to the Catholic Church and, having matured on Cooley's *Constitutional Limitations* and other social Darwinist-oriented writings, to *laissez faire* economics. His public statements consistently followed the same pattern of values—patriotism, morality and *laissez faire*. Voting in his first presidential election in 1888, he cast his vote for Cleveland and remained a Democrat thereafter. He entered politics briefly at the age of twenty-six when he was elected county attorney of Ramsey County, but after serving two terms returned to private practice while remaining a behind-the-scenes political adviser to Minnesota governors. He eventually won a reputation as one of the country's greatest trial lawyers. Although a formidable antagonist, particularly tough in cross examination, he had a good sense of humor and was well liked by his fellow lawyers. An unfriendly critic suggests that the "secret of his success was a brutal, domineering intimidation of witnesses [with] . . . no charm or intellectual quality about his work, only shrewd, driving energy."[10] Butler argued the *Minnesota Rate Cases* in 1912 and although he lost, Justice Hughes said that his brief was "one of the ablest, most comprehensive and most careful briefs ever submitted to this court."[11]

On the advice of many people, including Attorney General Harry M. Daugherty, Chief Justice Taft, and Justice Van Devanter, Harding named Pierce Butler to the Court on 22 November 1922 and he took his seat on 2 January 1923. Senator La Follette, on the basis of Butler's economic views, led the fight against confirmation, but eventually the Senate approved the nomination by a vote of 61-8 with twenty-seven abstentions. On the bench Butler was more sensitive than his colleagues to questions of procedural due process, but on substantive issues of free speech he voted against the individual in over two-thirds of the cases in which he participated.[12] He would not, for example, sustain the civil liberties claims of Bland, MacIntosh, Schwimmer, Gitlow, Abrams or Pierce. He has been called a "slow and ponderous thinker" whose decisions were "'dull and uninspiring,"[13] and characterized as a man whose world was "of either-or, of black or white, a world in which principle could never be sacrificed to expediency."[14] During Taft's headship Butler was a helpful ally in the judicial struggle against those who would alter the nation's economy through government regulation, but in the thirties his rigidity, and surely his principles, pushed him out of the mainstream of American economic and political, and subsequently constitutional thought.

Harding's fourth and final appointee to the Court was Edward T. Sanford of Tennessee, an able but colorless middle-of-the-roader who left no permanent mark on the Court's history. Sanford was born in Knoxville of a wealthy Connecticut father and French Swiss mother who gave him every educational advantage. He graduated first in his class from the University of Tennessee, and was one of the editors of the *Harvard Law Review*, graduating from the Harvard Law School in 1889. After practicing law in Knoxville for twenty years he was appointed assistant attorney general of the United States in 1907 where he served under McReynolds. The following year he was named to the federal district court in Tennessee where he labored until 1922 when, upon the resignation of Justice Pitney, he was elevated to the Supreme Court. Although an economic conservative, he saw the necessity for competition and voted consistently to enforce the anti-trust laws, which placed him in dissent in some of the Sherman Act cases, notably *Maple Flooring Manufacturing Association* v. *United States* [15] and *Cement Manufacturing Protective Association* v. *United States*. [16] He voted for the government in the well known *Gitlow* and *Whitney* cases involving freedom of speech, but against it in *Fiske* v. *Kansas* [17] in which he wrote the opinion holding that the Kansas Syndicalism Act was not applicable to the Industrial Workers of the World. He also dissented along with Holmes and Brandeis in the *Schwimmer* case. [18]

The last judge to serve under Taft and later to become chief Justice himself was a Coolidge appointee, Harlan Fiske Stone of New York. Stone was born in Chesterfield, New Hampshire, on 11 October 1872, a direct descendant of Captain Peter Stone, Revolutionary soldier, and the first of the Stone to settle in Chesterfield. Having resolved that their children should enjoy the best possible educational opportunities, Stone's parents moved to the college town of Amherst, Massachusetts, in 1874. Stone grew up in Amherst and received all his pre-legal, formal education there, and also acquired "enduring qualities of mind and heart—independence, self-reliance, sound judgment, a sense of civic responsibility, love of freedom." [19] He attended Massachusetts Agricultural College (now the University of Massachusetts) for just short of two years, having been dismissed for disorderly conduct such as roughing up a professor during a general student fracas in the chapel. Although Amherst College had a rule against admitting any student not in good standing at another institution, Stone gained admission to the class of 1894 after a direct appeal to the president. An able student, he acquitted himself with distinction. His first job was teaching school in Newburyport, Massachusetts, a job that he later said he liked so much that he "came near never leaving it." [20] Yet he remained there for only one year as he was so strongly pulled by the desire to study law. He was graduated from Columbia Law School in 1898, and set out on a long and successful legal career.

For twenty-five years Stone combined two professions as he practiced and taught law in New York City. For thirteen of the twenty-five he was Dean of the Columbia Law School. He accepted Coolidge's appointment as attorney general in 1924 and became an associate justice of the Supreme Court a year later. President Roosevelt promoted him to chief justice in 1941. Constitutional law had not been his specialty either in teaching or in his law practice, and he had, in fact, argued only one case before the United States Supreme Court prior to joining it. Unlike the other Harding-Coolidge appointees to the Court, Stone was not a hidebound conservative. But the terms "conservative" or "liberal" are not applicable to Stone in any event. He may be understood only with reference to the concept of judicial self-restraint: the idea that there is a distinction between judgment and will, between the desirability or wisdom of legislation and its constitutionality. Strongly adhering to this principle, Stone was often in dissent from 1925 until 1937. He believed that his conservative brethren simply equated regulatory economic legislation with unconstitutionality, and after 1937 he was at odds with the liberal or left wingers of the Court who, in Stone's view, sought to implant their personal ideas in the Constitution. At the end of his twenty-one years on the Court he was characterized as a "careful and wise judge, who after two industrious decades has left the mark of wisdom on almost every type of case which comes before the Supreme Court." [21] One biographer gives this succinct estimate of Stone:

He took seriously the 'aphorisms of his trade.' This meant thorough probing of ambiguous statutes for the intent of the legislator; it meant according legislation he distrusted the full estimate of the 'presumption of constitutionality.' Nothing delighted Stone more than to take a morass of conflicting decisions, sort them all out, and then restate the rule with reasons having solid substance. His skillful trimming, elaborating, and blending of the Brandeis and Holmes approach makes him one of the great creative judges of our time. [22]

Serving with Taft, then, during his eight years as chief were McKenna, Day, Pitney and Clarke, all sitting briefly, and Holmes, Van Devanter, McReynolds, Brandeis, Sutherland, Butler, Sanford and Stone who were with Taft during all or a major part of his time on the Court. In addition to handing down some miscellaneous decisions of some importance, the Court dealt essentially with three areas of constitutional interpretation: the commerce clause, economic due process, and civil liberties cases in increasing numbers.

Regulation of Commerce

Among the first cases the Taft Court was to hear under the commerce clause was *Railroad Commission of Wisconsin v. C.B. and Q. R.R.* [23] in which the chief justice, for a unanimous Court, went beyond past decisions to uphold the Transportation Act of 1920 and to approve the control of intrastate railroad rates by the Interstate Commerce Commission. Under the existing situation in Wisconsin a passenger traveling between two points within the state paid two cents a mile as contrasted with better than three and a half cents a mile paid by persons bound for points outside the state. In approving the upward revision of the intrastate rate by the I.C.C. Taft declared that it was the duty of the commission under the act to secure fair income for the railroad, and if intrastate rates were too low, the road would need to charge higher interstate rates to secure fair total income. Said Taft:

Under the Constitution, interstate and intrastate commerce are ordinarily subject to regulation by different sovereignties, yet when they are so mingled together that the supreme authority, the nation, cannot exercise complete, effective

control over interstate commerce without incidental regulation of intrastate commerce, such incidental regulation is not
an invasion of State authority. [24]

After this decision the commission, for all practical purposes, was
able to control all railroad rates since the old legal distinction
between intra- and interstate regulation was no longer a valid one.

On the surface the decision is in the spirit of nationalism and
national regulation of the economy, but one wonders what this
conservative Court would have done had the commission equalized
the rates by ordering the interstate charge lowered. It was
relatively easy to uphold national regulation when it redounded to
the profit of the railroads, but in general the Taft court was willing
to uphold the federal government when regulations involved
goods, persons, or transactions across state lines. For example, in
Stafford v. *Wallace*, the chief justice wrote the opinion upholding
the Packers and Stockyards Act of 1922 which intended to break
up monopoly price fixing and restore free competition in the meat
packing business. Referring to the *Swift* case, [25] in which the
Sherman Act had been held applicable to the meat packers, Taft
emphasized the "stream of commerce" doctrine or "flow theory."
He pointed out that the stockyards were not a place of "rest or
final destination," that they were "but a throat through which the
current flows," and that the transactions were "only incident to
this current from the West to the East and from one State to
another." Taft could not mass the entire Court; Justice McReynolds dissented, and in a similar case using similar reasoning in
which the Grain Futures Act was upheld, Sutherland joined
McReynolds in dissent. [26] Both cases were important precedents
for the Court when, fifteen years later, it extended the meaning of
the commerce clause to include labor relations. [27] Taft was able to
produce unanimity when he wrote the opinion upholding the
recapture provisions of the Transportation Act of 1920. [28] Under
the law the I.C.C. might divert earnings of a railroad in excess of
six percent to other roads whose earnings were less. The
Dayton-Goose Railway Company of Texas had earned $33
thousand above the six percent limitation in 1921, and was
ordered to place half of the sum in a reserve fund, and to remit the
other half under the law. Taft distinguished between profits

earned from investment in an ordinary business as opposed to the profits of one dedicated to public service, declaring that in the latter one "cannot expect either high or speculative dividends" but only a fair and reasonable return. Recapture, he said, was not confiscation because, by law, recaptured earnings had never been the road's property at all.

A year later, unanimity prevailed again as Taft wrote the opinion sustaining the Motor Vehicle Theft Act of 1919. [29] In this instance the chief justice drew upon the pure food and white slave cases as precedents, even though the theft of an automobile took place before any movement in commerce across state lines. The child labor case [30] was ignored, but in the future it would become impossible to separate conditions under which goods were manufactured from all other transactions that took place prior to entering commerce but which then used the channels of commerce to perpetuate a social evil. But the Taft Court continued to show its bias in behalf of business and against labor when it upheld an injunction against a stonecutters' union that had instructed its locals not to work on stone which had been cut by nonunion labor. [31] In spite of the fact that the stone had ceased to move in interstate commerce, and that the boycotts complained of were local in nature, the Court held that the refusal to work was an interference with the stream of commerce, and since commerce was directly affected, the union was violating the anti-trust laws. Thus, conditions of manufacturing were recognized as a part of commerce when they adversely affected the manufacturer, but not when they harmed the laborer. It was only a question of time before the law would be held to cut both ways.

Economic Due Process

Although the Court, including its most conservative members, could agree much of the time that national regulation of the economy was necessary, the justices could not agree on the validity of state regulatory measures. With a hard consistency the Court struck down law after law. It voided a Pennsylvania statute forbidding the mining of coal in such a way as to damage surface habitations, reasoning that the statute impaired the value of property in mines and so violated due process. [32] The Court also held violative of due process a Kansas statute that declared the food, clothing, fuel, transportation, and public utility businesses to be affected with a public interest and thereby vested a commission with authority to settle wage disputes in these industries by fixing wages and other terms of employment. [33] The Court declared unconstitutional a Nebraska statute fixing a standard of weight for bread, [34] a Pennsylvania law prohibiting the use of shoddy in the manufacture of mattresses, [35] a New York statute regulating the resale price of theater tickets (Holmes, Brandeis and Stone dissenting), [36] a New Jersey statute licensing employment agencies and empowering a state commissioner of labor to refuse a license if the proposed schedule of fees was excessive, [37] and a Tennessee statute authorizing a state commissioner of finance to fix gasoline prices. [38] In all of the above cases the businesses to be regulated were held not to be "affected with a public interest" and therefore beyond the scope of the state police power. Although generally Congress was not restrained by substantive due process, due in part to its positive constitutional power over commerce, an exception was made in *Adkins* v. *Children's Hospital* in 1923. [39] Congress, legislating in the manner of a state rather than nationally over all the states, had enacted a minimum wage law for the District of Columbia in which a board was given the power to fix minimum wages for women and children. In line with its decisions invalidating state laws dealing with price and wage fixing, the Court declared the law unconstitutional. Sutherland, for a majority of five, admitted that there was no absolute freedom of contract, but maintained, nevertheless, that freedom was the general rule, and restraint the exception. In a somewhat confusing opinion, Sutherland argued as follows: first, the *Lochner* case [40] in which the Court held that New York's attempt to limit hours of labor in bake shops was controlling; second that *Bunting* v. *Oregon* [41] and *Muller* v. *Oregon*, [42] both of which had upheld regulation of hours (in the latter case exclusively for women), were inapposite since they dealt with hours, not wages, and besides *Muller* differed from *Lochner* in that it involved only women. The rule that Sutherland fashioned was: all regulation of wages is bad; regulation of hours for men is also bad, but regulation of hours for women may be permissible, for there is a connection between a woman's health and the number of hours she works. The last point was barely conceded as Sutherland suggested that the differences between men and women "have come now almost, if not quite, to the vanishing point." Even the conservative Taft could not accept the opinion, and he joined the dissenters, however reluctantly. He suggested that *Lochner* had been overruled *sub silentio* because of *Bunting*, and furthermore he saw no valid distinction between fixing minimum wages and regulating maximum hours.

Individual Liberties

While the Court in the twenties used a rigid concept of due process of law as a barrier to economic regulation by the states, it was inconsistent in its application of due process to other forms of state interference with individual liberty. Probably the most significant doctrinal development during the period was the absorption of freedom of speech and press of the First Amendment into the due process clause of the Fourteenth in *Gitlow* v. *New York* [43] in 1925. Although the Court upheld Benjamin Gitlow's conviction under the New York criminal anarchy act, declaring the statute a reasonable limitation since it punished behavior inherently unlawful under a constitutional government, the rule that a part of the Bill of Rights was a restriction on state as well as national power was revolutionary, and as it became regular constitutional practice to limit the states through the Bill of Rights, the American federal system underwent considerable alteration. But even prior to *Gitlow* the Court twice used due process in behalf of personal liberty. It declared unconstitutional a Nebraska statute that prohibited the teaching of modern foreign languages to children in the first eight grades. Justice McReynolds for a majority of seven (Holmes and Sutherland dissenting) declared that the liberty guaranteed by the Fourteenth Amendment included the right of parents to educate children, within reason, according to their own conscience. [44] And in *Pierce* v. *Society of Sisters* [45] the Court invalidated an Oregon statute requiring children between the ages of eight and sixteen to attend public school. Although reasoning that parents had the right to raise children as they saw fit, McReynolds added that the law destroyed property rights in private schools. In line with *Gitlow* the Court heard a free speech case originating in California in which a criminal syndicalism law was under attack. [46] The law, which punished advocacy of crime, sabotage, or terrorism as a means of accomplishing political change, or a change in industrial ownership, was upheld since the First Amendment, said Sutherland, "does not confer an absolute right to speak" or "unbridled license," and the state may punish those who abuse freedom by "utterances inimical to the public welfare."

Cases involving alleged violation of procedural rights in criminal actions had not begun to come before the Supreme Court in large numbers until the 1930s, but the Taft court set several enduring precedents in this area in a small number of cases. It held that a mob-dominated trial was a violation of due process, and more important, that a federal court might determine independently the facts of a state criminal trial, [47] thus setting the stage for more appeals from the state courts to the federal courts in criminal cases. It abolished an unfair procedure by invalidating an Ohio law that permitted magistrates in courts of lowest jurisdiction to share in fines paid by prohibition violators. [48] A judge, said the Court, who profited from a conviction could not be impartial. Taft formulated two rules involving the Fourth Amendment. In one, which remains unchanged today, the Court ruled that the Fourth Amendment did not bar the search of a moving automobile without a warrant if probable cause exists. [49] In the other, Taft maintained that the Fourth Amendment did not prohibit wire tapping. [50] He went back to the common law to show that admissibility of evidence was not affected by the illegality of its acquisition, but in any event there was no searching and no seizing.

Rounding out the description of the Taft Court are three cases, each in a different constitutional category and yet having in common an alleged abuse of power. After the Court had declared the Child Labor Law of 1916 unconstitutional because, among other reasons, the commerce clause did not cover the subject matter, Congress, using its power of taxation as its instrument, enacted the Child Labor Law of 1919. Under the terms of this law a ten percent tax was levied upon the net profits of any firm employing children. For a majority Taft invalidated the law, first, because it was an attempt to regulate a matter reserved to the states; and second, because on its face the tax was a penalty rather than a revenue raising measure. [51] Said Taft:

> The good sought in unconstitutional legislation is an insidious feature because it leads citizens and legislators of good purpose to promote it without thought of the serious breach it will make in the ark of our covenant, or the harm which will come from breaking down recognized standards. . . . But in the act before us, the presumption of validity cannot prevail, because the proof of the contrary is found in the very face of its provisions. . . . To give such magic to the word 'tax' would be to break down all constitutional limitation of the powers of Congress and completely wipe out the sovereignty of the states. [52]

In another case the Court upheld the grant-in-aid principle, a device whereby the national government appropriated funds for social services of various kinds administered by the states. At the same time the Court formulated the rule that a taxpayer has no standing to challenge the spending power of Congress. [53] The case involved the Sheppard-Towner Maternity Act which created a cooperative federal-state program to reduce infant and maternal mortality. Both the state of Massachusetts and a citizen of the state sought to enjoin the operation of the law, and both were dismissed on jurisdictional grounds. The former was held to be an invalid attempt on the part of the state to act as a representative of its citizens against the national government, and the latter an invalid taxpayer's suit. Sutherland declared that a taxpayer's interest in "the moneys of the Treasury . . . is shared with millions of others; is comparatively minute and indeterminable; and the effect upon future taxation, of any payment out of the funds so remote, fluctuating and uncertain, that no basis is afforded for an appeal to the preventive powers of a court of equity."

The final decision of importance dealt with an issue close to Taft's heart, that of presidential authority. It involved the case of Frank Myers, a postmaster who had been appointed by President Wilson in 1917 and removed by him in 1920. [54] Since Wilson had not obtained senatorial consent to the removal, which a law of

1876 required, Myers brought suit, arguing that he had been illegally removed. Chief Justice Taft, for a majority of six, upheld the president, relying on two arguments, one historical, the other practical. He pointed out that after a long debate in 1789 Congress voted to make the secretary of state removable by the president without the consent of the Senate. Then Taft argued that since the president was charged with the faithful execution of the laws, he could not carry out this constitutional mandate unless he had complete control over his subordinates. Theoretically, Taft is correct, but one might make a distinction between a cabinet level officer and a postmaster. McReynolds, Brandeis and Holmes, in dissent, had no doubt that Congress might require senatorial consent to the removal of some officials.

Taft's health began to fail in 1929 and he resigned from the Court on 3 February 1930. He was replaced as chief justice by Charles Evans Hughes who was destined to lead the Court through one of its most difficult periods. Fundamentally, the Court crisis of the 1930s had its origin in the Wall Street crash of 1929 and the ensuing economic depression which soon took on catastrophic proportions. From 1929 to 1932 national income dropped from $81 billion to $40 billion as salaries and wages declined from $49 billion to $29 billion. Similarly production fell from an index of 125 to 59, and concomitantly unemployment reached 15 million as businesses and banks went bankrupt. [55] President Hoover simply applied old techniques to a situation that required something new and daring. In fact, by concentrating on balancing the budget and retaining the gold standard, the government contributed to further deflation in an already overdeflated economy. It was in the midst of the worst domestic crisis since the Civil War that Hoover designated Hughes chief justice, and in doing so he ran into a fury of protest. The opposition came from two normally antagonistic quarters, the Senate liberals (actually the remnant of the Progressives) and the southern conservatives. They were in agreement on one matter, namely that a man who leaves the bench for the political world ought not to be put back on the Court. But after that the two sides had different reasons for opposing Hughes. Senators George Norris, William Borah, Robert La Follette and Burton Wheeler disliked Hughes' property-business oriented views, whereas Senator Carter Glass argued that Hughes had an antipathy to states' rights. But Hughes had a good deal of support, including the two Democratic Senators from New York, Robert Wagner and Royal Copeland, and after several days of debate the Senate confirmed the nomination by a vote of 52-26.

With the exception of two important changes, the old Taft Court was to be the new Hughes Court. Justice Sanford died on 8 March 1930 and Justice Holmes resigned on 12 January 1932. To replace Sanford President Hoover nominated Judge John J. Parker of North Carolina, but the Senate denied confirmation primarily on the grounds that, while campaigning for the office of governor, he had made some derogatory remarks about Negroes, and as a judge, had written anti-union opinions. The president then named Owen J. Roberts, an attorney with a national reputation in legal circles whose political and economic views were not well known, or at least not well publicized, and the Senate promptly confirmed the appointment.

Roberts was born 2 May 1875 in Philadelphia. He graduated from Germantown Academy, the University of Pennsylvania, and *cum laude* from the University of Pennsylvania Law School where, for a time, he was a member of the faculty and later Dean. His career generally was that of a practicing attorney, although he served as district attorney of Philadelphia County for three years and as special attorney to represent the government in the litigation growing out of the Teapot Dome scandal. Roberts was a very modest man. When he resigned from the Court in 1945 he wrote: "I have no illusions about my judicial career. But one can only do what one can. Who am I to revile the good God that he did not make me a Marshall, a Taney, a Bradley, a Holmes, a Brandeis, or a Cardozo." [56] Justice Felix Frankfurter, writing in 1955 at the time of Roberts' death, asserted that Roberts was unfair to himself, that he brought great wisdom to the Court, and that he restrained his imagination in his opinions. [57] To the general public Roberts' judicial position seemed unclear and confused, a position which led eventually to his being characterized unflatteringly as the swing man between the hard core conservatives and liberals, as a man who switched from a conservative to a liberal position when the public and official pressure became unbearable. The basis for the charge was that on 1 June 1936 Roberts voted with the majority in the New York minimum wage case [58] to reaffirm the *Adkins* case and retain the concept of economic due process as a limitation on state power, and then, less than a year later, on 29 March 1937, he voted with the majority to overrule *Adkins*. [59] Years later Frankfurter presented a memorandum by Roberts in which Roberts indicated that he was willing to overrule *Adkins* in the New York case, but since a majority for overruling could not be obtained, he agreed that the New York statute was indistinguishable from the law challenged in *Adkins*, and furthermore New York did not ask the Court to overrule *Adkins* but merely to distinguish the two cases. This Roberts could not do. Ironically Chief Justice Hughes in his opinion in 1937 virtually destroying the concept of liberty of contract, relied heavily on Roberts' opinion in *Nebbia* v. *New York* [60] in which the Court brought an end to the "business affected with a public interest" doctrine as a limitation on state regulation of prices. Justice Roberts was able, hard working and energetic, but to some observers he appeared to be judicially inconsistent.

President Hoover's third and final appointee to the Court was the distinguished chief justice of the Supreme Court of New York, Benjamin N. Cardozo. [61] Cardozo was descended from a group of Spanish, Portuguese and English families who had immigrated to America prior to the Revolution. His father, Albert, a brilliant judge on the Supreme Court of New York, became involved with the scandals of the Tweed ring and resigned before an investigation of the judiciary was concluded. Benjamin was born on 24 May 1870. He was tutored privately by Horatio Alger of whom he said just before entering Columbia College: "He did not do as successful a job for me as he did with the careers of his newsboy heroes." [62] Cardozo graduated from Columbia at the age of nineteen, first in his class and a member of Phi Beta Kappa. He attended Columbia Law School but was admitted to the bar without finishing his degree. For twenty-two years he was primarily a counsel for other lawyers, a barrister unknown to the general public but held in high regard by the bench and bar of New York. In 1913 he was elected to the Court of Appeals of New York (the state's highest court) and was subsequently elected chief judge, a post which he held until his appointment to the United States Supreme Court in 1932. It was a severe wrench for Cardozo to leave New York. He was completely happy with his work and with a close circle of friends, and he took his seat on the supreme bench with great reluctance. He died in 1938 after serving only six years, but those years were among the most tempestuous in the Court's history. Cardozo was a poet, a philosopher and a scholar, and in addition to his judicial opinions he wrote four books, [63] all of which have become classic legal treatises reflecting a "tough mind" and a "gentle heart." [64] Frankfurter maintained that "Cardozo was second only to Holmes in making of the judicial process a blend of continuity and creativeness" and that his opinions reflected not the "friction and passion of their day, but the abiding spirit of the Constitution." [65] And Justice William O. Douglas characterized him as "gentle—almost self-effacing, an indefatigable worker, a stylist" and "craftsman supreme." [66] Certainly no judge made a more enduring contribution to American constitutional law in such a brief period of service. Ideologically he joined Brandeis and Stone in voting to uphold the government in matters of economic regulation, but he voted against the government whenever it interfered arbitrarily with individual liberty. In this sense Cardozo epitomized the twentieth century liberal spirit.

What historians now refer to as the New Deal Court—they would be more accurate to call it the anti-New Deal Court—consisted of four unswerving nineteenth century liberals (now called economic conservatives), Sutherland, Butler, Van Devanter and McReynolds. Generally in opposition to the conservative bloc were the new-style liberals who believed in the necessity of a measure of government control over the economy, Brandeis, Cardozo and Stone. Tending toward the conservative side, but not unbending were the chief justice and Owen Roberts. Although the term "revolution" is used everywhere to describe the New Deal, it seems more accurate to rely on Charles and Mary Beard's analysis that the New Deal was simply a culmination of long-standing agitation. [67] As they point out, there was no overthrow of one class by another, no wholesale transfer of property. The Agricultural Adjustment Act deprived no farmer or landowner of his land, nor did the National Industrial Recovery Act strip any corporation of its holdings. By aiding banks in trouble, the government saved the depositors and ultimately the banks, and the credit and money legislation protected holders of securities and enabled those burdened by debt to avoid bankruptcy. [68] But if the New Deal was not a revolution it changed the direction of the American system by "tying private interests more closely into a single network, making the fate of each increasingly dependent upon the fate of all," [69] and in doing so it repudiated social Darwinism with a finality that shocked those who were convinced of its rightness and its efficacy, including those members of the Supreme Court who had been reared on Spencer and Cooley and their disciples.

Before reviewing those decisions of the Court that brought about the most serious constitutional crisis since the post Civil War era, one ought to gain a balanced perspective on judicial review in the 1930s by viewing other questions of public law, particularly the area of civil liberty on which the Court spent a larger and larger portion of its time. These may be divided into three categories: freedom of speech and press, due process in criminal proceedings, and equal protection of the laws.

Freedom of Speech and Press

On 8 May 1931 Chief Justice Hughes wrote the opinion of the Court in *Stromberg* v. *California*, [70] a case involving nineteen-year-old Yetta Stromberg, a member of the Young Communist League, who had led children at a summer camp in a pledge of allegiance to a red flag which was supposed to symbolize the cause of the working class. Miss Stromberg was convicted of violating a California statute which provided that any person who displayed a red flag in a public assembly as (1) a sign of opposition to organized government or (2) an invitation to anarchistic action or (3) as an aid to propaganda that is of a seditious character, is guilty of a felony. Chief Justice Hughes said that under the instructions given to the jury it was impossible to separate the three clauses of the statute and to tell which of the three was used to convict. He concluded, therefore, that if any of the clauses was invalid, the conviction could not stand. Hughes went on to argue that, as construed by the state court, the clause that made it a criminal offense to display a flag as a sign of opposition to organized government was so vague and indefinite that it violated the liberty guaranteed by the due process clause of the Fourteenth Amendment. The statute in question interfered with the "opportunity for free discussion" and the concept of lawful means to obtain change and to keep government responsive to the will of the people.

In *United States v. MacIntosh*, [71] also in 1931, the Court, over the protesting dissent of the chief justice, ruled that under the act of Congress which required an applicant for citizenship to take an oath to "support and defend the Constitution and laws of the United States against all enemies, foreign and domestic, and bear true faith and allegiance to the same," a person who would not promise unconditionally to bear arms in defense of the United States could not be admitted to citizenship. The case turned on the narrow issue of whether the language of the statute required a promise to bear arms, and the Court never reached the question of whether Congress might require such an oath. In Hughes' view Congress had expressed no such intent, and he argued forcefully that there "is abundant room for maintaining . . . the conception of the supremacy of law as essential to orderly government, without demanding that either citizens or applicants for citizenship shall assume by oath an obligation to regard allegiance to God as subordinate to allegiance to civil power." [72]

In a third case decided in 1931 the Court for the first time declared a state law invalid on the ground that it violated the First Amendment as made applicable to the states through the Fourteenth. [73] The state of Minnesota had sought to enjoin the publication of a newspaper that had, in a series of nine articles, charged that local officials were guilty of gross neglect of duty and were in collusion with gangsters, gamblers and racketeers. The statute involved in the case provided for the abatement, as a public nuisance, of a "malicious, scandalous and defamatory newspaper, magazine or other periodical" and permitted truth with "good motives and for justifiable ends" as a defense. A lower court had adjudged the newspaper to be a public nuisance and had enjoined it from further publication. Hughes wrote an eloquent opinion in which he pointed out that the statute was not aimed at the redress of private wrongs but at the distribution of defamatory material, and that its object was suppression and censorship, not punishment in the usual sense. The fact that freedom of the press might be abused, said Hughes, by "miscreant purveyors of scandal does not make any the less necessary the immunity of the press from previous restraints in dealing with official misconduct," since the theory of the constitutional guarantee of freedom of the press is that "even a more serious public evil would be caused by authority to prevent publication."

Due Process in Criminal Proceedings

In two cases of permanent significance in the 1930s the Court held the states to a more rigid concept of due process than ever before. In *Powell* v. *Alabama* [74] Justice Sutherland wrote an opinion in which the Court held that a state had constitutionally deprived a criminal defendant of due process of law by not assigning counsel for his defense, whether requested or not. Although it was a narrowly drawn opinion in that the rule applied to the specific facts of the case—a capital crime in which the defendant was indigent, illiterate, and incapable of employing counsel or making his own defense—it set the stage for the development of the rule that, inherent in due process, is the right to counsel in all state criminal cases. The right is, of course, guaranteed directly by the Sixth Amendment in federal cases. In *Mooney* v. *Holohan* [75] the Court, in a *per curiam* opinion, although denying Mooney's petition for writ of habeas corpus without prejudice on the ground that he had not exhausted his state remedies, nevertheless was constrained to agree with Mooney's position that due process was violated if his conviction had been obtained by the state through a deliberate presentation of testimony known to be perjured. Due process, said the Court, "embodies the fundamental conceptions of justice which lie at the base of our civil and political institutions." In *Brown* v. *Mississippi* [76] the Court again cut through technical procedures in order to achieve a just result. For a unanimous Court Hughes wrote an opinion overturning a conviction of three ignorant Negroes based solely on a confession obtained through beating, whipping, hanging and generally brutal treatment. While the state argued that the Supreme Court lacked jurisdiction since counsel for the defendants had failed to move for exclusion of the evidence at the trial, the Court answered that the state, while retaining its right to exercise discretion as to the forms of a trial, may not "substitute trial by ordeal."

In all of these cases involving procedural due process, as well as those involving freedom of expression, the Court was developing a new concept, namely that due process of law does not require a simple adherence to traditional forms, but demands that fundamental and substantial justice be done. It was not until the 1950s and 1960s that this idea came to full fruition, and then it occasioned another constitutional crisis.

Equal Protection of the Laws

In the 1930s the Negro began to move into the courts with a new intensity and vigor to attack repressive state measures, using the equal protection of the laws clause of the Fourteenth Amendment as his constitutional shield. Among the actions that the southern states had taken to restrict Negro suffrage was the so-called white primary, a system which permitted only whites to vote in party primaries at which candidates were nominated. For lack of a strong Republican organization in the former states of the Confederacy, nomination by the Democratic primary was an assurance of election, and while Negroes, because of the Fifteenth Amendment, could not be excluded from general elections, the southern states took the position that political parties were private organizations akin to private clubs and that exclusion of Negroes from party affairs was constitutionally permissible. This conclusion was based on the doctrine of the *Civil Rights Cases* [77] which said that while the Fourteenth Amendment prohibits the states from discriminating against Negroes, it does not prohibit private discrimination. The distinction between private and public or state action is often subtle, and the entire issue was to be debated on and off the Court for years to come. Back in 1923 the Texas legislature enacted a law that excluded Negroes from participating in the Democratic primary of that state, but this was held to be state action, rather obviously, and therefore invalid. [78] The Texas legislature then passed a new law which authorized the state executive committee of any political party to determine who might vote in its primaries, and the executive committee of the Democratic party promptly excluded Negroes from membership. Speaking for the Court in *Nixon* v. *Condon* [79] Justice Cardozo invalidated the law and the party regulation on the ground that the discrimination was clearly authorized by the state. But when a convention of the Democratic party of Texas, acting without statutory authorization, resolved that the party membership was restricted to whites, the Court unanimously held, in an opinion by Justice Roberts, that the action in question was private and not public, that a political party was not an instrument of the state. [80] This decision was to be overruled nine years later, [81] but temporarily it severely curtailed the progress of equality in voting. But if the Court adhered to a rather narrow concept of state action, it pulled the state up short when discrimination was clearly public. In *Norris* v. *Alabama* [82] the Court held unanimously that the exclusion from juries, grand or trial, of Negroes on racial grounds, whether by statute or by judicial or administrative practice, was a denial of equal protection of the laws. The Court went so far as to hold that even in the absence of specific evidence of exclusion, racial discrimination was practiced upon a showing that large numbers of eligible Negroes had never been called for jury duty.

A Liberal Majority?

Prior to the series of cases that precipitated a constitutional crisis, the Court rendered two opinions which indicated the existence of a liberal majority that appeared to be sympathetic to the legislative response to the popular needs of the times. The first of these was the case of *Home Building and Loan Association* v. *Blaisdell* [83] in which Chief Justice Hughes, for a majority of five, upheld the Minnesota Mortgage Moratorium Act. The act was an attempt to grant relief to the farmer who found himself in alarming difficulty as a result of the economic depression of 1929. By 1932 farm income throughout the nation had dropped from $12 billion to just over $5 billion and although agricultural production declined six percent, prices had fallen sixty-three percent. About half the land was subject to mortgages, most of which had been incurred when the farm price level was four times as high as at the close of 1932. Inevitably many farms were foreclosed and placed on the market only to drive land prices down. It was clear to the legislature of Minnesota, as well as to those of other farm states, that if something were not done large numbers of people would lose their homes and their only means of support. Given these conditions Minnesota enacted a law that provided for relief during the emergency not to be extended beyond 1 May 1935. Under its terms foreclosure of mortgages and execution of sales thereunder might be postponed, and periods of redemption extended "for such additional time as the court may deem just and equitable." The courts were to determine a reasonable rental value of the property and to permit the mortgagor to retain possession while at the same time paying a reasonable amount toward taxes, insurance, interest and principal. This appeared to be the very kind of law the contract clause of the Constitution was designed to prevent, and to fall within the precedent of *Bronson* v. *Kinzie*[84] in which Chief Justice Taney had invalidated similar laws supposedly enacted to aid mortgage debtors. But Chief Justice Hughes, speaking for Brandeis, Cardozo, Roberts and Stone, upheld the law. In a masterful opinion Hughes swept away the impressive array of precedent by dwelling essentially on three points. First, he appealed to a line of cases such as *Stone* v. *Mississippi*[85] in which the Court had accepted the police power as a limit on the contract clause, although none of the cases was precisely like the one at hand. Second, he emphasized the *emergency* and the *temporary* nature of the Minnesota law. What is the relation of emergency to constitutional power, he asked? "Emergency," he answered, "does not create power . . . does not increase granted power . . . [but] may furnish the occasion for the exercise of power." He implied that some limitations in the Constitution, such as the prohibition against the states' coining money, are absolute while others, like due process, are subject to judicial and legislative discretion. The contract clause in Hughes' view falls into the latter category. Finally Hughes argued for a particular kind of judicial interpretation of the Constitution, a Constitution, in Marshall's words, "intended to endure for ages to come, and, consequently, to be adapted to the various crises of human affairs."[86] Or in the words of the great Holmes, also summoned by Hughes, "The case before us must be considered in the light of our whole experience and not merely in that of what was said a hundred years ago."[87] Fundamentally

Hughes reasoned that the Constitution must be viewed in terms of events and needs, not in terms of the literal intent of the framers. Justices Sutherland, Butler, Van Devanter and McReynolds disagreed.

In one of his finest opinions Justice Sutherland answered the chief justice point by point. The Constitution, he observed, was not "a mere collection of political maxims to be adhered to or disregarded according to the prevailing sentiment," but a law enacted by the people in their sovereign capacity. Furthermore it was not a matter of interpreting the Constitution. The instrument carried its own interpretation in "plain English words," and the judge's duty was simply to apply it. Certainly, Sutherland continued, circumstances cannot change the Constitution, for "if the provisions . . . be not upheld when they pinch as well as when they comfort, they may as well be abandoned."

Both Hughes and Sutherland were caught in the dilemma of all written constitutions, namely, how literally to interpret their provisions, and they divided into loose and strict constructionists just as Marshall and Jefferson divided over a century earlier. There was little room for optimism for the New Deal as a result of the *Blaisdell* case for the 5-4 division was the closest possible, and, moreover, the four conservatives were clearly *never* going to support regulatory schemes, whereas of the five who voted to uphold Minnesota, three had been Republicans, two, Hughes and Roberts, fairly conservative ones. But the coalition hung together on another important case in 1934, *Nebbia* v. *New York*. [88] In an opinion by Justice Roberts the Court upheld a New York law that provided for maximum and minimum prices on milk. Although calling attention to the public nature of the milk business, Roberts did not choose to define "business affected with a public interest" in the way it had been defined since 1877. [89] Instead, he discarded the entire doctrine when he declared: "It is clear that there is no closed class or category of business affected with a public interest. . . . The phrase 'affected with a public interest' can, in the nature of things, mean no more than that an industry, for adequate reason, is subject to control for the public good." The line-up of the justices in this decision seemed a particularly good omen, since just two years earlier both Hughes and Roberts had joined in an opinion by Sutherland to strike down an Oklahoma statute that attempted to regulate the ice business.[90] Selling ice, they had contended, was essentially a private business and therefore beyond the state's police power; the minority now having dwindled to four, adhered to that opinion in *Nebbia*.

Court Against the New Deal

If 1934 sounded a note of optimism for the Roosevelt program, 1935 and 1936 were years of despair. From January of 1935 through June 1936 the Supreme Court handed down twelve decisions which, taken together, persuaded President Roosevelt that there was little hope that the Court would validate such coming measures as the Social Security Act, the National Labor Relations Act and the Public Utility Holding Company Act. It was on this basis that the president decided upon a plan of reform that was to cause him greater political damage than some of the substantive New Deal measures themselves.[91] Rather than place the twelve notorious decisions into constitutional categories, it might be wise to take them chronologically. Seven of the twelve were decided in 1935, the remaining five in 1936.

The first case in which the Court swept away a key piece in the New Deal structure was *Panama Refining Co.. v. Ryan*,[92] popularly known as the Hot Oil Case. Under the National Industrial Recovery Act of 1933 Congress had established codes of fair competition for all major industries, including the oil industry which had fallen into a decline because of overproduction and wasteful competition. The code prescribed production quotas for each state, permitting the states to divide up the total allocation among the operators within the state. The act also authorized the president to prohibit transportation, in interstate and foreign commerce, of petroleum products produced or withdrawn from storage in excess of the amount permitted by any state law. In an Executive Order issued on 11 July 1933 President Roosevelt prohibited the transportation of oil in excess of the amounts permitted by the states, and almost immediately an owner of a refinery and an oil producer attacked the validity of that section of the act (9e) authorizing the president's action. They claimed that the law unconstitutionally delegated legislative power to the president and additionally that Congress had transcended its authority under the commerce clause. Chief Justice Hughes and seven of his brethren agreed that Congress had indeed invalidly delegated legislative power, and it was the first time ever that an act of Congress had failed on those grounds. Nowhere in the law had Congress declared a firm policy with respect to prohibiting the shipment of excess oil in interstate commerce, Hughes observed, nor had Congress fixed a standard for legislative action. The act, said Hughes, gave "to the President an unlimited authority to determine the policy and to lay down the prohibition, or not to lay it down, as he may see fit. And disobedience to his order is made a crime punishable by fine and imprisonment." In sum, Congress had left the whole matter to the president to be dealt with as he pleased, had given him "uncontrolled legislative power." In the lone dissent Justice Cardozo, while agreeing that a valid delegation of legislative power required that Congress proclaim a policy and fix definite standards, nevertheless purported to find both in the general context of the law.

Within a month two decisions were handed down which, although upholding the government, did so by a narrow 5-4 margin, and even the majority was critical of the administration. These were the so-called *Gold Clause Cases* [93] which arose as a result of the devaluation of the dollar through a decrease in its gold content by 40.94 percent. In addition Congress had passed a joint resolution declaring that every obligation containing a provision that the obligee had a right to require payment in gold or its equivalent was against public policy and void. One case involved a claim by the holder of a railroad bond bearing an interest coupon payable in gold with face value of $22.50 for its equivalent in current dollars or $38.10. For a majority of five Chief Justice Hughes denied the claim and upheld the resolution of Congress. He argued that contracts involving payment in gold were not commodity contracts but money contracts, and unquestionably Congress had the authority under Article I, Section Eight to establish and regulate the nation's currency. Said Hughes: "There is no constitutional ground for denying to the Congress the power expressly to prohibit and invalidate contracts previously made, and valid when made, when they interfere with the carrying out of the policy it is free to adopt."

In a second case the Court encountered a more difficult problem. What about contracts in which the national government was the obligee? That is, could a person who held an obligation of the United States providing that "the principal and interest hereof are payable in United States gold coin of the present standard of value" collect gold coin or its equivalent in current dollars from the government? Again the chief justice, speaking for a majority of five, wrote the opinion which he divided, for strategic purposes, into two distinct parts. First he admonished Congress that when the government undertakes an obligation, it remains binding on the "conscience of the sovereign," and the joint resolution changing the gold content of the dollar, insofar as it overrode the contractual obligation, went beyond the power of Congress. At the same time, however, Hughes wrote, the plaintiff sustained no loss in purchasing power and to pay him in gold or its equivalent "would appear to constitute . . . an unjustified enrichment." Thus Hughes rapped the knuckles of the Congress and the administration but he could not take the responsibility for increasing the national debt by several billion dollars. The dissenters, however, found the judging of the cases more simple. The government was morally and constitutionally wrong. In the words of Justice McReynolds, the "loss of reputation for honorable dealing will bring us unending humiliation; the impending legal and moral chaos is appalling." Reading his opinion from the bench, McReynolds turned on his colleagues in a rage, shouting "this is Nero at his worst. The Constitution is gone."

The victory for the New Deal in the *Gold Clause Cases* was not a comfortable one, and it raised the old question about ultimate determination of public policy hinging on the personal predilections and opinions of one man. But the worst was yet to come. Before the end of the term in 1935 the Court was to invalidate four administration measures, three by a unanimous vote. First the Court declared unconstitutional the Railway Retirement Act [94] under the provisions of which Congress had established a compulsory retirement and pension system for all common carriers subject to the Interstate Commerce Act. Turning the anti-New Deal minority into a majority, Justice Roberts in an opinion reminiscent of that in *Hammer* v. *Dagenhart* [95] declared that the act's purpose and effect was not to regulate commerce within the meaning of the Constitution. If it were, Roberts continued, Congress might require free medical attendance, housing, food, or the education of children to relieve the employee of strain and worry, just as providing for security in this instance is supposed to increase efficiency and morale. Writing the dissent for the minority of four was the chief justice who regarded the majority opinion as a serious barrier to all legislation of the type here involved. Furthermore, it was out of tune with previous decisions which had included in the concept of regulation the right to foster, protect, control, and restrain "with appropriate regard for the welfare of those who are immediately concerned and of the public at large." Certainly a pension plan, said Hughes, is closely related to the proper conduct of business enterprise.

In the second case the Court unanimously declared the Frazier-Lemke Act invalid. [96] By its terms Congress had attempted to deal with the sorry condition of farm mortgage debtors who were threatened with foreclosure. Under its authority to deal with bankruptcy, Congress had provided that a mortgagor might submit a plan to the mortgagee to purchase the mortgaged property, and if the mortgagee refused consent, the bankruptcy court might stay all proceedings for a period of five years during which the bankrupt person would retain possession of the property, provided he pay a reasonable rental. At the end of five years, or sooner, the debtor could discharge his obligation by paying into court, for the benefit of the mortgagee, the appraised value of the property. For the Court, Justice Brandeis maintained that the test of constitutionality of mortgage relief laws was whether "substantive rights of mortgagees were being impaired," and in this instance they were. Although Congress is not prohibited from impairing the obligation of contracts, its power over bankruptcy is limited by the Fifth Amendment, said Brandeis, and in enacting this measure Congress has contravened the amendment's requirement that private property may not be taken without just compensation.

In the third case, *Humphrey's Executor* v. *United States*, [97] the Court held unanimously that Congress might limit the removal power of the president. At first glance this appeared to be at odds with the *Myers* case. Justice Sutherland who wrote the opinion, along with Justices Van Devanter, Butler and Stone, had voted with Taft back in 1926 to hold that the president's power of removal over executive officers was unlimited. But Sutherland easily distinguished the two cases. Myers was a postmaster, and the office of postmaster was essentially unlike that of a federal trade commissioner, the position involved in this case. A postmaster is an executive officer and restricted to the performance of executive duties whereas a member of an independent commission is required by Congress to use his discretion in the implementation of legislative and judicial policies. Congress may, therefore, protect its creature with tenure, Sutherland declared, "for it is quite evident that one who holds his office only during the pleasure of another, cannot be depended upon to maintain an attitude of independence against the latter's will."

On the same day, 27 May, that saw the end of the Frazier-Lemke Act and a new restriction on the president's removal power, the Court also declared unconstitutional one of the key New Deal recovery measures, the National Industrial Recovery Act of 1933.[98] The justices unanimously agreed that the act was bad on two counts. First, it involved an invalid delegation of legislative power, and second, it was an improper regulation of interstate commerce. The act had been passed to promote industry-wide agreements on wages, hours, and trade practices in an effort to restore economic stability and to prevent cutthroat competition. Under its terms the various trade associations proposed agreements to the president, who then promulgated a code of fair competition for governing a given industry. If an industry could not or did not offer an acceptable agreement, the president could prescribe a governing code, and in either case, violation of the code was made a punishable offense. In this instance a New York poultry dealer, convicted for violating the live poultry code, challenged the constitutionality of some of its provisions. The chief justice pointed out that the act prescribed no standards or rules to guide administrative conduct, and that the discretion of the president was "virtually unfettered." Even Justice Cardozo, who had dissented in *Panama Refining Co., v. Ryan,*[99] agreed; he called the law "delegation running riot." But if the act had fixed appropriate standards to guide the president, it was unconstitutional in any event since it purported to regulate interstate commerce. The transactions involved were local in nature, and any effect on interstate commerce was indirect. Hughes observed that the traditional distinction between direct and indirect effect on interstate commerce must be maintained lest federal authority "embrace practically all the activities of the people."

If the end of the 1934-35 term of the Court closed on a note of despair for the New Deal and for the president's leadership, there was always hope that a new term of the Court might show a change in judicial attitude. But from January through June 1936 the decisions of the Court continued to frustrate political innovation by raising the barrier of constitutional limitation. The first such decision came in January when the Court invalidated the Agricultural Adjustment Act of 1933 in *United States* v. *Butler*. [100] The goal of the act was to aid farm producers by paying farmers to reduce crop acreage, and the funds for payment were to be obtained through a tax on food processors. With Justices Stone, Brandeis and Cardozo in dissent, Justice Roberts speaking for the majority consigned the act to the unconstitutional scrap heap on several grounds. The alleged tax was not a tax at all but a regulatory measure. And what did it purport to regulate? Agriculture. This Congress could not do since agriculture was a local matter and a subject reserved to the states under the Tenth Amendment. But if this were not bad enough, the act was coercive. Although a farmer might elect not to accept the benefits of the act, those who did cooperate might undersell the recalcitrant. Thus, ran Roberts' logic, the statute had a coerciive purpose and intent since it limited the farmer's choice through economic pressure. This might well be called the "revival case" since the majority had to revive judicial doctrines long since dead and buried. It revived the "tax as a penalty" concept, not used since 1922. [101] It also revived "dual federalism" in attributing limits to national power under the Tenth Amendment, not used since 1918. [102] Finally, it revived the idea that recipients of government largess are in some way coerced into actions they would otherwise not undertake. Even the chief justice accepted the Roberts position. It was in this case, incidentally, that Roberts set forth the simplistic analysis of judicial review (also a revival), when he said:

When an act of Congress is appropriately challenged in the courts as not conforming to the constitutional mandate the judicial branch of the Government has only one duty—to lay the article of the Constitution which is invoked beside the statute which is challenged and to decide whether the latter squares with the former. . . . This court neither approves nor condemns any legislative policy.

A month after the decision in *Butler* the Court upheld the constitutionality of the Tennessee Valley Authority over the lonely protest of Justice McReynolds. Although the administration won an apparent victory, it was a limited one and not a cause for rejoicing. The Court first faced the question whether to entertain the suit at all. The plaintiffs were holders of preferred stock in the Alabama Power Company which had entered into an agreement with the TVA to sell to it transmission lines, substations and other property and to interchange hydroelectric energy under certain conditions. The stockholders believed the arrangement to be injurious to the company and sought to have it enjoined, and thereby restrict the activities of the authority. The government had hoped that no justiciable question could be raised and that the Court would not be able to pass on the constitutionality of the act, but Hughes joined Van Devanter, Butler, Sutherland and McReynolds to form a majority that affirmed the right of the stockholders to sue. Then the entire Court agreed that the construction of a dam was an appropriate exercise of the war and commerce powers of Congress, that the government might convert water power into electric energy, and that such energy might be disposed of. McReynolds dissented, however, when the Court upheld the authority of the government to acquire transmission lines for the disposal of electric energy. He maintained that the primary purpose of the transaction was to put the national government into the business of selling electric power in certain areas, to expel the power companies in those areas, and to control the marketing of electricity. The chief justice answered that the broad question of government ownership of competitive enterprise was really not at issue since the government was not using water power to establish an industry or business but simply acquiring transmission lines to dispose of electrical energy. Although the Court upheld a specific contract in this instance, whether it would uphold a general policy of the government's running a network of generating plants around the nation was another matter. Also unsettling to the administration was the possibility that every contract made between a corporation and the government might be subject to attack by a dissatisfied stockholder.

In April 1936 the Court decided a case that did not involve a constitutional issue, but the decision indicated that a majority of the justices saw an evil in the growing power of administrative agencies. This was the case of *Jones v. Securities and Exchange Commission* [103] which involved the following facts: Jones had registered a statement with the SEC describing a proposed issue of trust certificates. After an investigation the commission concluded that the registration statement contained misleading or possibly fraudulent information, and subpoenaed Jones to produce certain papers. Jones then attempted to withdraw his original statement, assuming that this would end the commissions's jurisdiction over the entire affair. The commission, however, sought the aid of the courts to force Jones to appear at a hearing, thus raising the question whether a person could voluntarily withdraw from an SEC investigation. Over the protests of Justices Brandeis, Cardozo, and Stone, Justice Sutherland wrote the opinion holding that Jones might withdraw, and that to continue the investigation under the circumstances was in the nature of a "fishing expedition," and one wholly "unreasonable and arbitrary." He concluded that Jones' abandonment of his application "was of no concern to anyone but the registrant. The possibility of any other interest in the matter is so shadowy, indefinite, and equivocal that it must be put out of consideration as altogether unreal." Cardozo, on the other hand, was worried about the "host of impoverished investors" and suggested that Jones had beat a "precipitate retreat on the eve of exposure." Commenting on the decision Robert Jackson, soon to join the Supreme Court himself, declared that "the majority used the occasion to write an opinion which did all that a court's opinion could do to discredit the commission, its motives, its methods, and its existence." [104]

Within a month the Court staged, in a manner of speaking, a full-dress debate on the crucial constitutional issue of the day, namely the extent to which federal authority might be used to deal with matters traditionally handled by the states. [105] As a theoretical proposition the issue was the perennial one of loose versus strict construction of the Constitution; practically speaking it was a matter of updating the Constitution to fit the needs of the times. It is difficult to determine which side was the most logical (if judicial politics is ever logical), but for the moment the magic number five carried the day for the conservatives with Justice Roberts joining the four stalwarts. The Guffey Coal Act (Bituminous Coal Conservation Act) of 1935 purported to promote the interstate commerce of coal through a scheme under which the mine owners of the nation were to agree to a code that would regulate wages, hours, and prices throughout the industry. In order to secure compliance a sales tax was levied on all coal mined, the proceeds of which would be returned to those owners agreeing to the code. In the act itself Congress had declared that the various provisions were separable and the possible invalidity of any should not affect the constitutional status of the others.

Justice Sutherland, speaking for the majority, began his opinion with an analysis of the federal system. He defined it in rigid terms, declaring that the Constitution intended to preserve a "fixed balance" of powers and that "every addition to the national legislative power to some extent detracts from or invades the power of the states." Given this premise, the validity of the act then hinged upon the meaning of the commerce clause. What precisely does interstate commerce embrace in the constitutional sense? Calling upon eminent authorities including John Marshall and Melville Fuller, Sutherland defined commerce as "intercourse for the purposes of trade." He then concluded that the incidents leading up to and culminating in the mining of coal such as employment, wages, hours of work and working conditions all constitute intercourse for the purposes of *production* but not trade. Production, not being commerce, is therefore outside the congressional reach and a matter for the states to control if it is to be controlled at all. Of course, continued Sutherland, the production of every commodity intended for sale in interstate commerce has some effect on commerce, but the effect is indirect. And the fact that the coal industry is nationwide is irrelevant since it is not a question of the *extent* of the effect but the *relation* between the activity and the effect. But what about the price-fixing provisions? They were not simply a local matter but were a part of trade, of movement in commerce. Sutherland disposed of this problem by asserting that prices and wages were so closely related that one part of the act could not stand without the other. We cannot gainsay Sutherland's biographer who declared that this opinion "struck the idea of American nationalism a blow such as it has seldom, if ever, received." [106] Chief Justice Hughes, while approving the basic doctrinal approach of Sutherland, disagreed with the cavalier disposal of the price-fixing provisions of the act. These, said Hughes, must be considered separately, and were subject only to the constitutional restriction of the due process clause. In a dissent concurred in by Justices Brandeis and Stone, Justice Cardozo, reserving judgment on the labor regulations, argued that the price-fixing provisions were constitutional.

On 1 June, just two weeks after the decision in the *Carter Coal* case, the Court declared New York's minimum wage law for women unconstitutional. [107] The law made it a punishable offense for an employer to employ any woman at a wage that was less than the fair and reasonable value of the services rendered, and less than sufficient to meet the minimum cost of living necessary for health. The act then set forth procedures for determining minimum wages more precisely. Justice Butler wrote the opinion for the majority which included Van Devanter, McReynolds, Sutherland and Roberts. Primarily the Court dealt with the contention that the New York law was distinguishable from the act of Congress at issue in the *Adkins* case since the New York law, in addition to the "good health" standard, had the added requirement that the minimum wage must not exceed the fair and reasonable value of services rendered. For Butler and his brethren, however, the additional standard was not relevant. Minimum wage laws are an arbitrary denial of liberty and property without due process of law, and qualifications of any kind, so the tone of the opinion indicated, will not save them from invalidity. Technically the Court was simply asked to distinguish the New York case from *Adkins* and not to consider the fundamental issue of constitutionality, but had they viewed it from the latter standpoint, the sympathetic wording of the opinion suggests that all but Roberts would have voted to invalidate. What Roberts would have done is not clear since he said later that he had cast his vote only on the technical point of distinction. Chief Justice Hughes dissented, arguing that the "fair wage" standard was enough to differentiate the New York case from *Adkins*, but Justices Stone, Brandeis and Cardozo, while concurring with Hughes, would have taken another step and overruled *Adkins*.

Those were the decisions of the Supreme Court that caused a major constitutional crisis. Of the twelve decisions, three were unanimous (all three against the government), and of the remaining nine cases Cardozo supported the government in all, Brandeis and Stone in eight each, Hughes in five, Roberts in three, Van Devanter, Sutherland and Butler in one each, and McReynolds in none. Clearly, four of the justices were irrevocably committed to an economic and constitutional philosophy that would permit little, if any, compromise with the principles of the New Deal, and much of the time they were joined in their opinions by a fifth justice, some of the time by a sixth. Although the crisis of the spring and summer of 1937 was precipitated by an angry president, Congress was sympathetic to judicial reform and might have moved against the Court even in the absence of executive pressure. There were, after all, over 150 proposals introduced in Congress during this period that would in some way have diminished the role of the Supreme Court. [108] Although there are many reasons why the Court was left untouched, one reason was the president himself. His tactics and his refusal to compromise turned what might have been a victory into defeat.

Roosevelt's Remedy

On 31 May 1936, just four days after the Court had declared the National Industrial Recovery Act unconstitutional, President Roosevelt allegedly talked with Felix Frankfurter and former NRA Administrator Hugh S. Johnson about his determination to bring the Supreme Court into line, but neither gave the president his support. [109] During the summer of the 1936 campaign the president worked with Attorney General Homer Cummings on various plans that would constitutionally remove an obstructionist judiciary, and they settled ultimately on a scheme that would deal with the Court's personnel but, at the same time, would not alter the structure of the government nor go beyond what the Constitution permitted. It was not until 5 February 1937, after he won the election of 1936, that the president sent a draft bill and an accompanying message to Congress. The bill authorized the president to appoint a federal judge when any incumbent with at least ten years' service had served six months after reaching the age of seventy and failed to resign or retire. Within this framework the president might name as many as six additional judges to the Supreme Court and up to fifty throughout the entire federal judiciary system. Completing the package were an authorization for the chief justice to assign extra district or circuit judges to any district or circuit court of appeal where a press of business occurred and permission for the Supreme Court to appoint a proctor to watch over the status of litigation, investigate the need for assigning extra judges to congested courts and recommend their assignment to the chief justice.

In his covering message the president emphasized judicial delay and inefficiency, injustices to the poor because of a clogged judicial system and the incapacity of the older judges to deal with modern questions. In the president's words: "New facts become blurred through old glasses fitted, as it were, for the needs of another generation; older men, assuming that the scene is the same as it was in the past, cease to explore or inquire into the present or the future." The message then pointed out that in the previous fiscal year the Supreme Court had received 867 petitions for review and declined to hear 717 of them. And in those cases in which the government was not a party to the dispute, the Court heard only 108 out of 803 applications. The president asked: "But can it be said that full justice is achieved when a court is forced by the sheer necessity of keeping up with its business to decline, without even an explanation, to hear eighty-seven percent of the cases presented to it by private litigants?" Although the message alluded to older men not being in tune with the times, its main theme was the need for more judges to handle the workload.

When the bill reached Congress Senator Joseph Robinson, the majority leader, announced his support, as did Speaker William Bankhead of the House. As might be expected, Republicans generally opposed the measure along with some conservative Democrats including Representative Hatton Sumners of Texas, Senator Edward Burke of Nebraska, and the two Virginia Senators, Carter Glass and Harry Flood Byrd. With a few exceptions, notably the *Nation* and the *New Republic*, the national press emitted a general roar of protest, and congressional mail ran 9-1 against the plan. [110] Although the reaction surprised the president, he continued to believe, partly as a result of the 1936 election, that the people would support him. On 19 February 1937 an informal poll taken in the House of Representatives indicated that only about one hundred members would vote for the bill, but the president presumed a majority would be had eventually. In the Senate there were seventy-five Democrats, sixteen Republicans, one Progressive (La Follette), one Independent (Norris) and two Farmer-Laborites (Shipstead and Lundeen of Minnesota). In spite of the fact that only thirty were committed to the bill, and that some New Deal supporters had publicly voiced their opposition, notably Senators Joseph O'Mahoney of Wyoming and Tom Connally of Texas, the president was reasonably confident of attaining the requisite votes. Meanwhile, Republican strategy embodied in the leadership of Senators Charles McNary, William Borah and Arthur Vandenberg was to remain silent in the hope that dissident Democrats would defeat the bill themselves. And it seemed to work perfectly as Senator Burton Wheeler of Montana, a notable liberal Democrat, became leader of the opposition to the plan and convinced Senators Gerald Nye, Lynn Frazier and Henrik Shipstead to join him.

The president's advisers were in disagreement over strategy. [111] One group, led by Charles West, wanted the president to compromise and announce his willingness to accept a constitutional amendment on which the opposition could agree and for which they would guarantee the required two-thirds majority. Others, including Thomas Corcoran, Benjamin Cohen and Assistant Attorney General Robert Jackson, believed that the president should stick to his original plan. It was the latter group that prevailed, although one gets the impression that given the president's mood he would not have compromised even if his advisers had been unanimous in suggesting it. It is likely, however, that some sort of curb on the Court would have emerged under a compromise situation since most of those in Congress who opposed the president's plan had plans of their own. For example, Senator Wheeler proposed a recall of judicial decisions by a two-thirds vote of Congress after one intervening election; Senator Borah would have revised the Fourteenth Amendment to permit the states to enact social and economic measures which the Court had denied to the national government; Senator Burke opted for a straight judicial retirement age; and Senator O'Mahoney would have required a majority of seven justices to invalidate an act of Congress.

On 10 March the Senate Committee on the Judiciary began hearings. Of the eighteen members eight were for the proposal, eight were opposed and two were undecided, [112] and on 18 May, after weeks of hearings, the Committee voted ten to eight against the bill. The intervening period saw one of the greatest debates in American history over the nature of judicial power and the role of the Supreme Court in the American system of government. In the Index to the Congressional Record for that year there are more than 350 entries under *Supreme Court of the United States* encompassing public addresses and remarks on the floor by senators and representatives, proposed bills and constitutional amendments, addresses and articles by journalists and legal commentators, and memorials from state legislatures both for and against the bill. [113] Writing at the time of the debates Charles and Mary Beard point out that "Respectability" was divided over the plan in the same way that it was over the *Dred Scott* decision. [114] College presidents argued for and against the proposal; deans of law schools testified for and against it; legal scholars proclaimed their positions for and against. This was considerably different from the crisis of 1896 when "Respectability" arose to defend the Court against populism and anarchy. Two other interesting aspects of the controversy are pointed up in the Beards' analysis. First, even those who opposed the president's tampering with the judiciary in this particular way admitted that the Court had brought the opprobrium upon itself through the rendering of some very bad opinions. Second, and this is more fundamental, the old idea that the justices did not make law but merely found it, was laid to rest for all time. What every student of the Court had always known was now, for better or worse, tossed into the public arena. Probably the short-run impact of a public admission that judges were not political neutrals, that personal preferences did enter into judicial opinions, was to impair the prestige of the

Supreme Court, but in the long run the elimination of a myth strengthened the institution and that peculiarly American practice of judicial review. For now judicial review could stand or fall on its merits without any illusions or false pretensions about the process of judging.

Congress Considers

Before the Judiciary Committee sent its final report to the Senate in June, actions by the Supreme Court, both personal and collective, added considerable weight to the opposition to the president's bill. First was the letter sent by Chief Justice Hughes to Senator Wheeler, who in turn read it to the committee. According to newspaper reporters Joseph Alsop and Turner Catledge, Senators Wheeler, William King and Warren Austin had tried unsuccessfully to persuade the chief justice to appear before the committee. [115] They had then turned to Brandeis, who also declined to appear, but who suggested the letter from Hughes. Wheeler, appearing as witness before the Judiciary Committee on 22 March, read the text of the letter which amounted to a refutation of the president's charge that the Supreme Court was not keeping up with its work. [116] On the matter of petitions for certiorari Hughes contended that about sixty percent were wholly without merit and that, if anything, the Court had been overgenerous in granting as many as it had in the past. On the question of increasing the Court's size Hughes argued that as long as the Court acts as a unit this could only impair its efficiency since there would be "more judges to hear, more judges to confer, more judges to be convinced and to decide." In answer to the suggestion that the Court might divide up the work in such a way that not all judges would participate in all cases, Hughes declared that such a practice would be in contravention of the Constitution which vests judicial power "in one Supreme Court," *not* in two or more Supreme Courts, or parts of a Supreme Court functioning as separate Courts. The letter had very little, if any, effect on the Committee's deliberations, but it did indicate to the public at large that as far as the Supreme Court was concerned the president's charge of inefficiency was simply a cover for a disagreement over the outcome of particular cases.

But more significant in their effect on preventing reorganization of the judiciary, as court-packing is euphemistically called, were three major decisions handed down on 29 March, 12 April and 24 May. In the first, *West Coast Hotel* v. *Parrish*, [117] the Court upheld a minimum wage law for women enacted by the state of Washington. Speaking for a majority of five, the chief justice specifically overruled the *Adkins* case [118] and brought an abrupt end to the doctrine of "freedom of contract" and to the concept that due process of law prevented wages and hours legislation. Justice Sutherland, writing for himself, Van Devanter, Butler and McReynolds, accused the majority of amending rather than interpreting the Constitution. "To miss the point of difference between the two," said Sutherland, "is to miss all that the phrase 'supreme law of the land' stands for and to convert what was intended as inescapable and enduring mandates into mere moral reflections."

On 12 April came the decision in the *Jones and Laughlin Steel* case [119] in which the Court construed the commerce clause broadly enough to encompass the entire area of labor relations including collective bargaining. A key piece of the more permanent New Deal construct, the National Labor Relations Act, had now been upheld. Once again the chief justice spoke for a majority of five. Essentially Hughes argued that the steel company was not simply a local operation, that it engaged in "far-flung activities" across state lines, and that any work stoppage by industrial strife "would have a most serious effect upon interstate commerce." He relied primarily on the doctrine announced in *Stafford* v. *Wallace* [120] that although a specific transaction is local, if it is a part of the "current" or "flow" of commerce, it may be properly regulated by Congress. As for the recently decided *Schechter* [121] and *Carter Coal* cases, [122] Hughes distinguished the former on the ground that "the effect there was so remote as to be beyond the federal power" and the latter on the ground that the statute involved was invalid on several counts and not simply as an unconstitutional regulation of interstate commerce. This time Justice McReynolds, speaking for the four holdouts, maintained that Hughes and the majority had departed from the principles of *Schechter* and *Carter* and that the effect of labor relations on commerce was indirect and remote.

Finally on 24 May the same 5-4 majority upheld the old-age and unemployment provisions of the Social Security Act of 1935. [123] Justice Cardozo maintained first that Congress may validly tax and spend money in order to provide for the general welfare, and then answered the objections to the tax point by point: the tax is an excise and is laid with uniformity throughout the United States; the statute is not a denial of due process under the Fifth Amendment simply because it does not apply to agricultural or domestic labor; it does not coerce the states in violation of the Tenth Amendment; nor does it call for a surrender of state powers essential to their quasi-sovereign existence.

What is obvious to even the most cursory observer is that the same Court that had been invalidating much of the New Deal program was now upholding it, albeit by the change of only one vote. It is perhaps too easy to explain the new majority by attributing a change of attitude to Justice Roberts and to a lesser extent to Chief Justice Hughes, a change effected by the pressure of the president's proposal. Unquestionably both Roberts and Hughes were aware that continued invalidation by the Court of measures for social reform would bring about some retaliatory legislation, even though the president's specific plan seemed doomed before the Court's decisions of March, April and May. In all fairness to these justices, leaving aside motive which can never be determined precisely anyway, both voted to uphold the government several times prior to 1937 and Roberts, it will be recalled, wrote the opinion in *Nebbia* [124] which buried the old "business affected with a public interest" doctrine and opened up a broad area of state regulatory power.

In June the Judiciary Committee issued its adverse report [125] castigating the Court bill and indirectly the president. The report called the proposed bill "needless," "futile" and an "utterly dangerous abandonment of constitutional principle." The bill would "destroy the independence of the judiciary" and "subjugate the courts to the will of Congress and the President." In fact, continued the report, the "proposal violates every sacred tradition of American democracy" and "should be so emphatically rejected that its parallel will never again be presented to the free representatives of the free people of America." Moreover, the bill was presented in such a way, said the report, that it obscured its real purpose. Not only was the president attempting to subvert the Constitution and American institutions, he was a practitioner of deception and fraud. As the Beards saw it, "Those were contemptuous words for seven Democrats to hurl at the leader of their party, the President of the United States." [126]

Meanwhile the president suggested to Senator Robinson that he might work out a compromise, one which would, moreover, put Robinson on the Court. In a meeting with Senators Barkley and Minton, Robinson came up with a new plan by which the president would appoint one coadjutor justice for any justice who reached the age of seventy-five and failed to retire, with the proviso that no more than one such appointment be made in any one year. [127] But on 14 July in the midst of Robinson's attempt to build support for the compromise measure, he died of a heart attack, and with him went the president's last remaining hope of "packing the Court." In July by a vote of 70-20 the Senate recommitted the bill to the Judiciary Committee with the understanding that another bill to reform the judiciary would be reported out within ten days, a bill that would not alter the Supreme Court but would deal only with the lower federal courts. The Senate passed the Judicial Procedure Reform Act on 24 August in just fifty-seven minutes of consideration. Actually the bill took care of some needed reforms. It required the judges of the lower federal courts to notify the attorney general whenever the constitutionality of an act of Congress was drawn in question in a lawsuit between private parties, and the government might then enter the suit and present arguments on the question of validity. The law also shored up the injunctive procedure by abolishing injunctions issued by a single judge in cases in which an act of Congress might be suspended on grounds of unconstitutionality. Substituted was the three-judge requirement whereby an injunction might issue only before a panel of three judges including one circuit judge, such injunction to run for sixty days and to be made permanent or dissolved by the Supreme Court on fast appeal.

Thus ended the most serious crisis over judicial review since the congressional reaction to the *Dred Scott* decision, and perhaps the only time in our history that a congressional majority might have been mustered which would have seriously altered the Supreme

Court's role in the American system. Ironically the president's intransigence and lack of complete honesty may have been instrumental in saving the Court from an act of Congress that would have curtailed its functions in some way. But in the final analysis both the president and the Court had their victories. In the perceptive phrase of Robert Jackson, "In politics the black-robed reactionary justices had won over the master liberal politicians of our day. In law the president defeated the recalcitrant justices in their own Court." [128] Surely no statute altered the Supreme Court's organization or impaired its functions, but over the next eighteen years only two minor acts of Congress were declared unconstitutional [129] and for six years after the fight not a single act of Congress was invalidated. To suggest that the justices were intimidated is again to judge motives, but without question the high bench received a severe shock and for some time judicial review seemed moribund, if not dead. But by the 1950s a reinvigorated Court was able to sally forth once again to do battle over public policy, but this time the ingredients of the crisis differed substantially from any of the past.

7. Stone, Vinson & Warren:
Retreat, Rejuvenation & a
New Crisis

WHEN Harlan Fiske Stone became chief justice in 1941 the general tone of the Court's opinions had already changed considerably from the pre-1937 era. In fact, the change in attitude was discernible immediately after the 1937 crisis before President Roosevelt had the opportunity to name any new justices. (In addition to elevating Stone to Chief from associate, President Roosevelt appointed eight new justices prior to his death. Justice Roberts did not retire until the beginning of the Truman incumbency.) The decade 1937-47 might best be characterized as a revisionist period in which the justices scrupulously avoided the overturning of acts of Congress while declaring unconstitutional numerous state laws in areas varying in kind from the rights of Negroes to intergovernmental tax immunity. While the Court had recognized the changed and ever-changing role of the states in the Union since the Civil War, from the late 1930s onward there appeared to be a greater judicial awareness that the United States had truly become a nation and that any doctrinaire defense of "states rights" made little sense practically or constitutionally. Thus, the new revisionism recognized that the national government alone was capable of dealing with national problems, and concomitantly that the states must not interfere with the enlarged national sphere. This was not, however, a creative judicial period, but simply one in which the Court took into account the force of history in writing its opinions. At the same time it was a cautious Court in that it did not go as far as it might have to contain the powers of the states. Nevertheless much of what it began was extended sharply in the 1950s and 1960s, and some of the Roosevelt appointees were instrumental in effecting both the revision of the 1940s and the expansion and innovation of the two following decades.

Without question the men whom President Roosevelt named to the Supreme Court were, as a group, the most distinguished choices made by any president in American history. Excepting James F. Byrnes who served too briefly (one term) for one to make an informed judgment and Harlan F. Stone, who, although a capable justice, was not originally a Roosevelt selection since the president promoted rather than appointed him, the others were intellectually exciting, individually committed, unusually able, judicial craftsmen. By all odds the two outstanding judges, preeminent not only for their time but for all time, were Hugo Black and Felix Frankfurter who, by the mid-1940s, had become judicial antagonists and had assumed the leadership of two opposing wings of the Court.

Hugo LaFayette Black was born in 1886, the eighth and last child of William and Martha Black, in Clay County, Alabama, where his father farmed the land and kept a store.[1] Clay County was outside the "black belt" which meant that only a small part of the population was non-white and may account in part for the deep-South, rural-bred Black never having acquired a strongly racist attitude. At least, Black never evidenced any racial bias during his many years in national public life, and while on the Court he has consistently advanced the cause of Negro rights along with all civil liberty. At the age of seventeen Black enrolled in the Birmingham Medical College but left, after one year, to enter the two-year program at the University of Alabama Law School. After graduating in 1906 he set up law practice in Ashland, but closed up shop after just a year for lack of business. He moved to Birmingham where he slowly built up a practice of almost exclusively small businessmen. For two years he served as a police court judge disposing of petty crimes committed by the cast-offs of society—vagrants, drunkards, dope users—very often indigent blacks. In 1914 he was elected to a three-year term as county solicitor, later served in World War I for a year, married, and became a "respectable" member of the community. In 1923 he joined the Birmingham chapter of the Ku Klux Klan, and although he realized that he was not sympathetic with much of what the Klan stood for and resigned in 1925, it was the one act that almost lost him his appointment to the Court. He was elected to the United States Senate in 1926 where he spent most of his spare time in self-education since formally he had had only a high school education and some technical law training.

After Black's reelection to the Senate he became an active supporter of FDR and the New Deal and in 1937 was rewarded by being Roosevelt's first appointment to the Court. Why Black? In addition to the fact that he was a loyal, capable Democrat of personal integrity, he was a senator, a fact which would guarantee his confirmation by the Senate. Roosevelt wanted no argument over confirmation after the protracted Court-packing struggle. Secondly, the president could have his revenge against the conservatives in and out of the Senate by appointing an unabashed liberal. Herbert Hoover commented that the Court was "one-ninth packed" and the *Chicago Tribune* declared that the president had "picked the one who would be generally regarded as the worst he could find". The Senate confirmed Black by a vote of 63-16 (ten Republicans and six Democrats voting against him), and the new justice left for a European vacation. Meanwhile the *Pittsburgh Gazette* ran a series of articles presenting evidence that Black had belonged to the Klan. The articles aroused a good deal of anti-Black sentiment and when Black returned to the United States on 30 September he made a national radio address in which he defended his public record and pledged to the American people that he would be a fair and impartial judge. In more than thirty years on the bench he has not broken that pledge. Throughout his tenure he has remained the unswerving champion of individual liberty, and through consistent and persuasive logic has convinced a majority of the Court that the Bill of Rights must be applied to the states as well as to the national government and that freedom of speech must be given extraordinary judicial protection. Always there were those on and off the Court who disagreed with Justice Black, but all but the petty have accorded him the respect due a bright and bold mind.

If Franklin D. Roosevelt had deliberately set out to find someone whose background and temperament were as different from Hugo Black's as possible, the most suitable candidate would have been Felix Frankfurter. An immigrant Jew born in Vienna in 1882 of a poor merchant father, Frankfurter rose to eminence in a nation suspicious of the foreign-born and anti-Semitic to a shameful degree. He came to the United States at the age of twelve, graduated from City College of New York at nineteen and the Harvard Law School with honors at twenty-three. He entered public service shortly after graduation when he was made the assistant to Henry L. Stimson, then U.S. attorney in New York. For his work in trust busting he received a personal commendation from President Theodore Roosevelt. In 1914 he was appointed to the Harvard Law faculty where he remained on and off until his appointment to the Supreme Court in 1939. By that time he already had been an adviser to presidents, held a variety of government positions and had fought publicly for many social causes. He had assisted Louis Brandeis in preparing briefs and arguing cases before the Supreme Court, served in several government positions during World War I, and attended the Versailles Peace Conference where he represented the Zionist cause. In his postwar years at Harvard he became a careful student and critic of the Supreme Court, wrote prodigiously, helped found the American Civil Liberties Union, was an original stockholder in the *New Republic* and was closely involved with the National Association for the Advancement of Colored People. Had he never been appointed to the Supreme Court, history would always remember him for his crusade in behalf of Sacco and Vanzetti, the anarchists who had been convicted of murdering a Boston paymaster. His article in the *Atlantic Monthly* analysing the evidence and calling their trial a miscarriage of justice brought the case to the attention of the world. It also, incidentally, split the Harvard faculty and is reputed to have cost the university about a million dollars in reduced contributions. Frankfurter's plea was essentially for a new trial free of error and judicial prejudice rather than for the innocence of Sacco and Vanzetti. As an unofficial adviser to FDR during the early days of the New Deal, Frankfurter had a substantial influence on public policy. He also sent able young men to fill positions in the new administration.

On 4 January 1939 the president called Frankfurter on the telephone and said he was submitting his name for the Supreme Court at noon the next day. As might be expected his nomination was attacked violently by the far right, but he was confirmed without objection by a voice vote in the Senate. With his unusually broad outlook, he seemed uniquely qualified for the post. He read everything—law, philosophy, science, many newspapers (including British newspapers, for after his year as visiting professor at Oxford from 1933 to 1934 he was enamored of everything English)—all in addition to state, national, and international law reports. He knew many great men of his day personally—poets, prime ministers, judges, actors—and he had a tremendous impact on everyone he met.

Once on the Court it was not long before he became the eloquent spokesman for the principle of judicial self-restraint, and thus became a disappointment to the intellectual left which he had brilliantly served and led. But as a judge Frankfurter maintained the position that his personal views, his passions, his convictions, were irrelevant to his judicial duty. He strongly opposed the death penalty but joined in opinions upholding convictions where the death penalty was involved; he was not in sympathy with the anti-communist measures of the day but he voted to sustain them; he was aware of the unfairnesses in two systems of justice perpetrated by an outdated federal system, yet he would not vote to cut away some of the artificial insulation. In terms of results Frankfurter became the spokesman for government authority while Black defended the individual. When observers of the Court chose sides, the constitutional arguments between Black and Frankfurter afforded the opportunity for national debates of a high caliber. When Justice Frankfurter retired in 1963, the American Bar Association conferred upon him its highest honor, the gold medal for "conspicuous service to the cause of American jurisprudence," and President Kennedy presented him with the Medal of Freedom, the highest award a president can bestow on a civilian.

After appointing Hugo Black and prior to naming Felix Frankfurter, President Roosevelt sent to the Court Stanley Forman Reed who has been characterized as the "least controversial, least intellectually gifted (save one-term Byrnes) and most conventionally law-minded of the Roosevelt Justices." [2] Reed was born in Maysville, Kentucky in 1884 of colonial ancestry. His father, a well-to-do physician, sent him to Kentucky Wesleyan, Yale University, the law schools of Virginia and Columbia, and to the Sorbonne for a year of study. He became a successful lawyer in Kentucky and was first appointed to a government post, that of counsel for the Reconstruction Finance Corporation, by Herbert Hoover. After Roosevelt's election, he became a faithful servant of the New Deal, and as solicitor general he argued and won many of the government's cases. It was in 1938, when serving as the government's advocate, that FDR rewarded him with an appointment to the Court. Reed became identified as a conservative since he, like Frankfurter, was reluctant to strike down regulatory powers of the government, including anti-civil liberties measures, unless a strong case of unconstitutionality could be established. He wrote over 300 opinions during his nineteen years on the Court, many dealing with the intricacies of finance. In the 1940s he joined occasionally with Justices Douglas, Black, Rutledge and Murphy to curb government interference with freedom of speech. He wrote the Court's opinion when it declared that the white primary and segregation in interstate transportation were unconstitutional; and he joined the majority in subsequent desegregation decisions which came just prior to his retirement in 1957.

William O. Douglas was one of those bright young men of the 1930s who especially appealed to President Roosevelt. He became the president's fourth appointee, in 1939, when he was elevated from the chairmanship of the Securities and Exchange Commission. Douglas was born in Ottertail County, Minnesota in 1898, but his family moved to Yakima, Washington when he was still a baby. From childhood on he conquered adversity—the death of his father when he was six, infantile paralysis, poverty. He earned his way through Whitman College (Phi Beta Kappa), and rode east on a freight car to enter Columbia Law School from which he graduated the second in his class. He practised law for a period in New York, accepted a post on the Columbia law faculty, then moved to the Yale Law School in 1928. At age forty-one, in 1939, Douglas was the youngest man to go to the Court since Joseph Story in 1811. Until the end of World War II he strongly supported the government, even in civil liberties cases, but after the mid-1940s he became the most consistent supporter of individual liberty on the Court. In the minds of some observers Douglas was almost too predictably doctrinaire; that is, he seemed willing to free criminals on minor technicalities, or to defend even violent demonstrations or protests as protected by the First

Amendment, when fellow liberals like Justice Black, or later Chief Justice Warren, voted to sustain the government. Perhaps Justice Jackson's sharp dissent in the *Terminiello* case,[3] in which he suggested that the Court ought to temper its doctrinaire logic with a little practical wisdom, was a reasonable criticism of Justice Douglas who had authored the majority opinion. In spite of any shortcomings, however, Douglas has produced many enduring opinions of quality in his thirty-two years on the bench.

Also in the liberal mold of Black and Douglas, but somewhat less intellectually rigorous than either, was Frank Murphy whom the President chose as his fifth justice in 1940. Born the son of a lawyer in Harbor Beach, Michigan, Murphy was a graduate of the University of Michigan Law School and studied law at both Lincoln's Inn, London, and Trinity College, Dublin. After serving in World War I he opened a law office in Detroit, but moved quickly into public service when he accepted an appointment as assistant U.S. attorney for the Eastern District of Michigan. He first won elective office as mayor of Detroit, and was later appointed governor general of the Philippines where he remained as high commissioner when the Philippines became a common-wealth in 1935. He planned to remain in that office, but under pressure from FDR who considered Michigan a "doubtful state" in 1936, he ran for governor of Michigan. He won by 30 thousand votes but the president's plurality was over 300 thousand. He succeeded Homer Cummings as attorney general in 1939 and the following year was nominated to the seat of Pierce Butler, thus carrying on a tradition of a Roman Catholic on the bench. He died of a heart attack on 19 July 1949. What Justice Murphy would have done with the problems of the 1950s and 1960s is, of course, conjecture, but in the 1940s he was not merely a *protector* of individual liberty, he was a *crusader*. He went beyond his liberal colleagues, Black and Douglas, to write stirring dissents in the cases involving the exclusion from the West coast of American citizens of Japanese descent, and he upheld the rights of Nazi spies, Japanese generals, and the vehemently anti-Catholic Jehovah's Witnesses.

After a long career in the House and Senate James F. Byrnes took his seat on the Court in 1941 as Justice McReynolds' replacement, but at the request of the president in 1942 he resigned to take over the post of director of economic stabilization. He became in effect an assistant president for economic affairs whose primary task was to keep a tight hand on inflation. After the war he returned to South Carolina where he became governor. He also became a severe critic of the Supreme Court after the 1954 desegregation decisions, apparently unable, or at least unwilling, to transcend the parochial white supremacy of a lifetime.

A judge who could combine wit, eloquence, charm, and clarity in his judicial opinions as few others before him was Robert H. Jackson, the seventh Roosevelt appointee and eighty-seventh justice to sit on the Court. Born in 1892 on a family farm in Spring Creek township, Pennsylvania where his father ran a livery stable, two farms, a general store, and bred horses, Jackson later attended public schools in Frewsburg and Jamestown, New York. He read law for one year under the old apprentice system, attended the Albany Law School for a time, and "read" for another year before fulfilling the New York requirement to practice law in the state. Eventually he became one of the ablest trial lawyers and business counsellors in western New York. In 1934 he left a comfortable life at the persuasive request of Secretary of the Treasury, Henry Morgenthau, to become general counsel to the Bureau of Internal Revenue. At the same time he became a prominent spokesman for the New Deal, forthrightly defending the incisive overhauling of the economic system. He also became the most articulate administration spokesman for "packing" the Supreme Court. In 1938 the president appointed him solicitor general, a position which he handled with phenomenal success. Under his advocacy the government won fifty-seven out of eighty-nine cases before the Supreme Court, Jackson personally arguing twenty-one cases, losing but four. When President Roosevelt appointed Frank Murphy to the Court in 1940, he named Jackson attorney general. In that year Jackson wrote a book entitled *The Struggle for Judicial Supremacy*, of which the greater part was a critical analysis of the Supreme Court during the years 1933-37. The following year he joined the Court himself. At the close of World War II he left the Court temporarily to act as chief counsel at Nuremberg in preparing and prosecuting the charges of atrocities and war crimes against the German leadership under Hitler.

On the Supreme Court Jackson was generally unpredictable and often unorthodox, but he wrote with a vigor and style that is unsurpassed to this day. He strongly believed in judicial self-abnegation—both before and after his appointment—and thus joined forces with Frankfurter against Black, Douglas and Murphy. But if he could often vote to uphold the government in free speech cases—as he phrased it, "liberty with order, or anarchy without either"—he could also write the oft-quoted, rhetorically flawless opinion upholding the right of a Jehovah's Witness to refuse to salute the American flag. Unfortunately, he and Justice Black were not only doctrinally antagonistic but apparently had personal differences which, in part, caused Chief Justice Stone to acquire a reputation for being unable to control a feuding Court. At one point Jackson strained judicial propriety to the limit by disclosing the discussion of a Court conference and publicly criticising Black, but in spite of his occasional lack of self-control, he must be placed among the best of his time, possibly of all time.

When James Byrnes resigned from the Court in October of 1942 President Roosevelt named Wiley B. Rutledge, his eighth and final appointee. Born in Cloverport, Kentucky in 1894 Wiley Rutledge grew up in Maryville, Tennessee where he attended Maryville College. He graduated from the University of Wisconsin in 1914 and from the University of Colorado Law School in 1922. After practising law for two years he joined the law faculty at Colorado, but soon moved to Washington University in St. Louis where he became dean of the Law School in 1931. He was appointed dean of the Iowa Law School in 1935, serving until 1939 when the president selected him for the U.S. Court of Appeals for the District of Columbia. Rutledge's appointment to the Supreme Court was considered nonpersonal and nonpolitical, probably made as a result of considerable pressure put on the president by Irving Brant, the distinguished journalist and Madison biographer. Individual rights transcended all else in Rutledge's mind, and he logically joined with the liberal triumvirate, Black, Douglas and Murphy. In slightly more than six years on the Court he made several enduring contributions to public law, among which were his dissent in the *Everson* case[4] in 1947 which became the prevailing view in prayer and Bible-reading cases in the 1960s, and his disagreement with the majority in *Wolf* v. *Colorado*[5] in 1945 which became the law in *Mapp* v. *Ohio*[6] in 1962. Justice Rutledge was extremely well liked and highly respected by everyone who knew him.

As I suggested above, the period beginning with the end of the Court fight in 1937 and ending with the appointment of Chief Justice Vinson was one of cautious revisionism. The Roosevelt justices joined the Court over a five-year period, making their influence piecemeal and individual rather than collective, and after Stone became chief justice the personal and intellectual divisions among prima donnas like Frankfurter, Black, Jackson, Douglas and Murphy presented the public with an image of a Court badly in need of leadership. At least there appeared to be a good deal more open hostility among the brethren than there had been under Hughes and Taft. It was, however, a hard working crew that built for the future. Broadly speaking the litigation embraced three categories of special significance: national power, conflicts in the federal system, and civil liberties.

National Power

Certainly the most important case to arise under the commerce clause during the decade from 1937 to 1947 was *United States* v. *Darby*[7] which involved the Fair Labor Standards Act of 1938. The act prohibited the shipment in interstate commerce of goods made by child labor, or manufactured by workers who were paid less than legally specified minimum wages, or who had worked beyond legally ascertained maximum hours. Overruling *Hammer* v. *Dagenhart*[8] the Court forthrightly abandoned the old distinction between "production" and "transportation", holding that Congress may prohibit the shipment of goods manufactured under substandard labor conditions from entering the channels of commerce. It was in this case that another old doctrine, dual federalism, was discarded as the Court held that the Tenth Amendment was not a limitation on the enumerated powers of Congress but was simply a "declaration of the relationship between the national and state governments as it had been established by the Constitution before the Amendment." Adhering to the general theme of the *Darby* case, the Court upheld the wheat-marketing quota provisions of the Agricultural Adjustment Act of 1938.[9] Speaking for the majority, Justice Jackson approved the application of the law to a farmer who raised only twenty-three acres of wheat for use on his own farm, none of which was intended for interstate commerce. Jackson not only repudiated the old distinction between direct and indirect effect, but he argued forcefully that "questions of the power of Congress are not to be decided by reference to any formula which would give controlling force to nomenclature such as 'production' and 'indirect'." These cases should not seem startling to students of constitutional history, for they are logical extensions of two doctrines enunciated at the turn of the century, the "current of commerce" and "harmful result" theories of *Swift & Co.* v. *United States*[10] and *Champion* v. *Ames*[11] respectively. A broad use of national power over navigable streams was validated by the Court in two cases decided in 1940[12] and 1941,[13] indicating again the willingness on the part of the justices to view with equanimity the everwidening incursions of Congress into what once was considered a local matter. And in 1944 the Court overturned a long-standing precedent when it held that the insurance business was interstate commerce, and that as a consequence it was subject to the Sherman Act.[14] Although it did not specifically overrule the old case of *Paul* v. *Virginia*,[15] the effect of the decision, as Chief Justice Stone said in dissent, was to "withdraw from the states in large measure, the regulation of insurance and to confer it on the national government. . . ."

Conflicts in the Federal System

During this period when the Court was permitting broad regulatory powers to Congress under the commerce clause, it did not generally raise the federal commerce power as a barrier to state taxation, or to state police measures which touched on the subject matter of interstate commerce.[16] But there were some notable exceptions. State taxes were struck down if, in the Court's view, they imposed a multiple burden on a company, thereby producing an effect on interstate commerce, [17] or if the tax discriminated against out-of-state trade. [18] Actually the Court was often divided over the issue with Justices Black and Douglas urging the view, and occasionally convincing a majority, that the Court should not interfere with any non-discriminatory state tax laws which happen to affect interstate commerce. Seemingly in a special category were cases in which the state's police power denied the individual his civil liberties. Notable in this regard were *Edwards* v. *California* [19] and *Morgan* v. *Virginia*. [20] In the former the Court unanimously invalidated California's "anti-Okie law" which made it a misdeameanor to transport an indigent person into the state. The purpose of the law was to stop the immigration of southwestern farmers who were fleeing the "dust bowl," but ended up only swelling California's relief rolls. Transportation of people across state lines, observed Justice Byrnes, is interstate commerce, and California was clearly restraining that commerce. In the latter case the Court held unconstitutional a Virginia statute requiring segregation on interstate buses. Justice Reed based his opinion in part on an old case, *Hall* v. *De Cuir*, [21] in which the Court had struck down a Louisiana law prohibiting racial discrimination on common carriers. Justice Burton pointed out, correctly, that now all state laws *prohibiting* segregation on interstate carriers would also be unconstitutional. The dilemma had to be faced just two years later, after Chief Justice Vinson had joined the Court, in *Bob-Lo Excursion Co.* v. *Michigan* [22] which involved an interpretation of the Michigan Civil Rights Act guaranteeing equal accommodations on all public conveyances. A local steamship line had refused accommodations to a Negro for a trip to a Canadian resort island and had been prosecuted under the law. This was certainly a question of state regulation of foreign commerce, and the *Morgan* precedent should have determined the outcome. Splitting three ways, the Court upheld the law. A majority emphasized the local character of the commerce and thus decided that under the *Cooley* rule Michigan might regulate it. Justices Black and Douglas would have sustained the statute under equal protection of the laws, but Justices Vinson and Jackson, standing on legal precedent, argued that the law was unconstitutional.

In line with the revisionist spirit of 1937 to 1947 was the significant case of *Erie Railroad* v. *Tompkins*[23] which overruled *Swift* v. *Tyson*,[24] a precedent of almost a hundred years' standing. Under the *Swift* doctrine, when the federal courts were hearing diversity of citizenship cases in which no state law covered a particular question, the federal courts might determine for themselves what the law was, independently of the judge-made common law rules of a state. In his opinion for the Court, Justice Brandeis observed that the old rule promoted lack of uniformity since the state and federal courts often ruled differently on similar questions, thus causing a variation in the general law depending upon which court was hearing the case, and thus effectively denying equal protection of the laws.

In the area of intergovernmental tax immunity the Court continued to revise the decisions of the past. In general the Court narrowed the scope of the state and federal governments' reciprocal immunity from taxation and in some instances voided the immunity altogether. Such was the case in *Graves* v. *New York ex rel. O'Keefe*[25] in which the Court overruled *Collector* v. *Day*[26] and thus permitted each government to tax the salaries of employees of the other under a valid income tax law.

Civil Liberties

Of all the revisionism during the decade under discussion the most spectacular and revolutionary changes in judicial attitude, and consequently in constitutional law, were in the area of civil liberty. The stage had been set back in 1925 when the Court ruled in *Gitlow* v. *New York*[27] that the First Amendment's guarantee of freedom of speech had become a limitation on the states by its absorption into the due process clause of the Fourteenth Amendment. Moreover a majority of the justices had elevated Chief Justice Stone's earlier dictum in the *Carolene Products* case,[28] that is, that First Amendment freedoms held a preferred status in our constitutional hierarchy of values, to a rule to be followed by the Court. A bare majority led by Justices Rutledge and Murphy then embraced a logical extension which said that since freedom of speech, press, assembly, and religion are of such vital importance to a free society, any laws which appear to restrict them will be presumed unconstitutional, and the burden of proof of constitutionality will rest with the government. For a brief period at least, since within a few years a majority would no longer agree to adhere to these principles, the Court made this significant exception to the old rule that any law under constitutional attack would be presumed valid, and invalidity must be proved by the attacker.

Certainly the largest number of cases, and some of the most significant, were those involving the free exercise of religion, a majority of which were initiated by the religious sect known as Jehovah's Witnesses. In a series of cases the Court upheld the right to distribute religious literature in public places without the necessity of obtaining a permit from a city official, [29] the right to enter the property of a private householder and ring the doorbell for the purpose of distributing religious tracts, [30] the right to circulate religious literature in a company-owned town [31] or in a federal housing project, [32] and the right to play phonograph records in a residential neighborhood on Sunday mornings attacking other religions, notably the Roman Catholic church. [33] The Court also held that a license tax on those who sell publications on the streets or house-to-house may not be applied to a person who sells religious literature, [34] even to one who makes his entire living in this fashion. [35] At the same time the Court maintained that Jehovah's Witnesses were subject to a reasonable fee for using the streets for parades of a religious nature, so long as the fee did not discriminate against religious groups, [36] and that a state child labor law was applicable to children of Witnesses who sold religious literature on the streets. [37] In a notable opinion, replete with libertarian rhetoric, Justice Jackson spoke for a majority in 1943 [38] to overturn a precedent of only three years standing, [39] holding that a pupil in the public schools could not be compelled to salute the American flag if it were against his religious scruples. In yet another instance the Court revised an old doctrine in overruling three cases [40] by holding that a Seventh Day Adventist who was unwilling to bear arms but who would willingly perform non-combat service could not be refused American citizenship. [41] As a result of the above decisions it is a fair generalization that individuals or groups may publicly practice and proselytize their religious views without interference by the state, except minimally and peripherally, on the basis of preserving order.

For the first time in its history the Court dealt with the "establishment of religion" clause of the First Amendment when it decided *Everson* v. *Board of Education*[42] in 1947. New Jersey had authorized the use of public monies to pay the cost of transporting children to all schools not operated for profit, a category that included Catholic parochial schools. The question was raised whether tax money thus used amounted to a governmental support for religion. Justice Black, speaking for a majority of five, upheld the New Jersey law on the ground that the money was used not to aid the Catholic church but to benefit all children, to get them safely to and from schools, public or religious. Since the First Amendment requires the government to be neutral in religious matters, said Black, the state may not handicap religion any more than it may bestow favors upon it. Justices Jackson, Frankfurter, Rutledge and Harold Burton, (appointed in 1945), thought this a tortured construction of the First Amendment and would have struck down the New Jersey scheme. If the doctrine of the *Everson* case remains in force, and it has so far, it opens up myriad possibilities for direct governmental aid to students who attend either public or church-supported schools.

The Court decided relatively few cases involving freedom of speech and press, but in those that were before it, the Court ruled against the government and in behalf of free expression. In three cases persons had published material either seeking to influence a judicial proceeding or actually accusing a court of misconduct.[43] All were convicted of contempt of court, but the Supreme Court reversed all convictions as unconstitutional restrictions on freedom of the press, and observed that persons might be in contempt of court only if what they said constituted a clear and present danger to the administration of justice. In another group of cases the Court brought peaceful picketing within the protection of the First Amendment[44] although it qualified the principle to the extent of permitting the enjoining of picketing, peaceful in itself, but enmeshed with contemporaneous violent conduct that was concededly against the law.[45] Even during World War II the Court continued to protect dissent, in stark contrast to its approval of government infractions of free speech during World War I. For conduct very similar to that engaged in by Schenck in 1918—distributing pamphlets opposing the war—a man named Elmer Hartzel was convicted of violating the Espionage Act of 1917. But unlike Schenck, Hartzel did not go to jail, because on appeal the Court reversed his conviction, holding that his activities did not constitute a clear and present danger to the nation's security. [46]

At the same time that the Court was looking disapprovingly at government interference with free expression, in a series of aberrent decisions it upheld military orders providing for a curfew for all Japanese-Americans, aliens and citizens alike, [47] and even more reprehensible, gave a judicial stamp of approval to forcible evacuation of Japanese-Americans from the west coast to War Relocation Centers in inland states. [48] The latter decision was made over the strong protests of Justices Murphy, Jackson and Roberts who argued that not only was the order based on racial discrimination, but in any event individual loyalty hearings should have been held. However, the inadvisability of substituting judicial for military judgment during wartime carried the day for the majority. A third decision, although rendered at a time when the relocation centers were already being dismantled, held that an American citizen of Japanese ancestry whose loyalty to the United States had been established must be unconditionally released. [49]

Two cases which were to be overruled eventually, but nevertheless held up for almost two decades were *Betts* v. *Brady* [50] and *Adamson* v. *California*. [51] Both cases were concerned with the meaning of due process of law in state criminal proceedings, and in both the Court adhered to the rule enunciated by Justice Cardozo in *Palko* v. *Connecticut* [52] that the Fourteenth Amendment did not incorporate the entire Bill of Rights but only those necessary to a scheme of ordered liberty, e.g. the rights of the First Amendment. In *Betts* the Court said that due process does not require a state to provide counsel in all cases in which the defendant is unable to provide his own, and that whether a lack of counsel constitutes a denial of due process depends upon the "appraisal of the totality of facts in a given case." And in *Adamson* the majority upheld a California law permitting a prosecutor to comment on, and the jury to consider, the fact that a defendant failed to testify at his own trial. Self-incrimination, said the Court, is not included in due process of law except in circumstances involving coerced confessions or unfair convictions. Justice Black, who remained on the Court long enough to see his ideas prevail, wrote a long plea for incorporating the first eight amendments to the Constitution into the Fourteenth, and thus to require identical procedures in the national and state courts. Although it took Justice Black several years to convince his brethren of the soundness of his position, the seeds of revisionism in another constitutional area were being sown in the 1940s.

It was the post-1937 Court that also began to take a new look at Negro rights. While by no means ready to abandon the old "separate but equal" doctrine, the Court nevertheless began to call the states up short for certain discriminatory practices. Probably most important was *Smith* v. *Allwright*[53] which outlawed the white primary, the system used by southern states to exclude Negroes from the party nominating process and thus effectively to disenfranchise all blacks. Overruling the nine-year old precedent of *Grovey* v. *Townsend*[54] the Court declared that the primary election was an integral part of the state's election machinery, and that racial discrimination violated both equal protection of the laws and the Fifteenth Amendment. In two instances the Court dealt positively with racial discrimination in labor unions by holding that labor unions could not bargain collectively under the Railway Labor Act for the entire union as long as they continued to exclude Negroes from the bargaining process,[55] and that an association of federal mail clerks could not claim immunity from the operation of a New York statute prohibiting racial discrimination in labor organizations.[56] In addition to the *Morgan* case[57] discussed earlier, the Court began to insist firmly on equal treatment of the races while permitting de facto segregation. It ordered the Interstate Commerce Commission to insist on equality of treatment in interstate travel,[58] and in what may be considered the beginning of the end of segregation in education, the Court declared that Negroes must be provided with educational facilities essentially equal to those provided for whites.[59] In this instance the Court ordered Missouri to admit a Negro applicant to its state-supported law school or build a new one for Negroes. For the first time in decades two federal civil rights statutes of the

Reconstruction period were resurrected and applied, albeit cautiously. One makes it a crime for anyone acting under color of any law, statute or ordinance willfully to deprive any citizen of rights guaranteed him by the Constitution or laws of the United States. The second forbids conspiracies (two or more persons) to interfere with federally guaranteed rights. One of these was used to prosecute an election official who falsified the returns in a congressional primary in New Orleans, and the Court, upholding the conviction, declared that the right to vote in a congressional primary and to have one's vote counted honestly is a right of national citizenship. [60] In a second case the Court held that the same statute was a proper basis for prosecuting a Georgia sheriff who had beaten a Negro prisoner to death. [61] On a technicality, however, the Court reversed the sheriff's conviction since the jury had not been clearly charged that they might convict only if there had been a "willful" deprivation of a federally guaranteed right, in this instance the right not to be deprived of life without due process of law.

During the last term of Chief Justice Stone's tenure the remaining pre-Roosevelt justice (other than Stone himself), Owen Roberts, retired, and President Harry S. Truman selected his first Supreme Court appointee, Harold H. Burton, in 1945. Mr. Truman was to appoint four men to the bench, three of whom were moderately competent but undistinguished. (To the surprise of most observers of the Washington scene, the fourth, Tom Clark of Texas, developed into an able and somewhat creative justice.) Harold Burton had been mayor of Cleveland and senator from Ohio before his old friend and Senate colleague placed him on the Court. Justice Burton, the only Republican appointee of either Presidents Roosevelt or Truman, was moderately conservative and generally voted with the Frankfurter wing of the Court, although he could, on occasion, display an independence of spirit. He served well into the Eisenhower years, retiring in October 1958.

Before receiving the nomination of President Truman as chief justice in June 1946, Fred M. Vinson had already had a long career in Democratic politics and seemed well qualified for the position. Born in 1890 of relatively poor parents in Lawrence County, Kentucky, he managed to acquire an education primarily through the aid and pressures of his mother. He graduated at the head of his class from Kentucky Normal in 1908 and began the practice of law in Louisa, Kentucky, at the age of twenty-one. He acquired a good deal of legal experience in serving as city attorney for Louisa, commonwealth attorney for the state of Kentucky, and associate justice of the United States Court of Appeals for the District of Columbia. He also served long and well in both the legislative and executive branches of the national government—fourteen years in the House of Representatives and several years in top administrative posts including that of secretary of the treasury. At the time of his appointment it was reported that a leading factor in his selection was his talent as a mediator. This kind of talent was needed to heal the divisions on the Court. Actually, when he died seven years later the Court was still divided, often 5-4, but personal squabbles, if they existed, were limited to the conference room. Vinson, himself, was of a conservative mind, and the Court tended toward an even greater conservatism in free speech cases than it had under Stone. In the notorious *Dennis* decision,[62] for example, the vote was 7-2 upholding the Smith Act and sending leaders of the Communist party to jail. Only Justices Douglas and Black raised serious objections. At the same time the chief and those who followed Justice Frankfurter's theory of restraint could form a solid front with the liberals in a series of cases that advanced the cause of black Americans. In a procedural sense the Court was rather lazy under Vinson as it reached a new low in cases decided by opinion, slipping from 142 in the 1946-47 term to 88 in the 1950-51 term, and up slightly in his final term to 104. He personally wrote considerably fewer opinions than his colleagues, although those that he did write were reasonably clear and succinct. He was a competent chief justice but not a great one.

When Justice Murphy died in 1949 President Truman chose Attorney General Tom C. Clark as his replacement. Born in 1899 the son of a Dallas lawyer, Clark was raised in a comfortable middle class background, educated at Virginia Military Institute and the University of Texas Law School. He left private practice in 1937 to work in the Department of Justice where he became a career man, eventually heading up the Antitrust Division, the Criminal Division and finally the entire department as attorney general. When President Truman nominated Clark to the Supreme Court, both influential persons and major newspapers voiced strong opposition, charging that he was not only generally incompetent but insensitive to civil liberties and downright hostile to the American Negro. To the amazement of his critics he became a highly respected justice and the best of the Truman appointees to the Court. In every significant case involving the rights of Negroes he voted to advance their cause and in many instances he was sympathetic to the rights of criminal defendants and to individuals alleging a denial of rights under the First Amendment.

Mr. Truman's final selection to the Court was Sherman Minton, an amiable, decent, but no more than routinely competent judge. A native of Georgetown, Indiana, he worked part time to supplement the family income very early in life. He became a three-letter man in high school where he starred in football, baseball and track, but also excelled in debate. At Indiana University he graduated with a law degree in 1915 at the head of his class, and went on to receive an advanced law degree from Yale the following year. He won a Senate seat in 1934, became an ardent New Dealer, and fought hard for FDR's program, including the Court-packing plan. His enthusiasm for the radical politics of the thirties was too much for the conservatives of Indiana, and they retired him from the Senate after one term. He was not long unemployed, however, for President Roosevelt awarded his service with a seat on the United States Court of Appeals for the Seventh Circuit. While in the Senate his desk had been next to that of Senator Harry S. Truman, an accident of history which was to place him on the Supreme Court of the United States some fifteen years after a firm friendship had been formed. Justice Minton resigned from the Court because of ill health just prior to the opening of the October term in 1956.

The Vinson Court

Between 1947 and 1953 the Supreme Court under Chief Justice Vinson was somewhat uncertain of itself as it began to spend more and more of its time in civil liberties cases. On occasion it could take a strong libertarian view as it did in *Burstyn* v. *Wilson* [63] when it brought movies under the protection of the First Amendment, but at other times it was unwilling to afford American radicals, particularly those on the left, the freedom of speech guaranteed to all Americans under the Constitution. As a result of this reluctance some critics of the Vinson court suggested that it was illiberal and unwilling to protect civil liberties. Such charges are unfair since much of what the Court did during this period was either a continuation of what it had begun under Stone or the beginning of what it was to extend imaginatively under Warren. The fact is that the Court was helping to complete the transition that had started in 1937. By the late 1940s the Roosevelt Court was already breaking up, for Mr. Truman had appointed Justice Burton just prior to his nomination of Chief Justice Vinson. Before Vinson's death in 1953 two more Truman men had joined the Court, and all four Truman appointees were less activist and less civil liberties-minded than those whom they replaced.

The charge that the Vinson Court was not as careful as it might have been in upholding individual liberty stands up best in those cases involving subversion, loyalty, and the internal Communist threat. The first major case dealing with the Communist question was *American Communications Association* v. *Douds* [64] which turned on a provision of the Taft-Hartley Law requiring officers of labor unions to file affidavits declaring that they were not members of the Communist Party. Chief Justice Vinson, for the majority, while admitting that the provision discouraged political freedom, argued nevertheless that the requirement was a proper exercise of the commerce power. The following year in the previously mentioned Dennis decision, the Court sustained 7-2 the convictions of the top eleven Communist leaders in the United States under a section of the Smith Act which made it unlawful to advocate or teach the overthrow of any government of the United States by force or violence. Chief Justice Vinson, although claiming to adhere to the clear and present danger rule, modified it in such a way as to make it inoperable and unrecognizable. In each case, said Vinson, "the Court must ask whether the gravity of the 'evil', discounted by its improbability, justifies such invasion of free speech as is necessary to avoid the evil." Justices Black and Douglas maintained that such an interpretation practically destroyed the concept of clear and present danger, and that the Smith Act, in any event was a "virulent form of prior censorship of speech and press" and was therefore unconstitutional. Although given the chance to rule on the sensitive issues of the Truman loyalty program, the Court, instead of meeting the challenge head-on, took refuge in legalisms and remained on the periphery. [65] At the same time it dealt with a variety of state loyalty programs, upholding some and invalidating others. Essentially the position of the majority was that no one has an unqualified right to be employed by the government and that the states might require loyalty oaths to the effect that an employee did not believe in or was not actually engaged in, activities that might lead to the overthrow of any organized government in the United States by force or violence. As long as the law requiring such loyalty oaths or affidavits distinguished between "knowing" as opposed to "innocent" membership in an alleged subversive organization, a person might be discharged for either refusing to take an oath or refusing to testify as to Communist affiliations, assuming that adequate procedural safeguards surrounded the dismissal. [66]

In eight significant cases dealing with state police measures that in some manner restricted free expression, the Court ruled against the individual in exactly half, indicating the division, and one might add soul-searching, among the justices as they dealt with the perennial question of liberty versus order. Those cases in which the Court supported the government were *Beauharnais* v. *Illinois* [67] upholding a group libel law as applied to the head of the "White Circle League" who had been convicted for distributing anti-Negro pamphlets; *Breard* v. *Alexandria* [68] upholding a municipal ordinance forbidding salesmen from attempting to solicit orders from private residences except with the consent of the owner; *Feiner* v. *New York* [69] upholding a conviction of a street corner speaker under a New York statute forbidding speaking with intent to breach the peace, in this instance an attempt to galvanize Negroes into action against whites; and *Kovacs* v. *Cooper* [70] which held valid an ordinance of Trenton, New Jersey, prohibiting the operation of sound trucks emitting "loud and raucous noises." At the same time the Court ruled against the government in *Saia* v. *New York* [71] when it struck down a city ordinance giving the chief of police unbridled discretion—the ordinance lacked proper standards—to license sound trucks and electronic amplifying equipment in public parks; in *Burstyn* v. *Wilson* [72] as mentioned previously, by bringing motion pictures under the protection of the First Amendment; in *Terminiello* v. *Chicago* [73] when it overturned the conviction of an auditorium speaker, who had actually caused a riot, on a strained construction of a breach of the peace statute; and in *Kunz* v. *New York* [74] when it invalidated as prior restraint a New York City ordinance that authorized, without appropriate standards, an administrative official to grant or refuse permission to persons who wished to speak on the city streets.

Although in 1947 a majority of five had accepted the principle of aid to parochial school children, the Court in the following year stood firmly against religious instruction to public school children in the school building on school time. In *McCollum* v. *Board of Education* [75] the Court ended the old "released time" idea when by a vote of eight to one, Justice Reed being the lone dissenter, it invalidated a system of religious instruction in the schools given by members of the various faiths who came in once a week to hold classes. Four years later, however, a New York City "dismissed time" program, which permitted students to attend religious instruction on school time but not in the school building, was held valid. [76] Justices Black, Frankfurter and Jackson saw no essential difference in the two situations.

A final group of cases decided under Fred Vinson's chief justiceship which support the thesis of a Court uncertain yet progressive, are those dealing with the rights of Negroes. *Shelley* v. *Kraemer* [77] stands out as a major breakthrough in the sense that constitutional barriers to freedom of choice in housing were removed finally and completely. A unanimous Court, while adhering to the doctrine of the *Civil Rights Cases* [78] that the Fourteenth Amendment outlawed state action but not private discrimination, nevertheless was able to destroy the pernicious restrictive covenant. Chief Justice Vinson, while conceding that a restrictive covenant is a private agreement, ruled that once a state court enforces that covenant the state becomes a party to the discrimination. The effect of the ruling was to make a racial or religious covenant in a property deed unenforceable in court. [79] In a series of cases regarding segregation in state universities the Court laid the foundation for the *Brown* decision of 1954 [80] which invalidated racial segregation in all public educational facilities. *Sipuel* v. *Board of Regents* [81] involved the refusal of the state of Oklahoma to admit a qualified Negro to the state law school. In a *per curiam* opinion the Court ordered the state to admit Sipuel to the law school or furnish equivalent legal training within the state. Two years later in *Sweatt* v. *Painter* [82] the Court, while not technically outlawing segregation altogether, made it practically impossible for state universities to maintain all-white student bodies. Texas had built a law school for Negroes in order to satisfy the *Sipuel* dictum only to find that the Negro law school simply was not equal to that run by the University of Texas. For the first time the Court, in assessing equality, took into account qualitative factors such as reputation of faculty, opportunities for contacts with future lawyers and judges, and other general factors not susceptible of quantitative measurement which make for greatness in an institution. The practical effect of the decision was to say that separate educational facilities can never be equal, and that on the graduate level at least, state education for Negroes and whites must be identical. Reemphasizing the principle, the Court ruled in *McLaurin* v. *Oklahoma State Regents* [83] that once a Negro was admitted to a state university he could not be segregated within the institution, or treated differently in any way. In a final desegregation case the Vinson Court interpreted a clause of the Interstate Commerce Act of 1887, which prohibited carriers from subjecting "any particular person to any undue or unreasonable prejudice or disadvantage," as forbidding the practice on railroad dining cars of forcing Negroes to eat in a special curtained-off section. [84] Without actually declaring that segregation of the races by law was a violation of the Constitution, the Court had reoriented its position on legalized racial discrimination to the point where a direct attack on the concept of segregation was implicitly invited and inevitably made.

The Warren Era: Phase One

Not since John Marshall's day had a chief justice exerted the kind of leadership over the Court that entitled him to be identified totally and unreservedly with its work until the advent of Earl Warren, the fourteenth chief justice to be appointed since 1789.

And virtually no one, including President Eisenhower who nominated him, anticipated either the leadership, the direction it would take, or the impact the "Warren Court" would have on public policy and on America's future. Although those who make up the extreme Right in the United States invested money in a silly array of buttons, bumper stickers and billboard signs reading "Impeach Earl Warren," the general public and the responsible press characterized Warren variously as gracious, honest, forthright, hard-working, trustworthy, kindly, thoughtful and able. One of his biographers, John Weaver, observed that Warren developed slowly but demonstrated an extraordinary capacity for growth and an ability to change his perspective. [85] Not a crusader, essentially a cautious man, Warren liked to quote Lincoln: "I am a slow walker, but I never walk backward." [86]

Earl Warren was born in Los Angeles in 1891 of Norwegian immigrant parents. His father was born Methias Varran and changed his name when he came to the United States. The future chief justice received his undergraduate training and his law degree from the University of California at Berkeley, practiced law briefly, and then entered upon a life of public service. As district attorney in the San Francisco Bay area from 1925 to 1939 he never had a conviction reversed on appeal. He became attorney general of California in 1939, and in 1943 was elected governor, becoming the only three-term governor in the state's history. As attorney general he appalled liberals as he urged the evacuation of Japanese-Americans from their homes and farms, but as governor he proposed countless and far-reaching liberal reforms, including fair employment practices legislation. Although the legislature would not support him on the latter, much of his program was enacted into law. He ran for vice-president with Thomas Dewey in 1948 and was an active contender for the Republican presidential nomination in 1952.

If Earl Warren did not display any extraordinary talent as a lawyer or legal scholar, does he lay any claim to greatness as a judge? Unfortunately not. His opinions, though competent, are somewhat loose and rambling, often devoid of even elementary legal reasoning, and to the judicial craftsman, they are shockingly without precedents as a basis for decision. His learned, as opposed to his uninformed, critics have argued with justification that his style is one of "ipse dixit" (it's so because I say it's so), and that his opinions are conceived in terms of pragmatic desirability. Three decisions as significant as any in all American history, in which the chief justice authored the opinion, give ample evidence that the critics are right. In his opinion in the initial desegregation cases [87] the main reliance was not on law but on the shifting sands of sociological and psychological evidence; in the Colorado reapportionment case in which the one man-one vote principle was given constitutional status, [88] he refused to grapple with historical evidence to the contrary; and in *Miranda* v. *Arizona* [89] he gave the Fifth Amendment's self-incrimination clause a drastically new twist solely on the basis of his (and four of his brethren's) notion of fairness. Neither a great lawyer nor an exceptional legal scholar, Warren combined those subtle, perhaps indefinable qualities that gave him an authority that both his colleagues and the American people were willing to accept. In spite of what seem to be insurmountable shortcomings, Earl Warren was truly a leader for his time, a man of vision and wisdom, if not technical know-how. By the sheer force of personality he changed the course of history and must be ranked second to John Marshall, the chief justice whom, by design or accident, he most resembled. He infused the Supreme Court with a new spirit that manifested itself in bold judicial innovation and much needed constitutional reform.

Joining the Court as the additional choices of President Eisenhower in 1954, 1956, and 1959 respectively were Justices John Harlan, William Brennan and Charles Whittaker. A man named John Marshall Harlan must have been destined to sit on the Supreme Court from birth. Named after his grandfather who served on the Court from 1877-1911, himself named after the great Marshall, Harlan was born in Chicago in 1899 of a Bull Moose Progressive father who was the reform mayor of Chicago. He came to the Court from a genteel, upper class background with an education of the highest quality—Chicago Latin School, Appleby School, Lake Placid School, Princeton, and Oxford as a Rhodes scholar. With the exception of a period of service in the Eighth Air Force during World War II, he practiced law in New York until the president appointed him to a Federal Court of Appeals in February 1954. He was advanced to the Supreme Court in November of the same year upon the death of Justice Jackson. By background, temperament, and training Justice Harlan is a conservative in the best sense of the word. He joined Frankfurter in a posture of self-restraint until Frankfurter's death, and then Harlan became the leading spokesman for the conservative wing of the Court. He views the Court's function as a limited one, and he suggests that much of the time deficiencies in the system might better be corrected by other than judicial means. While an outspoken dissenter from many of the decisions altering the rules in criminal procedure, and those highly permissive in the area of free expression and innovative in the area of reapportionment, he is a strong defender of civil rights. He wrote the opinion in *Yates* v. *United States*,[90] protecting the right to advocate violent overthrow of the government so long as it is not tied to specific action. He is respected as a man of quality, ability, and unquestioned integrity by friend and foe alike. Although he often holds to a minority point of view on the Court, it is nevertheless a viewpoint entertained by many of his fellow citizens. Always concerned with precedent and other links to the past, he served as a healthy balance to the judicial inventiveness of Chief Justice Warren and those who agreed with the chief's constitutional orientation.

William Brennan's father was an Irish immigrant who began at the bottom and worked his way up to the position of director of public safety for the city of Newark. That is where young Brennan was born in 1906. Educated at the University of Pennsylvania and the Harvard Law School, his private law practice was only interrupted for service in World War II, until Governor Driscoll of New Jersey appointed him to the state supreme court in 1952. When Justice Minton retired in the fall of 1956 President Eisenhower could not have found a candidate for his replacement more ideally suitable from the standpoint of "good politics." Brennan was a Roman Catholic, and none had sat on the Court since Murphy's death in 1949; Brennan was a Democrat, and Eisenhower's image of nonpartisan leadership would be further enhanced; Brennan was already a judge, commending him to all those who believe that Supreme Court justices should have prior judicial experience, a group to which President Eisenhower belonged. He turned out to be creative and generally, but not always, in tune with the chief justice's liberal activism. He wrote the opinion in the landmark reapportionment case of *Baker* v. *Carr* [91] and subsequently became the Court's authoritative spokesman in obscenity cases. Prior to his appointment Brennan had publicly criticized the controversial muckraker, Senator Joseph McCarthy, and the senator repaid him in kind by casting the only dissenting vote in the Senate when he was confirmed.

The least effective of the Eisenhower appointees was Charles Evans Whittaker who retired from the Court after serving for only three years. A native of Kansas, he finished high school and went to law school at night and in the afternoon while working as an office boy in a Kansas City law firm. Coming up the hard way he eventually became a leading practitioner in Missouri. He was first selected by President Eisenhower for a federal district judgeship in 1954, promoted to the Court of Appeals for the eighth circuit in 1958, and elevated to the Supreme Court in 1959. From the beginning, he found the Court's volume of work overwhelming and he admitted that it had brought him to the point of physical exhaustion. He voted fairly consistently with Frankfurter and Harlan to uphold the government in various civil liberties areas, and probably would have joined them in dissent in the reapportionment cases decided immediately after his retirement.

The Crisis of 1957-58

Running through the key decisions of the Warren period are the twin themes of fairness and equality, two democratic ideals which, when put into practice anywhere, shake the establishment and the vested interests, always somewhat privileged in any system. Consequently, the Court moved swiftly to a major confrontation with Congress in the late 1950s, but even after winning that battle, continued to be buffeted by legislative attacks into the late 1960s. There was a crucial distinction between the crisis over the Warren Court and all the judicial crises of the past, with the possible exception of that over the Marshall Court which was, in modern terminology, an identity crisis. That is, the Court under John Marshall, in addition to exerting influence on the direction a newly founded government would take, was attempting to establish its role in the American system. In this sense the periods are similar since the Court under Warren, and to a lesser degree under Vinson, was in the process of redefining its role or establishing a new role in a system considerably changed in substance if not in form. However, between the times of John Marshall and Earl Warren conflicts between the Supreme Court and Congress or the President occurred as a result of a conservative judiciary applying brakes to reformist economic policies. In recent times exactly the reverse has been true. The Supreme Court moved ahead of the elected branches of the government and possibly ahead of a majority of the people, although in the decisive showdown the unwillingness of Congress to restrain the Court may indicate that most of the controversial decisions were never out of tune with the will of the majority. A more realistic, perhaps cynical view is that in the short run the *threat* of a curb on the Court is just as effective as the real thing—at least this appeared true in 1937—and the more perceptive of the Court's detractors are presumably aware that in the long run they might welcome judicial protection.

The course of the controversy began on 17 May 1954 when the Court unanimously outlawed racial segregation in the public schools,[92] the chief justice acting as spokesman. In an opinion as important as any in the Court's history Chief Justice Warren declared that separation of the races in state-supported educational institutions was barred by the Fourteenth Amendment, that the old doctrine of "separate but equal" had no place in public education since separate facilities are "inherently unequal." Within two years the Court had made clear its intention to erase legal segregation from public life, as it applied the principle enunciated in the *Brown* case to public beaches and bathhouses,[93] public golf courses,[94] and city bus transportation.[95] The southern reaction was a combination of anger, shock and indignation. Certainly there should have been no surprise since the new rules had been in the making for over fifteen years, but perhaps even those southerners who were conversant with the Court's work could not believe that the judiciary which had protected the southern way of life for so long had really reversed its position.

Another group of decisions which offended the already agitated critics involved an assertion of federal supremacy. In 1955 the Court held that the federal labor relations acts pre-empted the right of the Missouri Supreme Court to bar by injunction a strike against the Anheuser-Busch brewing company in St. Louis, [96] and in 1956 the Railway Labor Act which provides in part that notwithstanding the law of any state a carrier and a union may sign a union shop contract was held to prevail over the "right to work" provision of the Nebraska constitution. [97] In the same year the Court pushed the doctrine of pre-emption to its extreme when it reversed the conviction of Steve Nelson who had been tried under the Pennsylvania Sedition Act, holding that Congress, even though no statute had specifically so stated, intended to occupy the field of sedition to the exclusion of parallel state action. [98] The effect of this decision was to invalidate anti-Communist laws in forty-two states.

In another trio of decisions the Court, although not reaching the constitutional issues, considerably circumscribed official actions under the federal loyalty-security regulations, a program designed primarily to keep out of government employment Communists and Communist sympathizers. In one loyalty proceeding the decision went against the government on the ground that the Loyalty Review Board, in reopening the case on its own motion, had exceeded its powers under the law. [99] In a second case, *Cole* v. *Young*, [100] the Court invalidated an executive order which implemented an act of Congress insofar as it permitted agency heads to discharge summarily employees accused of disloyalty, without making a determination with respect to the relationship between the employee's retention and the national security. The effect of the ruling was to preclude summary dismissals from nonsensitive positions. In another case the Court decided that the secretary of state had not followed proper procedures in discharging a diplomat solely on the recommendation of the Loyalty Review Board of the Civil Service Commission. [101] While these decisions were a part of the judicial construct that brought on the wrath of Congress, it should be pointed out that in none of them was an act of Congress declared unconstitutional. The Court was critical only of the ways in which such laws were administered. In the case of *Watkins* v. *United States* [102] the chief justice, for a majority of eight, overturned a conviction for contempt of the House Un-American Activities Committee, and for the first time in many years Congress was on the receiving end of a lecture on how not to conduct investigations. Chief Justice Warren, suggesting that Congress was not a "law enforcement agency," declared that these functions belong to the executive and judicial branches of the government. Moreover, he continued, no inquiry is an end in itself, but must be related to and be in furtherance of a legitimate task of Congress. Striking at the greatest evil of congressional investigations, the chief justice observed that investigations conducted solely for the personal aggrandizement of the investigators, or to punish those investigated, are indefensible. Warren then decided the case on the very narrow point that, given the fact that the committee's legislative mandate was "loosely worded" and "excessively broad," the witness had not been adequately apprised of the pertinency of the questions to the investigation. Since he could not determine whether he was within his rights in refusing to answer questions, his conviction for contempt was a violation of due process of law.

In the *Watkins* case the Court, in addition to administering a judicial warning against sloppy investigating methods, was attempting to protect the individual during a period of anti-Communist hysteria. This was also true in three other cases, all of which turned on technical points but essentially dealt with legalized persecution of alleged Communists or Communist sympathizers. These cases, along with *Watkins*, *Nelson*, and the loyalty cases, frustrated a congressional policy which appeared to have considerable popular support. In *Mesarosh* v. *United States* [103] the Court ordered a new trial for five Communists who had been convicted under the Smith Act on the ground that one of the witnesses, a paid informer of the government, may have been lying. Since his credibility was at least doubtful, the Court said that the trial was "tainted." In *Jencks* v. *United States* [104] a labor leader had been tried for falsely taking the non-Communist oath required by the Taft-Hartley Act. At the trial Jencks' attorney had asked two government witnesses if they could recall what they had reported to the Federal Bureau of Investigation about Jencks at an earlier date. Since they could not, the defense attorney asked the Court to order the FBI to produce the documents in question in order to see if there were any discrepancies between the oral testimony and the earlier written reports. The trial judge refused the request, and Jencks was convicted of perjury. Reversing the conviction, the Supreme Court held that a defendant was entitled to an order directing the government to produce FBI reports, and that only after inspection might the trial judge determine the admissibility of their contents. In the event that the government withheld the reports, the criminal action must be dismissed.

The most significant of the three cases, *Yates v. United States* [105] was fundamentally a reinterpretation of the *Dennis* ruling of some six years earlier. In reversing the convictions of fourteen Communist leaders under the Smith Act, Justice Harlan, speaking for the Court, made two points. First, he maintained that the trial judge had not clearly distinguished between advocacy of an abstract doctrine and incitement to illegal action. As he saw it, the "essential distinction is that those to whom advocacy is addressed must be urged to *do* something, now or in the future, rather than merely to *believe* in something." Unless incitement to action had been proved, the jury could not convict. Second, the term "organize" as used in the Smith Act, said Harlan, refers only to acts entering into the creation of a new organization. Since the Communist party had been organized in 1945 and the indictment had not been returned until 1951, the prosecution on this charge was barred by a three-year statute of limitations. The effect of the ruling was to make all but impossible the prosecution of Communists under the conspiracy and advocacy sections of the Smith Act, and to give broad official tolerance to critical, political speeches, including the preaching of revolutionary overthrow of the government.

In two cases involving investigation of subversion and loyalty at the state level, the Court served notice that the states, as well as the national government, would be bound by fair procedures. In *Slochower v. Board of Education* [106] the Court held that a city college could not dismiss one of its professors solely on the ground that he had plead self-incrimination before a congressional investigating committee. Justice Clark condemned "the practice of imputing a sinister meaning to the exercise of a person's constitutional right under the Fifth Amendment." *Sweezy v. New Hampshire,* [107] the state counterpart of *Watkins,* involved a professor at the University of New Hampshire who refused to answer questions put to him by the state's attorney general who was acting as a one man committee investigating subversion. The interrogation covered the professor's political beliefs and affiliations as well as his classroom lectures. Overturning the contempt citation the chief justice concluded that the authorization for the investigation failed to fix ascertainable limits to the inquiry. In a similar vein the Court ruled against the state in two bar admission proceedings. [108] The New Mexico State Board of Bar Examiners had refused to admit a lawyer to practice on the ground that he lacked good moral character, this having been determined on the basis of his admitted membership in the Communist party during the 1930s, his use of aliases (allegedly to avoid anti-Semitism), and his record of several arrests. Black's opinion for the Court contended that none of these charges could support a judgment of bad character. In the second case California's bar examiners had refused to admit an applicant on the basis of his published criticisms of America's position during the Korean War, his alleged attendance at Communist party meetings in 1941 (testified to by an ex-Communist), and his refusal to tell the board whether he was or had ever been a Communist. Again a majority of the Court were of the opinion that neither membership in the party, criticism of United States foreign policy, nor even the petitioner's refusal to answer questions on the ground that the Constitution forbade the type of inquiry the examiners were engaged in, could support an inference of bad moral character. Now, elements of the legal profession, the entire South, and many senators, congressmen and state legislators had been offended by the new judicial activism.

If this were not enough, the Court added the police to the anti-Court forces. It did so with the decision in *Mallory* v. *United States* [109] which was basically an extension of the *McNabb* rule [110] fashioned by the Court fourteen years earlier. Andrew Mallory, a mentally deficient Negro youth, had been convicted of brutally raping a woman in the city of Washington. Under the Federal Rules of Criminal Procedure an arrested person is to be brought before a commissioner for arraignment "without unnecessary delay," but the District of Columbia police questioned Mallory some seven and one-half hours, persuaded him to submit to a lie detector test, and finally drew a confession from him before abiding by the arraignment requirement. Speaking for a unanimous Court, Justice Frankfurter held that Mallory's confession was inadmissible in court since it had been obtained while Mallory was illegally detained by the police. Without unnecessary delay, said Frankfurter, means "as quickly as possible" and such a requirement does not permit the police to hold and question a suspect prior to arraignment. Although the rule "does not call for mechanical or automatic obedience," wrote Frankfurter, "the delay must not be of a nature to give opportunity for the extraction of a confession." While this rule applied only to federal police, local and state police officials were concerned that the Court might extend it to them as well. It was not idle conjecture, for within ten years local police departments were to be covered by stringent constitutional rules surrounding arrest and interrogation practices.

As noted above, in none of the cases discussed so far did the Court declare an act of Congress unconstitutional. In only one case during the years between 1953 and 1958, *Toth* v. *Quarles*, [111] did the Court exercise that ultimate power when it invalidated Article 3(a) of the Uniform Code of Military Justice which subjected a discharged serviceman to trial by court martial for offenses committed by him while in service. Such a provision, said the Court, violated the doctrine of civil supremacy and was a deprivation of the constitutional safeguards protecting persons accused of a crime in the federal courts. This was the first major act of Congress, or section thereof, that the Court had invalidated since 1936. [112] While not unusually significant in itself, the case added supporting evidence to the charge that the Court was becoming overly activist, meaning in the minds of its critics that it was now engaged in policy-making as opposed to law-enforcing. "Activist" and "judicial policy-making" are code words which really mean that many influential persons and groups in American society disagreed with what the Court was doing.

That disagreement was expressed with a vengeance in the Eighty-Fifth Congress when some thirty proposals were introduced to alter the Court's work or its functions in some manner. They fell roughly into three categories: (1) those aimed at reversing the Court's interpretation of certain statutes; (2) those which would have limited the jurisdiction of the Court; and (3) those which would have fixed qualifications for judicial service. In the first category were fifteen bills which would have reversed the doctrine of implied pre-emption enunciated in the *Nelson* case, a doctrine that raised havoc with the anti-Communist laws of the states. Six were narrowly aimed at the Nelson ruling [113] whereas the remaining nine outlawed pre-emption in general terms. [114] In addition, a special subcommittee of the House Judiciary Committee was ordered on 2 July 1957 to study the possibility of legislation to counteract the Court's decisions in the *Jencks, Watkins* and *Yates* cases. All of these proposals, while peripherally an attack on the Supreme Court, did not really aim at altering the Court's functions or interfering with its institutional integrity. Not even the staunchest defender of judicial power could seriously contend that Congress may not overrule the Court on a matter of statutory interpretation or on questions of judicial procedures. This interaction of the two branches is all a part of the intricate system of checks and balances that the Constitution outlines either specifically or by implication. At the same time once the congressional mood becomes one of hostility toward the judiciary, Congress may begin by working its will through statutory repeal of a Court's decision and end with a major overhaul of judicial authority, which in the final analysis alters the delicate balance of power in the system itself. The remaining proposals indicate that the attitude of a substantial part of Congress had gone beyond reasonable disagreement with the Court to an unreasoning vendetta bent on a fundamental rearrangement of powers.

Five bills would have denied federal court jurisdiction over any matter relating to the administration of the public school system of any state or its subdivision. [115] One would have required the Supreme Court to grant hearings to litigants in all cases it accepts for review, [116] and two proposed bills which provided that the lower courts shall not be bound by any decision of the Supreme Court which conflicts with legal precedent, or is based on any consideration other than legal. [117] At the extremity was a proposed constitutional amendment that would have granted the states exclusive jurisdiction over matters of health, morals, education, marriage, and good order. [118]

A third group of bills sought to improve the caliber of the justices by fixing certain qualifications for service. Individually

they would have required that: (1) each justice be a member of
the bar with ten years' experience in the practice of law, and have
five years' judicial experience; [119] (2) at least one of two successive
nominees to the Court have a minimum of ten years' prior judicial
service; [120] (3) half the nominees to the Court possess at least six
years' judicial experience; [121] (4) each nominee have five years of
judicial service. [122] Another bill would have barred from federal
court service anyone who, in the five years previous to his
appointment, had been vice-president, a senator or representative,
head or assistant head of any major federal agency, or governor,
lieutenant governor or department head of any state or
territory. [123] Finally, a proposed amendment to the Constitution
would have limited the terms of Supreme Court justices to twelve
years, unless reappointed with the advice and consent of the
Senate. [124]

Amid a great deal of public shouting from the Senate, the
House, the press, and various organizations throughout the
country—mostly, but not completely, anti-Supreme Court—the
Congress gave seven measures serious consideration. [125] Of the
seven only one, the Jencks bill, was enacted into law. The House
approved five additional bills, two of which reached the Senate for
a crucial test of anti-Court strength. Both were defeated by narrow
margins. The seventh and most important in terms of its content
and the national drama surrounding its consideration was the
Jenner-Butler bill (S 2646) [126] introduced on 26 July 1957 by
Senator William E. Jenner of Indiana, and subsequently amended
by Senator John Marshall Butler of Maryland.

The original Jencks bill was drafted by the Department of
Justice and as Senate bill S 2377, was introduced by Senator
O'Mahoney of Wyoming, a life-long liberal and generally a
supporter of the Supreme Court. O'Mahoney and the Justice
Department thought of the bill as a codification and reform of
judicial procedure, and not as a curb on the Court, although the
overtones of anti-Court sentiment were always present as the bill
went through the labyrinth of congressional procedures. As finally
passed, the law was less a rebuke and more a confirmation of what
the Court had argued in the *Jencks* case. It permitted the defense
in a prosecution by the government to request statements (defined
as written statements signed or approved by the witness, or

stenographic or mechanical recordings, or transcriptions made contemporaneous with an oral statement) in possession of the United States only after a witness had testified in a criminal prosecution. The judge would inspect such documents *in camera* and decide which statements the defense might be permitted to see. If the government chose not to produce the documents, the judge might either strike the testimony of the witness from the trial or declare a mistrial.[127]

Passed by the House in March was HR 8361, an old proposal that had originally been introduced in the Eighty-Fourth Congress, which would have limited the Court's power of review on writs of habeas corpus.[128] Under existing procedures a prisoner convicted in a state court, if denied certiorari, might seek a writ of habeas corpus in a federal district court, and upon denial there, appeal to the Supreme Court. Critical of this system of double review were both state officials and some lower court federal judges who saw an overcrowding of dockets because of the Supreme Court's granting new hearings on the basis of what the critics believed to be frivolous grounds. The bill, drafted by a committee of the Judicial Conference of the United States in cooperation with the Conference of State Chief Justices, would have allowed state prisoners to petition for habeas corpus only if the following conditions had been met in the state courts: (1) a question of federal constitutional right had not been previously raised and determined; (2) the petitioner had not had a fair opportunity to raise the federal question; and (3) the issue could not subsequently be raised. This bill was a respectable means of attacking the Court since it enabled the critics to identify with judges who were interested in more efficient judicial administration.[129]

In July the House passed three bills, all with large majorities, which would have the effect of reversing three major decisions. The first dealt with the *Mallory* case and provided that evidence otherwise admissible should not be deemed inadmissible solely because of delay by the police in bringing a suspect before a magistrate. A second section, however, made inadmissible as evidence any statement made by the accused, unless he were first advised of his right to remain silent and warned that something he said might be used against him.[130] The second bill would have altered the ruling in *Cole* v. *Young* by extending the coverage of the Summary Suspension Act of 1950 to all federal jobs, sensitive or non-sensitive, [131] and the third would have dealt with the *Nelson* ruling and pre-emption generally. It provided that no act of Congress should be construed as indicating an intent on the part of Congress to occupy a field to the exclusion of state laws on the same subject, unless the law contained an express provision to that effect, or unless there were such a direct conflict between state and federal laws that the two could not be reconciled. [132] And in August 1957 the House sought to alter the Court's narrow interpretation of the term "organize" in the Smith Act by defining it as a continuing process of organizing groups and recruiting new members, and not merely the original organization of a subversive group such as the Communist party. [133] The two bills which were cleared for vote in the Senate were those dealing with pre-emption and the *Mallory* rule on illegal detention. The former barely missed passage as it lost by a single vote, 41-40. [134] The latter actually passed the Senate in a slightly different version from that of the House, but the conference committee had added new material to the bill, a violation of Senate Rule XXVII, and the liberals in the Senate were able to force burial of the bill just a few minutes before final adjournment in 1958. [135]

On 26 July 1957 Senator William E. Jenner of Indiana arose in the Senate to make one of the most vitriolic and ungracious attacks ever made on the Supreme Court. In recent years only southern legislators have equalled his venom. The speech was a prelude to the introduction of the most sweeping legislative measure, and the most fundamental in its intent, of any brought to a conclusive vote in the Eighty-Fifth Congress. Unlike the proposals which aimed only at modifying particular decisions, the Jenner bill would have cut down the authority of the Supreme Court by removing jurisdiction in five categories of cases: (1) contempt of Congress; (2) the Federal Loyalty-Security Program; (3) state anti-sedition statutes; (4) regulations of employment and subversive activity in schools; (5) admission to the practice of law in any state. As can be seen at a glance, the Jenner bill would have undone all of the important civil liberties work of the Court during the period 1953-57. In its original form the bill had no chance of passage, but ultimately, as amended on the initiative of Senator John Marshall Butler of Maryland (and subsequently known as the Jenner-Butler bill), it became the major test of anti-Court sentiment. And it came very close to gaining Senate approval. In its final form the bill would have prohibited the Court's taking jurisdiction of cases involving the admission of persons to the practice of law and of cases involving the pertinency of questions asked witnesses by congressional investigating committees. The remainder of the bill overrode the *Nelson* and *Yates* cases by permitting the operation of state antisubversion laws, and by allowing prosecutions under the Smith Act for advocating forcible overthrow of the government in the abstract. The term "organize" in the Smith Act was redefined as a continuous process rather than as the single, original act of organization.

While the hearings on the bill before the Internal Security Subcommittee brought forth critics of the Supreme Court from the vast reaches of the American union, the weight of the testimony in terms of "respectability" was against the proposal. Senator Thomas Hennings of Missouri, a minority member of the sub-committee, was able to line up a formidable array of Court supporters, including not only the obvious organizations like the American Civil Liberties Union and the Americans for Democratic Action, but leading practicing attorneys, law school deans, and law professors as well. [136] It was Hennings who, in the end, moved to table the Jenner-Butler bill. His motion carried by a vote of 49-41, a narrow margin indeed, but nevertheless a victory for the Court and its supporters. Although some of the old Court-curbing proposals were resurrected in the Eighty-Sixth Congress, they came to naught, for the critical stage of the battle was over with the demise of the Jenner-Butler bill. As in previous times of crisis the Court had received a congressional tongue-lashing and a public buffeting but had come through it all, institutionally unchanged.

Why the crisis in the 1950s? The superficial causes precipitating it were adeptly analysed by Professor Walter Murphy at the time. [137] The Court had gored "assorted oxen on a wholesale scale," arousing an "alliance of powerful enemies," he said. There were strident dissenting opinions, particularly Justice Clark's, asking Congress to correct the majority's errors, thus reflecting a division on the Court and an inability to present a solid front to the public. The technical skill of the Court was considerably less than distinguished, a deficiency that produced sloppy and "disjointed, emotional essays rather than crisp legal opinions." Furthermore, the justices lacked the ability to dramatize their opinions with exciting phrases, to "communicate and popularize their ideals and goals." All of these statements by Professor Murphy are factually true, but one must ask whether the crisis would have been avoided had all the controversial decisions been unanimous, and had they been models of judicial craftsmanship replete with moving rhetoric to rally the support of the man in the street. I think not.

In the 1950s the Supreme Court had become almost a day-to-day defender of individual liberty when it vigorously assumed its new role as the guarantor to the individual of human dignity, equality of opportunity, freedom from oppressive majorities and/or selfish minorities, freedom from arbitrary and capricious actions by public officials, and freedom to express a broad variety of ideas. The Court's new role was the inevitable consequence of a combination of historical events that created pressures which, in turn, became irresistible to the justices.

Converging almost simultaneously upon the Court were problems that required judicial attention either because they had not been dealt with at all by other agencies of government, or because they had been handled in a haphazard or unsatisfactory manner. Responsible for the problems were several historical currents, none of which has yet run its course. First was the rise of a new class of educated Negroes who understood the American system and were making it painfully clear to the American conscience that professed principles must be practiced. There is no doubt that the movement towards legal, social, and political equality for the Negro might have been accelerated with less friction through statutory rather than judicial means, and perhaps state legislation would have been preferable to acts of Congress in the sense that local majorities would have been responsible for the realignment of social mores with constitutional ethics. But, the fact was that the quickest road to equality for the Negro was through the federal judiciary. This was not true in 1857 when the *Dred Scott* case [138] was decided; nor was it true in 1883 when the Court held that the Fourteenth Amendment permitted no positive congressional protection for civil rights; [139] and it was not true in

1896 when the Court stamped judicial approval on segregation of the races. [140] Reasons abound for the Supreme Court's about-face in the 1950s: a change had occurred in the moral sense of a sizable segment of white America; the scientific data produced by anthropologists, sociologists, and psychologists had tended to destroy the irrational and empirical basis of racism; and whites and Negroes had undergone the ameliorative influences of inter-mingling in the armed forces in three major wars. But these factors produced no significant change in the attitude toward the rights of Negroes in the legislatures of South Carolina or Louisiana, or even in the American Congress. The old racial order began to crumble when the Negro lawyer organized his facts and presented his written briefs and oral arguments to the Supreme Court. The time was ripe for a break with the past, but the only channel open for a successful attack was in the federal courts.

The second historical trend which thrust many civil liberties issues upon the Court for consideration was the rise of new ideological theories of societal organization, the purposes of which were to free the oppressed worker from industrial serfdom under systems of unrestrained capitalism. Although the American system was able to absorb the shocks of a class struggle which carried overtones of violent revolution and the anomalous goals of either anarchy or bureaucratic collectivism, it did not do so without dislocations in a governmental arrangement dedicated to free and open advocacy of ideas. Except for the short-lived Alien and Sedition Laws, the national government did not indulge in any legislative harrassment of persons who expressed ideas outside the mainstream of American political tradition until 1917 and 1918 when the Espionage Acts were passed. [141] Nor did the states. The only statutes on the state level which might properly be termed sedition laws, and then peripherally, were those in the South which aimed at the abolitionist movement. Except for the Civil War period there is only one reported case of sedition in the state courts in the nineteenth century, and the defendant was found not guilty. [142] New York, in passing the Criminal Anarchy Act of 1902, [143] constructed the prototype on which over 300 state and federal statutes aimed at subversion were later to be based. [144] Congress copied the New York statute almost verbatim when it enacted the Smith Act, [145] the first peacetime federal sedition law in 142 years. It was invoked only once [146] from the time of its passage until 1948 when the leaders of the American Communist Party were convicted under its provisions. Combined with prosecutions under the various sedition laws were legislative investigations of subversion on both the state and national levels. These became less objective factfinding bodies and more inquisitorial expeditions into personal beliefs, reaching a fever pitch in national life in the late 1940s and early 1950s with the shrill, maniacal ravings of Senator Joseph McCarthy of Wisconsin. Many of these investigations raised not only the substantive issue of freedom of speech and political association, but were conducted with such procedural irregularities as to cast considerable doubt on the integrity of the investigations and, in some instances, on the investigators. As a result witnesses could argue with justification that they were being accorded something less than the fair hearing guaranteed by the due process clause of either the Fifth or Fourteenth Amendments, depending upon the jurisdiction, state or federal, of the investigation. Given this state of facts, it was inevitable that the Supreme Court would be faced with cases in which glaring abridgement of constitutional rights compelled judicial correction.

A third historical trend was the inexorable movement toward national unity which by its very nature was increasing the powers of the national government while subordinating state authority to an overriding national will. Here again the Court was constrained to deal with constitutional questions growing out of vast changes in the attitudes and practices of a new federalism. The Supreme Court's role as guardian of the individual against arbitrary action by the states was constitutionally non-existent until the adoption of the Fourteenth Amendment in 1868, and in practice it was not until after World War I that the Court actively intervened in the affairs of the states in behalf of personal liberty and governmental fair dealing. [147] Reading cases in the Supreme Court since 1925 which allege deprivation of federal constitutional rights by state authorities gives one the impression that popular majorities in the states became less responsible as the nation matured. And very often the state courts were just as unwilling to protect traditional civil liberties as were legislative majorities. Whether in the area of free expression or that of procedural due process the states have not been as careful as the Constitution orders them to be. There is no logical reason why Alabama could not have vindicated the constitutional rights of the Scottsboro boys, [148] Minnesota the rights of J.M. Near, [149] or Missouri the rights of Lloyd Gaines. [150] But ultimately in these cases it was a national agency, the Supreme Court, that had to order the states to conform to the mandates of the Bill of Rights.

It can be said with justification that the political branches of government on both the state and national levels had abdicated their responsibility for preserving constitutional rights, and what followed was a judicial guardianship of personal liberties for want of legislative and administrative protection. Blame for the constitutional crisis of the 1950s should be placed not on the Court but on legislatures, governors, and presidents. The Supreme Court did not seek its role; it was drawn into a vacuum created by irresponsible politics, and it did not shirk its duty.

Why, once again, did the attempt to curb the Court's power fail? Because there were enough determined and responsible men in the Senate—men like Hubert Humphrey, Paul Douglas, Thomas Hennings, Wayne Morse, Joseph Clark, Jacob Javits, John Sherman Cooper, and above all, Lyndon Johnson, the majority leader [151] —who held the view that the existing rules under which the Court exercised judicial review made more sense as they were than as some people desired them to be. The irony of the crisis is that for the first time in American history the Supreme Court was in trouble for insisting that the *substance* of democracy must be fulfilled as well as the form.

8. Aftermath: 1958-1969

Excerpt for its desegregation rulings, the Warren Court's early decisions seem almost insignificant compared to its later, revolutionary pronouncements. In fact, Professor Harold Chase's observation in 1960 that the Warren Court had been "exceptionally deferential to Congress," and that it had not done enough to uphold individual liberty under the Bill of Rights[1] makes considerably more sense than the view that the justices were usurping legislative power. Of course, the Court had not been deferential to the states, and it was the curtailment of state interference with constitutional rights, particularly in the desegregation cases, that precipitated legislative proposals aimed at reducing judicial power. Congress reacts to decisions of the Supreme Court not only in its capacity as a national legislature but also as a body representing powerful state interests, and in the latter sense the 1958 crisis was similar to all those of the past because it was a crisis in federalism. And the Court's decisions of the past ten years indicate that the American federal system is in a continuous crisis. That is, a majority of the significant decisions of the Warren Court, both before and after 1958, are those which have either directly curbed state power or have revised the rules governing state administrative practices.

From 1958 to the time of the chief justice's retirement after the 1968-69 term, three presidents had appointed five new justices, but the amalgam that was called the Warren Court—the appointees of five presidents beginning with Franklin Roosevelt—continued to break new ground, to deal creatively with problems that had been swept under the political and judicial rugs for years. President Eisenhower named his final Supreme Court justice, Potter Stewart, in 1958 upon the retirement of Harold Burton. Stewart, the offspring of a well-to-do Cincinnati lawyer, attended schools of prestige and quality—Hotchkiss, Yale (Phi Beta Kappa), Cambridge, and Yale Law—before joining a New York law firm. After serving as a naval officer during World War II he returned to Cincinnati where he was elected to the city council in 1949, and where he later served as vice-mayor. He actively supported Eisenhower for the presidency and was rewarded in 1954 when the president named him to the United States Court of Appeals for the Sixth Circuit. Four years later he was promoted to the nation's highest tribunal. Justice Stewart has been a competent and careful judge dedicated to justice in the highest sense, not easily categorized as conservative or liberal, but for the most part on the side of restraint. With notable exceptions, particularly in the areas of desegregation and freedom of speech, Stewart has generally been found in the conservative bloc voting against the chief justice and the cluster of liberals.

With the retirement of Justice Frankfurter in 1962 President Kennedy had the opportunity to make his first appointment to the Court, and he chose his secretary of labor, Arthur Goldberg. Goldberg was born in Chicago where his father, a Ukrainian immigrant, was a fruit peddler. Growing up in a tough, slum neighborhood Goldberg worked his way through school, including the Northwestern Law School where he graduated first in his class. He became one of the nation's most prominent labor lawyers during the 1930s and 1940s and in 1948 became general counsel for the Congress of Industrial Organizations and for the Steelworkers Union. His appointment to the Supreme Court received almost unanimous approval from the public, but he resigned within three years to accept the American ambassadorship to the United Nations. In spite of his brief tenure, Goldberg had more than a routine impact on the making of public law since his liberal orientation and activist attitude aligned him with Justices Black, Douglas, Brennan, and the chief justice, making a liberal majority of five in close cases. Frankfurter, whom he replaced, had of course tipped the scales the other way. It would be improper, however, to attribute to Goldberg some special influence. Many cases were decided unanimously or by majorities greater than 5-4 while he sat on the bench, and the most important activist-liberal case of the decade, *Baker* v. *Carr*, [2] was decided before he joined the Court.

President Kennedy's second and last appointment to the Court was Byron R. White who replaced Justice Whittaker in 1962. White, born of a relatively poor family in Colorado, was a top student and fine athlete in high school, qualities which won him a scholarship to the University of Colorado, a Phi Beta Kappa key, selection to an All-American football roster, a Rhodes scholarship to Oxford, and a Yale law degree, the latter studies having been interrupted by a five-year military break. White had met John F. Kennedy twice, once in Europe and again in the Solomon Islands when as an intelligence officer, he wrote the official report on the accident in which Kennedy's PT boat was sunk. After graduating from the Yale Law School White became Chief Justice Vinson's law clerk for a time before joining a law firm in Denver. He was an early Kennedy supporter, and he joined the new Kennedy Administration as deputy attorney general prior to his elevation to the Court. In the close and difficult cases Justice White often joined with Justices Harlan, Clark, and Stewart in a restraint-conservative position. He has been a careful, competent judge but not an exciting one either in terms of originality or rhetorical phrase-making.

The remaining justices to be associated with the Warren era were the two selections of President Lyndon Johnson, Abe Fortas and Thurgood Marshall. After Fortas had been nominated, Anthony Lewis wrote: "In intellect and breadth of experience and sheer ability as a lawyer, Fortas would stand high on any list of possible Justices. The fact that he is a hard-boiled character seemingly unworried by the pressure of having to decide, will do no harm."[3] Both before and after his appointment the adjective most used to describe Fortas was "brilliant," and with justification. He was born in Memphis in 1910, the son of a Jewish cabinetmaker who had emigrated from England. He went to Southwestern College in Memphis and to the Yale Law School where he edited the *Yale Law Journal*. After graduation he accepted an appointment to the staff of the law school, but he was soon attracted to Washington where initially he worked for William O. Douglas at the Securities and Exchange Commission. He moved on to other New Deal agencies and became under secretary of the interior at the age of thirty-two. It was during the New Deal days that Fortas met a young Texas Democrat named

Lyndon B. Johnson, and in 1948 he performed a never-to-be-forgotten bit of legal service for the future president. Johnson had won the Democratic nomination for the Senate in the Texas primary by a mere eighty-seven votes, but a federal district judge had enjoined the party from placing Johnson on the ballot as the nominee until after an inquiry into alleged malpractices. As Johnson's attorney Fortas went before the Supreme Court (actually before Justice Black, since the Court was in summer recess and the controversy had originated in Black's circuit) and obtained an order vacating the injunction on the ground that it was an improper interference with the state election process.

After Lyndon Johnson became president, Abe Fortas was one of his closest unofficial advisers, and had he chosen, he could have had a top official post. Apparently his only interest was in the Supreme Court before which he had argued and won many important cases, including the landmark case of *Gideon* v. *Wainwright*[4] in which the right to counsel of the Sixth Amendment was held to apply to the states through the Fourteenth. Once on the Court Justice Fortas was usually found on the side of the libertarians as was Goldberg whom he replaced. The new justice, however, was not a follower but an intellectual leader, a proper heir to the seat on the bench which had been occupied by Holmes, Cardozo, Frankfurter, and Goldberg. His opinions were scholarly, methodical and occasionally innovative. In mid-1968 one could have predicted that he would carry on the liberal-activist traditions of Warren, Black, Douglas, and of his hero, Louis Brandeis, to whom he was often compared. But fate destined otherwise.

In June 1968 the chief justice announced his intention of retiring contingent upon the confirmation of a successor. The president promptly nominated Justice Fortas for the chief justiceship. In July, when he appeared before the Senate Judiciary Committee, he disclosed that he had participated in White House conferences on urban unrest and the Vietnam war while a justice. As a result he was criticized by some senators for a lack of judicial propriety and he became the center of an unusual but not unprecedented political controversy. Led by Michigan Republican Robert Griffin, the Senate refused to cut off debate on whether it should take up the nomination, thus making the confirmation impossible. At Justice Fortas' request, the president withdrew the nomination, and the Supreme Court began the 1968-69 term with Warren still presiding and Fortas continuing as an associate justice. Less than a year later Fortas was to resign under heavy public criticism, the first justice ever to do so in the Court's history. Fortas left the Court in May 1969, just ten days after *Life* magazine had disclosed that the justice had accepted—and returned eleven months later—a fee of $20 thousand from Louis E. Wolfson, a financier then serving a one-year prison sentence for selling unregistered securities. The money was the first of annual payments for which Fortas was to render continuous service to the Wolfson Foundation. In the wake of growing criticism by the press, as well as by the Senate in which there had been talk of impeachment, Fortas wrote a letter to Chief Justice Warren declaring that there had been no wrongdoing on his part but that he was resigning "in order that the court may not continue to be subjected to extraneous stress which may adversely affect the performance of its important functions."

President Johnson's second appointment to the Court was Thurgood Marshall, the first Negro to join the high bench. Born in Baltimore in 1908, the son of a Pullman car steward, Marshall obtained an excellent education through the encouragement and sacrifices of his parents. He graduated from Lincoln University in Pennsylvania and received his law degree at Howard University where he was at the top of his class. Years before joining the Court in 1967 he was well-known nationally because of his long service as counsel for the N.A.A.C.P. Legal Defense and Educational Fund. It was in large part his efforts that convinced the Supreme Court that legal barriers to segregation must be ended. Arguing thirty-two cases before the Court alleging a denial of rights under segregation laws or practices, he emerged victorious twenty-nine times. His greatest triumph was in 1954 when the Court agreed with his contentions and invalidated racial segregation in the public schools. In 1961 President Kennedy appointed Marshall to the United States Court of Appeals for the Second Circuit where he served until President Johnson named him Solicitor General in 1965. Twenty-two months later he took his seat on the Supreme Court. Unquestionably the fact that Marshall is a Negro had strong political implications at a time when militant blacks were insisting on being heard in the councils of government, but he had earned the appointment in his own right as an able, dedicated, successful advocate.

The Warren Court: 1958-1969

In Edward S. Corwin's succinct and perceptive introduction to the annotated *Constitution of the United States of America*, published in January 1953, he divided the work of the Supreme Court into four periods, and he suggested that during the period ushered in by World War I the Court had replaced the "Constitution of Rights with a Constitution of Powers," and, moreover, had shifted the base of power from the federal system to a consolidated nationalism. [5] Professor Corwin's analysis was correct, but even as he wrote, the Court had entered upon a fifth period in which the "Constitution of Powers" would be transformed into a "Constitution of Equalities," or more precisely, a constitution in which national power would be used to emphasize equality. Throughout the original Constitution and the Bill of Rights "power" and "right" appear frequently, but until the adoption of the Fourteenth Amendment the work "equal" appears in only two sections, and both refer to equality among the states in the union. [6] The new constitutional theory came about in the first instance in response to the socialist criticism of liberalism in the nineteenth century for neglecting equality in the economic sphere, for permitting a rapacious individualism to produce shocking inequalities. Under heavy pressure in the 1930s the Supreme Court legitimated a national welfare state in which equality came to dominate constitutional theory. That domination extended logically into various pathways of adjudication, gathering momentum under an egalitarian chief justice, and broke many patterns of the past beginning with the pattern of racial inequality which had distorted and belied American ideals for over two hundred years.

After 1958 the Court wove the equality theme into the entire fabric of constitutional liberty. In terms of impact on the American system, the reapportionment decisions which demanded equality of voting power with the maxim "one man, one vote" may have been the most significant. Initially, the Court entered the reapportionment controversy by permitting the lower courts to order that districts from which members of the lower house of a state legislature were chosen be equal in population.[7] Eventually, it extended the principle to congressional districts,[8] to both houses of state legislatures[9] even when the people of a state amended their constitution to structure senatorial districts based on combined population and area,[10] and to local governing bodies.[11] These decisions hinged on an interpretation of "equal protection of the laws" as did the desegregation cases, but unlike the latter, the Court was uncompromisingly divided as Justices Frankfurter, Harlan, Clark, and Stewart registered strong dissents against what they called the majority's value judgment that the Constitution espoused a particular theory of representation. Congress again mounted an attack with the introduction of over one hundred bills designed to overrule these decisions. A bill introduced by Representative William Tuck of Virginia, which would have denied jurisdiction to all federal courts in matters pertaining to state legislative reapportionment, passed the House by a vote of 218-175, but was easily defeated in the Senate, 56-26.[12] On the other hand a proposed constitutional amendment introduced by Republican minority leader, Senator Everett M. Dirksen of Illinois, had considerable support and came very close to passing. Unlike the Tuck bill, the Dirksen amendment did not interfere with the Court's jurisdiction, but would have had the effect of reversing the Court in *Reynolds* v. *Sims* by permitting the people of a state to apportion one house of a bicameral legislature using factors other than population. On two separate occasions, 4 August 1965 and 20 April 1966, the proposal failed of passage by seven votes, just short of the two-thirds required to propose a constitutional amendment.[13]

Volumes have been written defending and condemning the reapportionment decisions, and certainly some arguments on both sides of the issue have merit; but clearly the fact remains that legislatures had rigged a representative system to dilute the voting power of millions of citizens, an arrangement that had resulted in a lopsided view of public policy. Such a state of affairs had frustrated so many people for so long that they had bypassed their state legislatures and turned to Washington. The damage had already been done, however, for even Washington could not right the wrongs perpetrated on metropolitan areas by decades of rurally-dominated legislatures. But many of those who saw the facts of the matter clearly maintained that malapportionment was not a proper question for judicial scrutiny, or even if it was, that the Constitution nowhere demanded equality of voting power in both houses of a state legislature. This position was taken by a minority of the justices themselves. The majority saw continued frustration of majority rule if the one man, one vote principle were not applied to the entire legislative body. Whether one agrees or disagrees with the reasoning of the majority in the reapportionment opinions, the decisions can be defended on the ground that they provided popular majorities with the opportunity to decide for themselves whether to operate under straight-out majoritarianism or to maintain the old system in which geographic areas, rather than numbers, dominated public policy. In the decisive showdown in the Senate, the old system lost as the forces of reaction could not quite muster the votes to overrule the Court. How ironical that the judicial oligarchy should be the vehicle for attaining majority rule!

Equality became the dominating principle in scores of decisions dealing with freedom of speech and press. Although the terms immediately following the 1957-58 crisis saw a judicial retreat in the area of sedition, subversion, and loyalty, [14] by 1968 the Warren Court had clearly guaranteed equality of status for seditious as well as constructive ideas, and equality of treatment for members of the Communist party in the United States. For example, the Court held that Congress could not deny passports to members of the Communist party, [15] that Congress could not prevent a member of the party from serving as an officer or employee of a labor union, [16] that it was unconstitutional to require members of the Communist party to register with the government, [17] and that a member of a Communist-action group might not be prohibited from working in a federal defense facility on the ground that the group to which he belonged was under a final order to register with the government. [18] The pertinent section of the Subversive Activities Control Act of 1950 according to Chief Justice Warren contained "the fatal defect of overbreadth" because it sought to "bar employment both for association which may be proscribed and for association which may not be proscribed consistently with First Amendment rights." The Court also virtually ruled out the loyalty oath for teachers as it invalidated loyalty oath laws in Washington,[19] Arizona,[20] and New York.[21] As it tackled one of the most difficult aspects of free expression, obscenity, the Court constructed a new standard that constitutionally guaranteed equality of status for all printed matter except patently offensive, hard-core pornography[22] and insisted on applying the principles equally to other media of communications.[23] When the Court outlawed Bible reading and official prayers in the public schools,[24] it was also applying the equality principle in the sense not only of equality of all religions, but of equality of status for believer and non-believer. Congressional proposals to overrule or modify the Court's decisions were unsuccessful.

With uninterrupted regularity the justices continued to advance the cause of racial equality to which they had given such a powerful impetus back in 1954. Upholding Title II of the Civil Rights Act of 1964 which prohibited racial discrimination in "any place of public accommodation" whose operations affect interstate commerce, Justice Clark, harking back to John Marshall in *Gibbons* v. *Ogden* declared that "determinative of the exercise of power by Congress under the Commerce Clause is simply whether the activity sought to be regulated is 'commerce which concerns more than one state' and has a real and substantial relation to the national interest."[25] Justice Clark also wrote the opinion of the Court holding that a local restaurant serving local people was properly covered by the law's provisions barring racial discrimination in any restaurant "if a substantial portion of the food which it serves . . . has moved in interstate commerce."[26] Calling on Justice Jackson's opinion in *Wickard* v. *Filburn* for support, Clark observed that the contribution of one person or enterprise, although trivial by itself, when taken with others similarly situated is not trivial and is, therefore, within the scope of federal regulation. In 1967 the Court struck down Virginia's antimiscegenation statute, thereby ending the long-standing policy against interracial marriages then in force in sixteen states.[27] In the same year the Court declared unconstitutional a section of California's constitution which permitted a person to sell, lease or rent property to anyone in his absolute discretion.[28] On the surface the provision seemed perfectly valid, but the Court took into account the section's historical context. Justice White emphasized the fact that California had once had a fair housing ordinance but then had submitted the question of open housing to the people in a referendum in which the anti-discrimination policy was reversed. Thus the state was not really neutral in the matter since the new section of the constitution "was intended to authorize and did authorize, racial discrimination in the housing market."

The most recent application of the equality theme has been in the area of criminal procedure where the Court moved simultaneously on two fronts. First, it has come very close to requiring identical constitutional standards for both the states and national governments by extending the doctrine of *Gitlow* v. *New York* [29] and incorporating into the due process clause of the Fourteenth Amendment all the major procedural guarantees of the Bill of Rights, [30] a move that Justice Black had been urging for many years. The Court recognized openly that the federal system with its independent state jurisdictions was a barrier to the fair administration of criminal justice, for it had become tortuously difficult to maintain that a just nation guarantees an accused criminal a lawyer in one jurisdiction but not in another, that it safeguards the right of an accused against self-incrimination in some courts but not in others. There are constitutional referents to which all jurisdictions must conform if a system of justice is to have stability, consistency, and the respect of those caught up in it as well as of those who administer it, and those who support it with their votes, their taxes, and other obligatory duties of citizenship. The old "states as laboratories" argument makes little sense where constitutional rights and guarantees are involved, unless the experiments are undertaken within the framework of a single constitutional standard. The nation suffers much today from the long period during which each state handled the rights of Negroes in its own way. The "independent sovereigns" concept may have been essential rhetoric to launch the American union, but the Civil War and the Fourteenth Amendment settled the argument long ago. Now the Warren Court had said that justice, like sovereignty, is indivisible, and that anyone accused of a crime must be accorded the same treatment in all jurisdictions in the United States.

But the Court under Warren not only updated the federal system by requiring equality of treatment in all American courts, it also fashioned a new set of constitutional rules for the police. Although the rules were developed in several cases over a period of time, they were best embodied in the capstone case of *Miranda* v. *Arizona* [31] by Chief Justice Warren. At minimum, Warren asserted, the new rules would include: a warning to a suspect prior to any questioning that he had a right to remain silent, that any statement made by a suspect might be used against him, and that he had the right to the presence of an attorney, appointed or retained, during the police interrogation. Although these or any other rights might be waived, the waiver must be made "voluntarily, knowingly and intelligently". To answer some questions does not constitute a waiver since the suspect may at any point in the proceedings refuse to be interrogated further until he has consulted with an attorney. Thus the Court extended the constitutional guarantees of the right to counsel and the right against self incrimination to the arrest and interrogation level. [32] The holding rested on the assumption that if these rights do not come into play until a person is formally charged with a crime, they are hollow rights indeed since a person under interrogation may have been illegally arrested and/or searched, pressured into making incriminating statements without legal advice, and all without having been informed that he has any rights whatsoever. Once again it is the equality norm that supports the alteration in the rules. A knowledgeable man of means has always insisted upon his rights, privileges, and immunities at the moment of contact with the police, and he was accorded them; the indigent, the unschooled, or the diffident has either been afraid to suggest that the officers of the government may not mistreat him, or he has been completely ignorant of the Constitution which is supposed to preserve what little dignity he may have. And given America's racial history, the legal inequality cut deeper than ever; it not only differentiated the have from the have-not, but singled out the Negro for separate treatment, and was a particularly cruel system for the black have-not whether he lived above or below the Mason-Dixon line.

The decisions setting forth new rules in criminal procedure came at a time when the nation was witnessing a shocking increase in the crime rate, and it became a political expedient—often a euphemism for demagoguery—to lay the blame for America's unsafe streets and terroristic criminal activity at the doorstep of the Supreme Court. Although little, if any, evidence can be adduced to show that careful judicial protection of the rights of accused persons has any connection with an increasing crime rate, the popular mind seemed to believe otherwise and politicians were only too willing to feed misconception and hysteria. After a good deal of wrangling in committee and something less than high level debate in the House and Senate, Congress enacted the Omnibus Crime Control and Safe Streets Act in the summer of 1968.[33] The statute had its origins in a legislative proposal submitted by the president in early 1967. It had been called the Safe Streets and Crime Control Act and, in a modest way, provided for federal aid to local governments for modernizing law enforcement machinery and establishing crime-prevention activities in schools and welfare agencies. The bill that Congress finally enacted into law bore little resemblance to the president's request. It was a catch-all of dubious constitutionality, and was in part the most serious and irresponsible meddling of all time with what traditionally have been judicially determined constitutional rights.[34] Of the act's four sections, three dealt separately with federal aid to local law enforcement, permissive wiretapping by the police for the purpose of gaining evidence, and prohibition from the mails of revolvers and pistols. Each of these provisions was justly criticized—the gun control section, for example, was believed by many to be far short of what was needed, whereas the wiretapping measure created an unnecessary potential for the invasion of individual privacy—but it was the remaining section, Title II, that struck at the integrity of judicial review. It effectively reversed three of the Supreme Court's decisions on questions of constitutional interpretation, *Mallory* v. *United States*,[35] *Miranda* v. *Arizona*,[36] and *United States* v. *Wade*.[37]

It will be recalled that the decision in *Miranda* was aimed at eliminating the evil of coerced confessions by requiring the police to inform a suspect of his rights prior to an interrogation, particularly the right to counsel and the right against self incrimination. The new law undercut the guarantee by permitting a trial court to admit voluntary confessions in evidence even if the suspect had not been told of his rights. The *Wade* decision was handed down on 12 June 1967 while the Subcommittee on Criminal Laws and Procedures, chaired by anti-Court Senator John L. McClellan of Arkansas, was piecing together the new law. Following logically in the pattern of *Miranda*, the Court had held in *Wade* that when a suspect was placed in a police lineup to be viewed by witnesses to a crime, the proceeding had changed from investigatory to accusatory, and identification thus obtained was not admissible in court unless the defendant had been informed of his right to counsel. The new law provided that eyewitness testimony might be admissible in evidence even if the suspect had not had a lawyer when identified in a police lineup. Under the guise of using its proper power to reverse the Supreme Court on questions of statutory interpretation, the Congress had suddenly pre-empted the judicial authority by proclaiming itself the final oracle on constitutional rights.

In reversing the third decision, *Mallory* v. *United States*, a case can be made that this involved, in fact, a question of statutory construction, although an equally valid counter argument may be advanced that this too was essentially a question of constitutional interpretation. It will be recalled that in *Mallory* the Court held that Rule 5 (a) of the Federal Rules of Criminal Procedure bars the admission of evidence obtained by federal officers during a period of illegal detention. Under the rule an arrested person is to be brought before a commissioner for arraignment "without unnecessary delay," a phrase the Court interpreted to mean "as quickly as possible," [38] and as Justice Frankfurter wrote in the Court's opinion, "the delay must not be of a nature to give opportunity for the extraction of a confession." It is technically correct that the case involved the interpretation of a statute and was, therefore, subject to congressional revision. On the other hand one might suggest that *Mallory* must now be read in conjunction with more recent cases, particularly *Wong Sun* v. *United States* [39] which held that verbal statements obtained as a result of illegal police action, in this instance an illegal arrest after an illegal entry and search, were inadmissible as evidence in a federal court. In a typical *Mallory* case the only evidence at issue is voluntary oral incrimination obtained through illegal police action, and since *Wong Sun* excluded voluntary oral incrimination as a result of illegal police action on due process grounds, the *Mallory* rule ought to have constitutional due process status. [40] In short, if due process of law excludes oral confessions under one kind of police illegality, it must exclude them under *any kind* of police illegality. If we then add *Miranda* to the mixture as well, there seems to be little doubt that official holding of a suspect for the purpose of obtaining incriminating statements between the time of arrest and the time of arraignment involves the question of due process of law, and not simply a judgment of congressional intent.

Assuming that the Supreme Court and not the Congress is still the final determinant of constitutional questions, the high bench will sooner or later be faced with the task of ruling on the validity of Congress' handiwork. If the Court strikes down any or all of these measures, Congress may then do what it should have done in the first place, propose a constitutional amendment and put the questions to an extraordinary majority. In spite of the serious, although perhaps temporary, attack on the integrity of judicial review, the situation might have been worse. Senator Sam J. Ervin of North Carolina had attempted to place three highly restrictive amendments into the bill, all of which were defeated. One would have eliminated altogether the Supreme Court's jurisdiction over confessions in federal trials; another would have done the same in state trials; a third would have prohibited all federal courts from granting writs of habeas corpus to prisoners alleged to be wrongly held in confinement by the states. [41]

Whether one agrees with the Court's decisions in the general area of criminal procedure is not at issue. Four of the justices disagreed with the decision in *Miranda*. What is at issue is whether Congress can, and should, make collateral attacks on cases that have been decided and substitute its view on constitutionality for that of the Court. One can argue, of course, that such powers ought to be within the legislative perogative, but it is difficult to see how the rights and liberties guaranteed to the individual under a written constitution can be adequately protected by 535 legislators who are subjected to pressures that more often than not reflect group desires and passions rather than a concern for justice.

Why did this legislative assault on the Court in 1968 meet with partial success when just ten years earlier a similar attack failed? Senators Hennings and Douglas, two of the stalwarts in the 1958 fight, were no longer in the Senate, but some of the actors were in both scenarios, albeit in different roles. Hubert Humphrey, as vice-president of the United States, sat in the presiding officer's chair and exercised minimal influence. Lyndon Johnson, the majority leader in 1958 who lined up the pro-Court votes, now the president, could have exerted some pressure but chose not to do so. When the bill came back to his desk for signature, he held it the maximum ten days then reluctantly signed it with the statement that it contained more good than bad. In the course of the debates on the measure either in committee or on the floor, several Senators spoke against all or parts of it, but the bill's only consistent and vocal antagonists were Democrats Philip Hart of Michigan and Lee Metcalf of Montana, and Republicans John Sherman Cooper of Kentucky and Hiram Fong of Hawaii. Only those four men voted against the bill in the final showdown. Seventy-two Senators voted for it. Among the absentees only Senators Stephen Young, Wayne Morse and Ernest Gruening declared that they would have voted against it. Other normally responsible and influential senators who might have forced the adoption of a more sensible law, or at least have blocked the offensive parts of the bill, were too busy campaigning to return to the Senate, and for political or personal reasons they chose not to go on record. This group included such luminaries as Robert Kennedy, Eugene McCarthy, George McGovern, Fred Harris, Walter Mondale and Frank Church.

So the southern contingent led by John McClellan, Sam Ervin, James Eastland, Strom Thurmond and Russell Long, forever anti-Court because of its desegregation decisions, had an issue on which they carried the day. Now they could count not only on the Republican conservatives like Everett Dirksen and Roman Hruska, but actually received the support of liberals like Abraham Ribicoff and Mike Mansfield. Edward Kennedy, though absent, declared for the bill. Presidential candidate Richard Nixon also helped the Court foes by publicly blaming the Supreme Court for some of the current disorder in society and calling for legislation to redress the balance.

But probably more than anything else it was the coalescing of events that produced a law which, under less chaotic conditions, a saner Congress would have rejected. First, the war in Vietnam had divided the American people and had spawned bitterness and hatred unparalleled in modern times. As a result of the intense public reaction to the war many of the nation's responsible leaders chose to focus their attention on this issue. Second, 1968 was a presidential election year and an unusual one since the incumbent president had withdrawn his candidacy—primarily because of his unpopular, aggressive policy in Vietnam. With the race wide open for the Democratic presidential nomination the most influential senators in the Democratic party were either seeking the presidential nomination or assisting those who sought it. They were thus preoccupied with matters other than Senate business. Many Republicans were also spending much of their time on the campaign, and moreover, as members of the minority party, they had found the crime problem—expressed in the slogan "law and order"—an exploitable political issue. And within that slogan's framework, usually implied but often explicit, was the charge that the decisions of the Supreme Court were somehow responsible for the nation's domestic disorder. Finally, Congress was attempting to meet the public clamor that Washington "do something" to restore order to the nation's cities, even though the outcry was the result of confusion over a series of events—race riots, individual crimes against persons and property, and political assassinations. Though not totally unrelated, these manifestations of social estrangement and unrest were distinct phenomena, each of which required specialized treatment, and the very name "omnibus" in the crime bill reflected and perpetuated the confusion that the social evils could be remedied in one neat legislative package. In the end it was another tragic event—the killing of Senator Robert Kennedy—that propelled the House of Representatives into overly swift action. On 5 June, the day Senator Kennedy was shot, the House opened debate on the bill. The next day it voted 386-17 to accept the Senate version without amendment.

Even as Congress spoke, the Supreme Court was breaking new ground along the entire spectrum of constitutional rights, and it continued to do so to the end of the 1968-69 term when Chief Justice Warren retired to private life. Far reaching in its impact was the case of *Witherspoon* v. *Illinois* [42] which held that a person may not be given the death penalty by a jury from which persons who have conscientious scruples against it have been excluded. Such a jury, said Justice Stewart, is a stacked deck against the accused, but he took care to point out that the decision did not interfere with the state's right to dismiss prospective jurors who say they would never vote to impose the death penalty, but that it applied only to those who had some doubts about that penalty as a form of punishment. The old case of *Olmstead* v. *United States* [43] was overruled *sub silentio* when the Court brought wiretapping under the protection of the Fourth Amendment, [44] and the prohibition against unreasonable searches and seizures was given a new twist when the Court held that when a person is illegally detained by the police—that is, arrested without a warrant or any form of judicial authorization—fingerprints obtained during such detention amount to an illegal search of the person and are, therefore, inadmissible as evidence. [45] In this instance Justice Black dissented, warning that it was "high time . . . in the administration of criminal justice" to cut the Fourth Amendment "down to its intended size." But in spite of Justice Black's admonition, the Court continued to hold the police to stringent rules when conducting searches. Overruling two cases of some twenty years standing, [46] the Court reversed a defendant's conviction for burglary of a coin shop since the incriminating evidence had been obtained from the search of his home without a warrant. [47] Searches incidental to arrests, without search warrants, may encompass the search of a person and the area within his immediate control, said the Court, but there is no "justification . . . for routinely searching rooms other than that in which an arrest occurs—or, . . . for searching through all the desk drawers or other closed or concealed areas in that room itself." Adhering to a similar line of reasoning the Court held that a search of a person incidental to arrest may not extend: (a) from the point of arrest fifteen to twenty feet in front of his home to a search of the home itself; [48] or (b) to the ransacking of a sixteen-room house to find evidence after making an arrest. [49] Although upholding the "stop and frisk" principle embodied in several state and municipal laws, [50] the Court nevertheless limited the circumstances to those in which "a police officer observes unusual conduct which leads him reasonably to conclude . . . that criminal activity may be afoot." He may then "conduct a carefully limited search of the outer clothing . . . in an attempt to discover weapons which might be used to assault him."

During Warren's final year as chief justice the Court overturned convictions no less than seven times in cases involving freedom of speech, varying in content from protest marches, [51] to the wearing of black arm bands in high school, [52] to threatening the life of the president, [53] to criticizing and burning an American flag, [54] to the holding of rallies for unpopular causes. [55] In one of the latter cases the Court overruled *Whitney* v. *California*, [56] a precedent of some forty years standing. The Court also held that a state may not make the mere possession of obscene material a crime, [57] and that rules and regulations of the Federal Communications Commission which require broadcasters to offer free, equal time to persons attacked in broadcasts, and to opponents of candidates endorsed by a station, are consistent with the constitutional guarantee of freedom of speech. [58]

Warren's final months as chief saw no retreat in the areas of reapportionment and the rights of blacks. The Court decided that the "one man, one vote" rule applied to the election of county commissioners as well as of state legislators, [59] and it invalidated reapportionment statutes in Missouri [60] and in New York, [61] holding that limited population variances among congressional districts are permissible only if (1) they are unavoidable despite efforts in good faith to achieve absolute equality; or (2) justification for the variation is shown. Neither Missouri nor New York had satisfied the constitutional requirements. Cases from Virginia, Tennessee and Arkansas involving freedom of choice plans demonstrated the growing lack of judicial patience with southern foot-dragging in school desegregation. In New Kent County, Virginia, and in the Gould School District in Arkansas not a single white child had chosen to enroll in an all-Negro school. Although a number of Negro children were enrolled in other schools, more than eighty-five percent of the Negro children attended all-Negro schools. In the Court's view this plan was constitutionally inadequate to convert racially segregated schools to a nonracial system. [62] The plan in Jackson, Tennessee, permitted a child, after he had registered in his assigned school, to transfer to another school if space were available. After three years of operation under this arrangement, a formerly "Negro" junior high school was still completely "black", and one of two formerly "white" junior high schools was almost all "white." The Supreme Court ordered the school board to "fashion steps which promise realistically to convert promptly to a system without a 'white' school and a 'Negro' school, but just schools." [63]

Although many laws, state and federal, attempt to prohibit racial discrimination in housing, including a 1968 act of Congress, the Court recently enforced an old statute which had been enacted in 1866 to supplement the Thirteenth Amendment. The law in question provided that all citizens of the United States "shall have the same right . . . to inherit, purchase, lease, sell, hold, and convey real and personal property." This statute, said Justice Stewart, bars *all* racial discrimination, private as well as public, in the sale or rental of property. At the very least Congress may, under the Thirteenth Amendment, secure the freedom for a black man to buy whatever a white man can buy and the freedom to live wherever a white man can live. [64] Among the chief justice's final opinions was his ruling in *Allen* v. *Board of Elections* [65] holding that a trio of Mississippi laws which (a) altered voting arrangements for county supervisor; (b) changed the office of county superintendent of education from elective to appointive; and (c) stiffened requirements for an independent candidate to gain a position on the ballot, were unenforceable since the state had failed to obtain federal approval under Section Five of the Voting Rights Act of 1965. All of the state's actions involved in the case would have had the effect of inhibiting Negro participation in elections. In a similar vein Justice Douglas spoke for the majority in *Hadnott* v. *Amos* [66] when he declared that Alabama's disqualification of the predominantly black candidates of the National Democratic party for failure to meet filing requirements that had not been met by another party's candidates whose names were nevertheless placed on the ballot, constituted unequal application of the same law to different racial groups. And in *Gaston County* v. *United States* [67] the Court halted North Carolina's attempt to reinstate a literacy test for voters. Justice Harlan reasoned that adult blacks who had received an inferior education were discriminatorily affected by a literacy test, even when the test was impartially administered.

On 21 May 1969 President Richard Nixon nominated Warren Earl Burger, a sixty-one-year-old native of St. Paul, Minnesota to replace Earl Warren, who had announced earlier that the 1968-69 term would be his last on the Supreme Court. The new chief justice, a judge of the United States Court of Appeals for the District of Columbia since 1956, was confirmed immediately by the Senate. He was sworn in on June 23 and assumed leadership of the nation's highest tribunal at the opening of the 1969-70 term. Already a public controversy was in the making, not because of opposition to the Court's pronouncements, but as a result of a considerable disagreement both in and out of Congress with President Nixon's choice of a successor to former Justice Abe Fortas. In August the president sent to the Senate the name of Clement Furman Haynsworth of Greenville, South Carolina, the chief Judge of the Fourth Circuit Court of Appeals, and the first southerner to be nominated for the Court in twenty years. Opposition to Haynsworth became loud and sustained as organized labor suggested that he was guilty of a conflict of interest when he had cast a deciding vote in favor of a textile firm in dispute with a union. Haynsworth had been vice-president of—and had owned considerable stock in—a company doing business with the textile firm at the time. Black organizations opposed him because he had allegedly voted for racial segregation in several cases. Public criticism was reflected in the Senate as more and more senators proclaimed that they would vote against his confirmation. Although Haynsworth could not be accused of personal corruption or of having done anything illegal, a majority of the Senate became convinced that he should not be confirmed, and the nomination was defeated by a vote of 55-45. Senate antagonism seemed to be based on the feeling that his judgment and his intellectual powers fell short of the Court's requirements.

Not until 19 January 1970 did the president try again to bring the Supreme Court up to its full strength of nine. He nominated G. Harrold Carswell, a fifty-year-old judge of the United States Court of Appeals for the Fifth Circuit based in Tallahassee, Florida. Although it appeared at first that Carswell would be confirmed with relative ease, opposition began to build, and seventy-nine days after his selection the Senate voted 51-45 to reject the appointment. Initial antagonism to Judge Carswell came from civil rights forces who produced evidence that his background was tainted with racial bias. He had, for example, in a campaign in 1948 said that he would "yield to no man" in his "firm, vigorous belief in the principles of white supremacy"; he had in 1956 helped incorporate a private golf club in order to prevent desegregation of the city's public golf courses; he had sold a piece of land with a racially restrictive convenant attached; and he had drafted a charter for an all-white university booster club. These scattered events in Carswell's past neither made him a segregationist in 1970 nor precluded a future official judicial performance free of racial bias. In all probability these charges, although not trivial, would not have prevented his confirmation without something more.

That something more was provided when Dean Louis H. Pollak and Professor William Van Alstyne, respectively from the law schools of Yale and Duke, testified before the Judiciary Committee of the Senate and suggested that Carswell's legal attainments were extremely mediocre, a charge that was to be echoed by distinguished lawyers, by a segment of the press, and by some leading senators. When the Senate made its final decision it appeared that the scales tipped against Carswell because of his thin qualifications, his lack of stature. In a public reaction to the second Senate veto of one of his nominees to the Court, President Nixon declared that no southern federal appellate judge "who believes in a strict interpretation of the Constitution can be elevated to the Supreme Court." This is hardly true. Had the president selected a southern conservative of high quality whose public record was one of substantial achievement, and there are many, it is doubtful that either his background or his conservatism would have been a bar to approval by the Senate. Nevertheless, the president moved away from the South when he selected Judge Harry Andrew Blackmun of the United States Court of Appeals for the Eighth Circuit based in St. Louis. Blackmun, a product of Harvard (Phi Beta Kappa) and of the Harvard Law School, had lived and practiced law in Minnesota before President Eisenhower placed him on the federal bench in 1959. His legal and judicial career, while not exceptional enough to receive national attention, was nevertheless one of solid competence and meticulous craftmanship. He became the ninety-ninth justice to sit on the Court when the Senate, without a dissenting vote, confirmed his nomination on 12 May. After almost a year as chief justice, Warren Burger finally had a full bench, and as in the past, events only dimly seen would grow into public controversies that the Supreme Court in a new day and with some new talent would be asked to resolve.

A Plea for the Status Quo

While the history of the Supreme Court and of its role in the American system may be read as an institution immersed in perpetual conflict and periodic crisis, the Court has nevertheless survived, grown and contributed immensely to the development of a great nation. Moreover, it has creatively forced majorities to reconsider their proposals and very often has insisted that "the people" be more humane and just than they wished to be. Like all human institutions the Court has been guilty of miscalculation, of grievous error, of lack of vision and even of personal vindictiveness. But it has been an indispensable ingredient in a very complex mixture as it has interpreted and applied the rules under which the system is maintained. Although American democracy is conducted under a set of general regulations, or boundaries, without which popular sovereignty tends to become majoritarian tyranny, on those few occasions when the majority has insisted on getting its way, it resorted to a constitutional amendment which clearly and effectively reversed the Court and affixed a new standard to which the Court had to adhere. This is a sensible arrangement since it takes an appeal to an extraordinary rather than to a simple majority, and the mechanics are such that many people in various capacities must reflect upon the proposed change in fundamental law before it goes into effect. Essentially then, the Supreme Court has been and is the medium for accommodating rule by the people with the rule of law, a task which, by its very nature, has spawned conflict and crisis. The justices are duty-bound to decide legal controversies and no matter how cases are adjudicated, they are certain to arouse antagonism. Sometimes the opposition resorts only to anti-Court slogans like "judicial legislation" or "judicial tyranny", but often it initiates legislative proposals designed to reduce friction in the future. These hardy perennials may be divided into two groups: those that would change the makeup of the Court's personnel and those that would alter the exercise of judicial review.

In the first group one proposal that seems to have merit is the requirement of prior judicial experience for nominees to the Supreme Court. A close scrutiny of this remedy, however, gives one pause. Among the ninety-one justices who had served up to the time of the 1958 crisis, [68] only twenty had had prior judicial service of ten years or better, [69] and of these only three—Taft, Holmes and Cardozo—stand out. Holmes and Cardozo had gained their experience on state courts and both said later that it was of little use to them on the Supreme Court. [70] Of those who came to the Court after service on the lower federal benches, not one, with the possible exception of Taft, emerges as one of the great or near-great figures of the past. On the other hand, included among those who had *no* prior judicial experience were Marshall, Story, Taney, Chase, Bradley, Waite, Hughes, Brandeis, Sutherland, Stone, Frankfurter, and Warren. A five-year experience minimum would have eliminated both Whites, both Harlans, Rutledge and Black. A ten-year rule would have denied judgeships to William Johnson, Field and Murphy. If we look at the Court at the time of *Brown* v. *Board of Education*, the decision which renewed the demands for justices with prior experience, it is true that only Minton had substantial lower court service (eight years) prior to his appointment, but if Black had only a negligible year and one-half prior to his appointment to the Court, and Douglas, Jackson, Frankfurter, Clark, Reed and Burton had none, all had had a good deal of experience before joining in that historic unanimous ruling. And as Professor Fred Cahill reminds us, "if it is the overruling of precedent that is troublesome, let us recall that Mr. Justice Brandeis had been on the Court for twenty-two years when in *Erie Railway* v. *Tompkins* he overruled something like a hundred and fifty cases in one fell swoop." [71] To require prior judicial service of appointees to the Supreme Court is to narrow the field of choice with an irrelevant restriction, and as Justice Frankfurter asserted so aptly, "the correlation between prior judicial experience and fitness for the functions of the Supreme Court is zero . . . [and] it would be capricious, to attribute acknowledged greatness in the Court's history either to the fact that a justice had had judicial experience or that he had been without it." [72]

Recurring since the days of Jefferson is the proposal that justices should be elected for a fixed term. Whether elected judges are qualitatively better than those appointed by the executive might be the subject of a study in itself. It is done in some states without deleterious effects. Unquestionably some, perhaps all, of the towering figures of the Court would not have been elected a second time, and for reason of their independence of and divergence from popular opinion of the moment. It is doubtful that the Court should ever be concerned with popular acceptance of its day-to-day or even term-to-term work, for the Court's role, in its origin, in its operation and by its very nature is and must be at odds with the public opinion on occasion. To suggest that the Court rule on questions of public law in accordance with the wishes of the majority, and this is what an elective judiciary would tend to produce, is to place all three branches of the government in the hands of the people, a concept which removes the final element of qualitative balance from the American system. The framers intended that only one of the departments of the national government, the legislature, be popularly controlled. As the Constitution matured the Presidency also acquired a representative function, giving the people control over the executive department. If the last remaining department, the judiciary, becomes popularized, no check remains on the shifting winds of public opinion. Whatever the mass of people chooses to call free speech is free speech, and whatever the majority says is due process is due process. Under an elected Supreme Court the concept of individual rights and government under law would seem to have little chance of surviving majority tyranny, always a latent threat in a democracy.

Two remaining reforms dealing with the personnel of the Court are less destructive of the ends which the Court serves but do not offer any perceptible advantage over the present arrangement. First is the fixing of a retirement age for the justices. History tells us that advanced age, like judicial experience, has no correlation with greatness or fitness to serve. Some justices might better have retired in their fifties; others were doing great work in their seventies and eighties. In all fairness, if old age is to be a limit on judicial service, it ought to be a limit for Congress and the Presidency as well. On balance it is better that an occasional judge serve beyond his time than that most be retired before their time. Another periodic suggestion, one that received a thorough airing in 1936, is to augment the number of justices. Certainly nine is not a magic number but it is very reasonable and intensely practical. It is a small enough group so that all the justices can participate in all decisions at every level and yet large enough to bring diversity of background, personality and interest to bear on the terribly complex constitutional problems of the day. One can opt for nine without being arbitrary.

Of the reforms that concern the exercise of judicial review two have been around for a long time. The first is the alteration of the Court's appellate jurisdiction, generally a problem in federalism since most, although not all, such proposals have been aimed at taking the Court out of the states' constitutional affairs. A notable exception was the original Jenner bill which would have removed from the Court's jurisdiction litigation dealing with contempt of Congress and with the federal loyalty-security program. At the time of the 1958 showdown Senator Hennings labelled this kind of measure "kill the umpire" legislation and it is difficult to think of a better phrase. The Supreme Court is a guide for all the courts in the union, state and federal, and it provides for uniformity in applying the law of the Constitution. This "guiding" or "policing" or "umpire" function must reside in a final authority, and if it were removed from the Court, Congress would of necessity need to lodge the function elsewhere. Alexander Hamilton stated the case for the Supreme Court's appellate jurisdiction in *The Federalist* No. 80, and perhaps his reasoning makes more sense today than it did in 1788. He wrote:

What, for instance, would avail restrictions on the authority of the State legislatures without some constitutional mode of enforcing them? The States, by the plan of the convention, are prohibited from doing a variety of things, some of which are incompatible with the interests of the Union, and others with the principles of good government. . . . No man of sense will believe that such prohibitions would be scrupulously regarded without some effectual power in the government to restrain or correct the infractions of them. This power must either be a direct negative on the State laws or an authority in the federal courts to overrule such as might be in manifest contravention of the articles of Union. There is no third course that I can imagine. The latter appears to have been thought by the convention preferable to the former. [73]

Furthermore, continued Hamilton, the state tribunals may not be impartial either because the laws of the states have prejudged the question or because "judges, as men . . . feel a strong predilection to the claims of their own government." [74] A century and one-half later a prominent legal scholar, in summarizing the legislation dealing with the appellate jurisdiction of the Court, declared:

By the mid-twentieth century legislation governing the appellate jurisdiction of the Supreme Court of the United States clearly reflected the idea, and the fact, that that Court was no ordinary appellate tribunal. Implicit in the statutes which finally set the lines of its appellate burden was recognition of the Court's unique responsibilities: that it was one of the prime agencies to hold the federal balance in adjustment. [75]

To hold the federal balance in adjustment is precisely the reason for placing final authority over constitutional questions in a federated government in the Supreme Court. To remove jurisdiction in cases involving the police power is to eliminate national authority and stability of law exactly where it is needed most. Such a policy would cause individual liberty to vary from state to state thus creating a situation open to that existing under the Articles of Confederation. Those who would remove various aspects of appellate jurisdiction would surely wish it back one day, for short-sighted expedients do not make for permanent solutions. Legislative tampering with appellate jurisdiction could lead to the extreme in which Congress would withhold or grant jurisdiction to conform to each ephemeral public whim, a state of affairs potentially destructive to all constitutional and national unity. Justice Jackson's conclusion in 1941 is still sharply pertinent. He wrote: "It is now an accepted part of our constitutional doctrine that conflicts between state legislation and the federal Constitution are to be resolved by the Supreme Court, and had it not been, it is difficult to see how the Union could have survived."[76]

A final recurring proposal for change is the requirement of an extraordinary majority or even a unanimous vote by the justices to declare a statute unconstitutional. The effect of such a rule would be to cut down—possibly to the vanishing point—the exercise of judicial review, and would accomplish the purpose of giving broader leeway to legislative policy, once again enthroning majority rule in the legislature. On difficult constitutional questions the views of the minority rather than the majority of the justices would determine the outcome of the case. One can defend a judicial check on majority rule and oppose minority control on the Court itself without being inconsistent, since the procedures for arriving at a final decision in Congress and on the Court are of an entirely different dimension. Congress must reflect and refract mass emotions, private and powerful pressure groups and all that goes into making up that elusive entity called public opinion. The Court must determine individual rights and governmental powers under a constitution, and it seems wise that these matters be decided by the minimum number that can agree rather than by a maximum number that must agree. In civil liberties cases particularly the dice should not be loaded against the individual.

Much of the public friction resulting from the Supreme Court's labors stems in part from a misconception of its historic judicial-political role, and in part from a lack of agreement on what a Supreme Court justice is supposed to do. In the main the justices collectively and individually must act as the nation's conscience when they sit in judgment on the entire governmental process from the popular will to the actions of legislatures, presidents, governors, and a host of law-making and law-administering bodies. The intrinsic imprecision of statutes, ordinances, and even constitutions requires precision in their application, and the specific turn which judicial application takes depends on a variety of factors, not the least of which are the character and personal philosophy of the judge. Judicial character was aptly defined by Justice Frankfurter who called it that quality of objective detachment which enables the judge to recognize and retain the permanent essentials of constitutional government while discarding the temporary and the transient. [77] While all of life's experiences go into the making of that character, once a man sits on the Supreme Court of the United States, it is almost impossible for him to forget, and very few have forgotten, the awesome responsibilities of his office. The rendering of public and private justice is a formidable task and it requires an exacting standard of moral and mental greatness.

But even those judges who rate low in objectivity cannot rove at will over the constitutional spectrum. The discretion which the justices exercise is "a discretion informed by tradition, methodized by analogy, disciplined by system and subordinated to 'the primordial necessity of order in the social life' ". [78] Very often the justices can rely on precedent but *stare decisis* is at best an imperfect device in a dynamic social order. As Justice Cardozo pointed out, the hard judicial work begins when precedents are in conflict or are non-existent, but the hardest work of all confronts the judge when precedents are ample and clear but social justice demands that they be reversed. The law must then be refashioned for the litigants with startling consequences for the governed and the governors. [79] The judge performs a creative act not only by interpreting the social conscience, but by helping to "form and modify the conscience he interprets. Discovery and creation react upon each other." [80]

In our system in which lawsuits often determine the broad policies of government, if the old rules are unjust, the Supreme Court faces the responsibility of re-examining the hypotheses and reformulating the rules, and always it must defend the new rules with reasoned arguments that the body politic will accept. Although the legal realists were right in insisting that the Court be viewed as a human institution that makes law and does not simply find it, some of them have failed to understand the necessities of human nature and of the human condition when they attribute personal preference and nothing more to a judge's decision. Strong as the personal element may be, a judicial decision which either qualifies or reverses a statutory mandate must be based on a source of law superior to the statute. Without such a foundation the decision and ensuing governmental policy cannot be justified as law either in the conscience of the judge or in the minds of his countrymen. When the source is a written constitution, itself inexact in meaning, an ultimate appeal must be made to a universal standard of justice. The good customs are thus separated from the bad, and the governing rules will be based finally on the former.

Judicial review has survived because it has been the vehicle for providing the American people with sound, logical reasons for what the government can and cannot do. When the reasons given by the justices are not acceptable to large numbers of people, they can be overruled by available constitutional means, and it is a tribute to judicial responsibility that the Court has been checked so few times in just eighteen years short of two centuries. Undoubtedly there will be crises in the future as in the past, but they will be the result of new and difficult problems confronting the Republic and not the effect of institutional malaise. Government by lawsuit should continue to be an appropriate companion to government by the people, for as Alexis de Tocqueville declared long ago, "the power vested in American courts of justice of pronouncing a statute to be unconstitutional forms one of the most powerful barriers that have ever been devised against the tyranny of political assemblies."[81]

Notes

Notes to Chapter 1

1. As quoted in Francis R. Aumann, *The Changing American Legal System* (Columbus: Ohio State University Press, 1940), p. 52.
2. *Ibid.*
3. Records of the Suffolk County Court 1671-1680, Vol. 1 (Publications of the Colonial Society of Massachusetts, Vol. 29). See Aumann, *Legal System*, p. 51.
4. *Ibid.* See the introduction to the *Records of the Suffolk County Court* by Samuel Morison and Zechariah Chafee.
5. Aumann, *Legal System*, p. 52.
6. Roscoe Pound, *Organization of Courts* (Boston: Little, Brown, 1940), p. 27.
7. *Ibid.*
8. See Aumann, *Legal System*, p. 9.
9. See Francis N. Thorpe, *The Constitutional History of the United States* (Chicago: Callaghan, 1901), Vol. I, p. 181.
10. Pound, *Courts*, p. 5.
11. *Ibid.*, pp. 56-57.
12. *Ibid.*, pp. 28-29.
13. For a discussion of vice-admiralty courts and their importance, see Charles M. Andrews, *The Colonial Period of American History* (New Haven: Yale University Press, 1934), Vol. IV, pp. 222-271; see also Carl Ubbelohde, *The Vice-Admiralty Courts and the American Revolution* (Chapel Hill: University of North Carolina Press, 1960).
14. See Ubbelohde, *Vice-Admiralty*, pp. 202-214.
15. See Roscoe Pound, *Appellate Procedure in Civil Cases* (Boston: Little, Brown, 1941), Chap. I, for a discussion of the historical development of appeals procedure.
16. *Ibid.*, p. 9.
17. *Ibid.*, p. 10.
18. *Ibid.*, pp. 24-25.
19. *Ibid.*, p. 27.
20. *Ibid.*, p. 38.

21. *Ibid.*, p. 72.

22. See Joseph Henry Smith, *Appeals to the Privy Council from the American Plantations* (New York: Columbia University Press, 1950), pp. 523-537. See also Dudley Odell McGovney, "The British Privy Council's Power to Restrain the Legislatures of Colonial America: Power to Disallow Statutes: Power to Veto," 94 *University of Pennsylvania Law Review* (1945) 59-93 and "The British Origin of Judicial Review of Legislation," 93 *University of Pennsylvania Law Review* (1944) 1-49.

23. Smith, *Appeals*, p. 525.

24. *Ibid.*

25. Act for Preventing Frauds, and Regulating Abuses in the Plantation Trade, 7 and 8 Wm. III, C. 22 (1696). J.H. Smith suggests that this section was inserted at the recommendation of Chief Justice Holt who had earlier expressed judicial approval of the doctrine of *Bonham's Case* that acts of Parliament were void which ran counter to basic common law principles. It was Holt's conception that given a basic legal rule, dispositions contrary thereto could be declared void. As Holt said in *East India Company* v. *Sandys*, "if any law be made against any point of the Christian religion, that law is *ipso facto* void." Howell, State Trials, Vol. 10, p. 375. See Smith, *Appeals*, p. 527.

26. Smith, *Appeals*, p. 529.

27. *Ibid.*, p. 530.

28. See Jeremiah Dummer, *A Defense of the New England Charters* (London: W. Wilkins, 1721), pp. 66-76, as quoted in Smith, *Privy Council*, pp. 530-531.

29. See Robert L. Schuyler, *Parliament and the British Empire* (New York: Columbia University Press, 1929), pp. 19-22.

30. Smith, *Appeals*, p. 531.

31. See McGovney, *Privy Council*, p. 62.

32. *Ibid.*, pp. 71-72.

33. *Winthrop* v. *Lechmere*, 1727; *Philips* v. *Savage*, 1738; *Clark* v. *Tousey*, 1738; and *Camm* v. *Hansford and Moss (Parson's Cause)*, 1764.

34. Hampton L. Carson, *The History of the Supreme Court of the United States* (Philadelphia: P.W. Ziegler, 1902), p. 41.

35. *Ibid.*

36. *Journals of the Continental Congress*, Vol. 3, pp. 371-75.

37. Carson, *History*, p. 43.

38. Under this arrangement special committees heard the cases of: the *Thistle* (*Journals of the Continental Congress*, Vol. 5, p. 827), the *Elizabeth* (*Journals of the Continental Congress*, Vol. 5, p. 751), the *Charming Peggy* (*Journals of the Continental Congress*, Vol. 6, p. 885), the *Vulcan* (*Journals of the Continental Congress*, Vol. 6, p. 986), *Esek Hopkins* v. *Richard Darby* (*Journals of the Continental Congress*, Vol. 5, p. 545), the *Richmond* (*Journals of the Continental Congress*, Vol. 7, p. 13), the *Phoenix* (*Journals of the Continental Congress*, Vol. 7, p. 30).

39. *Journals of the Continental Congress*, Vol. 7, p. 75. The first standing committee consisted of James Wilson of Pennsylvania, Jonathan Sergeant of

New Jersey, William Ellery of Rhode Island, Samuel Chase of Maryland and Roger Sherman of Connecticut. The number was increased to eight for a brief period, but then reduced to five.

40. *Journals of the Continental Congress*, Vol. 16, p. 61. Congress elected as judges George Wythe of Virginia, William Paca of Maryland, and Titus Hosmer of Connecticut. Wythe declined and Cyrus Griffin of Virginia was chosen in his stead. Judge Hosmer died in August of 1780 and the work of the court was performed during the first two years of its existence by Paca and Griffin. In November of 1782, Paca resigned to become governor of Maryland. In December, 1782, George Read of Delaware and John Lowell of Massachusetts were chosen to serve with Judge Griffin.

41. *Journals of the Continental Congress*, Vol. 16, p. 61.

42. *Journals of the Continental Congress*, Vol. 30, p. 60.

43. *Journals of the Continental Congress*, Vol. 30, p. 423. See also J.C. Bancroft Davis in the Appendix to *U.S. Reports*, Vol. 131, p. 28.

44. *Journals of the Continental Congress*, Vol. 9, pp. 906-928.

45. See the essay by Thomas Sergeant in Peter DuPonceau, *The Jurisdiction of the Courts of the United States* (Philadelphia: A. Small, 1824), p. 152.

46. See *Journals of the American Congress*, Vol. 3, pp. 606-607 (1781) and Vol. 4, pp. 169-170 (1783).

47. *New Hampshire, New York, and Massachusetts v. Vermont; Pennsylvania v. Virginia; Pennsylvania v. Connecticut; New Jersey v. Virginia; Massachusetts v. New York*; and *South Carolina v. Georgia*.

48. *Pennsylvania v. Connecticut*.

49. See *Journals of the Continental Congress*, Vol. 21, *passim*.

50. *Ibid.*

51. *Journals of the Continental Congress*, Vol 22, pp. 121-126.

52. *Journals of the Continental Congress*, Vol. 19, pp. 402-420.

53. *Journals of the Continental Congress*, Vol. 22, p. 103.

54. *Journals of the Continental Congress*, Vol. 27, p. 606.

55. See J. Franklin Jameson, *Essays in the Constitutional History of the United States* (Boston: Houghton Mifflin, 1889), pp. 43-44. See also Carson, *History*, pp. 63-64.

56. For a discussion of precedents for judicial review prior to 1789, see: William M. Meigs, "The American Doctrine of Judicial Power, and Its Early Origin," 47 *American Law Review* 683 (Oct. 1913); Charles Grove Haines, *The American Doctrine of Judicial Supremacy* (Berkeley: University of California Press, 1932), pp. 88-121; Edward S. Corwin, "The Establishment of Judicial Review," 9 *Michigan Law Review* 102 (Dec. 1910) and 283 (Feb. 1911); William Winslow Crosskey, *Politics and the Constitution* (Chicago: University of Chicago Press, 1953), II, pp. 938-975.

57. See particularly Charles A. Beard, *The Supreme Court and the Constitution* (New York: Macmillan, 1912). At least one of the framers asserted flatly and unequivocally that the Supreme Court possessed the power of judicial review. See Alexander Hamilton's contention in *The Federalist*, No. 78.

58. See William Meigs, "Judicial Power," p. 689.

59. *Ibid.*

Notes to Chapter 2

1. *Chisholm* v. *Georgia*, 2 Dallas 419 (1793).
2. As quoted in David Loth, *Chief Justice John Marshall and the Supreme Court* (New York: Morton, 1949), p. 162.
3. Alexis de Tocqueville, *Democracy in America* (New York: Knopf, 1948), I, p. 151.
4. Ten of the twenty senators and eight members of the House had been among the fifty-five members of the Constitutional Convention and five senators and twenty-six representatives had been members of the state ratifying conventions.
5. Committee members who had been at the Convention were Oliver Ellsworth of Conn., William Paterson of N.J., Caleb Strong of Mass., Richard Bassett of Del., and William Few of Ga. The remaining members were William Maclay of Pa., Richard Henry Lee of Va., and Paine Wingate of N.H.
6. Voting against the Judiciary Bill were Pierce Butler of S.C., Richard Henry Lee and William Grayson of Va., John Langdon and Paine Wingate of N.H., and William Maclay of Pa.
7. *Journal of William Maclay* (New York: Albert and Charles Boni, 1927), p. 114.
8. *Ibid.*
9. 1 *Annals of Congress* 814.
10. *Ibid.*, 813. See also the arguments of James Jackson of Georgia, 1 *Annals of Congress* 832-833; Edanus Burke of South Carolina, 1 *Annals of Congress* 843; and Michael Stone of Maryland, 1 *Annals of Congress* 854-859.
11. See Felix Frankfurter and James Landis, *The Business of the Supreme Court* (New York: Macmillan, 1928), p. 12.
12. *Ibid.*, 14. Slight relief for circuit riding came with an act of Congress of 1793 whereby the justices were relieved of handling a fixed circuit and could take circuits in turn, and under which only one Supreme Court justice was required to sit on a circuit court.
13. James Richardson, *Messages and Papers of the Presidents*, I (Washington: Government Printing Office, 1896), p. 289.
14. Rutledge to Hamilton, 10 January 1801, as quoted in Albert Beveridge, *Life of John Marshall* (New York: Houghton Mifflin, 1944), II, p. 550.
15. The House passed the bill on 20 January by a vote of 51-43 (10 *Annals of Congress* 915) and the Senate approved the bill on 7 February by a vote of 16-4 (10 *Annals of Congress* 741-742).
16. John Spencer Bassett, *The Federalist System*, 1789-1801 (New York: Harper, 1906), p. 293.
17. Max Farrand, "The Judiciary Act of 1801," 5 *American Historical Review* 682-686 (1900).
18. Acts of 1809, 1875 and 1891.
19. Frankfurter and Landis, *Business*, pp. 24-25.
20. The message read: "The judiciary system of the United States and especially that portion of it recently erected, will of course present itself to the contemplation of Congress; and that they may be able to judge of the

proportion which the institution bears to the business it has to perform, I have caused to be procured from the several States, and now lay before Congress, an exact statement of all the causes decided since the first establishment of the courts, and of those which were depending when additional courts and judges were brought in to their aid." (*Writings*, Ford, ed., pp. 8, 123).

21. See William S. Carpenter, "Repeal of the Judiciary Act of 1801," 9 *American Political Science Review* (519 (1915).

22. The bill to repeal the Judiciary Act of 1801 passed the Senate on 3 February and the House on 3 March. See 11 *Annals of Congress* 1305-1306.

23. See speeches of Nathaniel Chipman of Vt., 11 *Annals of Congress* 123, 130; Uriah Tracy of Conn., 11 *Annals of Congress* 57; Simeon Alcott of N.H., 11 *Annals of Congress* 75; and William Wells of Del., 11 *Annals of Congress* 132.

24. See speech of Robert Wright of Md., 11 *Annals of Congress* 113 and Stephen B. Bradley of Vt., 11 *Annals of Congress* 167.

25. 11 *Annals of Congress* 547.

26. See speech of Thomas T. Davis of Kentucky, 11 *Annals of Congress* 556.

27. See speeches of Robert Wright of Maryland, 11 *Annals of Congress* 112 and Abraham Baldwin of Georgia, 11 *Annals of Congress* 102.

28. See speech of Nathaniel Chipman of Vermont, 11 *Annals of Congress* 122.

29. See speech of William Wells of Delaware, 11 *Annals of Congress* 132.

30. *Ibid.*, p. 133.

31. Henry Adams, *History of the United States* (New York: Scribners, 1898), I, p. 297.

32. 11 *Annals of Congress* 90, 91, 77.

33. *Ibid.*, 92.

34. Uncertain of this newly taken position, the Republicans enacted a bill which put off the next session of the Supreme Court until February, 1803, the August term in 1802 being omitted. (Act of 29 April 1802, 11 *Annals of Congress* 1332-1342).

35. See 11 *Annals of Congress* 179-180.

36. 10 *Annals of Congress* 101. See Charles Warren, *Congress, the Constitution and the Supreme Court* (Boston: Little, Brown, 1935) pp. 99-127, for a comprehensive discussion of the early congressional debates and the question of judicial review.

37. See John C. Miller, *The Federalist Era: 1789-1801* (New York: Harper, 1960), p. 125.

38. Scores of essays and books have been written about John Marshall. Most can be found in James A. Servies, *A Bibliography of John Marshall* (Washington: United States Commission for the Celebration of the Two Hundredth Anniversary of the Birth of John Marshall, 1956). Still the best biography is Albert J. Beveridge's monumental *The Life of John Marshall* (Boston and New York: Houghton Mifflin, 1916-1920). Published during the same period was Edward S. Corwin's *John Marshall and the Constitution*

(New Haven: Yale University Press, 1919). Two very able recent studies are John P. Roche, *John Marshall: Major Opinions and Writings* (Indianapolis and New York: Bobbs-Merrill, 1967), and Robert K. Faulkner, *The Jurisprudence of John Marshall* (Princeton: Princeton University Press, 1968).

39. Roche, *John Marshall*, pp. XXX-XXXI

40. Charles Warren, *The Supreme Court in United States History* (Boston: Little, Brown, 1923), II, p. 273.

41. 1 Cranch 137 (1803).

42. 4 Wheaton 316 (1819).

43. 9 Wheaton 1 (1824).

44. See Warren, *The Supreme Court in United States History*, I, p. 288.

45. Charles Grove Haines, *The Role of the Supreme Court in American Government and Politics, 1789-1835* (Berkeley: University of California Press, 1944), p. 333.

46. 6 Wheaton 264 (1821).

47. 8 Wheaton 1 (1823).

48. See 16 *Annals of Congress* 133.

49. See 16 *Annals of Congress* 133-147.

50. See 19 *Annals of Congress* 412, 20 February 1809.

51. 5 Cranch 115 (1809).

52. *Penhallow* v. *Doane's Administrators*, 3 Dallas 54 (1795).

53. *U.S.* v. *Judge Peters*, 5 Cranch 115 (1809).

54. See Allen Johnson (ed.), *Readings in American Constitutional History* (Boston: Houghton Mifflin, 1912), p. 254.

55. See John Schmidhauser, *The Supreme Court as Final Arbiter in Federal-State Relations, 1789-1957* (Chapel Hill: University of North Carolina Press, 1958), p. 39.

56. 1 Wheaton 304 (1816).

57. 6 Cranch 87 (1810).

58. 4 Wheaton 518 (1819).

59. 7 Cranch 164 (1812).

60. 4 Wheaton 122 (1819).

61. 4 Wheaton 316 (1819).

62. 8 Wheaton 464 (1823).

63. 8 Wheaton 1 (1823).

64. 9 Wheaton 738 (1824).

65. With the single exception of the slavery controversy, there has never been a cooperative spirit among the states to protect an abstract doctrine of states' rights. In general, a state which had a grievance against the national government (any or all of its branches) had to stand in isolation. In this instance Kentucky, in protesting against encroachments of the federal judiciary, was following the position taken by Virginia after the *Hunter's Lessee* and *Cohens* decisions. But Virginia supported the Supreme Court in *Green* v. *Biddle*. As Charles Warren pointed out, state opposition to judicial action depended upon a particular interest aided or injured and not upon a political theory held by the states. (*History*, I, p. 642).

66. For the text of the amendment, see 38 *Annals of Congress* 68.
67. See 38 *Annals of Congress* 68-91 for Senator Johnson's remarks.
68. 38 *Annals of Congress* 114.
69. 39 *Annals of Congress* 1682.
70. 41 *Annals of Congress* 28.
71. 41 *Annals of Congress* 336.
72. In the House the bill was debated January 4, 5, 6, 9, 10, 11, 12, 18, 19, 21, 23, 24, 25, April 17, 24, 28, May 7; in the Senate, April 7, 10, 11, 12, 13, 14, 15, May 3, 28.
73. See 2 *Register of Debates in Congress* 1086.
74. 5 *Stat.* 176. For a history of the bill, see 3 *Congressional Globe* 10, 27, 51, 185, 197, 209, 243, 251, 280.
75. *Brown* v. *Maryland*, 12 Wheaton 419 (1827).
76. 2 Peters 449 (1829).
77. 4 Peters 410 (1830).
78. Letter of 15 October 1830, as quoted in Warren, *History*, I, 727.
79. See 6 *Register of Debates in Congress* 22-452.
80. 7 *Register of Debates in Congress* 532.
81. *Ibid.*, 542.
82. *Ibid.*, 540.
83. See *Cherokee Nation* v. *Georgia*, 5 Peters 1 (1831).
84. *Worcester* v. *Georgia*, 6 Peters 515 (1832).
85. See Warren, *History*, I, pp. 764-765; see also Schmidhauser, *Final Arbiter*, pp. 33-36.
86. See Alfred H. Kelly and Winfred A. Harbison, *The American Constitution* (New York: Norton, 1955), p. 303.
87. See Richard P. Longaker, "Andrew Jackson and the Judiciary," 71 *Political Science Quarterly* 363 (1956).
88. See 9 *Register of Debates in Congress* 1903.
89. Robert G. McCloskey, *The American Supreme Court* (Chicago: University of Chicago Press, 1960), p. 72.

Notes to Chapter 3

1. *Charles River Bridge* v. *Warren Bridge*, 11 Peters 420 (1837).
2. Wallace Mendelson, *Capitalism, Democracy and The Supreme Court* (New York: Appleton-Century-Crofts, 1960).
3. *Ex parte Merryman*, 17 Fed. Cases 144, No. 9487 (CCD Md.) 1861.
4. Mendelson, *Capitalism*, p. 44.
5. *Brown* v. *Maryland*, 12 Wheaton 419 (1827).
6. *Craig* v. *Missouri*, 4 Peters 410 (1830).
7. *Ogden* v. *Saunders*, 12 Wheaton 212 (1827).
8. *Prigg* v. *Pennsylvania*, 16 Peters 539 (1842).
9. Louis Boudin, *Government by Judiciary*, II (New York: Goodwin, 1932), p. 2.
10. *Charles River Bridge* v. *Warren Bridge, supra.*

11. Twenty years after the ruling in *Bronson* v. *Kinzie* the Taney Court voided a decision of a state court which allegedly interfered with contract rights since it was at odds with the state court's earlier judicial decisions. *Gelpcke* v. *Dubuque*, 1 Wallace 175 (1864). This case extended further than ever before federal judicial protection of vested contractual rights.

12. 16 Howard 369 (1854) at 412.

13. 18 Howard 331 (1856).

14. *Armstrong* v. *Athens County*, 16 Peters 281 (1842) and *Philadelphia and Wilmington Railroad Co.* v. *Maryland*, 10 Howard 376 (1850).

15. *Gordon* v. *Appeal Tax Court*, 3 Howard 133 (1845).

16. 101 U.S. 814 (1880).

17. 11 Peters 420 (1837).

18. 6 Howard 507 (1848).

19. 8 Howard 163 (1850).

20. *Willson* v. *Blackbird Creek Marsh Co.*, 2 Peters 245 (1829).

21. *License Cases*, 5 Howard 504 (1847).

22. *Cooley* v. *Board of Port Wardens*, 12 Howard 299 (1851).

23. 14 Peters 526 (1840).

24. 14 Peters 540 (1840).

25. 16 Peters 367 (1842).

26. 16 Peters 1 (1842).

27. 12 Howard 443 (1851).

28. *The Thomas Jefferson*, 10 Wheaton 428 (1825).

29. 16 Peters 435 (1842).

30. 15 Peters 449 (1841).

31. 16 Peters 539 (1842).

32. *Rowan* v. *Runnels*, 5 Howard 134 (1847).

33. Carl Brent Swisher, *Roger B. Taney* (New York: Macmillan, 1935), p. 419.

34. *Jones* v. *Van Zandt*, 5 Howard 215 (1847).

35. *Moore* v. *Illinois*, 14 Howard 13 (1853).

36. 10 Howard 82 (1851).

37. 19 Howard 393 (1857). Professor Swisher states that the name, Sanford, is incorrectly spelled, Sandford, in the reports. There are many accounts of this case in the literature of American constitutional history including Professor Swisher's presentation in his biography of Taney. Recent detailed analyses include Stanley I. Kutler, *The Dred Scott Decision: Law or Politics* (Boston: Houghton Mifflin, 1967); Vincent C. Hopkins, S.J., *Dred Scott's Case* (New York: Atheneum, 1967). See also the brief narrative by Julius J. Marke in 12 *N.Y.U. Law Center Bulletin* 12 (Fall, 1963).

38. See Marke, 12 *N.Y.U. Law Center Bulletin* 12 (Fall, 1963).

39. 10 Howard 82 (1851).

40. Allan Nevins, *The Emergence of Lincoln* (New York: Scribners, 1950), pp. 473-477.

41. *Ibid.*, p. 475.

42. Arthur Bestor, "State Sovereignty and Slavery: A Reinterpretation of Proslavery Constitutional Doctrine, 1846-1860," *Journal of the Illinois State Historical Society* (Summer, 1961) 54, 148-74. Reprinted in Kutler, *Dred Scott*, p. 178.

43. Edward S. Corwin, "The Dred Scott Decision in the Light of Contemporary Legal Doctrines," 17 *The American Historical Review* (October 1911) 52-69. Reprinted in Kutler, *Dred Scott*, 128-129.

44. See 9 Congressional Globe 18, 26th Congress, 2d Session, 5 December 1840; 12 Congressional Globe 39, 27th Congress, 3d Session, 16 January 1843; 13 Congressional Globe 35, 304, 307, 14 December 1843, 20 February 1844, 21 February 1844.

45. 21 Congressional Globe 351 (Part I), 31st Congress, 1st Session, 13 February 1850.

46. Congressional Globe, 35th Congress, 1st Session, 18 January 1858, p. 320.

47. *Ibid.*

48. *Ibid.*

49. *Ibid.*, p. 341.

50. *Ibid.*, p. 342.

51. *Ibid.*, p. 345.

52. *Ibid.*, p. 617.

53. *Ibid.*, p. 620.

54. *Ibid.*, p. 943.

55. *Ibid.*, p. 1160.

56. *Ibid.*, p. 1115. See also the speech of Senator Hannibal Hamlin of Maine, pp. 1101-1106.

57. *Ibid.*, p. 327.

58. Congressional Globe, 35th Congress, 2d Session, App., pp. 72-75.

59. See Congressional Globe, 30 April 1866, p. 2299.

60. Congressional Globe, 36th Congress, 1st Session, 17 April 1860, App., p. 234.

61. *Ibid.*

62. *Ibid.*, pp. 234-236.

63. Congressional Globe, 35th Congress, 1st Session, 11 March 1858, p. 1066.

64. *Ibid.*, p. 1067.

65. *Ibid.*, p. 1070.

66. *Ibid.*, p. 1314.

67. *Ibid.*, p. 1316.

68. *Ibid.*, p. 1263.

69. Congressional Globe, 36th Congress, 1st Session, 19 December 1859, p. 179. See also Senator Pugh's speech of 12 January 1860, pp. 415-416.

70. See Robert G. McCloskey, *The American Supreme Court* (Chicago: University of Chicago Press, 1960).

71. 21 Howard 506 (1859).

72. 17 Fed. Cases 144, No. 9487 (CCD Md.) 1861.

Notes to Chapter 4

1. Lincoln's First Inaugural Address, 4 March 1861. Richardson, ed. *Messages and Papers*, Vol. VI, p. 5 ff.

2. *Ibid.*

3. See *Cong. Globe*, 37th Cong., 3rd Session, Feb. 20-26.

4. See David M. Silver, *Lincoln's Supreme Court* (Urbana: University of Illinois Press, 1956), pp. 83-88, for a detailed discussion of the legislation.

5. *Prize Cases*, 2 Black 635 (1863).

6. Silver, *Lincoln's Supreme Court*, p. 185.

7. *Ibid.*, p. 207.

8. See Benjamin F. Wright, *The Growth of American Constitutional Law* (Boston: Reynal and Hitchcock, 1942), p. 82.

9. *Mississippi* v. *Johnson*, 4 Wallace 475 (1867); *Georgia* v. *Stanton*, 6 Wallace 50 (1868); and *Ex parte McCardle*, 7 Wallace 506 (1869).

10. See Fred Rodell, *Nine Men* (New York: Random House, 1955), p. 144.

11. *Cong. Globe*, 37th Cong., 2nd Session, 4 December 1861, p. 8.

12. *Ibid.*, 9 December 1861, p. 27.

13. *Ibid.*, 20 December 1861, p. 155.

14. Charles Warren, *The Supreme Court in United States History*, III, (Boston: Little, Brown, 1923), p. 143.

15. *Cong. Globe*, 39th Cong., 1st Session, 26 February 1866, p. 1035.

16. *Ibid.*, July 1866, p. 3699.

17. *Ex parte Milligan*, 4 Wallace 2 (1866).

18. *Cong. Globe*, 39th Cong., 2nd Session, 31 January 1867, p. 251.

19. *Ibid.*, 16 January p. 502.

20. 4 Wallace 277 (1867).

21. 4 Wallace 333 (1867).

22. *Cong. Globe*, 39th Cong., 2nd Session, 22 January p. 646.

23. *Ibid.*, p. 671.

24. *Ibid.*, p. 672.

25. *Cong. Globe*, 40th Cong., 2nd Session, Part 1, 13 January 1868, p. 478.

26. *Ibid*, p. 479.

27. *Ibid.*, pp. 479-480.

28. *Ibid.*, p. 485.

29. *Ibid.*

30. *Ibid.*

31. *Ibid.*, p. 486.

32. *Ibid.*

33. *Ibid.*, p. 488.

34. 6 Wallace 318 (1868).

35. *Cong. Globe*, 40th Cong., 2nd Session, Part 2, 12 March 1865, p. 1881.

36. *Ibid.*, p. 1882.

37. *Ibid.*, pp. 1883-1884.

38. *Cong. Globe*, 40th Cong., 2nd Session, Part 3, 25 March 1865, p. 2094.

39. *Ibid.*, p. 2116.

40. *Ibid.*, p. 2118.
41. *Ibid.*, p. 2119.
42. *Ibid.*
43. *Ibid.*, p. 2122.
44. *Ibid.*
45. *Ibid.*, pp. 2126-2127.
46. *Ibid.*, p. 2168.
47. *Ibid.*
48. 5 Wallace 541 (1867).
49. *Cong. Globe*, 40th Cong., 2nd Session, Part 2, 12 March 1868, p. 2170.
50. *Ex parte McCardle*, 7 Wallace 506 (1869).
51. 8 Wallace 85 (1869).
52. *Cong. Globe*, 41st Cong., 2nd Session, Part 1, 6 December 1869, p. 2.
53. *Ibid.*, pp. 87-93.
54. *Hepburn* v. *Griswold*, 8 Wallace 603 (1870); *Knox* v. *Lee*, 12 Wallace 457 (1871).
55. *U.S.* v. *Reese*, 92 U.S. 214 (1876).
56. See Howard Jay Graham, "The Waite Court and the Fourteenth Amendment," 17 *Vanderbilt Law Review* 525 (March, 1964).
57. C. Peter Magrath, *Morrison R. Waite: The Triumph of Character* (New York: Macmillan, 1963), p. 72.
58. *Ibid.*, p. 274.
59. *Holmes-Pollock Letters,* Mark DeWolfe Howe, Ed., (Cambridge: Belknap Press of Harvard University Press, 1961).
60. See Magrath, *Morrison R. Waite,* p. 246.
61. Howard Jay Graham, *Vanderbilt Law Review*, p. 516.
62. See Paul H. Buck, *The Road to Reunion* (Boston: Little, Brown, 1937); Vincent P. De Santis, *Republicans Face the Southern Question 1877-1897* (Baltimore: Johns Hopkins Press, 1959); and William B. Hesseltine, "Economic Factors in the Abandonment of Reconstruction," XXII *Mississippi Valley Historical Review* 191 (1935).
63. See Wilfred E. Binkley, *American Political Parties* (New York: Knopf, 1945), p. 232.
64. Wallace Mendelson, *Capitalism, Democracy and the Supreme Court* (New York: Appleton-Century-Crofts, 1960), pp. 55-56.
65. 16 Wallace 36 (1873).
66. *Minor* v. *Happersett*, 21 Wallace 162 (1875).
67. *Walker* v. *Sauvinet*, 92 U.S. 90 (1876).
68. 110 U.S. 516 (1884).
69. 7 Peters 243 (1833).
70. 94 U.S. 113 (1877).
71. Edward S. Corwin, *Liberty Against Government* (Baton Rouge: L.S.U. Press, 1948), p. 138.
72. *Railroad Commission Cases,* 116 U.S. 307 (1886).

73. See Robert G. McCloskey, *The American Supreme Court* (Chicago: University of Chicago Press, 1960), pp. 130-131, and Edward S. Corwin, *Liberty Against Government*, p. 131.

74. See *Morgan Steamship Co.* v. *Louisiana*, 118 U.S. 455 (1886); *Transportation Co.* v. *Parkersburg*, 107 U.S. 691 (1883); *Beer Co.* v. *Massachusetts*, 97 U.S. 25 (1878); *Mugler* v. *Kansas*, 123 U.S. 623 (1887); *Antoni* v. *Greenhow*, 107 U.S. 769 (1883).

75. 101 U.S. 814 (1880).

76. *United States* v. *Reese*, 92 U.S. 214 (1876); *United States* v. *Cruikshank*, 92 U.S. 542 (1876).

77. *United States* v. *Harris*, 106 U.S. 629 (1883).

78. *Civil Rights Cases*, 109 U.S. 3 (1883).

79. *Ex parte Siebold*, 100 U.S. 371 (1880).

80. *Ex parte Yarbrough*, 110 U.S. 651 (1884).

81. *Strauder* v. *West Virginia*, 100 U.S. 303 (1880); *Ex parte Virginia*, 100 U.S. 339 (1880).

82. See *Philadelphia & Reading R.R.* v. *Pennsylvania*, 15 Wallace 232 (1873); *Welton* v. *Missouri*, 91 U.S. 275 (1876); *Inman Steamship Co.* v.*Tinker*, 94 U.S. 238 (1877); *Robbins* v. *Shelby County Taxing District*, 120 U.S. 489 (1887).

83. *Hannibal & St. Joseph R.R.* v. *Husen*, 95 U.S. 465 (1878); *Hall* v. *De Cuir*, 95 U.S. 485 (1878); *Pensacola Telegraph Co.* v. *Western Union Telegraph Co.*, 96 U.S. 1 (1878); *Bowman* v. *Chicago & Northwestern Railway*, 125 U.S. 465 (1888).

84. 118 U.S. 557 (1886).

85. *Springer* v. *U.S.*, 102 U.S. 586 (1881).

86. *Julliard* v. *Greenman*, 110 U.S. 421 (1884).

87. 99 U.S. 700 (1879).

Notes to Chapter 5

1. See Willard L. King, *Melville Weston Fuller* (New York: Macmillan, 1950), pp. 148-151 and Frankfurter and Landis, *The Business of the Supreme Court* (New York: Macmillan, 1928), pp. 93-102 for a discussion of the proposals and of the circumstances surrounding their adoption.

2. See King, *Melville Weston Fuller,* especially pp. 11, 22, 85, 97, 114, 364, for an assessment of Fuller.

3. King, *ibid.,* p. 114.

4. *Ibid.,* p. 85.

5. Quoted in Arnold M. Paul, *Conservative Crisis and the Rule of Law* (Ithaca: Cornell University Press, 1960), pp. 70-71.

6. 169 U.S. 366 (1898).

7. 198 U.S. 45 (1905).

8. Charles A. Kent, *Memoir of Henry Billings Brown* (New York, 1915), as quoted in King, *Melville Weston Fuller,* p. 156.

9. King, *ibid.*, p. 157.
10. *The Nation*, 1 June 1921.
11. *Lochner* v. *New York, supra.*
12. King, *Melville Weston Fuller*, pp. 229-230.
13. Mendelson, *Capitalism, Democracy and the Supreme Court* (New York: Appleton-Century-Crofts, 1960), p. 71.
14. *Ibid.*, p. 75.
15. Catherine Drinker Bowen, *Yankee from Olympus* (Boston: Little, Brown, 1946), p. VIII.
16. *Ibid.*
17. 135 U.S. 1 (1890).
18. 149 U.S. 698 (1893).
19. *Chae Chan Ping* v. *U.S.*, 130 U.S. 581 (1889).
20. 135 U.S. 100 (1890).
21. 5 Howard 504 (1847).
22. 143 U.S. 110 (1892).
23. 194 U.S. 497 (1904).
24. 16 Peters 1 (1842).
25. 143 U.S. 621 (1892).
26. *Chicago, Milwaukee & St. Paul Railway Co.* v. *Minnesota (Minnesota Rate Case)*, 134 U.S. 418 (1890).
27. *Ibid.*, p. 458.
28. 94 U.S. 113 (1877).
29. *Minnesota Rate Case, op. cit.*, p. 461.
30. *Ibid.*
31. 143 U.S. 517 (1892).
32. *Ibid.*, p. 551.
33. 153 U.S. 391 (1894).
34. 154 U.S. 362 (1894) at 397.
35. 156 U.S. 1 (1895).
36. 9 Wheaton 1 (1824).
37. 156 U.S. at 43.
38. 157 U.S. 429 (1895). See Arnold M. Paul, *Conservative Crisis*, pp. 185-220 for a thorough and careful analysis of the case.
39. *Hylton* v. *United States*, 3 Dallas 171 (1796).
40. *Springer* v. *United States*, 102 U.S. 586 (1881).
41. Paul, *Conservative Crisis*, p. 189.
42. *Pollock* v. *Farmers' Loan & Trust*, 158 U.S. 601 (1895).
43. King, *Melville Weston Fuller*, p. 200.
44. Principally *Hylton* v. *United States*, 3 Dallas 171 (1796); *Pacific Insurance Co.* v. *Soule*, 7 Wallace 433 (1869); *Springer* v. *United States*, 102 U.S. 586 (1881).
45. *Pollock* v. *Farmers' Loan & Trust Co., supra*, p. 671.
46. *Ibid.*, p. 695.

47.

	Justice	State	Per Capita Wealth*
	Fuller	Illinois	$1,324
Against	Field	California	2,097
the	Gray	Massachusetts	1,252
Tax	Brewer	Kansas	1,261
	Shiras	Pennsylvania	1,177
	Harlan	Kentucky	631
For	Brown	Michigan	1,001
the	Jackson	Tennessee	502
Tax	White	Louisiana	443

* According to the census of 1890.

48. *In re Debs*, 158 U.S. 564 (1895).
49. *Ibid.* at 583.
50. *Ibid.*
51. Alan Westin, "The Supreme Court, the Populist Movement and the Campaign of 1896," 15 *Journal of Politics* 3-41 (Feb. 1953), p. 40.
52. As quoted in Westin, *ibid.*, p. 28.
53. 163 U.S. 537 (1896).
54. *Ibid.* at 551.
55. *Ibid.* at 560.
56. 188 U.S. 321 (1903).
57. 195 U.S. 27 (1904).
58. 193 U.S. 197 (1904).
59. 196 U.S. 375 (1905).
60. *U.S.* v. *Trans-Missouri Freight Association*, 166 U.S. 290 (1897).
61. 221 U.S. 1 (1911).
62. 221 U.S. 106 (1911).
63. Chief Justice Fuller died on 4 July 1910, and White's appointment was made on 12 December.
64. 198 U.S. 45 (1905).
65. *Ibid.*, p. 57.
66. *Muller* v. *Oregon*, 208 U.S. 412 (1908).
67. *Adair* v. *United States*, 208 U.S. 161 (1908); *Coppage* v. *Kansas*, 236 U.S. 1 (1915); *Adkins* v.*Children's Hospital*, 261 U.S. 525 (1923).
68. *First Employers' Liability Cases*, 207 U.S. 463 (1908).
69. *Second Employers' Liability Cases*, 223 U.S. 1 (1912).
70. 209 U.S. 123 (1908).
71. John Rutledge was given a recess appointment by President Washington in 1795, but he was not confirmed by the Senate.
72. The factual material about Hughes' life is taken from Samuel Hendel, *Charles Evans Hughes and the Supreme Court* (New York: Kings Crown Press, 1951), pp. 2-15 and Alpheus T. Mason, *The Supreme Court from Taft to Warren* (Baton Rouge: Louisiana State University Press, 1958).

73. T.S. Pringle, *William Howard Taft* (New York: Farrar and Rinehart, 1939), p. 971.

74. Drew Pearson and Robert S. Allen, *The Nine Old Men* (New York: Doubleday, Doran and Co., 1936), p. 187.

75. *Hitchman Coal and Coke Co.* v. *Mitchell*, 245 U.S. 229 (1918).

76. *Duplex Printing Press* v. *Deering*, 254 U.S. 443 (1921).

77. *Eisner* v. *Macomber*, 252 U.S. 189 (1920).

78. Pearson and Allen, *Nine Old Men*, p. 222.

79. For the best account of the life of Brandeis, see Alpheus T. Mason, *Brandeis, A Free Man's Life* (New York: The Viking Press, 1946).

80. 208 U.S. 412 (1908).

81. Pearson and Allen, *Nine Old Men*, p. 225.

82. *Baltimore and Ohio R.R.* v. *I.C.C.*, 221 U.S. 612 (1911).

83. *Wilson* v. *New*, 243 U.S. 332 (1917).

84. *Hammer* v. *Dagenhart*, 247 U.S. 251 (1918).

85. *First Employers' Liability Cases, supra.*

86. *Second Employers' Liability Cases, supra.*

87. *Clark Distilling Co.* v. *Western Maryland Railway Co.*, 242 U.S. 311 (1917).

88. *Shreveport Rate Case (Houston, East and West Texas R.R.* v. *United States)*, 234 U.S. 342 (1914).

89. *Hammer* v. *Dagenhart, supra.*

90. See, for example, *City of Sault Ste. Marie* v. *International Transit Co.*, 234 U.S. 333 (1914) and *Adams Express Co.* v. *New York*, 232 U.S. 14 (1914).

91. *Chicago, B.&Q. R.R.* v. *McGuire*, 219 U.S. 549 (1911).

92. *Sturges and Burn Mfg. Co.* v. *Beauchamp*, 231 U.S. 320 (1913).

93. *Miller* v. *Wilson*, 236 U.S. 373 (1915).

94. 236 U.S. 1 (1915).

95. 219 U.S. 219 (1911).

96. 235 U.S. 151 (1914).

97. *Truax* v. *Raich*, 239 U.S. 33 (1915).

98. 249 U.S. 47 (1919).

99. 250 U.S. 616 (1919).

100. 252 U.S. 239 (1920).

101. In the *Selective Draft Law Cases*, 245 U.S. 366 (1918), the Court unanimously upheld compulsory military service. The Court also sustained the War Prohibition Act even though it had been passed after the armistice was signed. *Rupert* v. *Caffey*, 251 U.S. 264 (1920); *War Prohibition Cases*, 251 U.S. 146 (1919). The Army Appropriation Act authorizing presidential seizure of and operation of the railroads during wartime also received judicial approval. *Northern Pacific Ry. Co.* v. *North Dakota*, 250 U.S. 135 (1919).

102. *Rhode Island* v. *Palmer*, 253 U.S. 350 (1920).

103. *Missouri* v. *Holland*, 252 U.S. 416 (1920).

104. *Cong. Record*, Vol. 28, p. 897 (54th Cong., 1st Sess., 23 January 1896).

105. December 27, 1896; 19 March 1897 and 4 June 1897.

106. *Cong. Record*, Vol. 30, p. 1495 (55th Cong., Part 2, 1st Sess., 4 June 1897).

107. *Ibid.*, p. 1494.

108. *Cong. Record*, Vol. 31, p. 430 (55th Cong., 2nd Sess., 7 January 1898).

109. *New York Times*, 18 February 1923.

110. *New York Times*, 19 September 1924.

111. *Ives* v. *South Buffalo Railway Co.*, 201 N.Y. 271, 93 N.E. 431 (1911).

112. *State* v. *Clausen*, 65 Wash. 156, 117 Pac. 1101 (1911).

Notes to Chapter 6

1. See T. Harry Williams, Richard N. Current and Frank Friedel, *A History of the United States* (New York: Knopf, 1961), II, p. 410.

2. Alpheus T. Mason, *The Supreme Court from Taft to Warren* (Baton Rouge: Louisiana State University Press, 1958), p. 43.

3. T.S. Pringle, *William Howard Taft* (New York: Farrar & Rinehart, 1939), p. 967.

4. Mason, *Taft to Warren*, p. 47.

5. As quoted in Pringle, *Taft*, p. 963.

6. Joel Francis Paschal, *Mr. Justice Sutherland* (Princeton: Princeton University Press, 1951), p. 113.

7. The factual account of Sutherland's life is taken primarily from Paschal, *ibid.*

8. Paschal, *ibid.*, p. 242.

9. *Powell* v. *Alabama*, 287 U.S. 45 (1932).

10. Drew Pearson and Robert S. Allen, *Nine Old Men* (Garden City: Doubleday, Doran, 1936), p. 127.

11. 310 U.S. XVII (1940).

12. David J. Danelski, *A Supreme Court Justice Is Appointed* (New York: Random House, 1964), p. 181.

13. Pearson and Allen, *Nine Old Men*, p. 134.

14. Danelski, *Supreme Court Justice*, p. 19.

15. 268 U.S. 563 (1925).

16. 268 U.S. 587 (1925).

17. 274 U.S. 380 (1927).

18. For a discussion of Sanford see John W. Green, *Law and Lawyers* (Jackson, Tennessee: Mocowat-Mercer Press, 1950), pp. 64-69 and James A. Fowler, "Mr. Justice Edward Terry Sanford," 17 *American Bar Association Journal* 229-233 (1931).

19. Alpheus T. Mason, *Harlan Fiske Stone: Pillar of the Law* (New York: Viking, 1956), p. 20.

20. *Ibid.*, p. 65.

21. Walter Gardner, "Mr. Chief Justice Stone," 59 *Harvard Law Review* 1203 (1946), p. 1208.

22. Mason, *Taft to Warren*, p. 143.

23. 257 U.S. 563 (1922).

24. *Ibid.*, p. 588.

25. *Swift & Co. v. United States*, 196 U.S. 375 (1905).

26. *Chicago Board of Trade v. Olsen*, 262 U.S. 1 (1923).

27. *N.L.R.B. v. Jones & Laughlin Steel Corp.*, 301 U.S. 1 (1937).

28. *Dayton-Goose Creek Railway Co. v. United States*, 263 U.S. 456 (1924).

29. *Brooks v. United States*, 267 U.S. 432 (1925).

30. *Hammer v. Dagenhart*, 247 U.S. 251 (1918).

31. *Bedford Cut Stone Co. v. Journeymen Stone Cutters' Association*, 274 U.S. 37 (1927).

32. *Pennsylvania Coal Co, v Mahon*, 260 U.S. 393 (1922).

33. *Wolff Packing Co. v. Court of Industrial Relations*, 262 U.S. 522 (1923).

34. *Jay Burns Baking Co. v. Bryan*, 264 U.S. 504 (1924).

35. *Weaver v. Palmer Bros. Co.*, 270 U.S. 402 (1926).

36. *Tyson and Bros. v. Banton*, 273 U.S. 418 (1927).

37. *Ribnik v. McBride*, 277 U.S. 350 (1928).

38. *Williams v. Standard Oil Co.*, 278 U.S. 235 (1929).

39. 261 U.S. 525 (1923).

40. 198 U.S. 45 (1905).

41. 243 U.S. 426 (1917).

42. 208 U.S. 412 (1908).

43. 268 U.S. 652 (1925).

44. *Meyer v Nebraska*, 262 U.S. 390 (1923).

45. 268 U.S. 510 (1925).

46. *Whitney v. California*, 274 U.S. 357 (1927).

47. *Moore v. Dempsey*, 261 U.S. 86 (1923).

48. *Tumey v. Ohio*, 273 U.S. 510 (1927).

49. *Carroll v. United States*, 267 U.S. 132 (1925).

50. *Olmstead v. United States*, 277 U.S. 438 (1928). The case was virtually, if not actually, overruled in *Berger v. New York*, 388 U.S. 41 (1967).

51. *Bailey v. Drexel Furniture Co.*, 259 U.S. 20 (1922).

52. *Ibid.*, pp. 37-38.

53. *Massachusetts v. Mellon*, 262 U.S. 447 (1923).

54. *Myers v. United States*, 272 U.S. 52 (1926).

55. Merle Fainsod and Lincoln Gordon, *Government in the American Economy* (New York: W.W. Norton & Co., 1941), p. 13.

56. Felix Frankfurter, "Mr. Justice Roberts," 104 *University of Pennsylvania Law Review* 311 (Dec. 1955), p. 312.

57. *Ibid.*

58. *Morehead v. New York ex rel Tipaldo*, 298 U.S. 587 (1936).

59. *West Coast Hotel v. Parrish*, 300 U.S. 379 (1937).

60. 291 U.S. 502 (1934).

61. See George S. Hellman, *Benjamin N. Cardozo: American Judge* (New York: McGraw-Hill, 1940) for a discussion of Cardozo's life before his appointment to the Supreme Court.

62. *Ibid.*, p. 15.
63. The titles are: *The Nature of the Judicial Process* (1921); *The Growth of the Law* (1924); *The Paradoxes of Legal Science* (1928); *Law and Literature and Other Essays and Addresses* (1931).
64. Joseph P. Pollard, *Mr. Justice Cardozo* (New York: The Yorktown Press, 1935), p. 9.
65. Felix Frankfurter, *Dictionary of American Biography*, Volume 22, Supplement 2, p. 95.
66. William O. Douglas, "Mr. Justice Cardozo," 58 *Michigan Law Review* 349-350 (1959-60).
67. Charles A. Beard and Mary Beard, *America in Midpassage*, I, (New York: Macmillan, 1939), p. 248.
68. *Ibid.*, p. 249.
69. *Ibid.*
70. 283 U.S. 359 (1931).
71. 283 U.S. 605 (1931).
72. *Ibid.*, p. 634.
73. *Near* v. *Minnesota*, 283 U.S. 697 (1931).
74. 287 U.S. 45 (1932).
75. 294 U.S. 103 (1935).
76. 297 U.S. 278 (1936).
77. 109 U.S. 3 (1883).
78. *Nixon* v. *Herndon*, 273 U.S. 536 (1927).
79. 286 U.S. 73 (1932).
80. *Grovey* v. *Townsend*, 295 U.S. 45 (1935).
81. *Smith* v. *Allwright*, 321 U.S. 649 (1944).
82. 294 U.S. 587 (1935).
83. 290 U.S. 398 (1934).
84. 1 Howard 311 (1843).
85. 101 U.S. 814 (1880).
86. *McCulloch* v. *Maryland*, 4 Wheaton 316 (1819) at 415.
87. *Missouri* v. *Holland*, 252 U.S. 416 (1920) at 433.
88. 291 U.S. 502 (1934).
89. As enunciated for the first time in *Munn* v. *Illinois*, 94 U.S. 113 (1877).
90. *New State Ice Company* v. *Liebmann*, 285 U.S. 262 (1932).
91. See Franklin D. Roosevelt, "The Fight Goes On," *Collier's*, 20 September 1941, p. 17.
92. 293 U.S. 388 (1935).
93. *Norman* v. *Baltimore & Ohio R.R.*, 294 U.S. 240 (1935); *Perry* v. *U.S.* 294 U.S. 330 (1935).
94. *Railroad Retirement Board* v. *Alton R.R. Co.* 295 U.S. 330 (1935).
95. 247 U.S. 251 (1918).
96. *Louisville Joint Stock Land Bank* v. *Radford*, 295 U.S. 555 (1935).
97. 295 U.S. 602 (1935).
98. *Schechter Poultry Corp.* v. *United States*, 295 U.S. 495 (1935).
99. 293 U.S. 388 (1935).

100. 297 U.S. 1 (1936).

101. *Bailey* v. *Drexel Furniture Co.*, 259 U.S. 20 (1922).

102. *Hammer* v. *Dagenhart*, 247 U.S. 251 (1918).

103. 298 U.S. 1 (1936).

104. Robert H. Jackson, *The Struggle for Judicial Supremacy* (New York: Knopf, 1941), p. 152.

105. *Carter* v. *Carter Coal Co.*, 298 U.S. 238 (1936).

106. Joel Francis Paschal, *Mr. Justice Sutherland*, p. 198.

107. *Morehead* v. *New York ex rel Tipaldo*, 298 U.S. 587 (1936).

108. Merlo J. Pusey, *The Supreme Court Crisis* (New York: Macmillan, 1937), p. 89.

109. Joseph Alsop and Turner Catledge, *The 168 Days* (Garden City: Doubleday, Doran, 1938), p. 16.

110. *Ibid.*, p. 72.

111. *Ibid.*, pp. 113-119, 154-160.

112. Chairman Henry Ashurst and Senators Matthew Neely, W. Va.; Marvel Logan, Ky.; William Dieterich, Ill.; Key Pittman, Nev.; and James Hughes of Delaware were committed to the president's bill; Senator George Norris, Neb., was lukewarm and Senator George McGill, Kans., was publicly uncommitted but privately for it. Against it were Senators William King, Utah; Frederick Van Nuys, Ind.; Edward Burke, Neb.; Tom Connally, Tex.; William Borah, Idaho; Warren Austin, Vt.; Frederick Steiwer, Ore.; and Joseph O'Mahoney, Wyo. Uncommitted were Carl Hatch, N.M., and Patrick McCarran, Nev.

113. *Index to Congressional Record*, Vol. 81, Part 2, 75th Congress, 1st Session, Jan. 5-Aug. 21, 1937, pp. 534-539.

114. Charles and Mary Beard, *America In Midpassage*, I, (New York: Macmillan, 1939), pp. 354-358.

115. Alsop and Catledge, *168 Days*, p. 125.

116. For the text of the letter see *Congressional Record*, Vol. 81, Part 3, 75th Congress, 1st Session, pp. 2813-2814.

117. 300 U.S. 379 (1937).

118. *Adkins* v. *Children's Hospital, supra.*

119. *N.L.R.B.* v. *Jones and Laughlin Steel Corp.*, 301 U.S. 1 (1937).

120. 258 U.S. 495 (1922).

121. 295 U.S. 495 (1935).

122. 298 U.S. 238 (1936).

123. *Helvering* v. *Davis*, 301 U.S. 619 (1937) and *Steward Machine Co.* v. *Davis*, 301 U.S. 548 (1937).

124. *Nebbia* v. *New York*, 291 U.S. 502 (1934).

125. Senate Report No. 711, 75th Cong., 1st Session (1937).

126. Charles and Mary Beard, *America in Midpassage*, p. 358.

127. See Alsop and Catledge, *168 Days*, pp. 223-250.

128. Jackson, *Judicial Supremacy*, p. 196.

129. Section 2(f) of the Federal Firearms Act of 1938 establishing a presumption of guilt based on a prior conviction and present possession of a

firearm was held to violate the test of due process under the Fifth Amendment. *Tot* v. *United States*, 319 U.S. 463 (1943). Section 304 of the Urgent Deficiency Appropriations Act of 1943 providing that no salary should be paid to certain named federal employees out of moneys appropriated was held to violate Article I, Section Nine, Clause Three, forbidding bills of attainder. *United States* v. *Lovett*, 328 U.S. 303 (1946). The first major invalidation after 1937 was *Toth* v. *Quarles*, 350 U.S. 11 (1955) in which Article 3(a) of the Uniform Code of Military Justice subjecting civilian ex-servicemen to court martial for crimes committed while in military service was held to violate Article III, Section Two and the Fifth and Sixth Amendments to the Constitution.

Notes to Chapter 7

1. The account of Black's pre-Court career is taken primarily from John P. Frank, *Mr. Justice Black: The Man and His Opinions* (New York: Knopf, 1949).

2. Fred Rodell, *Nine Men: A Political History of the Supreme Court from 1790-1955* (New York: Random House, 1955), p. 268.

3. *Terminiello* v. *City of Chicago*, 337 U.S. 1 (1949).

4. *Everson* v. *Board of Education*, 330 U.S. 1 (1947).

5. 338 U.S. 25 (1949).

6. 367 U.S. 643 (1961).

7. 312 U.S. 100 (1941).

8. 247 U.S. 251 (1918).

9. *Wickard* v. *Filburn*, 317 U.S. 111 (1942).

10. 196 U.S. 375 (1905).

11. 188 U.S. 321 (1903).

12. *United States* v. *Appalachian Electric Power Co.*, 311 U.S. 377 (1940).

13. *Phillips* v. *Guy Atkinson Co.*, 313 U.S. 508 (1941).

14. *United States* v. *Southeastern Underwriters Association*, 322 U.S. 533 (1944).

15. 8 Wallace 168 (1869).

16. See *McGoldrick* v. *Berwind-White Coal Mining Co.*, 309 U.S. 33 (1940); *Nelson* v. *Sears, Roebuck & Co.*, 312 U.S. 359 (1941); *Nelson* v. *Montgomery Ward & Co.*, 312 U.S. 373 (1941); *Caskey Baking Co.* v. *Virginia*, 313 U.S. 117 (1941); *Independent Warehouses* v. *Scheele*, 331 U.S. 70 (1947); *International Harvester* v. *Evatt*, 329 U.S. 416 (1947); *Nashville C. & St. Louis Railway* v. *Browning*, 310 U.S. 362 (1940); *Milk Control Board* v. *Eisenberg Farm Products*, 306 U.S. 346 (1939); *Terminal R.R. Association* v. *Brotherhood of R.R. Trainmen*, 318 U.S. 1 (1943); *Parker* v. *Brown*, 317 U.S. 341 (1943).

17. See *Adams Mfg. Co.* v. *Storen*, 304 U.S. 307 (1938); *Gwin, White & Prince* v. *Henneford*, 305 U.S. 434 (1939); *Freeman* v. *Hewit*, 329 U.S. 249 (1946).

18. *Best & Co.* v. *Maxwell*, 311 U.S. 454 (1940).

19. 314 U.S. 160 (1941).

20. 328 U.S. 373 (1946).

21. 95 U.S. 485 (1878).

22. 333 U.S. 28 (1948).

23. 304 U.S. 64 (1938).

24. 16 Peters 1 (1842).

25. 306 U.S. 466 (1939).

26. 11 Wallace 113 (1871).

27. 268 U.S. 652 (1925).

28. 304 U.S. 144 (1938). This position is stated clearly by Justice Rutledge in *Thomas* v. *Collins,* 323 U.S. 516 (1945).

29. *Lovell* v. *Griffin,* 303 U.S. 444 (1938); *Schneider* v. *Irvington,* 308 U.S. 147 (1939); *Largent* v. *Texas,* 318 U.S. 418 (1943); *Jamison* v. *Texas,* 318 U.S. 413 (1943).

30. *Martin* v. *Struthers,* 319 U.S. 141 (1943).

31. *Marsh* v. *Alabama,* 326 U.S. 501 (1946).

32. *Tucker* v. *Texas,* 326 U.S. 517 (1946).

33. *Cantwell* v. *Connecticut,* 310 U.S. 296 (1940).

34. *Murdock* v. *Pennsylvania,* 319 U.S. 105 (1943).

35. *Follett* v. *McCormick,* 321 U.S. 573 (1944).

36. *Cox* v. *New Hampshire,* 312 U.S. 569 (1941).

37. *Prince* v. *Massachusetts,* 321 U.S. 158 (1944).

38. *West Virginia State Board of Education* v. *Barnette,* 319 U.S. 624 (1943).

39. *Minersville School District* v. *Gobitis,* 310 U.S. 586 (1940).

40. *United States* v. *Schwimmer,* 279 U.S. 644 (1929); *United States* v. *MacIntosh,* 283 U.S. 605 (1931), and *United States* v. *Bland,* 283 U.S. 636 (1931).

41. *Girouard* v. *United States,* 328 U.S. 61 (1946).

42. 330 U.S. 1 (1947).

43. *Bridges* v. *California,* 314 U.S. 252 (1941); *Pennekamp* v. *Florida,* 328 U.S. 331 (1946); *Craig* v. *Harney,* 331 U.S. 367 (1947).

44. *Thornhill* v. *Alabama,* 310 U.S. 88 (1940); *Carlson* v. *California,* 310 U.S. 106 (1940).

45. *Milk Wagon Drivers' Union* v. *Meadowmoor Dairies,* 312 U.S. 287 (1941).

46. *Hartzel* v. *United States,* 322 U.S. 680 (1944).

47. *Hirabayashi* v. *United States,* 320 U.S. 81 (1943).

48. *Korematsu* v. *United States,* 323 U.S. 214 (1944).

49. *Ex parte Endo,* 323 U.S. 283 (1944).

50. 316 U.S. 455 (1942).

51. 332 U.S. 46 (1947).

52. 302 U.S. 319 (1937).

53. 321 U.S. 649 (1944).

54. 295 U.S. 45 (1935).

55. *Steele* v. *L.&N. Rwy. Co.,* 323 U.S. 192 (1944); *Tunstall* v. *Brotherhood of Locomotive Firemen and Enginemen,* 323 U.S. 210 (1944).

56. *Railway Mail Association* v. *Corsi*, 326 U.S. 88 (1945).

57. *Morgan* v. *Virginia*, 328 U.S. 373 (1946).

58. *Mitchell* v. *United States*, 313 U.S. 80 (1941).

59. *Missouri ex rel. Gaines* v. *Canada*, 305 U.S. 337 (1938).

60. *United States* v. *Classic*, 313 U.S. 299 (1941).

61. *Screws* v. *United States*, 325 U.S. 91 (1945).

62. *Dennis* v. *United States*, 341 U.S. 494 (1951).

63. 343 U.S. 495 (1952).

64. 339 U.S. 382 (1950).

65. *Bailey* v. *Richardson*, 341 U.S. 918 (1951); *Joint Anti-Fascist Committee* v. *McGrath*, 341 U.S. 123 (1951).

66. See *Gerende* v. *Election Board*, 341 U.S. 56 (1951); *Garner* v. *Board of Public Works of Los Angeles*, 341 U.S. 716 (1951); *Adler* v. *Board of Education*, 342 U.S. 485 (1952); *Wieman* v. *Updegraff*, 344 U.S. 183 (1952).

67. 343 U.S. 250 (1952).

68. 341 U.S. 622 (1951).

69. 340 U.S. 315 (1951).

70. 336 U.S. 77 (1949).

71. 334 U.S. 558 (1948).

72. 343 U.S. 495 (1952).

73. 337 U.S. 1 (1949).

74. 340 U.S. 290 (1951).

75. 333 U.S. 203 (1948).

76. *Zorach* v. *Clauson*, 343 U.S. 306 (1952).

77. 334 U.S. 1 (1948).

78. 109 U.S. 3 (1883).

79. In the companion case of *Hurd* v. *Hodge*, 334 U.S. 24 (1948), the Court held that restrictive covenants were also unenforceable in the District of Columbia.

80. *Brown* v. *Board of Education*, 347 U.S. 483 (1954).

81. 332 U.S. 631 (1948).

82. 339 U.S. 629 (1950).

83. 339 U.S. 637 (1950).

84. *Henderson* v. *United States*, 339 U.S. 816 (1950).

85. John D. Weaver, *Warren: The Man, The Court, The Era* (Boston: Little, Brown, 1967), p. 10.

86. *Ibid.*, p. 347.

87. *Brown* v. *Board of Education, supra*.

88. *Reynolds* v. *Sims*, 377 U.S. 533 (1964).

89. 384 U.S. 436 (1966).

90. 354 U.S. 298 (1957).

91. 369 U.S. 186 (1962).

92. *Brown* v. *Board of Education, supra; Bolling* v. *Sharpe*, 347 U.S. 497 (1954).

93. *Baltimore City* v. *Dawson*, 350 U.S. 877 (1955).

94. *Holmes* v. *City of Atlanta*, 350 U.S. 879 (1955).

95. *Gayle* v. *Browder*, 352 U.S. 903 (1956).

96. *Weber* v. *Anheuser-Busch*, 348 U.S. 468 (1955).

97. *Railway Employees' Department* v. *Hanson*, 351 U.S. 225 (1956).

98. *Pennsylvania* v.*Nelson*, 350 U.S. 497 (1956).

99. *Peters* v. *Hobby*, 349 U.S. 331 (1955).

100. 351 U.S. 536 (1956).

101. *Service* v. *Dulles*, 354 U.S. 363 (1957).

102. 354 U.S. 178 (1957).

103. 352 U.S. 1 (1956).

104. 353 U.S. 657 (1957).

105. 354 U.S. 298 (1957).

106. 350 U.S. 551 (1956).

107. 354 U.S. 234 (1957).

108. *Schware* v. *New Mexico*, 353 U.S. 232 (1957); *Konigsberg* v. *California*, 353 U.S. 252 (1957).

109. 354 U.S. 449 (1957).

110. *McNabb* v. *United States*, 318 U.S. 332 (1943).

111. 350 U.S. 11 (1955).

112. *Tot* v. *United States*, 319 U.S. 463 (1943) and *United States* v. *Lovett*, 328 U.S. 303 (1946). See Chapter VI, Note 129.

113. S. 654 Sen. Styles Bridges (R. N.H.)
H.R. 744 Rep. Thomas J. Lane (D. Mass.)
H.R. 946 Rep. Lawrence Smith (R. Wisc.)
H.R. 1129 Rep. Dante B. Fascell (D. Fla.)
H.R. 1142 Rep. John E. Henderson (R. Ohio)
S. 2401 Sen. Strom Thurmond (D. S.C.)

114. S. 337 Sen. John L. McClellan (D. Ark.)
H.R. 3 Rep. Howard W. Smith (D. Va.)
H.R. 19 Rep. Armistead I. Selden Jr. (D. Ala.)
H.R. 513 Rep. Thomas G. Abernethy (D. Miss.)
H.R. 679 Rep. Edgar W. Hiestand (R. Cal.)
H.R. 6567 Rep. Edgar W. Hiestand (R. Cal.)
H.R. 1012 Rep. Jim Wright (D. Tex.)
H.R. 2240 Rep. Robert L. F. Sikes (D. Fla.)
H.R. 2417 Rep. William M. Colmer (D. Miss.)

115. S. 1183 Sen. Herman Talmadge (D. Ga.)
H.R. 175 Rep. E. L. Forrester (D. S.C.)
H.R. 1228 Rep. L. Mendel Rivers (D. S.C.)
H.R. 2020 Rep. D. R. Matthews (D. Fla.)
S. 2401 Sen. Strom Thurmond (D. S.C.)

116. S. 2258 Sen. Herman Talmadge (D. Ga.)

117. H.R. 463 Rep. Frank Smith (D. Miss.)
H.R. 692 Rep. George Huddleston (D. Ala.)

118. S.J. Res. 75 Sen. James O. Eastland (D. Miss.)
H.J. Res. 175 Rep. Jamie L. Whitten (D. Miss.)

119. H.R. 322 Rep. Henderson Lanham (D. Ga.)

120. S. Res. 96 Sen. John Stennis (D. Miss.)
H.R. 462 Rep. Frank E. Smith (D. Miss.)
121. S. 171 Sen. Russell B. Long (D. La.)
122. S. 283 Sen. George Smathers (D. Fla.)
S. 1184 Sen. Herman Talmadge (D. Ga.)
H.R. 512 Rep. Thomas G. Abernethy (D. Miss.)
123. H.R. 512
124. S.J. Res. 9 Sen. Russell B. Long (D. La.)
S.J. 114 Sen. James O. Eastland (D. Miss.) Terms of justices limited to four years with reappointment by Senate consent.
125. See Walter F. Murphy, *Congress and the Court* (Chicago: University of Chicago Press, 1962) for a detailed account of the legislative attack on the Supreme Court in the Eighty-Fifth Congress. See also C. Herman Pritchett, *Congress versus the Supreme Court, 1957-1960* (Minneapolis: University of Minnesota Press, 1961).
126. See 103 *Congressional Record* 12806-10, 26 July 1957.
127. Public Law 85-269; 71 Stat. 595 (1957).
128. 104 *Congressional Record* 4675, 18 March 1958.
129. Murphy, *Congress and the Court*, p. 177.
130. 104 *Congressional Record* 12940-12941, 2 July 1958.
131. *Ibid.*, p. 13416, 10 July 1958.
132. *Ibid.*, p. 14162, 17 July 1958.
133. *Ibid.*, p. 17171, 12 August 1958.
134. 104 *Congressional Record* 17426-17437, 21 August 1958.
135. *Ibid.*, pp. 19574-19576, 25 August 1958. Ten years later, in 1968, Congress enacted a law modifying *Mallory*. See Chapter VIII.
136. See Murphy, *Congress and the Court*, pp. 157-162 for a detailed list of spokesmen, pro and con.
137. *Ibid.*, pp. 120-123.
138. *Dred Scott* v. *Sandford*, 19 Howard 393 (1857).
139. *Civil Rights Cases*, 109 U.S. 3 (1883).
140. *Plessy* v.*Ferguson*, 163 U.S. 537 (1896).
141. 40 Stat. 217 (1917), repealed by 62 Stat. 862 (1948) and 40 Stat. 533 (1918), repealed by 41 Stat. 1359-60 (1921).
142. *Respublica* v. *Dennie*, 4 Yeats (Pa.) 267 (1805). See Note, 31 *Indiana Law Journal* 277 (Winter 1956).
143. Laws of 1902, c. 371; N.Y. Pen. Law, secs. 160-161.
144. See Walter Gellhorn, *The States and Subversion* (Ithaca: Cornell University Press, 1952). See also 31 *Indiana Law Journal* 280.
145. 54 Stat. 670 (1940).
146. *Dunne* v. *United States*, 138 F.2d 137 (8th Cir., 1943), Certiorari denied, 320 U.S. 790 (1943).
147. See *Gitlow* v. *New York*, 268 U.S. 652 (1925); *Norris* v. *Alabama*, 294 U.S. 587 (1935); *Powell* v. *Alabama*, 287 U.S. 45 (1932); *Missouri ex rel. Gaines* v. *Canada*, 305 U.S. 337 (1938).
148. See *Norris* v. *Alabama, supra* and *Powell* v. *Alabama, supra*.

149. See *Near* v. *Minnesota*, 283 U.S. 697 (1931).
150. *Missouri ex rel. Gaines* v. *Canada, supra.*
151. See 104 *Congressional Record*, Eighty-Fifth Congress, 2nd Session, 17125-17127; 17173-17226.

Notes to Chapter 8

1. Harold W. Chase, "The Warren Court and Congress", 44 *Minnesota Law Review* 595-637 (March 1960), p. 634.
2. 369 U.S. 186 (1962).
3. *The New York Times Magazine*, 8 August 1965.
4. 372 U.S. 335 (1963).
5. *The Constitution of the United States of America*, S. Doc. No. 39, Eighty-Eighth Congress, 2d Sess. 22-23 (1964).
6. Article II, Sec. 1 and Article V. The word, "equally", appears in Article I but it refers to a division of senators into three groups for election purposes and to a tie vote in the Senate which would require the vote of the vice-president to obtain a majority.
7. *Baker* v. *Carr*, 369 U.S. 186 (1962).
8. *Wesberry* v. *Sanders*, 376 U.S. 1 (1964).
9. *Reynolds* v. *Sims*, 377 U.S. 533 (1964).
10. *Lucas* v. *Forty-Fourth General Assembly of Colorado*, 377 U.S. 713 (1964).
11. *Avery* v. *Midland County, Texas*, 390 U.S. 474 (1968).
12. See *Congressional Record*, 88th Congress, 2d Sess. Vol. 110, Part 15, p. 20300.
13. See *Congressional Record*, 89th Congress, 1st Sess. Vol. 111, Part 14, p. 19373 and Vol. 112, Part 7, p. 8593.
14. See *Uphaus* v. *Wyman*, 360 U.S. 72 (1959); *Wilkinson* v. *United States*, 365 U.S. 399 (1961); *Braden* v. *United States*, 365 U.S. 431 (1961); *Barenblatt* v. *United States*, 360 U.S. 109 (1959).
15. *Aptheker* v. *Secretary of State*, 378 U.S. 500 (1964).
16. *United States* v. *Brown*, 381 U.S. 437 (1965).
17. *Albertson* v. *Subversive Activities Control Board*, 382 U.S. 70 (1965).
18. *United States* v. *Robel*, 389 U.S. 258 (1967).
19. *Baggett* v. *Bullitt*, 377 U.S. 360 (1964).
20. *Elfbrandt* v. *Russell*, 384 U.S. 11 (1966).
21. *Keyishian* v. *Board of Regents of State of New York*, 385 U.S. 589 (1967).
22. See *Roth* v. *United States*, 354 U.S. 476 (1957); *Alberts* v. *California*, 354 U.S. 476 (1957); *Manuel Enterprises, Inc.* v. *Day*, 370 U.S. 478 (1962); *Bantam Books* v. *Sullivan*, 372 U.S. 58 (1963); *Ginzburg* v. *United States*, 383 U.S. 463 (1966); *Mishkin* v. *New York*, 383 U.S. 502 (1966); *Fanny Hill Case (A Book Named "John Cleland's Woman of Pleasure")* v. *Mass.*, 383 U.S. 413 (1966); *Redrup* v. *New York*, 386 U.S. 767 (1967).

23. *Jacobellis* v. *Ohio*, 378 U.S. 184 (1964); *Freedman* v. *Maryland*, 380 U.S. 51 (1965); *Teitel Film Corp.* v. *Cusack*, 390 U.S. 139 (1968).

24. See *Engel* v. *Vitale*, 370 U.S. 421 (1962); *Abington School District* v. *Schempp and Murray* v. *Curlett*, 374 U.S. 203 (1963).

25. *Heart of Atlanta Motel, Inc.* v. *United States* 379 U.S. 241 (1964).

26. *Katzenbach* v. *McClung*, 379 U.S. 294 (1964).

27. *Loving* v. *Virginia*, 388 U.S. 1 (1967).

28. *Reitman* v. *Mulkey*, 387 U.S. 369 (1967).

29. 268 U.S. 652 (1925).

30. *Mapp* v. *Ohio*, 367 U.S. 643 (1961); *Robinson* v. *California*, 370 U.S. 660 (1962); *Gideon* v. *Wainwright*, 372 U.S. 335 (1963); *Malloy* v. *Hogan*, 378 U.S. 1 (1964); *Murphy* v. *Waterfront Commission of New York Harbor*, 378 U.S. 52 (1964); *Pointer* v. *Texas*, 380 U.S. 400 (1965); *Washington v. Texas*, 388 U.S. 14 (1967); *Klopfer* v. *North Carolina*, 386 U.S. 213 (1967); *Duncan* v. *Louisiana*, 391 U.S. 145 (1968); *Benton* v. *Maryland*, 395 U.S. 784 (1969).

31. 384 U.S. 436 (1966). Also included were the companion cases of *Vignera* v. *New York, Westover* v. *United States* and *California* v. *Stewart*.

32. See Robert J. Steamer, "The Court and the Criminal", 8 *William and Mary Law Review* 319-342 (Spring, 1967) for a detailed discussion of this development.

33. See Richard Harris, "Annals of Legislation", *The New Yorker*, 14 December 1968, pp. 68-179 for a superb account of the legislative history of the statute.

34. Public Law 90-351; 82 Stat. 197. See 26 *Congressional Quarterly*, No. 23, 7 June 1968 for an analytical summary of the law.

35. 354 U.S. 449 (1957).

36. 384 U.S. 436 (1966).

37. 388 U.S. 218 (1967).

38. *Mallory* v. *United States*, 354 U.S. 449 (1957) at 455.

39. 371 U.S. 471 (1963).

40. See Dale Broder, "Wong Sun v. United States, A Study in Faith and Hope", 48 *Nebraska Law Review* 483 (1963) for an analysis of this viewpoint.

41. See 26 *Congressional Quarterly, op. cit.*

42. 391 U.S. 510 (1968).

43. 277 U.S. 438 (1928).

44. *Berger* v. *New York*, 388 U.S. 41 (1967).

45. *Davis* v. *Mississippi*, 394 U.S. 721 (1969).

46. *United States* v *Rabinowitz*, 339 U.S. 56 (1950) and *Harris* v. *United States*, 331 U.S. 145 (1947).

47. *Chimel* v. *California*, 395 U.S. 752 (1969).

48. *Shipley* v. *California*, 395 U.S. 818 (1969).

49. *Von Cleef* v. *New Jersey*, 395 U.S. 814 (1969).

50. *Terry* v. *Ohio*, 392 U.S. 1 (1968) and *Sibron* v. *New York*, 392 U.S. 40 (1968).

51. *Gregory* v. *Chicago*, 394 U.S. 111 (1969) and *Shuttlesworth* v. *Birmingham*, 394 U.S. 147 (1969).

52. *Tinker* v. *Des Moines County School District*, 393 U.S. 503 (1969).

53. *Watts* v. *United States*, 394 U.S. 705 (1969).

54. *Street* v. *New York*, 394 U.S. 576 (1969).

55. *Carroll* v. *Commissioners of Princess Anne*, 393 U.S. 175 (1968) and *Brandenburg* v. *Ohio*, 395 U.S. 444 (1969).

56. 274 U.S. 357 (1927), overruled by *Brandenburg* v. *Ohio, supra*.

57. *Stanley* v. *Georgia*, 394 U.S. 557 (1969).

58. *Red Lion Broadcasting Co.* v. *F.C.C.* and *United States* v. *Radio Television News Directors Association*, 395 U.S. 367 (1969).

59. *Avery* v. *Midland County*, 390 U.S. 474 (1968).

60. *Kirkpatrick* v. *Preisler*, 394 U.S. 526 (1969).

61. *Wells* v. *Rockefeller*, 394 U.S. 542 (1969).

62. *Green* v. *School Board of New Kent County*, 391 U.S. 430 (1968) and *Raney* v. *Board of Education*, 391 U.S. 443 (1968).

63. *Monroe* v. *Board of Commissioners*, 391 U.S. 450 (1968).

64. *Jones* v. *Mayer Co.*, 392 U.S. 409 (1968).

65. 393 U.S. 544 (1969).

66. 394 U.S. 358 (1969).

67. 395 U.S. 285 (1969).

68. As of the 1957-58 Term ninety-one justices had sat on the bench although there had been ninety-six actual confirmed appointees. Robert H. Harrison of Maryland was nominated by President Washington, was confirmed and commissioned, but never served. John Rutledge, Edward Douglass White, Charles Evans Hughes, and Harlan Fiske Stone were each appointed twice, first as associate justice, then as chief justice.

69. See Robert J. Steamer, "Statesmanship or Craftsmanship: Current Conflict over the Supreme Court", 11 *Western Political Quarterly* 273 (June, 1958) for a list of the justices with prior experience.

70. Felix Frankfurter, "The Supreme Court in the Mirror of Justices", 105 *University of Pennsylvania Law Review* 786 (April, 1957).

71. Fred V. Cahill, Jr., "The Supreme Court—Friends and Foes". Paper delivered at the 1958 Annual Meeting of The American Political Science Association, St. Louis, Missouri.

72. Frankfurter, *"Mirror of Justices"*, p. 795, 784.

73. *The Federalist* (New York: Modern Library), p. 516.

74. *Ibid.*, p. 519.

75. James Willard Hurst, *The Growth of American Law* (Boston: Little, Brown, 1950), pp. 117-118.

76. Robert H. Jackson, *The Struggle for Judicial Supremacy* (New York: Knopf, 1941), p. 17.

77. Frankfurter, *"Mirror of Justices"*, p. 793.

78. Benjamin N. Cardozo, *The Growth of the Law* (New Haven: Yale University Press, 1924), p. 136.

79. See Benjamin N. Cardozo, *The Nature of the Judicial Process* (New Haven: Yale University Press, 1921), p. 21.

80. Cardozo, *The Growth of the Law*, pp. 96-97.

81. Alexis de Tocqueville, *Democracy in America* (New York: Knopf, 1948), I, p. 103.

Table of Cases

Index